MAJOR LEAGUE LOSERS

MAJOR LEAGUE *Losers*

THE REAL COST OF SPORTS AND WHO'S PAYING FOR IT

MARK S. ROSENTRAUB

BasicBooks
A Division of HarperCollins*Publishers*

Copyright © 1997 by Mark S. Rosentraub
Published by BasicBooks,
A Division of HarperCollins Publishers, Inc.

Data and text from Mark Rosentraub's and Sam Nunn's "Sports Wars: Suburbs and Center Cities in a Zero Sum Game," from *Journal of Sport and Social Issues* 21, no. 1 (1997), © 1997 by Journal of Sport and Social Issues, reprinted by permission of Sage Publications.

The author also wishes to thank the *Journal of Urban Affairs* and the Urban Affairs Association for permission to reproduce data from his previously published work (co-authors Michael Przybylski, Dan Mullins, and David Swindell).

FIRST EDITION

Designed by Elliott Beard

Library of Congress Cataloging-in-Publication Data
Rosentraub, Mark S., 1950–
    Major league losers : the real cost of sports and who's paying for it / by
Mark S. Rosentraub. — 1st ed.
        p.   cm.
    Includes bibliographical references.
    ISBN 0-465-08317-X
    1. Sports—Economic aspects—United States. 2. Sports teams—United
States—Costs. 3. Sports teams—United States—Finance. 4. Cities and
towns—United States—Economic conditions. 5. Sports team owners—
United States. I. Title.
    GV716.R67   1997
    338.4'3796'0973—dc20   96-26446

97 98 99 00 01 ❖/RRD 10 9 8 7 6 5 4 3 2

For Karen
David, Alexa, Natalie, and Sabrina

CONTENTS

ACKNOWLEDGMENTS

ALL THOSE WHO HAVE undertaken the task of writing a book know well the support required from others to complete the work. I was extremely fortunate to have the financial, professional, and personal networks that supported me in my work. If it were not for the Center for Urban Policy and the Environment at Indiana University–Purdue University Indianapolis, this work's scope would have been far more limited. The Center receives substantial financial support from the Lilly Endowment, and that support of scholarship, research, and inquiry is directly responsible for this book. To all who that shared the dream of an urban research center at Indiana University's metropolitan campus, I hope this book is worthy of your work, faith, and support.

The Center is part of Indiana University's School of Public and Environmental Affairs, and colleagues in both parts of my academic world helped make this project successful. The task of patiently entering (dare I say "typing") countless revisions, tables, and graphs fell to Carla Brock, Shannon Cooper, and Jeannine Smith. They probably know far more about cities and sports than they want, but their efforts as well as their questioning of different sections when they did not make sense to them meant more to me than they know. Research assistants are part of any professor's projects, and I was fortunate to have four who helped me time and time again. Nur Ungan,

Alicia Gebhardt, Paula Schwabe, and Amy McFadden became unwilling experts on sports, and I am sure they "bore" husbands and boyfriends with countless tales of the subsidies teams receive. I just hope their significant others do not resent me for any interference with their enjoyment of sports.

Books are always made better by editors who become critics, the reader who is always right, and the "wordsmith" professors' need to clarify their points and reach their intended audiences. It was my great fortune to have the Center's director of communications, Teresa Bennett, serve as editor. She was not only the reason the initial drafts of the book appeared so "clean" to the staff at BasicBooks, but her constant questioning of each chapter (and each paragraph) clarified and sharpened the book's focus and message. Producing "readable" research is no easy task, but when you have Teresa Bennett to review your work and make suggestions (as well as improvements in your words), the task is made far easier. I owe Teresa a huge debt of thanks for the time and effort she put into this book, and I apologize for making her far more knowledgeable about sports than she ever wanted to be.

Exchanging ideas with colleagues is the heart and soul (and greatest benefit) of the university community, and those conversations vastly improved this book. A. James Barnes provided the encouragement and advice that brought this project to BasicBooks. Andrew Zimbalist, Michael Przybylski, Dan Mullins, David Swindell, Sam Nunn, Scott Cummings, Karen Harlow, and Drew Klacik each gave me the opportunity to explain my ideas and concepts. Their critiques, criticisms, suggestions, and comments helped sharpen my focus. I am also very grateful for the help and information I received from Professor Pat Larkey and his graduate student team at the H. John Heinz School, Carnegie Mellon University. Their research into a new stadium for the Pittsburgh Pirates not only illustrated what graduate students and their final project can mean for a city, but it set a standard that many communities can look to for the work they require from consultants.

One of the great outcomes from projects of this nature are the friendships and working relationships one develops with the countless people that are interviewed. Tom Chema, who as executive director of the Gateway Redevelopment Corporation was part subject of this book, became, through interviews, a friend and colleague who then agreed to review a draft of my chapter on Cleveland. While Tom and I still cannot agree on all issues related to cities and sports, I am fortunate to have him as a colleague and I am extremely grateful for his willingness to discuss and disagree with my research. Three mayors of Indiana cities also helped me better understand what sports can and do mean for elected officials and their electoral careers and the cities they serve. I learned a great deal from my conversations with Stephen Goldsmith (Indianapolis), Paul Helmke (Fort Wayne), and William Hudnut (Indianapolis). Their insights into and experiences with sports helped expand my understandings and appreciation of the pressures and opportunities mayors must address.

My interest in studying cities and professional sports began in 1975, when I relocated to the Dallas/Fort Worth area and learned of different aspects of the contract that brought the Washington Senators to Arlington. Mayor Tom Vandergriff was at the center of the negotiations that brought an American League team to Texas. While the results of my research, and my many public presentations, may have annoyed him, Mayor Vandergriff never tired of my numerous questions. Throughout the years, and as I prepared this book, Mr. Vandergriff never refused to meet with me to discuss sports and cities and politics in the Dallas/Fort Worth region. While he and I probably still disagree on many points, our twenty-year discussion of sports and cities is something I continue to cherish. Our disagreements have never diminished my substantial respect and admiration for Tom Vandergriff's leadership and electoral career. Tom, I sincerely appreciate your willingness to both tolerate me and continue to meet with me.

In each of the cities profiled in this book several key individuals were gracious enough to discuss numerous aspects of their roles in sports; it was an honor and privilege to be able to discuss cities and sports with each of these people. Sen. Tom Eagleton and Mayor Richard Greene (Arlington, Texas) deserve special thanks and appreciation. Even though I frequently, and publicly, disagree with their views, they still gave me some of their time, advice, and guidance. Mayor Greene knows well our disagreements, but I trust he and Senator Eagleton also know the respect I have for their leadership and accomplishments. I remain for both men "the majesty's (most) loyal (and respectful) opposition." Mark Sauer, president of the Pittsburgh Pirates, gave me a glance into the world of surviving in a small baseball market, and Michael Collins, executive director of Three Rivers Stadium, helped me understand the intricacies of the problems faced by Pittsburgh's teams. In Toronto, Paul Godfrey was most gracious in explaining the relationship between Canadian investors and sports. David Shtern and Peter Tomlinson, public officials with Ontario Province and the city of Toronto, untangled the issues involved with Skydome and the investments made by those governments.

There are several personal debts I also owe. Two special people in my life and in this project's life did not live to see this book published. Michael Carroll, vice president of the Lilly Endowment, first heard my views of cities and sports in 1990. From that conversation grew our mutual interest in building an urban research center for Indiana University–Purdue University Indianapolis. Mike's intellectual and emotional support framed and helped create the Center for Urban Policy and the Environment. I hope he would find this book worthy of his aspirations for the Center's work. My love of sports began with my father; while I did not learn or know enough while he was alive to write this book, I think he would be proud to see how I was able to take my craziness and make it part of my career. My brother, my eternal co-conspirator in our family's love of sports, and my mother, who still must tolerate my sports mania, will have to gauge if this book would have burst Dad's chest. I hope they know how much their respect and love pushed this effort to completion and how much their respect and love mean to me.

Writing a book of this nature and magnitude has taught me how important one's immediate family is for providing the emotional support and confidence one needs to get the job done. I do not think my family knows how much their love and support meant to me during this project. Karen's career suffered from the burdens I had to place on her while this book became the all-encompassing part of my professional life. Alexa, Natalie, and Sabrina all had to forfeit one of our family vacations while I spent a summer visiting different cities and libraries and in our basement writing this book. Drafts of David's work went unread as I was always revising or changing one chapter or another. The hardest part of this book and my role as a father and husband is knowing the time my children and wife lost, and what I can never return to them. I am grateful, beyond words, for their understanding and support.

What follows is my responsibility. This work does not represent the views and ideas of the Lilly Endowment, the Center for Urban Policy and the Environment, nor Indiana University. I trust that what has been produced is worthy of all the support I have received. Sabrina, I promise not to spend another summer, or every evening while you are doing your homework, in the basement, working on "the book." Karen, I hope I can fulfill that promise.

INDIANAPOLIS
JUNE 1996

ACKNOWLEDGMENTS xvii

MAJOR LEAGUE LOSERS

1

Subsidizing Sports

The Real Economics of Cities
and Professional Teams

INTRODUCTION

A WELFARE SYSTEM EXISTS in this country that transfers hundreds of millions of dollars from taxpayers to wealthy investors and their extraordinarily well-paid employees. Who are these individuals profiting from this life on the dole? They are the owners of North America's professional sports teams and the athletes who play in each of the four major sports leagues (baseball, basketball, football, and hockey). This welfare system exists—indeed it thrives and continues to grow—because state and local government leaders, dazzled by promises of economic growth from sports, mesmerized by visions of enhanced images for their communities, and captivated by a mythology of the importance of professional sports, have failed to do their homework. They do not understand—or they choose to ignore—how small sports are as a part of any area's economy and how minuscule its impact is on a region, a city, or even a segment of a city. City and state leaders have also ignored or failed to realize just how few jobs professional sports teams produce and that businesses do not select an office or plant site because of the presence of a sports team. Few taxpayers and elected officials have invested the time needed to understand why this welfare system exists and just how profitable it is for the team owners and players who now control it.

This welfare system can be dismantled; and it can be changed so that taxpayers do not subsidize a very healthy industry and some of the wealthiest people in this country. However, if changes are to be made, and if providing hundreds of millions of dollars in welfare to millionaire owners and players is to end, elected officials and community leaders must understand why this welfare system exists, how it operates, and how taxpayers are its victims. To help end this perverse and unfair system, the mystique of sports and their mythical benefits must be unraveled. Only then will community leaders have the tools they need to deal with teams and their owners. If sports teams were treated as the *small* entertainment businesses they are, then it would be possible to end the welfare system that benefits team owners and players by taking money from taxpayers. This book has been produced in the hope of accomplishing that objective.

HOW DOES THE SPORTS
WELFARE SYSTEM WORK?

Once upon a time the investors who owned teams and hired players also paid most of the costs for building stadia and arenas. Prior to World War II public contributions to the building of playing facilities were quite modest. In the post–World War II era public participation in the financing of playing facilities did increase, but in most circumstances teams paid substantial rent for their use of a stadium or arena. The governments that were landlords to professional teams generally lost some money, but the franchises were required to pay for their use of the stadium or arena (Hamilton and Kahn, 1997). In addition, the public authorities who owned facilities frequently shared in the revenue collected from parking and the sale of food and beverages. To be sure, there were exceptions to these patterns, but through the 1960s and into the 1970s, for the most part, the professional sports leagues were able to operate without substantial subsidies from state and local governments. Expanding television revenues and favorable federal tax regulations, combined with the ability of each league to control the number of franchises that existed, created a profitable environment for team owners.

The financial world of professional sports has been substantially altered during the last two decades; these changes have reshaped the economics of stadium financing and have created the modern sports welfare system. First, as a result of court rulings and labor confrontations, players have secured expanded rights to sell their skills to the highest bidder. "Free agency" has become a slogan to describe a process whereby players' salaries sharply escalated. While many of us grew to adulthood amazed that Mickey Mantle, Willie Mays, or Henry Aaron could earn $100,000 by playing a game, suddenly $100,000 became "chump change." Multimillion-dollar contracts are now the expected norm for star players, and even average players command extraordinary salaries. By 1993 at least eighteen players had contracts and endorsements that guaranteed them an annual income of $6 million or more. Each of these players had contracts with their teams for no less than $3 million in annual pay (Meserole, 1995). In 1995, the minimum salary for players in the National Basketball Association (NBA) was $200,000, and the average salary in the National Hockey League (NHL) was more than $700,000 (Helyar, 1996). In 1996, $100-million contracts became part of the world of professional sports. Where could the owners find the money to pay these salaries and still earn the profits they had in previous years? Either someone else had to pay for the playing facilities, or the owners would lose their profits to the players and the "free agency" system.

Second, teams earn money from ticket sales, the broadcast of games and related programs, souvenir purchases, and the sale of food and beverages at stadia and arenas. As long as income from these sources continued to escalate, owners could pay players the new higher salaries and still earn the profits they wanted. However, when salaries began to escalate faster than these existing revenues, new revenue *sources* were needed. Some teams like the New York Yankees, Chicago Cubs, and Atlanta Braves were able to increase their revenues through cable television and "superstation" deals. Teams in smaller markets, however, could not access large cable television contracts, and not every team was owned by a media giant with a "superstation." New and different revenue sources were needed, and luxury suites and club seating, together with expanded restaurants, became the routes to financial success. What all team owners needed and wanted were playing facilities with luxury seating and restaurants that would create additional revenue streams and additional revenues from which players could be paid and profit levels maintained. If state and local governments could be convinced to pay a large portion of the capital costs for building these new facilities, then players could earn their astronomical salaries and owners could still earn their desired profits. All that was needed to make this system work were willing public-sector partners who could be persuaded to contribute large amounts of tax dollars to the building of arenas and stadia. The modern sports welfare system was born in the 1980s as willing governments were found that were only too eager to create the revenue streams owners and players wanted. These community leaders anticipated receiving a large return on their investments, and few bothered to ask whether cities could prosper from professional sports.

Each of the sports leagues had its own twists on this new welfare system, but the end result was similar. In the National Football League (NFL), the very lucrative national media contracts are shared by all teams; however, income from luxury seating, in-stadium advertising, in-stadium food and beverage purchases, and parking fees is not. In an era of free agency, the team with the most in-stadium revenue would have the most money to attract players and earn profits. The Dallas Cowboys and Miami Dolphins were two teams that were able to raise a substantial amount of money that did not have to be shared with other NFL team owners.

Prior to 1996, teams in the other major sport leagues retained all
of their own local media income, as well as their revenues from luxury seating and advertising. As a result, by the 1980s, baseball, basketball, and hockey teams in smaller media markets began to experience severe difficulties finding the dollars to pay star players.
Teams such as the Montreal Expos, Texas Rangers, Cleveland Indians, Cleveland Cavaliers, Indiana Pacers, Winnipeg Jets, and the
Quebec Nordiques found themselves at a decided disadvantage. For
example, the New York Yankees were able to earn more than $45
million from media contracts while baseball teams in smaller markets found themselves confined to paltry earnings of less than $20
million. The New York Knicks earned almost $21 million in media
revenues in 1994, but the Indiana Pacers, Milwaukee Bucks, Sacramento Kings, and San Antonio Spurs earned less than $14 million.
How could the small-market teams fill this revenue gap? Many owners knew what the answer was. They needed facilities with luxury
seating, and if the public sector would pay for these facilities, then
teams could not only survive but prosper in small markets.

Beginning in the 1980s many state and local governments
formed partnerships with teams to build new facilities; by the end of
the decade and into the 1990s, all of these facilities contained substantial numbers of luxury suites and club seats. Through these
public/private partnerships, the public sector's responsibility or
share of the cost of stadia and arenas actually declined. In the 1970s,
governments typically were responsible for 90 percent of the cost of
construction of the facilities used by professional sports teams. For
facilities built in the 1990s, the public sector was typically responsible for less than 60 percent of the cost (Swindell, 1996). At first
glance, then, these partnerships seem reasonable and hardly the cor-
nerstones of a multimillion-dollar welfare system. They are, however, a bit peculiar and do indeed produce a bizarre and regressive
subsidy system. How?

First, only one of the partners, the team, generally shares in
the revenues or profits earned from the operation of the facility.
If the public sector receives even a small portion of the revenues
from the operation of a stadium or arena, these funds are counted
as part of the private sector's contribution to the partnership. In

this manner the public sector does not receive a monetary return on its investment; fiscal returns on investments are reserved for the team owners while the public sector's investment—through taxes—does not generate any revenue or direct financial returns (from the operation of the facilities). (Chapters 4 and 5 will deal with the minuscule size of the other economic benefits that do accrue to cities.) *Second,* the private-sector partner, the team, generally passes the cost of its investment to fans who attend games, while the public-sector partner is forced to ask all citizens to support the playing facility through higher taxes.

How do teams develop partnerships like this? The steps taken are so familiar that the script is well known and has been played and replayed from Baltimore to Nashville, from San Antonio to Oakland, from Detroit to Tampa Bay, and from Minnesota to the Dallas/Fort Worth area.

Act I: The Portrait of a Noble Victim

The sports drama or community soap opera begins with a team owner, generally seated alone, bemoaning the current and unfair state of the economics of his or her sport. Our hero or heroine decries the state of the world and describes the litany of problems now all too familiar to sports fans and community leaders: Player salaries are escalating, travel and hotel costs keep rising, and large-market teams are amassing huge cash reserves they will use to buy the best players and win repeated championships. If help is not forthcoming, how will it ever be possible to save the family business and the community's pride?

The victim's opening monologue also contains the obligatory observation that he or she will have to leave the community, as unpleasant and repulsive as that thought is, if a satisfactory facility is not built that has the potential to substantially increase revenues (profits). In other versions of the play a team owner promises to come to your city if an acceptable public/private partnership can be developed. Regardless of the setting—the team will leave your community or come to your city—the first act always ends with a vivid description of the need for a new stadium or arena because players are demanding high salaries and large-market teams earn far more money from which they can pay the best players. The first act, then, paints the players as culprits or greedy rascals. The heroes or heroines never suggest that they should reduce their profits or wealth by paying the players higher salaries. Such an outcome could avoid subsidies and higher taxes. This option is rarely part of this soap opera.

Act II: The People Deserve a Champion: Who Will Stand with Me?

With good and evil clearly defined in Act I, the team owner then declares that if the new facility is not built and the additional revenues (from luxury seating, advertising, and the sale of food and beverages) not earned, the team is destined to be mediocre and unable to win the championship the fans deserve. As the owner wants to build a winner, a public-sector partner who shares this championship dream and fervor is sought. The owner also frequently suggests that the fans deserve a more comfortable stadium with the modern conveniences common in the newest facilities. Act II ends with a call to arms—actually a call for cash—to permit a championship team to exist so all the fans can see that championship banner flying proudly over or in a new, first-class stadium or arena that has all the modern conveniences the fans deserve.

Act III: We All Can Be Winners: One for All and All for One?

Once the challenge to help build a winner and a first-class facility to keep the fans comfortable is presented, reports usually circulate describing the economic and image benefits to a city and region of having a team that is a "winner" and from building a first-class facility. These benefits are identified as the "returns" to the public sector from its investment and its commitment to building a winning team, a first-class facility, and a first-class image. (The fiscal or money returns will, of course, accrue to the owners and the players. The city's benefits will be the "winning image.") This information is then used to counter any studies or stories that suggest that the direct economic benefits of a team are relatively small. If only the stadium or arena could be built, our hero or heroine cries at the end of Act III, we all could live in "Titletown, USA."

Act IV: The Nobility Joins the Visionary Leader

In the fourth act of this drama community leaders then emerge who proclaim the proposed arena or stadium as a potential civic asset and monument worthy of the public's support. In some instances this chorus proclaims the proposed stadium or arena as a "signature statement" for the community, an edifice or landmark for the ages that will proclaim the city's greatness and centrality in the American economy. These leaders also discuss the enhanced economic development that will result from the team's presence and the building of a new facility. Newspaper reports usually follow these discussions, and these articles always discuss the extensive "feelings" of community solidarity that the team will foster in their new home. Frequently, reporters are dispatched to other cities to describe the resurgence in civic pride that took place there after a team arrived or won a title or pennant. The fourth act concludes with a reading of these tributes and an enumeration of the achievements of the communities that were wise enough to build a stadium.

Act V: The Answer Is Provided and the Word Is Given

With a relatively friendly political environment established by the stories published in Act IV, an elected official—not desiring to be the one in office when a team moves or fails to come to town— develops a public/private partnership proposal for a new facility. The proposal is sometimes voted upon at a general election; other times a council or legislature simply ratifies the agreement. Regardless, the debate or vote is always accompanied by donations from facility and team supporters (and sometimes the team and its owners) that help secure the needed votes.

Where does all this typically lead? Generally it ends with the building of playing facilities that cost far more than initially projected and with most, if not all, revenues from the facilities belonging to the team. Conversely, much of the responsibility for cost over-runs is left to the public sector. Other inducements are also frequently given to owners to compete with the largesse others have received. For example, some cities have provided team owners with "moving expenses" that were so large that they amounted to nothing less than a bounty or one-time welfare payment for moving their teams. Other owners have received land, special investment opportunities, offices, luxury suites at the new stadium and arenas, and practice facilities for their teams. Most of these inducements, of course, are provided from the public's taxes.

The stadium and arena construction game has produced a welfare system in which subsidies from state and local government generate giant revenue pools for each franchise with a new facility. The control of this money has been the focus of each of the labor and management confrontations in professional baseball, basketball, football, and hockey. As some have commented, labor strife in professional sports is a battle between "the haves and the have mores." But what these two wealthy groups (the players and the owners) are now fighting over is a revenue pool built by the tax dollars of citizens who can only dream of million-dollar salaries. Elected leaders have permitted the leagues to operate as cartels with the ability to extract subsidies that generate substantial profits for all the actors in the professional sports world. All the actors, that is, except the cities and the taxpayers who provide this welfare while hoping for economic benefits, improved community images, and a new sense of community spirit.

DOES THE SPORTS INDUSTRY
NEED WELFARE TO EXIST?

This welfare system is not needed. By virtually any measure professional sports is an extremely successful business. The players—once underpaid and abused—are now enjoying princely salaries, and the vast majority of teams earn profits and generate substantial wealth for their owners through the escalating value of most franchises. In addition, sports as a business is having no serious problem attracting consumers. Fan interest, as measured by attendance, while declining in baseball and hockey from some earlier levels, is still quite robust. And for some baseball teams, it has never been stronger. In 1995, the Cleveland Indians became the first MLB team to sell all tickets to all of its games four months before the 1996 season started. Many football teams routinely sell all tickets to their games, and NBA teams are also playing before sold-out arenas or near-capacity crowds in numerous cities. Does such a business really need a public subsidy or welfare to exist?

To be sure, some teams are losing money, and some do not earn as much as other teams. The financial problems of the Pittsburgh Pirates are substantial, and fan support for the Montreal Expos remains an ongoing challenge. The different levels of income earned by some teams are also a problem. For example, in the NBA, the Indiana Pacers, Los Angeles Clippers, and Dallas Mavericks generate far less money than do the Chicago Bulls, New York Knicks, Detroit Pistons, or Los Angeles Lakers. In the NFL, as noted, few teams earn as much as the Dallas Cowboys, Miami Dolphins, San Francisco 49ers, and Philadelphia Eagles. Yet, despite these revenue differences and the financial problems of a handful of franchises, as an industry professional sports are very, very healthy and profitable. How profitable?

One report for the U.S. Congress evaluated the state of MLB when a congressional committee was reevaluating the sport's exemption from anti-trust laws during the 1994 strike and lock-out. This report found that seemingly profitable and unprofitable teams were increasing in value, thus generating substantial returns on the investments made by owners.

> Franchise revenues grew by nearly 12 percent per year from 1970 to 1991, a 6.3 percent annual growth rate over and above the rate of inflation. . . . The Baltimore Orioles, a profitable team, were sold for $12 million in 1979, $70 million in 1989, and again for $173 million in 1993 (with the benefit of a new stadium complex financed by Maryland taxpayers). The Seattle Mariners, long a financially weak team, were sold in 1981 for $13 million and again in 1988 for $89.5 million ($77.5 million changed hands with the buyer taking over

$12 million in liabilities). In 1992, they were sold again for $106 million to a group of local businesses that offered to invest an additional $19 million in the team. The Texas Rangers, also a weak team, were sold for $10.5 million in 1974 and for $79 million in 1989 (Cox & Zimmerman, 1995, p. 4).

MLB owners are not the only investors in sports with appreciating assets. NFL team owners have found their investments to be appreciating as well. The actual market value of NFL teams is probably best illustrated by the $175 million Jeff Lurie paid for the Philadelphia Eagles in 1994. *Financial World* magazine estimated the team's value in 1992 to be $149 million, but that figure, as illustrated by the 1994 price, was probably a bit conservative. In terms of understanding the value of an NFL franchise, it is also instructive to point out that the Eagles are not a perennial champion. They last won a championship in 1980 and have not appeared in a league championship game nor have they been a divisional champion since the 1980 season.

Wealth has been growing for team owners not only in terms of the value of their franchises but from the fees charged to individuals or groups who seek expansion teams. The successful bidders for these few scarce franchises pay an extremely large and arbitrarily defined fee for the right to have a franchise. These franchise fees are then equally divided among the existing owners, generating more income. The owners of the Florida Marlins and Colorado Rockies paid $95 million in 1991 to join MLB. The owners of the new MLB teams that will play in Phoenix and St. Petersburg each paid $130 million to join the major leagues. In three years, then, the value of a new MLB franchise increased 37 percent. How were these franchise fees chosen? At least some evidence suggests that these numbers were literally picked "out of the air" by the other owners, who then divided the funds received among themselves (Whitford, 1993).

The owners of the latest entries to the NBA, the Vancouver Grizzlies and the Toronto Raptors, paid $125 million (U.S. dollars) "2 Be Where the Action Is." For Toronto's owners this was another case of "pay me now or pay me (lots) later." The Toronto Huskies were part of the Basketball Association of America in 1946. That team folded at the end of its inaugural season. The surviving members of the Basketball Association of America merged with the National Basketball League to form the NBA in 1949. After World War II, basketball franchises in any league were available for nominal sums ($300). Had Toronto stayed in the NBA, the team's owners would have earned a substantial return on their investment.

It also costs a small fortune to join the NFL. The owners of the Carolina Cougars and the Jacksonville Jaguars each paid the NFL $140 million to become league members. These funds, of course, were then distributed to each existing owner. And NHL team owners saw their team's values increase 11.9 percent from 1991 to 1994 (Much & Friedman, 1995). With assets of this value it is hard to justify that any team owner deserves welfare or the subsidies they have been receiving from state and local governments.

The owners are not the only ones reaping substantial benefits from these subsidies. In the past, players did not receive a substantial share of the wealth produced by professional sports. Today, the situation is quite different from the world Bob Cousy, Willie Mays, Andy Bathgate, Johnny Unitas, Lenny Moore, Frank Gifford, and Ray Felix knew. Players in each of the four major sports are very well paid for their work, with "star" players receiving unimaginable amounts of money. By the 1990s, player salaries represented more than two-fifths of MLB team revenues, a 100 percent increase from the 1970s. By 1994, without the strike, it is reasonable to expect that half or more than half of all team revenues were consumed by players' salaries. In part, the strike and the subsequent labor impasse were a result of the owners' desire to return to the proportions that existed prior to the 1990s. The median salary for major league baseball players in 1994 was $500,000, and the game's top twenty stars earned in excess of $4 million (Zimbalist, 1992; Cox & Zimmerman, 1995).

While the "average" baseball player does not receive the salary of the star free agents, the salary received by at least 50 percent of all major league baseball players would make the vast majority of Americans feel as if they had won a lottery. Starting players in the NBA now earn in excess of $500,000, and several players on each team now earn more than $3 million each season. In 1994, *Financial*

World estimated that players earned more than half of the revenues received by baseball, football, and basketball teams and 41 percent of the revenues earned by NHL teams. While the estimates are subject to a considerable amount of criticism, it is safe to conclude that both owners and players are earning a great deal of money. It is difficult to find any real evidence that team owners or players need subsidies or welfare support. Sports is a very successful business for all involved with the only real issue being who, the owners or players, deserves a larger portion of an expanding pie.

So, given the money being made by players and owners, why are governments providing subsidies to this very healthy industry? Why do most public leaders believe that they must provide subsidies or match the offers made by other cities? Why is anyone subsidizing the stadia and arenas used by teams that generate wealth for owners and players alike?

These subsidies are even harder to explain in the 1990s if one takes even a casual look at the political landscape. During virtually every election, candidates from both parties present platforms and make promises to "privatize," "downsize," and "marketize" governments at all levels. From the U.S. Congress to every state legislature, Republicans and Democrats alike call for reduced welfare payments and smaller governments through the utilization of private firms to deliver services. At every turn in the political world one finds increasing calls for a reliance on free markets and market-based solutions to all of our policy dilemmas. And leaders of both political parties promise to reduce taxes or at least to fight tax increases. Yet, when it comes to sports, bigger governments, larger welfare packages, and tax increases are endorsed by both Republicans and Democrats, and more legislation and regulation to "protect" the sports leagues and the public are proposed. From areas as politically different as Maryland and Tennessee, state and local governments are willing to shower hundreds of millions of tax dollars on millionaire ballplayers and owners. We may demand that the elderly spend down their wealth before providing Medicaid benefits, but we shudder to ask team owners and players to do the same before providing subsidies and supporting increased taxes to build these big boys their big toys. Sports as a business hardly seems to deserve special protection from market forces. Yet the welfare payments to sports teams continue to grow.

MOVING ACROSS STATE LINES
FOR MORE WELFARE

Legislatures across the country debate welfare-for-work programs, reduced welfare payments for poor people, and the need to discourage people from moving to their state to receive welfare. But few elected officials raise a voice to protest hundred-million-dollar welfare programs for wealthy team owners and rich athletes, and most states seem eager to encourage teams to move inside their borders to receive public subsidies. At least five communities now provide or have proposed providing at least $250 million in subsidies for professional sports: Baltimore (and Maryland), Cincinnati, Cleveland, St. Louis (city and county in partnership with the state of Missouri), and Nashville. Between eighteen and twenty-four state and local governments have provided or have proposed to provide at least $100 million in subsidies to professional sports teams, and several of these subsidies will amount to almost $200 million.

The welfare system that now exists in professional sports is actually encouraging team owners to move their franchises to communities where more robust subsidies will be provided. Some teams move as a result of a loss of fan support or interest or out of a desire to locate in larger markets. Increasingly, though, the movement of teams has very little to do with fan support but a great deal to do with the subsidies or welfare teams receive from different communities and the amount of revenue the teams are permitted to keep from the tax-supported facilities built for them. What is now taking place that makes the recent moves of teams different from those in the past is that teams with substantial levels of fan support are drawn to other communities as a result of welfare packages.

Two of the most recent moves illustrate this process. The Oakland Raiders regularly sold out their home games at the Oakland-

Alameda Coliseum, but that did not stop the team's owner, Al Davis, from moving the team to Los Angeles in 1982. The driving force behind this move was the commitments local governments in Los Angeles were willing to make to have an NFL team. Why was Los Angeles interested in subsidizing professional football? The Los Angeles Rams had just left for Anaheim, and Los Angeles County and the city of Los Angeles wanted another team.

Los Angeles County lured the Raiders with promises of renovations to the aging Coliseum. The Los Angeles market never embraced the Raiders as the fans in Oakland had, and the Los Angeles area governments were not willing to respond to Al Davis's increasing requests for additional assistance. As a result, when Oakland increased the size of the subsidy it was willing to provide to the team, the Raiders returned home for the 1995 season.

The Cleveland Browns provide another example of a team moving to another state to take advantage of a better welfare program. From 1986 through 1994 the Browns averaged more than seventy thousand fans for each of their home games despite four straight years of below .500 teams (1990 through 1993). That level of fan support, together with the city of Cleveland's commitment to spend $175 million to improve Cleveland Stadium, did not stop Art Modell from taking his team and its five decades of history with the fans of Cleveland to Baltimore (Rushin, 1995). Baltimore, of course, had been left with its thirty years of memories of Alan Ameche, Johnny Unitas, Lenny Moore, Don Shula, and two Super Bowl appearances when the Colts moved to Indianapolis in 1984. At the current time, as detailed in Table 1–1, almost thirty teams have either threatened to move or have moved in an effort to secure a facility that would generate more income and that included a larger welfare bonus than they were currently able to secure. Teams are now moving across state lines to secure better welfare deals, and this process shows no signs of abating unless public officials do their homework and understand what sports mean and do not mean for their communities.

TABLE 1–1
The Status of Teams Seeking New Facilities

League/Team	Situation	Resolution
Major League Baseball		
Chicago White Sox	Threatened move to Florida	New stadium in 1991
Cincinnati Reds	Threatened move	New stadium approved
Cleveland Indians	Threatened move	New stadium in 1994
Detroit Tigers	Threatened move to suburbs	New stadium approved
Houston Astros	Threatened to leave the region	New stadium proposed
Milwaukee Brewers	Threatened to leave the region	New stadium approved
Montreal Expos	Low levels of fan support, revenue	Unresolved
New York Yankees	Threatening to leave New York City	Unresolved
Pittsburgh Pirates	Threatening to leave the region	Unresolved
San Francisco Giants	Threatened a move to Florida	Privately funded stadium
Seattle Mariners	Threatened to leave the region	New stadium approved
Texas Rangers	Threatened to leave Arlington	New stadium in 1994
National Basketball Association		
Indiana Pacers	Discussing a new arena	New arena planned
Dallas Mavericks	Threatening to move to suburbs	Unresolved
San Antonio Spurs	Threatening to move to New Orleans	Unresolved
Seattle Super Sonics	Threatened to leave the region	Remodeled arena
National Football League		
Arizona Cardinals	Interested in move to Los Angeles	Unresolved
Tampa Bay Buccaneers	Threatened to move	New stadium approved
Chicago Bears	Threatening to move to Indiana, Suburbs	New stadium proposed
Cincinnati Bengals	Threatened to move	New stadium approved
Cleveland Browns	New team by 1999	New stadium approved
Detroit Lions	Threatening a move within the region	New stadium in Detroit
Green Bay Packers	Needed more revenue from stadium	Stadium expanded
Houston Oilers	Move to Nashville announced	New stadium
Indianapolis Colts	Discussing revenue needs with city	Pending
Los Angeles Raiders	Moved to Oakland	Reconstruction of stadium
Los Angeles Rams	Moved to St. Louis	New stadium in St. Louis
Baltimore Ravens	Moved from Cleveland	New stadium approved
Seattle Seahawks	Threatening a move	Unresolved
National Hockey League		
Dallas Stars	Threatening to move within region	Unresolved
Florida Panthers	Threatening to move within region	New arena
New Jersey Devils	Threatened move to Nashville	New lease in New Jersey
Quebec Nordiques	Moved to Denver	New facility planned
Winnipeg Jets	Announced move to Phoenix	Using America West Arena

WHO PAYS FOR THE PUBLIC'S SUPPORT OF PROFESSIONAL SPORTS?

Do these welfare issues affect you? If you live in most places in North America they do. It is likely, no matter where you live, that you will be confronted with demands for a subsidy to help a "struggling" sports franchise. There are now 129 major league teams in fifty-six different cities in North America (Meserole, 1994). MLB will add two more teams for the 1998 season, and the NFL will likely add at least one more team to fill the void that exists in Los Angeles following the moves of the Rams and Raiders. NFL expansion into Canada appears likely before the end of the century, and another NFL team for Cleveland will also be created before 1999. European divisions for the NHL and NBA are being discussed as well, especially after the latter league's foray into Canada in 1995, and there are hundreds of minor league teams. If your county or province has a population of three hundred thousand people, you will likely deal with at least one professional sports team. If you live in a larger community, be prepared for demands for welfare from multiple teams.

Arlington Makes the Deal

In the early 1990s the Texas Rangers wanted a new stadium. Arlington Stadium, a remodeled minor league park, had almost 50 percent of its seats in the outfield. As a result, the team's revenues were among baseball's lowest. While the old field had good sight lines and everyone was close to the action, there were no sky boxes, club seats, or restaurants.

When the team began discussions for a new stadium they were quick to cast a roaming eye toward Dallas and St. Petersburg, Florida, where the unoccupied Sun Coast Dome beckoned. To convince the team to stay in Arlington, a "partnership" was created to build the ballpark in Arlington. During his campaign for the governorship of Texas, George Bush Jr., a minority owner of the Texas Rangers, proudly described the partnership as an example of his experience as an entrepreneur and in building successful partnerships for economic development. A close examination of the partnership reveals why national columnist George F. Will noted, "The safest way to gauge baseball disputes is to assume the owners are wrong" (Will, 1994).

To build the new facility, a structure that is an architectural masterpiece, a public/private partnership was developed. The city's investment was supported by a sales tax increment. The one-half percent increase in the sales tax will expire when the bonds are retired. The city of Arlington believes this will occur in 2002. Since Arlington is a retail, convention, and entertainment hub, the comptroller's office estimates that more than half of the sales tax dollars earned by Arlington are from nonresidents.

The investment by the Rangers consisted of its short-term commitment of lease revenues from luxury boxes. The city received 115 percent of the luxury suite revenue in the first year of the stadium's operation. In the second through fourth years of operation, the city received 5 percent of the luxury suite revenue. Corporations that lease luxury suites pay a rental fee in addition to the cost of the tickets.

To recoup its commitment of revenue from these various leases, the Rangers and Arlington agreed the team would charge a $1 per ticket fee on all seats sold. The revenues from this fee would repay the team for its cash commitment to financing the stadium. The team, then, committed revenues in the form of taxes from fans to build the stadium and then "recouped" this investment by increasing the price of the tickets. In addition, the team also committed the land it owned for the new stadium. However, this land was part of the original inducements given to attract the Rangers from Washington, D.C., and to retain them over the years. The land upon which the present and previous stadium existed was purchased through bonds which taxpayers had previously approved and supported with tax dollars. In this sense, one part of the team's investment took the form of the previous inducements it had received to relocate to Arlington and to remain in the city.

The team also received other benefits from the new stadium deal. The stadium included office space for the team and additional space that the team could rent to tenants. The baseball team retains all profits from any leases it negotiates and from any development of the land surrounding the stadium that the team owned.

What's wrong with this deal from the city's perspective? After all, the Rangers are a private business, and if they can get their consumers (fans) to purchase their product at rates sufficient to cover the cost of the stadium, what's the problem? The problem rests with the spending of taxes to increase the profitability of the team without the taxpayers sharing in that profitability. In other words, if the city of Arlington is investing tax dollars that increased the wealth of the team and its play-ers, what return should it earn on these funds? It is true the Rangers do pay rent for the use of the stadium, but that amount neither supports the costs of maintenance nor represents a fair return on the public's investment. Further, if the Texas Rangers are a successful business, able to pass along their share of the cost of the stadium to fans, why should the city subsidize any portion of the stadium's cost without sharing in the wealth created for team owners and players?

ENDING WELFARE AND SURVIVING SPORTS: THE CHAPTERS THAT FOLLOW

Will the subsidy game ever end? As this is being written, Maryland is considering a second investment to attract the Washington Red-skins, and a group of investors and local governments in northern Virginia is working together to attract an MLB team to the area. Negotiations are also under way between the New York Yankees and governments in the New York metropolitan region to provide or address the subsidies demanded by the franchise that is regarded by many as professional sports' most profitable and valuable team. Those discussions, as well as the initiatives for baseball and football teams in the Washington metropolitan region, will probably lead to another round of public-sector investments of tax money to guar-antee the wealth of team owners and their players. Each year it seems that the "ante" expected from cities by teams increases. More than one civic leader interviewed for this book responded that it was a good idea to subsidize an existing team because the costs of attract-ing another team after you have lost one escalate tremendously. The most frequently cited examples used to justify a subsidy to avoid a larger subsidy in the future are St. Louis and Baltimore. Both even-tually paid far more for replacement teams than the owners who left had demanded prior to moving their teams. The need for this book is probably best underscored by the number of civic leaders who accept the notion that subsidies for professional sports are very much a case of "pay me a little now, or pay me a great deal later."

WHY DO SO MANY PEOPLE
DEFEND WELFARE TO SPORTS TEAMS?

While the Republicans' "Contract with America" called for limits on welfare and prompted calls in several states for no additional support for moms on welfare who had another child, there is considerable support for providing welfare to wealthy owners and their ballplayers. Why is this? Why do voters and elected officials endorse welfare packages for sports teams that would be tossed out of a legislature faster than a Nolan Ryan fastball if the subject were unwed mothers or the homeless? As you read on, chapter 2 provides some answers to this question by analyzing why sports are so important to so many people. Putting an end to welfare programs, especially those that are so appealing to many legislators, national leaders, community leaders, and community organizations will not be easy. A mind-set exists in which sports are important, even critical, to a city's image and thus deserving of the public's largesse.

There is probably no better example of the extent to which sports manipulate the political agenda than the events that took place in early December 1995. During the days after Thanksgiving the United States had to decide whether or not to send troops to Bosnia to help support a peace treaty negotiated in Dayton, Ohio, between all parties to the dispute. During this same time, the President and the Congress were locked in a difficult battle over the U.S. budget that had already forced one partial shutdown of the federal government. A second shutdown loomed as both sides sought an acceptable balanced-budget proposal. During this time, what was the U.S. Senate doing? Indeed, there is some special irony—or perhaps a warped sense of priorities—in noting that the same week the United States committed troops to maintain peace in Bosnia, at the time that the President and the Congress were battling to define the parameters for balancing the federal budget, the U.S. Senate held hearings on the move of the Cleveland Browns to Baltimore. A budget accord did not exist, but drafts of proposed legislation to remedy the NFL's inability to stop Art Modell from leaving Cleveland were being prepared. The rights of Cleveland to subsidize the Browns and their wealthy owner and players were being jeopardized by a $270 million plus proposal from Maryland and Baltimore. Indignantly, Cleveland's Mayor Michael White, testifying before a Senate committee, demanded a "fair" hearing or level playing field from the NFL and Art Modell for his $175 million welfare proposal. Triumphantly, the mayor proclaimed, "Cleveland will not just go away." He never added the thought, "until someone accepts our welfare proposal and gives us an NFL team," but he could have. In 1995 alone, cities from Quebec and Winnipeg to Seattle, from Detroit and Milwaukee to Los Angeles, were debating whether or not to build facilities for professional sports teams. No matter what problems or issues confront your community or the nation, sports remain on the "front burner" and the "front page." If this welfare program is to be destroyed you need to understand why it exists in the first place. If it is ever to be stopped, the subtle ways in which sports cultivate their welfare status must be understood and appreciated. The roots of the welfare problem and the obstacles to its demise are discussed in chapter 2.

WHY DO SPORTS COST SO MUCH?

Why have professional sports become so expensive for cities and states? There are two overriding reasons. First, the leagues have been permitted to operate outside the free market. The leagues are permitted to specify not only how many teams will exist but where they will play. With the number of teams artificially controlled (or constrained), the value of each existing team escalates. Why do the sports leagues have this power? I'll detail that in chapter 3, but they do currently have the power, and neither the Congress nor any state legislature seems willing to take it away from them. How many teams would exist if a free market for professional sports were permitted to exist? I'll provide several estimates to illustrate the number of teams that should exist and what the ability to limit the number of teams means to owners and players.

Second, stadia and arenas need to be replaced far more often than they did ten or twenty years ago, and with the power to control the number of teams that exist, the leagues have established a system whereby local and state governments must frequently subsidize the cost of building and rebuilding these playing facilities. And why must these facilities be rebuilt so often? Because every ten or twenty years new ways emerge to earn money from them, and each team owner wants those revenues, as do the players. For example, private suites, club seating (with food and beverage services), and extensive food service outlets (restaurants and bars included in the facility and able to serve large numbers of people) were not part of the building plans for facilities developed in the 1970s and early 1980s. Yet, to maximize team profits, these amenities are necessary and do afford owners higher profits and the ability to pay players higher salaries. These amenities also guarantee that the market value of teams will increase.

How successful are teams at getting new facilities? Very success-ful. By 1996, Indianapolis's Market Square Arena, built in 1974, was the third oldest facility serving as a home for an NBA team. In the 1993–94 season, the Indiana Pacers repeatedly called for improve-ments and enhancements to the arena. By the 1994–95 season, Stephen Goldsmith, Indianapolis's fiscally conservative mayor, was convinced the Indiana Pacers would lose money even if every game was sold out. Dallas's Mavericks were also demanding a new facility to replace Reunion Arena in 1994 and 1995 despite the facility's age, fourteen years, and the fact that the city still owed $62 million for the bonds used to finance it. When the Maverick's owner, Don Carter, was asked what Dallas should do with Reunion Arena, he indicated it should be razed and replaced with a new facility. Indeed, even the Los Angeles Lakers and the New York Knicks, with their large cable television contracts, needed remodeled facilities. The current Madison Square Garden, built in 1968, received a $100 mil-lion renovation in the early 1990s, and proposals have also been developed to replace the Great Western Forum in Los Angeles. Of the NBA's twenty-seven teams, twenty-five are either playing in new facilities or arenas substantially upgraded over the past ten years.

The pressure to build new facilities for teams is also sustained by other cities without teams, which stand ready to demonstrate their commitment and love of sports through the incentives they will provide to be a "sports town." The most important incentive is to provide an owner with a new facility complete with all of the latest revenue-generating innovations. While all professional sports leagues regularly issue proclamations that they oppose team relocations, unless a region steadfastly refuses to support its team, an intense bidding war is common and this "civil war" takes place despite pleas from some elected officials and civic leaders that cities refrain from competing against each other for professional sports franchises and calls for legislation to restrict franchise movement.

WHY WOULD A CITY INVEST IN SPORTS?

What drives communities to subsidize sports teams and build facilities? Cities choose to get involved with sports for a variety of reasons. Some central cities seek teams to help them rebuild their downtown areas. Some communities hope for direct economic development. Other center cities seek teams to improve their identities, while still other cities fight to retain teams to avoid a loss of identity or to avoid a stigma of decline. Still other communities seek to redefine their image or establish their identity as a "major league" community. Indianapolis, Cleveland, and Baltimore tried to change their images through investments in sports. Arlington, Irving, St. Louis, San Antonio, Phoenix, and Portland wanted to underscore or establish their status as "big league" communities. Suburban cities sometimes seek teams to emphasize their economic vitality in an urban region. Other cities seek teams to enhance their entertainment image or to complement other entertainment venues. Some cities are speculators; these are the cities that build facilities in the hope of attracting a team. Sports teams have also become competitive assets within metropolitan areas. In the same way that some cities "steal" corporations from other communities in their region, teams are sometimes convinced to relocate within the same market area.

Each city that decides to provide subsidies to teams genuinely believes sports and the presence of a team are essential for a "big league" identity and economic development. Cities that cannot get major league teams believe a need exists to at least have a minor league team. But do cities really get anything from this self-defined and media-hyped "big league image"?

What do you get when you have a team? As detailed in chapters 4 and 5, there is very little economic gain. There are, however, psychological or intangible benefits. For example, something indeed important happens when millions of fans return to downtown areas to see sporting events. Even the harshest critics of sports and their economic impact must acknowledge the sense of vitality created by attracting almost four million people to downtown areas. There is also a community-building benefit from sports. The recent success of the Detroit Red Wings brought more than twenty thousand people each night back to downtown Detroit. Detroit's chief of police, commenting on the crowds and their return to downtown Detroit, noted, "It's almost an ecstatic feeling" (LaPointe, 1995). True, one booming business isn't going to change long-term economic trends; one successful team, even a possible Stanley Cup champion, won't reverse decades of negative image, some of it self-inflicted (LaPointe, 1995). Although the excitement and spirit generated by a winning team and its effects on communities should not be summarily removed from the analyses of the factors that make cities successful, are million-dollar subsidies really needed to produce these benefits? As I will demonstrate, those subsidies are not needed, and one can still have all the positive benefits noted above without any investment of tax dollars. Enhancing a city's ability to achieve the positive benefits of sports, without providing welfare to wealthy owners and players, is the goal of this book.

WHAT DID CITIES DO FOR SPORTS?
WHAT DID THEY GET FROM SPORTS?

The development of any plan to eliminate the welfare provided to teams must be grounded in the experiences of cities that have tried to use sports for economic development and to enhance their image. After all, if the money cities and states spend for sports teams generates substantial benefits, then maybe the subsidies provided are shrewd and strategic investments. While chapters 4 and 5 will identify elements of the larger economic contributions that are possible (and not possible or probable) from sports, case studies of the experiences of individual cities will identify (1) what cities tried to accomplish, (2) how they went about negotiating with teams and building the facilities required by owners, (3) the lessons learned from these experiences, and (4) the local impacts that did occur. Chapter 6 details the extensive sports and downtown development policies and programs developed by Indianapolis. No city has had as defined and articulated a program for downtown development that emphasized sports as did Indianapolis in the 70s, 80s, and early 90s. Indianapolis was committed to this strategy for more than twenty years. If sports could have any economic effects or impact on a city's economy, it would have happened in Indianapolis. From 1974 through 1995, and across the administrations of three mayors, Indianapolis used sports to redevelop its image and downtown region.

Chapter 7 analyzes Cleveland's extensive investments in Jacobs Field and Gund Arena and the proposed investment to either improve Cleveland Stadium for an NFL team or build a new facility. In 1990 Cleveland launched a public/private partnership designed to save the Indians and to bring the NBA's Cavs back to the downtown area from the suburbs. More than $300 million in tax dollars were pledged to the effort, and another $175 million was targeted for Cleveland Stadium. Together, then, Cleveland spent in excess of $475 million. Why? What did Cleveland get, and what lessons for cities and sports are learned from their experiences?

Chapter 8 focuses on another city that went to extraordinary lengths to get back into the NFL. St. Louis developed an extensive package of incentives that will likely commit the public sector to an investment of more than $700 million over a period of thirty years. St. Louis's desire to get a team at any price provides an opportunity to analyze the ability of a member of a sports cartel to dictate terms, demand and receive subsidies, and provide very little in return. The problems with American sports are carefully detailed in the analysis of St. Louis's efforts to get the Rams.

Canadian cities also provide subsidies for professional sports. Montreal and Toronto's experience with MLB details the hopes, success, and failure of two of Canada's largest experiments with the American pastime. Chapter 9 assesses the quest for economic identity in North America through emphasis on sports.

Small-market cities are particularly vulnerable to the manipulations of the sports leagues. In many of these areas several large firms have already left, and there are numerous examples of teams leaving smaller markets for larger areas. As such, these communities are especially sensitive to calls for large subsidies to offset the disadvantages of their smaller market sizes. An analysis of the efforts of Cincinnati and Pittsburgh to retain MLB teams and an NFL team is detailed in chapter 10 and is critical to the development of a market-based set of policies and programs that will permit professional sports to be played in smaller cities without extensive subsidies or cumbersome legislation.

Communities in several regions have fought among themselves to be the home for a professional sports team. In several instances, neighboring cities have increased the incentives or welfare provided to convince a team to move in a fashion that rivals the welfare provided when teams move between regions. Of course, when teams move within a metropolitan region, what sometimes happens in later years, is that the city initially left without a team then provides an even larger set of incentives to draw the team back "home." This game of "one-upmanship" between cities in a region raises taxes, increases subsidies, and raises the profits of team owners and the salaries players receive.

Why do communities within the same metropolitan region engage in raiding each other to be the host to a team? Each city seeks prestige and the economic growth they believe will follow the franchise to their doorstep. Can any city in a metropolitan area really capture the small benefits generated by a team's presence? That question, and the value of the prestige associated with hosting a team, is analyzed in chapter 11. The experience of the cities in this region that have invested in sports—Arlington, Irving, and Dallas— is compared to the economic growth in cities that did not invest in sports.

FUTURE CHOICES:
HOW CITIES AND THEIR TAXPAYERS CAN AVOID
SUBSIDIES AND BECOME TRUE PARTNERS IN
THE SPORTS BUSINESS

Chapter 12 details a plan for eliminating unneeded subsidies and welfare payments for professional sports teams. If these recommendations cannot be implemented, a set of guidelines and strategies to help local communities survive and benefit from professional sports is also provided. Having established why sports are so important in our culture, this chapter presents an alternative for completely ending the subsidies teams receive as well as a set of strategies for building real partnerships between teams and their communities. In this chapter, I will present a simple but effective way to permit all cities— even those that lose teams   to have new franchises, as well as a plan for effectively using market solutions to stop the spiraling subsidies. Cities, as well as team owners and players, can benefit and prosper from professional sports. To accomplish this objective, however, community leaders must learn what team owners knew and what players learned in the last twenty years: the real economics of cities and professional team sports.

2

Why Are Sports So Important to So Many People?

The sharpest memory of my first week in college is of walking toward the Purdue football stadium on a sunny, cool September afternoon, the noise of the marching band and the huge crowd in the distance, the anticipation of seeing the Boilermakers play Notre Dame. That event, over a generation ago, began a personal love affair with college sports.

—MURRAY SPERBER, *College Sports, Inc.*

When asked to define the greatest days of his life, Billy Crystal's character in *City Slickers* describes his first Yankee game, at age eight: "the beauty of the grass, the red clay running track, the smell of Yankee Stadium, my father holding my hand."

THE SUBSIDIES OR WELFARE given to professional sports teams is a result of two factors: (1) the privileged position accorded to and the importance placed on sports by our society and (2) the artificial scarcity and control owners have over the number of teams that exist. If the subsidies provided to teams are ever to be curtailed or eliminated, sports will need to be seen only as the interesting diversions and small businesses that they are. Their romanticized qualities will have to be removed from the mind-set of negotiators who represent cities in their discussions with teams and the professional leagues. Further, the authority the professional sports leagues have been given to control the number of teams that exist must be changed, and that too will require a recognition that sports are not deserving of the special treatment and reverence that they are accorded. Both of these alterations in the modern psyche will occur only if taxpayers and legislators challenge the mythology of sports. Before dealing with the evolution of the sports leagues and their acquisition of the power to control the number of franchises (chapter 3), it is important to understand the roots and extent of the romanticized elements of sports. Recognizing the emotional attachment that our society has to sports is the first step in a process that can lead to an end to the subsidies given to teams. If enough people understand the mythology of sports, then it may become easier to challenge the view that professional teams deserve welfare.

CAN ANYONE SEE THE MAN BEHIND THE CURTAIN?

Preparing for negotiations with a professional sports team or league requires more than just doing your homework on the economics of the business of professional sports. Developing a "game face" for the negotiations necessitates a clear understanding of how sports became so popular and how their importance in our society is exaggerated. Like Dorothy and Toto, you have to look at what is really behind the curtain or facade of sports to understand the forces that have made sports a modern-day Wizard of Oz. But, be warned. This facade is believed by a great many people, and the illusions created by sports are widely accepted. Beyond the emotional attachments many have to sports, professional sports are also thought to (1) stimulate economic development (Indianapolis, Arlington, Cleveland, Gary), (2) establish the national identity of cities and regions (Nashville, Jacksonville, St. Louis), (3) facilitate regional cooperation among governments (Charlotte), and (4) provide opportunities to bring people back to downtown areas and unify a community

(Baltimore, Cleveland, Detroit). At the same time that teams and their playing facilities accomplish all this for different communities, players have become crucial role models and spokespersons for a number of different social causes. Just as the residents of Oz believed the Wizard could do anything, large numbers of people believe sports, teams, and athletes are the elixirs for any number of social, economic, and political ailments. But, as Toto, Dorothy, the Lion, the Scarecrow, and the Tin Man learned, our modern-day Wizard of Oz relies on smoke and a bombastic display of revelry to illustrate its abilities and power. Is there any substance to this imagery, romanticism, and mysticism? Just what is it that makes sports so important to so many people, and why do people believe sports have a magical quality that can transform communities and their social settings? You must understand each of these factors when you negotiate with teams because not only will you encounter those who believe the myths, but team owners will manipulate the myths to their economic advantage.

Sports As an Elixir for Racial Conflict

Some people believe sports have a stabilizing influence that can minimize civil unrest. The Orioles teams of 1969–1971 had all the qualities of a dynasty: power hitting, superb pitching, defense, speed, and a blend of age and youth. The team won 318 games on its way to three American League pennants and one World Series championship. The Orioles' success was paralleled by that of the Colts, who won an NFL championship in 1968 and two years later, following the merger of the AFL and NFL, won the championship of the professional football world. The Baltimore Bullets of the National Basketball Association were also highly successful in these years.

The triumph of its (Baltimore) sports teams came at a psychologically critical moment for the city and for its political-business elite. After more than a decade of efforts at urban renewal, the riots of 1968 put into doubt the political leadership's master plan for reviving Baltimore. The triumphs of Baltimore's sports franchises were proof that the city still retained vitality. On April 10, 1968, a week after the murder of Martin Luther King, Jr., and less than two days after a modicum of order was restored to the areas where rioting occurred in the wake of the assassination, over 22,000 fans passed through a still-smoldering city to gather at Memorial Stadium for opening day. Mayor Thomas D'Alesandro III was present to throw out the first ball and to show the city's determination to continue about its normal business (Miller, 1990, p. 149).

The psychological attachment of people (especially men) to sports is extraordinary, rooted in the whimsical memories many of us have of our youthful years. Critics of sports like Murray Sperber know their lives were affected, if not partially defined, by sports. Fans like Billy Crystal know their experiences mirror the emotions of middle-age youngsters across North America. The escapism and fantasy of sports captures and absorbs men from the time they are about five years old. This fascination is something that never seems to end; men die with their love of sports intact.

How and why did this attachment develop? At one level there are few parts of life, from language to holiday celebrations, that are not touched, affected, and even partially defined by sports. This pervasiveness builds a number of emotional attachments to sports for men (and many women, too) that are exploited to justify taxes and subsidies for sports team. Individual teams and the professional leagues, as well as their advocates, use these psychological and sociological attachments as ploys to engender excitement and "tug at the hearts" of enthusiasts and nonenthusiasts when negotiations occur. This excitement or emotionalism often prevents cities and their citizens from remembering that the imagery and emotionalism of sports are part of the "show." Spectator sports as a form of escapism and entertainment can captivate and divert attention from dreary aspects of life. As a form of entertainment sports have the ability to create memorable events and develop memories that mark the passage of time and bond generations through shared activities. This romantic bond, coupled with opportunities to escape from the worries of the day, is what owners and leagues manipulate to get what they want from governments, fans, and taxpayers, even in an era of repeated calls for smaller governments and lower taxes.

Just How Popular Are Sports?
Some Important Examples

While the protracted labor problems that have plagued professional sports in recent years have tarnished its image and reduced its meaning for some fans, overall support and interest remain incredibly robust. This pattern is even evident for MLB, where fan resentment from the 1994 strike is clearly evident. In 1990, nearly fifty-five million tickets were sold by MLB teams. In 1994, had the entire season been completed, more than sixty-four million tickets would have been sold, not including the attendance at home games of the two expansion teams that began play in 1993. If the home attendance of the Rockies and Marlins is included, more than seventy-one millions tickets for baseball games would have been sold. In 1995, however, fan resentment over the labor dispute and the cancellation of the 1994 World Series was clearly evident as less than 51 million tickets were sold. Had the entire season been played, and including the attendance at Marlin and Rockies games, MLB sold less than 57 million tickets, or about the same number as sold in 1991.

For the other major sports, despite increasing ticket prices, attendance levels continue to soar. With several teams playing before capacity crowds, the NBA, which sold less than seventeen million tickets in 1991, sold more than eighteen million tickets in 1995. The NFL, another league in which many teams play before capacity crowds, also saw the number of tickets sold increase by more than 100,000 from 1993 to 1995 (excluding the attendance at home games of expansion teams). The NHL has also enjoyed a substantial rise in popularity, selling for the 1994/95 season almost four million additional tickets as compared to the 1991/1992 season. A portion of this increase was the result of the addition of expansions teams, but those teams were just another example of the increasing popularity of the NHL. The 1996/97 season will be a test for the NHL to see if their fans return to purchase tickets after the abbreviated 1995/96 season.

There has also been an unprecedented growth in the demand for minor league teams from small and medium-sized cities. Erie, Pennsylvania, population 108,718, recently spent $8.7 million to become a home for a minor league team. Some medium-sized cities have even been able to successfully support major league hockey and basketball teams.

The media's interest in broadcasting and telecasting games also has not waned despite an amazing proliferation of coverage. Sporting events dominate the list of the most watched television events. When the NFL feared a reduced bid from the networks for its games, the Fox network gave the league its largest contract ever. In 1995 ESPN signed a commitment to televise all of the games for the NCAA's women's basketball championship tournament. The nation's colleges have organized themselves into large blocks or leagues to negotiate profitable media packages, and Notre Dame University was able to negotiate its own contract with NBC to telecast its football games. Pay-per-view and other changes in the cable television industry continue to offer exceptional opportunities for teams and leagues as they seek to reach households in North America, Europe, and Asia. The NFL and the NBA regularly play games in Europe and Asia, and MLB will likely add Asia to its market very soon.

Has the popularity of sports diminished? Not at all!!

SPORTS, CULTURE, AND IMAGERY

Many members of my generation can remember where they were and what they were doing when they heard President Kennedy and Dr. King had died. Neil Armstrong's moon landing proclamation is similarly etched in our minds. Unfortunately for community leaders who deal with professional sports teams, many people also can remember where they were when the 1980 U.S. Olympic hockey team upset the Soviet Union and when the Amazing Mets of 1969 won the pennant. Most baseball fans also know what they were doing on any number of days when the Boston Red Sox collapsed. Probably no sports broadcast is replayed as often as the ending of the 1980 Olympic hockey upset when ABC's Al Michaels declared, "America, do you believe in miracles?"

The defining moments in my life include my first visit to Yankee Stadium; I was eight and can recreate that entire day in my memory, together with my first visions of that green grass and red clay running track circling the field. Just like Billy Crystal, I have never seen grass so green nor clay so red since. My father also held my hand as we descended closer and closer to our seats. I still remember that Yogi Berra had failed to shave before the game and had quite a shadow. Such are the things that eight-year-olds remember.

I also remember a warm November Saturday in the Los Angeles Coliseum. The University of Southern California football team was trailing Notre Dame 24–6, but as the sun set over the Coliseum on one of those glorious fall afternoons in southern California, the Trojans, led by Anthony Davis, Pat Haden, and J. K. McKay, scored seven straight touchdowns to defeat the Irish. I remember USC's band and horse, and the song girls celebrating the most improbable end to the game. Such are the things twenty-two-year-olds remember. These cherished memories, like those enjoyed by Murray Sperber and Billy Crystal, do mark my relationships and sense of time. It is emotions like these that frequently lead public officials to conclude that sports teams deserve subsidies because they create powerful and positive memories. If the welfare system that creates large profits for team owners and players is to end, taxpayers and community leaders must understand the psychological grip sports have on our society and decide not to let these emotions rule our pocketbooks. Sports play on the psyche of taxpayers and community leaders through (1) their image as a romanticized ideal, (2) their integral role in everyday life, (3) their importance to the media, (4) their political symbolism, and (5) their imagery for economic development. These powerful emotional forces must be demystified if the welfare system is ever to end.

SPORTS AS A ROMANTICIZED IDEAL

The romanticized view that many people have of sports has two primary threads. First, people are fond of telling each other that there are a number of positive values that can only (or easily) be taught through sports. These values include the merits and payoffs from hard work and practice, the importance of leadership, the meaning and benefits of team efforts to accomplish or reach a group's goal, and the value of individual sacrifice for group achievement. If these worthy attributes are not sufficient to create a sympathetic environment in which to discuss a sports subsidy, the second thread of the romanticized ideal of sport can be touted: Sports provide a complete set of activities in which parents and children can play together. As a result, for many people, a number of their memories of their parents and childhood are intertwined with these shared activities. Whether it is attending a game together, playing games together, or watching other family members play in their games, family life not only is interwoven with many dimensions of sports but is, at least partially, defined by sports.

To be sure, in recent years we have also become all too keenly aware of some of the negative psychological factors sports can impart. Many male athletes, exposed to levels of violence that are integral parts of certain sports, have had difficulty finding the appropriate boundaries for this physical violence in their nonsport lives. From excessive drug abuse to rapes and spousal abuse to inappropriate risk-taking, promiscuity, and gambling, there is certainly ample evidence that sports have contributed to several of society's pathologies (Lipsyte, 1995). But these extremely critical and important elements of the dark side of sports should not detract from the many positive outcomes that emanate from athletics and athletes.

Sports do teach the very positive values of teamwork, hard work, and sacrifice to attain goals. One cannot become a winner or champion without a substantial commitment to practice, and it is through that commitment that sports teach the value of working hard to achieve a goal. Sports can also teach people to challenge themselves, set goals, and work with others to reach objectives or goals that, without teamwork, could not be achieved. The commitment sports can require, and the team effort involved with all sports (coaches and players in nonteam sports make up a team as well), also form a set of powerful emotional relationships that affect people. It is these memories and the feelings of accomplishment and success that come from working with others that create many of the positive values or impressions of sports many people reference for their entire lives. Anything that supports these memories or underscores these positive values is seen as very desirable. That desirability is what team owners and the professional sports leagues rely on to increase the support they receive from cities and state governments. After all, without a team, what role models would a community use to extol the positive attributes of teamwork, hard work, and achievement?

The romanticized ideal of sports extends from these positive role-model issues to the memories sports create for parents and children. Sports, much like Disney World, create opportunities for parents and children to enjoy the same set of activities. From playing games together to watching games together, sports do create a level of bonding that is quite powerful. Whether it is a boy or girl remembering a game of catch or passing a soccer ball with a parent, games played through school years, or spectator events, sports are a powerful force that binds generations to each other. This emotionalism can affect people's desires to "land a team." Federico Peña, Denver's mayor during its successful drive to get an MLB team, and other civic leaders cited their desire to take their children to baseball games as part of the reason they wanted to bring major league baseball to Denver. These leaders carried their youthful emotions into their decision-making roles. And Denver did commit large amounts of the public's money to indulge and subsidize their bonding needs.

So, why is it important to remember these facets of sports as no more than a mythical ideal when negotiating for a team. First, each of these elements I've described is overly romanticized. It is certainly true that one can learn the value of hard work, teamwork, and sacrifice from sports, but those lessons can also be learned from many other activities and can be taught as a way of life through any number of activities or events. As a result, even though all the positive outcomes attributed to sports are probably true, these lessons can be learned without subsidizing professional teams to play in your city. A city does not need to subsidize a professional team to teach values to children through sports. While professional teams and athletes are usually fine examples of success from hard work, good habits can be taught to children through their own participation in sports, which does not require a subsidy for professional sports. Further, given how few jobs there are in professional sports for players, focusing the attention of young people on sports can distract them from other goals and their education, which can create a more stable economic future.

Second, parents and children can do things together without public subsidies for sports teams. Playing catch, shooting hoops, or passing a soccer ball do not require taxes to support stadia and arenas. Parents and children can find things to do together without sports stadia and arenas, and there is no guarantee that the existence of these facilities will actually encourage anyone to do anything with their children. With the current price charged for tickets to many games, parents and their children may have fewer opportunities to bond at these games than they realize.

Lastly, for all of the positive values that emanate from sports, there is certainly abundant evidence of the negative outcomes as well. Although it is impossible to determine the balance between the good and bad, it is sufficient to recognize that both exist. As such, remember that when your city's leadership says you need to have the team to provide recreation for families or to generate memories, they are taking you for a walk down memory lane. In sports, that translates into a subsidy for teams and the passage of new taxes.

SPORTS AND EVERYDAY LIFE

If you think about events in the United States at almost any point in recent history, other than when our attention was temporarily deflected by a national crisis, sports and the activities of its participants have been a dominant preoccupation. For example, for more than a year America was gripped by the trial of O. J. Simpson, and the preoccupation with his life and the trial was much more than media hype. True, the trial provided an opportunity for the mass media to produce relatively inexpensive "filler" for numerous tabloid television shows. However, America wanted more, much more coverage, and much more coverage from the "mainstream" of

America's media. Each network's evening news shows included daily updates on the trial; on many nights, CNN provided expanded coverage of issues and events associated with the trial. The early-morning network shows such as *Today* and *Good Morning, America* also included frequent updates on the trial through the use of special reporters. On the Internet, the global computer network, there was even an "OJNet" that included daily updates on the trial's progress and tidbits on O.J.'s life.

The media's attention was certainly out of proportion to the crime; other spousal abuse cases and trials are virtually ignored by the media unless there is a bizarre twist (for example, the Bobbitt case). But O. J. Simpson, as a sports star, was an American icon. And Americans wanted to know each and every detail of the inside life of a sports star. Lost amidst details of missing bags and misplaced or mishandled evidence was the death of another victim of spousal abuse and a young man who may have simply been in the wrong place at the wrong time.

The sensationalism of the Simpson trial and the public's desire to know about it were interrupted, only briefly, by Michael Jordan's return to basketball. Newspapers across the country carried front-page stories of the "Second Coming" of his "Airness," and residents of Chicago were enthralled. During this same time period, Mike Tyson, a boxing champion convicted of rape, was released from prison, and his initial activities and press conference were reported by the media with a level of intensity not even reserved for visiting leaders of foreign countries. Indeed, it is safe to argue that Americans were probably more interested in the trial of O. J. Simpson, Michael Jordan's decision to return to professional basketball, and the life of Mike Tyson than the statements and opinions of many elected officials and leaders of other countries. Each of these events and the substantial public attention directed by the mass media underscore the importance of sports and help to establish the environment in which subsidies can be developed and supported.

SPORTS AND LANGUAGE

To underscore the importance of sports to everyday life, one does not have to focus upon the celebrity status of Michael Jordan or the notoriety of O. J. Simpson and Mike Tyson. The first way sports defines our culture and lifestyle is in the very use of language. Sports metaphors are intertwined throughout everyday language, and we define ourselves, events, situations, and outcomes in sports terms. Are you a "winner" or "loser"? Do you want your city to be "major league," or do you want to be the mayor that "lost" the team? Would you rather be the city that "won" a bidding war for a team and proved it had the ability to "go the distance"? See, we can even use sports metaphors to convince you that you should want a team in your city. The use of sports in our language is seemingly endless.

Deadlines and the need for critical actions or decisions are frequently described as "ninth-inning" decisions or actions. The need for a large or major effort to overcome a difficult or even hopeless situation is frequently described as "fourth and long." Midlife crises are described as "halftime" in the game of life. By extension, maybe midlife crises are nothing more than a form of halftime entertainment you engage in while you wait for the older team to take the field. "Going all the way" refers to success, as does "bringing it home." Unlikely, but favorable, outcomes are "long shots," or "three-point shots" from "downtown." Unfavorable outcomes or events for which no advance warning is provided are frequently described as being "blindsided" as when an unsuspecting quarterback is tackled by rushing defensive players. Keeping people updated on items is to give them a "heads-up" as in looking for a fly ball or pass. To confront someone or to negotiate strenuously is "to play hardball." Someone who is a forceful leader "knows how to take it to the hole." If someone is aggressive in arguments, it is an "in your face" discussion. Sticking to a problem or a situation is to do battle until the "ninth inning" or the "fourth quarter." Do-or-die situations begin when the "two-minute warning" is received. Loyal employees are "team players," and much of the thinking that has dominated administrative reform, from Ford's Quality Circles to all aspects of the total quality management concept, emphasize the "team approach" to problem solving and getting to be "Number 1." Sales meetings across the country are dominated by winning coaches and athletes who can impart the "winning" and "team spirit." Important elections or primaries are the "Super Bowls" of the election process. Key debates between candidates become a "World or Championship Series." National leaders, corporate leaders, civic and community leaders, citizens, students, men and women, rich and poor—probably everyone at one time or another has used sports metaphors. Here is an example.

> I am the Cal Ripken candidate if people are interested in performance, consistency, a person they can trust . . . winning the devotion of people who revere the idea of a person constantly being there to witness goodness to his family, to witness faithfulness to a lifetime of work and striving for excellence, to witness fair play and enthusiasm for the achievement of others, to witness the healthy example of a leader who says no to personal vices and to marital infidelity (Stuteville, 1995).
> —SENATOR RICHARD LUGAR (R-Indiana), discussing his candidacy for the Republican nomination for president

What does it mean when the language of a culture begins to include metaphors from something such as sports? It means that at one level, maybe subconsciously, maybe not, the importance of sports in life and for communication is underscored. If sports define something so basic as the language we use to communicate, then are they not deserving of public support, subsidies, and special attention? Shouldn't we treat sports differently from other items that the public must consider. Aren't sports the way we shape values and mold people to be successful adults? As a form of public education don't sports warrant a subsidy?

SPORTS AND SCHOOLS

The inclusion of sports in everyday life does not end with language. Language is clearly an important socializing element, and to the extent that sports are part of our language, we are each socialized to think of them as an important facet of everyday life. The socialization of young people into the world of sports does not begin or end with language. Indeed, maybe our schools underscore more than do metaphors the importance of sports to and in our society.

From alumni reunions or homecomings to parents' day at most universities to establishing school spirit, sports are part of our educational experiences from grade school to graduate school. Residential colleges have turned sports into an industry filled with ritual, bands, midnight practices, school planes and buses, and tutors who help balance an athlete's academic and sports life. But the pageantry and excess that are college sports do not begin with college life. They begin with grade school teams, with cheerleading camps, and with band camps, which define life for youngsters across North America.

Books and movies that highlight high school sports and their importance for young people, their parents, and their communities abound. The attachments these works describe clearly convey sports as a part of life. During one's high school years Friday nights are dominated by high school events that encircle "the game." Sports are even intertwined with the entire process of dating as the weekly games become the arenas within which young men and women learn about the opposite sex and how to relate to it. Romantic relationships sometimes begin at a school's athletic events or the events organized to complement a game. As a result, it is not uncommon to find people believing sports are very important to their lives.

There is also an industry of sorts within this school sports world that helps focus the attention of young people. High school coaches seek to become college coaches and junior high school or middle school coaches seek to advance to the high school level. A sure route to success is to develop young players who can win and thus be attracted to high schools or colleges. To advance in the ranks, coaches at lower levels must develop and encourage young people to become players and improve. As they develop this talent, both coaches and players can move to higher levels.

Much of the association or connection between sports and school is also built around a series of justifications. Frequently any excesses in a coach's or player's behavior are excused or defended because sports mold character and teach people to win. Sports have also been credited with encouraging people to extend their grasp beyond their reach and to dream of glories hard work can produce. How could we not subsidize sports?

SPORTS AND HOLIDAYS

Sports are intrinsically linked to life-cycle events through the placement of "key" sporting events around holidays. Think about it for a minute. What do most families do on Thanksgiving? Eat turkey and watch professional football. What do they do on the Friday after Thanksgiving? Eat leftovers, shop, and watch college football. What do we Americans do on national holidays such as the Fourth of July, Memorial Day, Labor Day, New Year's Day, and Martin Luther King Day? We go to the ole ballpark (or arena) or watch the games on television. We have baseball games on the Fourth of July, complete with fireworks afterwards, and on Memorial Day and Labor Day. Teams even have special afternoon basketball games for Martin Luther King Day.

The largest single sporting event itself, the Indianapolis 500, is scheduled for Memorial Day weekend, moved to Sunday only to give organizers an extra day for the race in the event of rain. What would New Year's Day be without a college bowl game, or actually eight college bowl games? Only parts of Christmas Day have remained protected from the domination of sports. The NBA's Christmas Day present to fans, a choice game between contending teams, usually doesn't start until after noon, but Christmas Eve and Christmas night have long been "fair game" for sports programming. With the potential that more and more football games would be played on Christmas night, the NBA countered in 1995 with not one, but with two, Christmas presents, back-to-back games to fill those idle hours after opening presents and lunch. There is no holy day, Sabbath (Jewish or Christian), or holiday that is not now defined by sports. Sundays belong to the NFL; Saturdays to college football. Basketball, hockey, and baseball at various levels are played on Saturday and Sunday. How many ministers in Texas have been advised to keep their sermons short to avoid conflicting with the Cowboys' kickoffs? As a team that plays in the central time zone, Cowboys games frequently begin at noon. I still remember one Yom Kippur service, the holiest day in the Jewish calendar, when the "buzz" in the congregation was so intense that a very orthodox rabbi agreed to announce the score of the World Series if we could then return to prayer. When sports cannot be part of the life cycle, it is usually best to change the life cycle. Try to plan an event for "Super Bowl Sunday" or the Saturday of the weekend when the final-four teams in college basketball play for the berths in the championship game. If you don't change your event, attendance will suffer, or attendees will be quite distracted.

Just how extensive is sports programming on the holidays? Here is a partial listing for a typical Thanksgiving, Christmas Day, and New Year's Eve and Day (all times eastern standard).

Thanksgiving Day, 1995

11:00	College Football, Georgia v. Georgia Tech
12:30	NFL Football, Minnesota v. Detroit
4:00	NFL Football, Kansas City v. Dallas
4:00	Figure Skating: Skate International, France

Christmas Day, 1995

Noon	Kelly Tires Blue/Gray College All Star Football Classic
3:30	Jeep Eagle Aloha Bowl, College Football, Kansas v. UCLA
3:30	NBA Basketball Doubleheader, Game 1: San Antonio v. Phoenix
6:00	NBA Basketball Doubleheader, Game 2: Houston v. Orlando
9:00	NFL Football, Dallas v. Arizona

New Year's Eve

12:30	NFL Football, Atlanta v. Green Bay (playoff game)
2:00	Anderson Consulting World Championship, Golf
3:30	NFL Football, Indianapolis v. San Diego (playoff game)
7:00	Nokia Sugar Bowl, Virginia Tech v. Texas

New Year's Day

9:00	High School Basketball Hall of Fame Game (Indiana Only)
12:30	Gator Bowl, Clemson v. Syracuse
1:00	Citrus Bowl, Ohio State v. Tennessee
1:30	Cotton Bowl, Colorado v. Oregon
4:30	Rose Bowl, Northwestern v. USC
8:00	Orange Bowl, Florida State v. Notre Dame

The Christmas Day schedule has sports programs available from noon to midnight eastern time, or from nine in the morning until nine in the evening in the Pacific time zone.

What do all these sports events as part of our natural life cycle of events mean for state and local governments that are negotiating with teams? It means that many civic and community leaders, having their holidays and life cycle defined, in part, by sports, might believe that sports are such an important factor that they deserve subsidies from government and from taxpayers.

Emotionalism and a City's Negotiating Style: Denver Gives Away the Store

David Whitford, in *Playing Hardball*, provides an excellent description of how the emotional commitment to sports can affect community leaders when they "try to make the deal." This emotionalism produced a lease for the Colorado Rockies that the team's president, Carl Barger, described in the following terms: "Ha Ha—Ha Ha! It's a great lease. I gotta hand it to those people who negotiated it, it's a hell of lease, boy! In fact, it's unbelievable" (Whitford, 1993, p. 87).

The taxpayers in the Denver metropolitan region voted to provide up to $100 million, or 70 percent of the cost, for a stadium if a team was awarded to the area. Voters approved a one-tenth of 1 percent increase in a regional sales tax to extend for as long as necessary to retire the bonds for this investment. While the voters in the city of Denver alone would have rejected the tax, with the aid of suburban voters, the measure passed with 54 percent of the popular vote. It was known that the stadium would cost more than $100 million. The measure was written so that voters were assured that 30 percent of the cost of the stadium would be supported by private money from such sources as parking, private investment, advertising at the stadium, concessions, and so on. However, the citizens never got what they voted to support.

When the time came to submit Denver's bid to MLB for a team, problems emerged with the proposed ownership group. A great deal of money was needed to secure the team. MLB required a $95 million fee from prospective owners to receive the franchise. To operate the team until revenues began to accrue, each potential ownership group was reminded that another $20 million in cash was needed.

With more than $100 million required from private investors, "flexibility" in the financing of the stadium was required to attract investors or companies who could pay what MLB demanded for a new team. Led by the governor of Colorado, the planning group for the future franchise found that unless potential team owners were given all of the stadium's revenues, investors would not be found. The mayor of Denver, Federico Peña, who had already invested substantial political capital to secure a team, was also eager to provide whatever was necessary to attract the team and an acceptable ownership group. After hearing of the financial problems faced by an emerging ownership group, he wrote, "I assure you the city and county of Denver will cooperate with franchise owners to make Mile High Stadium available on terms that are fair and reasonable" (Whitford, 1993, p. 99).

For the first and second year of its existence, and while a new stadium was being built, the Colorado baseball team would have to play in Mile High Stadium. This stadium was built for the Denver Broncos of the NFL. As a result, two leases were actually developed: one for the use of Mile High Stadium for two years and one for the new stadium.

The mayor was true to his word. For the two years during which the team would need to use Mile High Stadium, it paid no rent. In each of these years the team drew approximately four million fans. The city also gave the team 92 percent of the revenues from concessions.

In terms of the new stadium, it was agreed that the public sector would pay the entire cost of construction, $156 million. The Rockies were to be responsible for all operating and maintenance costs and make payments of $550,000 each year to a capital repair fund. The team also agreed to pay the district that oversees the stadium $.25 for each ticket sold above 2.25 million; $.50 for each ticket between 2.5 and 3.0 million; and $1 for each ticket sold over 3 million. The seating capacity of the new stadium is fifty thousand, so there is a potential to sell more than 4 million tickets each year. If four million fans attend games in any season at the new stadium, the government would receive $1,312,500.

To calculate the percentage of the costs for the new stadium paid by the team and the public sector, I assumed the team would always draw four million fans and that it would continue to make payments of $500,000 to the capital fund. If this was done for twenty-two years at a 6 percent discount rate, the contribution by the Rockies to the stadium, in 1995 dollars, is $21,157,986, or an amount equal to 13.6 percent of the construction cost. If an 8-percent discount rate is used for the twenty-two-year revenue stream, the contribution by the team would be $17,591,560 (in 1995 dollars). This would represent 11.3 percent of the cost of the stadium. Each of these figures is below the 30 percent anticipated by the voters who supported the tax increase to build the stadium and is dependent on the team selling four million tickets every year. While this does not seem to be a particularly difficult target in the team's initial years, the Mets, Yankees, Cubs, White Sox, Dodgers, and Angels, playing in much larger markets than the Rockies, have not been able to sustain attendance at that level. The Toronto Blue Jays have been the only other team to sustain attendance figures at the four million level, but they have also recently won two World Series crowns. In 1995, even if the entire season had been played, the Rockies would have drawn "only" 3.8 million fans.

While the team's contribution never matched what was originally expected, this did not stop the public sector from providing even more revenue for the owners. The new stadium was named Coors Field. The brewing company paid $15 million to the owners to name the stadium, and these revenues also accrued to the team.

Why did Denver "have" to enhance its original commitment for the new stadium? The lease made a big impression on the (existing MLB) owners, exactly as it was intended to do. During the question-answer period (after the presentation of Denver's proposal to MLB) Warren Giles (from the Phillies) was moved to ask Jacobs, "Will you come to Philadelphia and negotiate my lease? This is the best lease I've ever read." Later, Bill White (National League president), after he'd had a chance to fully digest its terms, would label Denver's lease "the proto-type of what we ask our teams to look at" (Whitford, 1993, p. 130).

Denver's political leadership feared that without a subsidy of this nature they could not get an ownership group that could pay MLB's franchise fee and have sufficient revenues to operate the team. Yet, should the Denver region have provided this level of subsidy to support sports and baseball? Clearly, the emotional attachments to sports and baseball in particular helped convince some civic leaders that they had to bring baseball to Denver. After all, repeated efforts to secure a team had failed in the past, and the honor of the city, as well as the memories that could be generated by families attending a game, were at stake. These psychological pressures were sufficient to produce a very generous rental lease agreement for the new owners of the Rockies and permit these people to pay MLB $95 million to bring a franchise to the Rocky Mountains. Federico Peña can now take his children to an MLB game in Denver.

SPORTS AS THE MEDIA'S BREAD AND BUTTER

A great deal of the public's attention on sports is driven by the mass media. Media corporations argue that they are simply responding to consumers who have an insatiable appetite for sports. While there is certainly a good deal of interest in sports to which the media do respond, the media also have a substantial self-interest in cultivating, nurturing, and extending the public's attraction for sports. As a result, a portion of the importance placed on sports develops as a result of the media's interest in having people focused on sports.

Sports are a critical asset for the mass media and directly contribute, in several ways, to the profitability of newspapers, television stations, and radio stations. First, sports fans have an almost insatiable desire for news and information about their teams. Even those fans who attend a game or watch on television want to read about it in the paper. When there is a big game, when a season begins, or when there is an important series, pregame programs are usually part of the "broadcast" day. The print media will publish story after story that is read and reread. As a result, advertisers, eager to reach people interested in sports (males between the ages of eighteen and fifty-four), purchase space or broadcast time. Most importantly for the media, however, is the fact that the cost of producing these stories is very low. Athletes and coaches will frequently talk to the media (to increase their own visibility), and if they will not talk to the media, that too can be covered in great detail. So, sports represent an inexpensive source of news that is consumed by a market group that is very attractive to advertisers. Sports information and news account for approximately 20 percent of the material included in newspapers. To attract the audience most desired by advertisers, newspapers limit their coverage of sports to those with greatest middle- and upper-class appeal: baseball, football, hockey, basketball, and auto racing, with far less attention directed toward wrestling and boxing (Stevens, 1987).

Second, sporting events are both a drama and a form of escapism. For the broadcast media, games represent a virtually endless supply of live entertainment with unknown outcomes. Each game includes limitless examples of success and failure, triumph, despair, ecstasy with risk, and just rewards for hard work. All of these emotions are graphically portrayed in a neatly packaged two- or three-hour time period that has sufficient "breaks" during which advertisers can appeal to fans. Indeed, where additional opportunities for advertisers are needed, extra time-outs are added to the game. This has been done for football and basketball games for years. Baseball requires no additional TV time-outs, with planned breaks in the action every half inning and each time a new pitcher is brought in from the bull pen. The mass media, then, want people to crave sports. Inexpensive dramas and copy are produced for which advertisers will pay handsomely as long as the demand for sports remains high. A never-ending and mutually reinforcing network or linkage exists between sports and the media. If the media can help their "bread and butter" receive a subsidy for a stadium, not only are more profits and copy generated during the discussions for the new facilities, but the media have more incentive to help the teams succeed in getting their new stadia and arenas.

Civic leaders must also recognize that stations pay the teams for the right to transmit games. Since the media are paying for entertainment, it is not surprising that broadcast stations want entertainment and not news. As a result, "hard" news issues or topics may be avoided. For example, when issues were raised about the death of

Celtic star Reggie Lewis and the possible connection to cocaine abuse, it was the *Wall Street Journal* that reported the story, not any of the major networks that broadcast NBA games for their entertainment value or newspapers with sports sections whose revenues are so important to the fiscal success of the paper.

For the print media, sporting events also produce new outcomes or events to be reported daily. Games can be easily rehashed and reviewed with important plays and turning points dissected and analyzed. All of this information or "news" will be gladly and gleefully consumed by readers in one of the best possible age cohorts for advertisers. Neither medium, broadcast nor print, has to invest a great deal of money to produce these events or to train reporters. For the print media, their employees are provided with free attendance at games as the leagues crave the free publicity. While the broadcast media must pay teams or leagues for the rights to televise or broadcast games, given the size of these contracts, it is clear the broadcast media realize substantial profits from sporting events. Multiyear contracts in excess of $1 billion are now common for the television rights to football, basketball, or baseball. While these sums are clearly extraordinary, it is the teams that must produce the events to be broadcast. In this sense the network purchases a series of dramas and the teams must provide the actors (players), the officials, and the stage (arena, stadium) where the play unfolds. If a government can be convinced to pay for the stage, then both the network and team or league realize excess profits as part of the cost of production is passed to the public sector. Teams are merely troupes of actors for multiple dramas (a season of games) telecast in every part of North America and, increasingly, in sections of Europe and Asia.

Some have argued that the attractiveness of sports to the media and the audiences they serve lies in the similarities between sports and life. There is success and failure; ecstasy and disappointment; boredom and unnerving tension; individual and group accomplishments; shared joy and sorrow; violence, within limits; and the potential risk of injury. There are also the ever present committee meetings that dominate life and that are integral to all team sports. Football teams huddle after each play; baseball managers, catchers, and pitchers regularly confer to discuss strategy in the middle of the business day (game), and basketball teams usually meet up to seven times during a game (time-outs). These meetings (huddles, time-outs, discussions with pitchers on the mound) not only provide opportune times for commercials but underscore the similarity between the games and the workday lives of viewers where meetings also precede action. Sports, then, imitate life. Before the action at baseball games begins, there is a meeting at home plate between the managers and the umpires, even though the ground rules and line-ups are well known to everyone. The meetings held among the officials (referees and umpires) might be the most similar to events in real life. Here, a group of authority figures meet to make a decision, interpret actions and subjective rules, and make decisions that can affect life. Everyone can relate to a process like this over which they have little control. Sports provide this, and a wide range of other emotions and events within a short time period. Sports are the ultimate soap opera, parroting life and providing joys and sorrow to viewers in a three-hour lifetime. Each athletic event, with its varied outcomes, upsets, winners and losers, whether broadcast or reported in newspapers or magazines, is different. There is endless variety from sports and the competition between teams and individuals. This variety and its finality, the presence of a winner and loser, create the perfect psychodrama for all mass media outlets.

At least six dimensions or facets to any sporting event account for its appeal to fans. These attributes also assure television and radio programmers of ever-changing dramas. First, in every game or sporting event there is a level of competition with a winner and a loser. From both winners and losers there are emotional reactions. Fans can enjoy their own emotional reactions and observe others from a safe distance, realizing that the outcomes really do not create lasting positive or negative consequences. (Of course, for gamblers such outcomes may produce very real consequences; but for this illustration I am talking about fans who do not gamble to the point of risking their financial stability.)

Second, no two games or events are ever identical. Every contest is different, with separate nuances and possible outcomes, so there is never a "rerun." For the programmers this means a constant source of new mini-dramas that can be endlessly reviewed and discussed.

Third, there are frequent upsets in which an underdog or modern-day David overcomes obstacles to conquer a Goliath. This creates, for fans who may be Davids in their own life, a sense of hope that they too might overcome some large obstacle. Even if a fan does not need to see a David beat a Goliath, the possibility of an upset creates a constant drama for each event or game. Northwestern University's improbable arrival at the 1996 Rose Bowl permitted NBC to focus everyone's attention on the Cinderella season of this highly regarded academic institution. Northwestern's stellar academic achievements, however, were the "sidebar" to the fact that its team was the Big Ten football champion. The fact that the university had placed fifty-five players on the Academic All-American team in the past decade never brought it the exposure it received for its first Big Ten football championship in several decades.

Fourth, most games end with a winner and loser (ties are possible in some sports but recent rule changes make this increasingly unlikely), so a finality or clear-cut outcome is produced in a relatively short period of time. However, since ties are unlikely even where possible, fans are virtually assured of a clear-cut ending to the drama.

Fifth, there is always hope for the losers, for there is a tomorrow in the form of a new season or another game that can be won. This provides hope at the end of every drama, no matter how desperate the situation or outcome from the game played.

Sixth, while participants are rarely seriously hurt as a direct result of events in a game, there are sufficient injuries that become badges of courage to be seen, witnessed, and analyzed through innumerable replays. In addition, physical injuries become the random and uncontrollable events that can affect outcomes. This establishes a strong parallel with each fan's life. Events sometimes happen that cannot be controlled but change what is likely to occur. Injuries, in a sense, provide this random element, which both gives hope (as when an opponent's players are injured) and generates fear (one of our players might be hurt, contributing to our loss). The endless variety of outcomes, the emotions produced, and the bounded time frame within which these dramas take place are perfectly designed for the mass media. With their growing dependence on sports for revenues and income, can the mass media be relied upon to report on sports news and the politics and economics associated with teams seeking "deals" from cities?

The profitability of sports means few newspapers or broadcast stations have much interest in the politics and economics of sports. Most media prefer to focus on the entertainment value of sports. Howard Cosell was the first, and clearly the best, of a very small group of hard news reporters who concentrated on the broader issues defined by and interlaced with sports. The *New York Times,* the *Wall Street Journal,* the *Washington Post,* the *Los Angeles Times,* and selected other papers do have reporters who detail the politics and economics of sports; so do a few of the networks. But these examples, together with *Sports Illustrated,* are the exceptions, not the rule. The media has discovered a "golden goose" in sports and that goose is rarely analyzed for local officials who must decide whether or not a subsidy is needed.

It is important for citizens and their officials to know and be aware of the attraction of sports to the broadcast and print media. The media's need for sporting events to fill pages or broadcast times with live programs establishes television stations, radio stations, and newspapers as potential advocates for the presence of local teams. Teams mean income and readily available quality programming for the broadcast media, and this can sometimes mean these stations will support efforts to bring a team to a city. The financial importance of sports to the media is probably best illustrated by the impact sports have on the sale of newspapers. During the 1994–95 labor disruption in the NHL, the daily circulation of newspapers in both Montreal and Toronto declined by at least four thousand copies. The *Dallas Morning News* also reported that its largest daily sales were on the Sundays that the Dallas Cowboys played in the Super Bowls and the Mondays after their victories.

Sporting events also comprise virtually all of the ten most watched television programs of all time. What all this means is that when state and local officials negotiate with teams the media will (1) likely be strong supporters of any deal needed to bring a team to a community, (2) be unlikely to critically report or investigate the negative implications or aspects of any partnership that brings a team to a community, (3) provide substantial coverage of the positive impacts of, or benefits from, a team's presence in the community and, (4) provide substantial coverage of any lost opportunities or events that surround the movement of a team from a city to another community. As a result, substantial pressure is likely to be generated by the media to support any effort to secure a team's location. Elected officials know well the power of the media to highlight negative outcomes. As such, they may be unwilling to "take on" the media, and they may be very receptive to supporting sports issues if it means favorable exposure in the media.

In some communities major media sources have a direct financial interest in the success of a team. This results from their ownership of the team or the stadium (arena) in which the team plays. While arrangements of this nature are a clear example of media firms participating in the building of their communities, they also establish an important, if not critical, conflict of interest. If the newspaper or a broadcast station has a direct financial investment in a team or the playing facilities built in a city, how can that same community expect the media to provide a balanced appraisal of the benefits, costs, liabilities, and alternatives to any financing program presented by the city or region's political leadership? How can elected leaders and citizens be confident that the media will provide a balanced and fair review of issues if a particular newspaper or station is also an owner of an arena or stadium?

The Mass Media and Financing Sports Stadia: Who Should Pay for the Stage?

When state and local officials think about ways to finance the construction of stadia and arenas, it is important to remember that through the mass media many individuals "attend" or "view" games. In other words, stadia and arenas should be thought of as stages on which melodramas are performed. Some members of the audience are present for the performance; others consume it directly through a live broadcast. Still others consume it through local newscasts (highlights), through detailed descriptions in newspapers, through special sports reporting shows (ESPN's *Sports Center*), or through endless talk shows (radio and television). If those who "attend" the event in any of these various forms are assessed a small fee to support the construction of the stage for these melodramas, there may be no need for state and local governments and their taxpayers to support the cost of a stadium or arena. A failure to collect this fee increases profits for media owners as they base their advertising rates on viewers or newspapers sold.

The importance of broadcast games to teams is probably best underscored by the impact of media markets on a team's value. In 1994, *Financial World* ranked the value of the New York Yankees as the greatest of any of the twenty-eight MLB teams, and the New York Mets were ranked third. Yet, in that year, the paid attendance at Yankee games ranked sixteenth among the twenty-eight teams, and the attendance at Mets games was the third worst in the league (twenty-sixth). In 1993, the Yankees had the sixteenth highest attendance level and the Mets had the twenty-fourth highest. The value of the two New York teams, then, was a direct result of the size of their media markets. These fans or "viewers" of Mets and Yankee games paid nothing to the city of New York for the cost of the "stage" on which the team performed. Yet, the media market was a direct factor in accounting for the value of the team. When cities finance stadia they need to consider shifting the cost of the stadium to all fans who "watch" or "listen" to the game. This can be done by charging an "admissions tax" to those who watch games from the comfort of their homes. Since the value of the team does not depend only on those fans in attendance at games, the financing of the stadium should be borne by all fans, including those who attend that game through the mass media.

SPORTS AND POLITICS

Attention is, of course, power, alluring those who would appropriate that attention to different ends than those which generated it in the first place.

—JOHN MACALOON (1987, p. 116)

The importance of sports for the public sector and as something governments should support is repeatedly underscored by the use of sports in politics. Most members of my generation grew to adulthood amid images of Adolf Hitler's use of the 1936 Olympics to illustrate the virtues, values, and triumph of Nazi society. When groups in the 1960s wanted to highlight the contributions of African Americans, many recalled, with great joy, the triumph of Jesse Owens over the athletes from the Third Reich and Hitler's inability to graciously acknowledge Owens's accomplishments. Of course one does not have to return to the 1930s to see examples of the use of sports for political messages and efforts.

In 1980, President Jimmy Carter used the Olympics to protest the Soviet Union's invasion of Afghanistan when he refused to send the U.S. team to the Moscow games. The Soviet Union retaliated, of course, by refusing to participate in the 1984 Olympics in Los Angeles. Virtually every nation that hosts the Olympics uses the events to showcase their country and society. Large events have always served this purpose, but often the attention sports commands makes them showcases for political statements.

Beyond the international politics associated with sports, domestic and intraregional confrontations also use sports as the vehicle to deliver their messages. From the protests by African Americans for their treatment in the United States at the 1968 Olympics to the capture and death of Israeli athletes at the 1972 Olympic games in Munich, sports, because of the attention they attract, create a forum within which national, regional, and international politics are also played.

Sports have also been used to validate cultures and establish both prestige and image. This was very important to the Communist nations during the cold war when they tried to counter the West's consumer lifestyle with a lifestyle that focused on national prestige and not consumption. Capitalists also wanted to see their athletes win. Roone Arledge, ABC Television's director of sports for many years, once noted that at the height of the cold war he could have televised any event involving a Russian and an American and had a solid audience. Americans rejoiced when our hockey team defeated the Soviet Union in 1980, and we all relished in the NBA's "Dream Team" and their accomplishments in the 1992 Olympics after seeing our collegians lose to foreign basketball teams in several preceding Olympic and Pan-American contests.

Why is the association or linkage between politics and sports important in terms of the subsidies teams receive? Because sports are often used to make political statements, establish identities, and achieve a certain status. The use of sports in national and international politics underscores the importance or prestige that comes from sports or from being associated with sports. If our athletes beat theirs, our culture or country or town is somehow better. Winning teams and athletes validate cultures, economic systems, value systems, and establish, for many people, an external identity. But if you don't have a team, do you have an identity? Better pay what it takes to get a team, right?

The use of sports to celebrate or validate a culture is not a new phenomenon. Sports were a central part of Roman culture; from the Colosseum in Rome to the chariot races that framed *Ben-Hur* to the gladiators themselves, sports were an important part of that culture. Greek culture gave the world the concept of the Olympic games. Some might argue we remember the Roman Colosseum and the concept of the Olympics more than the Roman Senate or any of the other achievements of those two societies. Finally, the importance of sports to ancient cultures is not limited to European societies. Mexico's native tribes used sports to celebrate their culture and holidays. A basketball-like game played at Chichen Itza in Mexico's Yucatán peninsula was part of ritual celebrations within the Mayan culture.

Across cultures, economic systems, and time, societies have used sports to define themselves and illustrate their ability to dominate other cities, cultures, and systems. Sports generate prestige and reputations. When the Packers were winning, Green Bay was "Titletown, USA." The Dallas Cowboys, when they win, are "America's Team." The Bears defined Chicago as the "Monsters of the Midway." Brooklyn had "dem Bums," but now has no team. Indianapolis was a "cemetery with lights," but now is a capital for amateur sports and home to a winning basketball team. And would New York be New York without the Yankees? Better beware of what sports mean and what they can mean when your city starts to negotiate for the "deal" to bring or keep a team.

SPORTS, A COMMUNITY'S IMAGE, AND ECONOMIC DEVELOPMENT

Without them, we're a cow town.
—CHRISTOPHER FLORES, *Sports Illustrated,* March 13,
1995, commenting on the importance of St. Louis's
attracting the Los Angeles Rams

Sports represents a significant opportunity to generate economic development for a city. Leveraging sports to create jobs and expand business paid off handsomely for Indianapolis during the 1980s.

—WILLIAM H. HUDNUT III,
four-term mayor of Indianapolis

During D'Alesandro's three terms as mayor (1940s and 1950s), Baltimore built new schools and roads, public housing, a major airport, and, of course, Memorial Stadium. He wanted to bring baseball to the city to show that Baltimore was a big league town (Miller, 1990, p. 29).

—On the importance of the Orioles'
move to Baltimore in 1954

The media's attention to sports has encouraged many cities to reshape or establish their images and reputations through sports. Indianapolis is frequently mentioned as a city that used its reputation as the "amateur sports capital" to undo a non-image and negative stereotypes as a sleepy city that came to life one day a year. Buffalo, New York's, resurgence involved the building of new facilities for its football and minor league baseball teams. Cleveland attempted to overhaul its image and redevelop its downtown with more than $400 million in sports-related construction. St. Louis and St. Petersburg both built domed stadia in the effort to attract sport teams to their cities. Oklahoma City is planning a major redevelopment of its downtown area around a minor league baseball stadium, a twenty-thousand-seat indoor facility for hockey and other events, and a renovated convention center. These efforts have been described as the most significant events in Oklahoma City's history since the land run (Hamilton, 1995). Gary, Indiana, and its surrounding county were seriously considering the merits of a local income tax to generate sufficient money to attract the Chicago Bears, who would play ten games a year in a new publicly subsidized new stadium.

Cleveland's recent investments in new homes for the Indians and Cavaliers were not the first attempts by this city to try to use sports to "jump-start" economic development. In 1928 city officials asked voters to approve a $2.5 million bond to build a municipal enterprise known as Municipal Stadium. "City officials, in this case led by city manager William R. Hopkins, viewed sports as an economic benefit for the city. A city-owned facility would generate rental revenues from sports teams. In addition, the Mayor also promised that a large, modern facility would attract conventions and other programs to Cleveland which, in turn, would generate economic growth. The supposed ability of sports to drive a service economy has been part of our mythology for decades. Despite cost overruns and setbacks caused by the Depression, the stadium was completed on July 1, 1931" (Grabowski, 1992, pp. 46–47).

Many college presidents and officials are also convinced that the only way to become a "real university" is to have a sports program that attracts attention and students and maintains alumni. The mythology of the importance of sports is pervasive in the halls of the academy.

Making the University of Texas at Arlington a Real University

Ryan C. Amacher served as president of the University of Texas at Arlington (UTA) for several years in the early 1990s. Located in the center of the Dallas/Fort Worth region, the largely commuter campus has faced continuing challenges in establishing its identity. Home to several fine schools and more than twenty thousand students, UTA lacked name recognition and identity. As president, Amacher sought to develop the university's image through sports. The following is an excerpt from an open letter he sent to alumni shortly before his resignation.

"Let me explain why I believe Division I NCAA athletics can contribute to the development of universities in general and of UTA in particular. Another major college president recently told me: 'Real universities do athletics.' This seems obvious to me, but perhaps we should ask the question: Why do (real) universities do athletics?

First, universities do athletics because athletic programs attract many good students. Students are drawn to universities for various educational and leadership enhancing programs besides the regular offerings: theater, student newspapers, band, debate, and athletics. At present UTA has about 325 student-athletes. These students would not be here if we did not play Division I athletics. They would instead be at Texas Tech or North Texas or another school that recruited them. These same students are going to be successful, loyal alums [sic].

Second, student-athletes have a work ethic sought by employers. Recently, I asked many Metroplex human relations personnel what they found most lacking in recent university graduates—ours and others. The most common response was a lack of competitive spirit and commitment to the teamwork of the company. Those are the very skills developed by participation in athletics. . . .

Third, athletics are good for alums and students. They develop a sense of spirit and camaraderie. Many universities build their development efforts around this spirit. When I visit community alumni groups, they ask about UTA athletics more frequently than anything else. In our society, athletics provide a place where we can all come together—regardless of career interest or race. They create a common bond. . . .

Finally, let's return for a moment to the proposition that real universities do athletics. Let's play the wannabe game. List five public universities that you would aspire for UTA to challenge. Write them down. Now that you've done that, think of their athletic programs. My guess is that the universities you listed have invested significantly in athletics. Perhaps you even know of them because of their athletic programs. . . . In ten years, return to your list of five public universities you wish UTA could be 'more like.' My guess is that you will agree with my presidential colleague who said 'real universities do athletics.' I think she is correct."

Many of the points made by Dr. Amacher are valid in the sense that they represent perceptions rampant in our society. What

Dr. Amacher ignores are the negative issues associated with professional sports. First, many athletic programs lose money for their colleges and universities (Blum, 1994). Second, there is no certainty that winning sports programs, or sports programs in general, are associated with increased alumni donations and activities (Lederman, 1988). Third, college sports programs have generated a myriad of management and ethical problems (Sperber, 1990). Fourth, when considering the educational mission of college sports, Sperber (1990) noted, "The main purpose of college sports is commercial entertainment. Within most universities with big-time intercollegiate programs, the athletic department operates as a separate business and has almost no connection to the education departments and functions of the school—even the research into and teaching of sports is done by the physical education department. The reason elite athletes are in universities has nothing to do with the educational missions of their schools. Athletes are the only group of students recruited for entertainment" (p. 1). Fifth, virtually every year there are sports programs that are placed on probation as a result of recruiting and other program administration violations.

Consider the problems that have emerged within the last few years. The University of Georgia admitted to manipulating grade reports to permit players to compete (Bowen, 1986). At least three Texas universities, two of which are located in the same metropolitan area as UTA—Texas Christian, Southern Methodist, and Texas A&M—were placed on probation because student-athletes received illegal payments (McNaab, 1986). Barry Switzer resigned from his head coaching position at the University of Oklahoma amidst reports of illegal activities by several football players. Despite placing programs on probation and forcing SMU to abandon its football program, neither the NCAA nor selected university administrations have been able to control certain athletic programs. In 1995, *Sports Illustrated* reviewed in great detail the excesses at the University of Miami's football program. The problems were so severe that the magazine's story called the program "Broken Beyond Repair" and called upon the university's president to terminate its football team (Wolff, 1995). Are these problems and issues worth the gains UTA's former president hoped to achieve? Are sports needed to develop a "real" public metropolitan university?

Sports and imagery can be a sort of "double-edged sword," even if one believes that hosting winning teams does attract economic development. James Edward Miller, in his wonderful history of the Baltimore Orioles, noted that longtime sports scribe Roger Angell frequently described a "deep pessimism" that was part of the city of Baltimore during its team's repeated losses to New York teams in baseball, football, and basketball (Miller, 1990, p. 153). Residents of Boston have long had to live with the repeated failures of the Boston Red Sox, which many link to the trade (actually, he was "sold" to the New York team for $100,000 to help finance the Boston team owner's Broadway production of *No, No, Nanette*) of Babe Ruth to the hated Yankees in the 1920s. That legacy, however, has had little negative impact on the rise and fall of Boston's economy over the years, and the (continuing) staggering importance of its educational, health, and finance centers. Boston's redevelopment and revitalization also seem to have continued without many sports championships.

The facilities built for sports teams and events, because of their size and the number of people they attract, also have become defining elements or architectural statements for many cities and regions. While the Roman Colosseum remains one of the important legacies of Imperial Rome, the facilities built by cities throughout the world generate substantial levels of civic pride. Popular author James A. Michener was among the first to underscore the levels of civic pride generated by these new facilities. Maybe public stadia are even a required part of the definition of a city. In *Sports in America* (1976) Michener noted:

> The real reason is that a city needs a big public stadium because that's one of the things that distinguishes a city. I would not elect to live in a city that did not have a spacious public building in which to play games, and as a taxpayer I would be willing to have the city use my dollars to help build such a stadium, if that were necessary. I am therefore unequivocally in support of public stadiums (p. 338).

Ah, but isn't that the heart of the matter? Is it necessary? Michener continues:

> My reasons are not all pragmatic. I believe that each era of civilization generates its peculiar architectural symbol, and that this acquires a spiritual significance far beyond its mere utilitarian purpose. First we had the Age of Pyramids in which I would include such edifices as the Ziggurat in Babylon, Borobudur in Java, and Angkor Wat in Cambodia. . . . Those societies which built well in this age of massive structures are well remembered. . . . Then came the Age of Temples, symbolized by the Parthenon, followed by the Age of Stadia, symbolized by the Coliseum [sic](Rome). Then came the glorious Age of Cathedrals, and much later the Age of Bridges when flying arches were thrown across all the rivers of the world. One of the best periods, architecturally, was the Age of the Railroad Stations.

Sporting arenas built by the Romans also dot parts of Turkey and Israel, and one in Israel is still used for concerts.

Michener's observations may ring with more truth today when cities across North America use sport facilities to establish their identities, anchor development, and lead redevelopment efforts. For more than twenty-five years, sports facilities have been presented to voters and taxpayers as packages to "establish identities," "make us big league," "define our city," "give character to our city," and to "redevelop," "invigorate," "stimulate," or "rebuild" downtowns, declining areas, or faltering economies.

In 1974 Indianapolis launched the redevelopment of its downtown area with the building of Market Square Arena (home to the NBA's Pacers) to anchor the eastern edge of the then new downtown. Slightly more than two decades later Indianapolis completed its redevelopment of downtown with a new baseball stadium for its minor league team on the downtown's western edge and across the street from the RCA Dome, home to the NFL's Colts. Likewise, Cleveland's Gateway Economic Development Corporation led efforts to rebuild downtown Cleveland with two new sports facilities and a restaurant and entertainment district and mall. Temple

University's president and Philadelphia's mayor were both interested in redeveloping north Philadelphia in 1995 through the construction of at least one new sports facility for the university's teams.

Basking in the architectural and critical acclaim for the "Ballpark in Arlington," a facility cast in the nostalgic mode of Baltimore's Camden Yards and home to MLB's Texas Rangers, Arlington, Texas's, civic leadership was eager to build another facility for an NBA team, the Dallas Mavericks. The city's leaders wanted to build this second facility to continue to foster Arlington's reputation as a sports and recreation capital. The watershed for the latest round of sports as a redevelopment tool was Oriole Park at Camden Yards, which capped that city's redevelopment of its inner harbor. If imitation is the highest form of flattery, Baltimore's effort may have been a particularly significant factor in continuing society's preoccupation with sports and encouraging teams to push cities to build architectural statements for their new home-court advantages.

How Far Will a City Go for Civic Pride? St. Louis and Jacksonville Seek NFL Teams

The city of St. Louis lost its football team, the Cardinals, to Phoenix in 1988. In 1993, the NFL decided to add two new teams, and many believed St. Louis would receive one of these franchises as compensation for the Cardinals. Problems with the establishment of a local ownership group in St. Louis encouraged the NFL to award its new franchises to Charlotte and Jacksonville, which left St. Louis with no hope for a team unless it could convince an existing franchise to relocate. To establish itself as a potential home for an existing team, the city of St. Louis and St. Louis County, with help from the state, built a $260-million domed stadium

One team that was ready to listen to St. Louis's siren call was the Los Angeles Rams. The Los Angeles region, despite being the nation's second largest population center, has only one "first-class" facility for football. That facility, the Rose Bowl, has never been home to a professional team. When the Rams moved from Cleveland to Los Angeles in the 1950s they selected as their home the Los Angeles Coliseum. With approximately a hundred thousand seats and its proximity to downtown, the Coliseum was an acceptable location for the Rams. However, the Coliseum, built for the 1932 Olympic games, has numerous drawbacks, including a running track that surrounds the football field, creating a substantial distance between the players and the fans. Some seats were also so far from the field that they were seldom purchased, and the Coliseum's design militated against the development of luxury seating and suites.

As the region's population grew and dispersed, the Rams sought a different facility. Unable to conclude negotiations with the Coliseum Commission for substantial renovations or a new facility, the Rams moved to the suburban city of Anaheim and began using the same facility as MLB's California Angels.

As fan support for the Rams substantially declined, attendance dropped below fifty thousand fans per game, and their market value, as estimated by *Financial World,* fell below the average for all NFL teams in 1995. Thus, the Rams were a possible "target" for a city willing to provide a football-only facility and other inducements.

To entice the Rams from Anaheim, the city and county of St. Louis offered the team 100 percent of all concession revenues, 75 percent of advertising income from the facility, and 90 percent in any year that more than $6 million in advertising income was earned. A local corporate group guaranteed that 85 percent of the luxury boxes and club seats would be sold for fifteen years. The Rams were also promised all income from these seats. Through the sale of seat options to prospective fans, the city and county of St. Louis also agreed to provide the funds to pay the team's indemnity to Anaheim, all moving expenses, and a portion of the costs associated with building a practice facility. The Rams received twelve hundred parking spots for each game at a cost of $2 per spot as well. The team may distribute or sell these as they desire.

For all of these incentives or provisions, the Rams make an annual rental payment of $250,000, and pay between $250,000 and $300,000 for game-day expenses associated with the use of the facility. There is the potential for the Rams to "cover" the annual cost of their lease from the advertising they sell in the stadium built for them with taxpayers' funds. In this sense, then, the Rams were even provided with the source of the revenue to pay for the use of their "stage," leaving the team to use all ticket, concession, luxury seating, and media revenues for its own profits. If the present value of the Rams' costs for use of the stadium through 2016 are calculated in 1995 dollars, their investment ranges from $39.1 million (using a 6 percent discount rate) to $30.6 million (using an 8 percent discount rate). This amounts to either 15 percent of the public sector's investment (at a 6 percent discount rate) or 11.8 percent (at an 8 percent discount rate). Some have estimated the total cost to state and local taxpayers for attracting the Rams to St. Louis to be $720 million (Burstein & Rolnick, 1995).

When the Rams presented their request to move to the NFL's other owners—a team wishing to move from its metropolitan region needs the support of three-quarters of their fellow owners—the league rejected the proposed relocation. The owners cited their concern that their own procedures for documenting a lack of community support for a team had not been followed by the Rams. Some owners even argued that the Rams were supported by southern California but that the team's owners were unfairly operating in a manner to encourage a lack of support so they could move the team. There was also substantial concern that the loss of one of the two teams in the Los Angeles market (one from each conference) would reduce television revenues for all teams if television ratings declined and the Fox network sought a refund. When Fox made its offer to the NFL to televise national conference games, there was a national conference team in Los Angeles. With the move of the Rams, Fox would be without a team in the nation's second largest market. St. Louis is the nation's twentieth largest media market. The other owners wanted compensation or a share in the excellent lease the Rams had secured in exchange for the risks they would have to assume if reduced television revenues resulted from the team's move.

The Rams initially offered to give the league $25 million to permit the move. When that proposal was rejected, the Rams met with their fellow owners and agreed to the following terms: (1) give to the league 34 percent, or $17 million, of their seat licensing revenue; (2) pay a relocation fee of $29 million; (3) agree to forgo their share of any expansion revenues from a new Los Angeles–area team if the league expands before 2005; (4) if the Fox broadcasting network suffers a severe ratings drop because there is only one team in the Los Angeles market, the Rams will be responsible for 50 percent of any rebates up to $12.5 million; and, (5) if the league decides to realign its teams into new divisions, the Rams will accept any decision made regarding its own placement. The Rams thus agreed to pay $46 million in cash and could lose up to $71.5 million in their move to St. Louis. They were able to afford to do this because of the public subsidies they received.

The city of Jacksonville agreed to improve its Gator Bowl for the Jacksonville Jaguars when it and a private ownership group applied for an NFL franchise. These renovations to the stadium would cost $121 million. The team was also given a thirty-year lease that provides for the team's total control over concessions, stadium advertising, luxury suites, and parking revenues. The public sector is responsible for maintenance and repair of the facility and game-day expenses. The Jaguars agreed to pay the city $2.50 for each ticket sold and $2 for each car that is parked at the facility on game days.

If the Jaguars sell all seventy-three thousand tickets to all games (eight regular season and two exhibition games), the city will receive $1,825,000 in annual payments from the team. The public sector would also receive revenue from parking at the stadium. If the team sells out every game through 2016, and twenty thousand cars used the lots controlled by the team, the public sector would receive an amount equal to 26.8 percent of its investment in renovations (at a 6 percent discount rate) and 22.7 percent of its investment at an 8 percent discount rate. These calculations included no value of the public sector's initial investment in the stadium. However, the public sector does have complete responsibility for all maintenance, repair, and operational expenses for the stadium.

Undoubtedly the presence of an NFL team adds to a community's quality of life and enhances its image. Jacksonville has its team, and St. Louis is, again, home to an NFL team. Did the amount of money these communities invested in professional sports actually reflect an improved "quality of life" and the enhancement of their civic reputation?

SPORTS AND ECONOMIC DEVELOPMENT II: BEWARE OF THE GROWTH COALITION

On one philosophical point I am adamant. Ninety-nine out of the hundred greatest buildings in world history—pyramids, Parthenon, Chartres Cathedral, Rockefeller Center— would never have been built if approval from the general public had been required. You cannot construct a beautiful city by plebiscite; someone with vision must force the issue, override trivial objections, and ensure that the job is finished artistically. Therefore, I would not want the building of great stadiums to be subjected to picayune supervision by the general public. Let the project be explained, justified, and funded honestly, then let the men and women of vision proceed with the actual work.

—JAMES A. MICHENER, *Sports in America* (p. 346)

Cleveland entered the 1980s having just come out of fiscal default (in 1978 it was the first major American city to default on its fiscal obligations since the depression) with the realization that its old industrial economy was no longer viable. Service industries such as banks, hospitals, restaurants, entertainment facilities, and hotels would now be the core of the economy. Sports would be a critical ingredient in two ways: Winning teams not only boost the city's image through their national exposure but also bring needed revenues to the community. The place of sports in civic life had come 180 degrees from its origins. Play was now work, and sporting pastimes were economic products of greater or equal value than previous products such as agricultural crops, or the iron and steel produced by Cleveland's once vast mills. By the end of the decade many believed the city had achieved a renaissance as it escaped default. New construction projects filled the downtown area, and Cleveland earned national recognition as an "All American City."

—JOHN J. GRABOWSKI, *Sports in Cleveland* (p. 84)

There is a great deal of money to be made from the stadia and arenas that cities and states build to attract and retain teams. There are bonds to be sold that create income for lawyers and the financial community. There is land to be purchased and developed, and that means money for banks, real estate developers, landowners, and lawyers. When facilities are built, frequently the land adjacent to the arena or stadium escalates in value. There is profit to be made here too. As already noted, the local media will also benefit from the location of a team. And then there is the increase in value the team owners enjoy. When new facilities are built, the value of teams usually increases, and the increases are quite substantial. The value of the Texas Rangers, as estimated by *Financial World,* increased from $106 million to $132 million after the Ballpark in Arlington opened. This represented a 24.5-percent increase in the wealth of the team's owners. This occurred in a year when the value of the average MLB franchise actually declined by $1 million. The ownership of the Cleveland Indians enjoyed a similar return after Jacobs Field opened. The 1993 team value was $81 million and increased to $100 million in 1994, an increase of 23.5 percent. The owners of the Phoenix Suns saw the value of their investment increase from $71 million to $108 million after the opening of the America West Arena. This represented a 52.1-percent increase in the value of the team.

> As capitalist firms grow in size and strategic importance, they become more public than private, forcing the state and local governments to consider them more as partners than as private actors. . . . This convergence of interest explains why, despite the fact that many businessmen are apprehensive about the expansion of government, they can be quite tolerant of government action when it serves their interest. Their support of the ideology of free enterprise does not prevent them from occasionally seeking help from the government when profits are endangered. The ideology of the free market does serve a purpose, however; for it allows businessmen to reject the idea of quid pro quo for government assistance. . . . Sport capitalists have learned these lessons well, lobbying for government protection (and assistance) when profits are threatened, appealing for more market freedoms when opportunities for gain arise.
>
> —JOHN WILSON, *Playing by the Rules* (p. 29)

The collection of financial interests who stand to benefit, even if the investment does not generate substantial economic growth or new tax revenues for state and local governments, is sometimes referred to as a "growth coalition" or "growth machine" (Molotch, 1993). These coalitions or machines are comprised of the people who will benefit politically or economically from the team's presence and who use their political, social, and economic connections to facilitate, encourage, and even lead the effort for the development of a sports facility. It is also possible that the very elected leaders who negotiate with teams and the professional sports leagues are, themselves, members of the growth coalition. This is most common in areas where mayors are part-time officials who also have other jobs. If the elected officials are not a direct part of the growth coalition, they are frequently dependent on these economic actors and their institutions for campaign funds. In addition, mayors in all cities can also enjoy substantial benefits from voters who enjoy sports. That support is a frequent factor in explaining why most mayors seek to attract and retain sports teams (Fort, 1997).

Growth coalitions do provide important leadership for the development of many cities, and without such influence many medium-sized cities find their developmental efforts seriously hampered. Yet, when it comes to sports and ensuring public guarantees for professional teams, taxpayers and civic leaders would be wise to question the proposals made by growth coalitions.

The frequent refrain when cities and states are approached for subsidies is that the team cannot afford to operate without tax support. However, consider this point. In 1994, the Milwaukee Bucks gave Glenn Robinson a multiyear $68 million contract. In 1996, the Los Angeles Lakers gave Shaquille O'Neal a $120 million multiyear contract. If someone could afford to pay a player $68 or more than $120 million, you can be sure someone or some group of people, other than the player, are able to earn a profit from this player's activities. Who are these people? They are the owners of teams, those who own land in the area near the location of the arena or stadium, and the businesses that prosper from the location of a team. All of these "winners" from professional sports make up the growth coalition that pressures for tax support for stadia and arenas. They may be the same people who contribute to the campaign coffers of elected officials, or they may be the business tycoons who whisper to mayors about the need to be a "major league city." We all need to be cautious when the siren song is sung by a growth coalition. Michener's prediction may well be true. Many large projects would be defeated if placed before the public for a vote, especially if the public believes they will not benefit from the project.

There are examples where the public has decided to support the actions of a growth coalition. When voters in Arlington, Texas, were asked to support an increase in their sales tax to pay for the city's share of the cost of constructing the Ballpark in Arlington, the measure was supported by two-thirds of those who voted. The growth coalition did use players from the Rangers in advertisements that asked voters to "Keep us in Arlington." Members of the growth coalition fought hard for the measure and it was supported by the voters. While some might argue the city and its taxpayers should not have subsidized the team, contrary to Michener's fears the project was completed even after the people were asked. One could argue that the voters did not understand who would gain and how much they would have to pay. They might also have misunderstood how to finance a stadium without public subsidies, but they did support the tax increase.

THE IMPORTANCE OF SPORTS

Why do citizens accept and support the subsidies provided to teams? The emotional attachment to sports, cultivated by institutions that also profit from sports, has clouded their judgment and established a set of unrealistic priorities. *Consumer Reports* always advises its readers to avoid emotional attachments to any one car when negotiating with dealers. That's good advice to taxpayers and their community leaders when they deal with professional sports teams. Understand the emotional attachments to sports; be sensitive to the ways in which these bonds affect decision making and logic; and try to remember that sports, as entertainment, is but one way a city can establish its world-class image and its civic reputation. As enjoyable as sports are, there is no need to subsidize them. Be aware of the growth coalition that emerges to support sports. From the media to developers you will hear calls to be major league. Understand why they make these calls and the profits they are likely to earn.

Sports are important, but nothing that has been described here could or should be used to justify a subsidy or welfare payment to the owners of teams. Nevertheless, when negotiating with teams or leagues it is critical to understand the range of emotional issues that can surface and the institutions that will capitalize on these feelings to secure a team. The first step toward reducing the welfare paid to professional sports teams involves pulling back of the curtain and understanding that the men manipulating the smoke and pageantry of sports are presenting an illusion steeped in the traditions and culture of our society. Just as the lion learned that he had all the courage he needed, the professional sports wizards cannot give us anything that we do not already possess. Sports can teach valuable lessons, but so can any number of other institutions. Sports can provide entertainment, but so do movies, concerts, nature trails, bicycle paths, and countless other activities. Sports can bring people to downtown areas, but so can other civic events. Sports are a helpful and beneficial diversion, but they do not have the power and abilities ascribed to them by believers in the Wizard. Now, why did we give these wizards who own teams the power to control where teams play and where they will not?

3

Maintaining Scarcity

Why All Cities That Want Teams Can't Have Them

LIKE ANY BUSINESS, professional sports teams can increase their profits if they reduce or eliminate competition. Most businesses must accomplish this objective by producing the best possible product at the lowest price. The professional sports leagues, however, have been able to establish a protected environment and eliminate competition while maintaining the illusion of a free market. All the professional sports leagues are, in reality, cartels or private business associations insulated from the competitive pressures of a free market. These cartels control the number of teams that exist, allowing association members to extract subsidies and welfare from state and local governments that want one of the controlled franchises to locate within their borders. The subsidies ensure that substantial economic gains will be made by either those who own teams or the players. The fewer teams that exist, the more likely it is that cities and states will offer substantial incentives to owners. In the past only the owners benefited from the cartel structure of sports; now, the players benefit as well as salaries have soared. The labor strife that has dominated each of the leagues in the last several years is really a battle for control of the cartels' profits, with neither players nor owners desiring a market-based environment that would end the subsidies provided by governments.

The power to limit the number of teams is a direct result of the formation of leagues by the owners of professional sports teams. When initially formed, the leagues were not designed to be the cartels or ownership groups that wield the sort of power they do today. Leagues were formed to organize and regularize seasons and aspects of competition, and to attract other investors who might be willing to assume the risks of team ownership. Yet, over time, the leagues evolved into powerful economic and political institutions concerned with both profitability and the rules for playing games. The leagues that now exist control their markets and eliminate competition in ways that GM, IBM, AT&T, Microsoft, and Boeing cannot. While more teams would mean more jobs for players, fewer, more profitable and valuable teams can mean higher salaries for those who do play. The paradox that fewer teams could mean more money was best summarized by one of the participants in the sale of the Oakland A's, who noted, "If we're going to make baseball a purely money deal based on the value of franchises, we should just put all the franchises on the East Coast and West Coast and a team in Chicago and call it a day" (Whitford, 1993, p. 33).

Before any solutions or changes in this environment can be proposed it is necessary to understand: (1) why leagues developed, (2) the economic fear and insecurity that drive the desire to have leagues function as powerful cartels, (3) how each cartel member earns money and benefits from the existing system, and (4) the powerful incentives that exist for both players and owners to perpetuate this system. Professional sports *are* different from any other business, and those differences do establish the need for very limited special arrangements. However, the ability to declare where teams will play and the cities that will have teams is a disruption in market forces that guarantees a shortage in the number of teams that exist. In such an environment subsidies will flow and fans and taxpayers will pay more for sports than they should. Ending this system requires an understanding of its development, why some struggle to protect it, how it is maintained, and the current state of affairs.

HOW MANY TEAMS CAN EXIST?

How successful have the sports leagues been in establishing their control over the number of teams that exist? There are no fewer than *four ways* to illustrate just how scarce the supply of teams has become, or how many teams could exist if markets rather than cartels controlled the supply of franchises. First, focusing on the supply of players for baseball teams, Zimbalist (1992) illustrated the potential for additional, *high-quality* teams. In 1903 there were 320 major league baseball players drawn from a population of eighty million people in the United States, or one player for every 250,000 people. The 650 major leaguers in 1990, drawn from a population of approximately 250 million people, amounted to one player for every 385,000 people in the United States. One frequent lament is that we cannot create more teams because the quality of the players is decreasing or not keeping pace with the expanding number of teams. In terms of the distribution of baseball players, as Zimbalist has pointed out, that simply is not the case. With 320 players drawn from a population of 80 million in 1903, there were four players per 1 million people. Using this ratio, in 1990, with a population of 250 million people, American should have been able to produce a thousand baseball players; with approximately twenty-five players on each team, the current population is sufficiently large to produce enough players for forty teams.

As convincing as this analysis is for the potential existence of more teams with high-quality players, the situation is actually even more advantageous. In 1990 the major leagues were drawing talent from all racial groups, something that was not done in 1903. This means the pool of available talent in the 1990s is actually *much larger* than the pool from which major league players were selected in 1903. With improved nutritional levels and training programs, a greater number of quality athletes also can be expected to exist. In addition, even if one were to argue that some athletic talent is now drawn to other sports (basketball, hockey, and football), restricting the actual number of athletes available for baseball teams, the few hundred athletes who are members of the teams in these other leagues are more than offset by further expansion of the pool of athletic talent for all sports teams by drawing players from Central and South America, the Caribbean Islands, Europe, the former Soviet Union, and Japan. Simply put, the internationalization of baseball, basketball, and hockey means there is no shortage of talent from which to supply *additional* competitive baseball teams or teams for any of the professional sports leagues.

Second, it is also possible to use the size and increases in the population of the United States to illustrate the shortage of teams (see Table 3–1). The market for all sports teams has increased far faster than the supply of teams; as cities and the nation have grown in size, there are now more communities that can financially support a team. For example, in 1990, Milwaukee, the metropolitan area with the smallest population base, supported an MLB team. While the team has had several financial challenges, it has been fiscally successful in the past and, with a new stadium, will likely be successful again. Currently, at least nine other metropolitan areas have populations larger than that of the Milwaukee region. At a minimum, then, the population of the United States is large enough to support at least thirty-three major league baseball teams. With two teams already in Canada, MLB should have at least thirty-five teams. There may be other cities in Canada or Mexico that could also support MLB teams.

In professional football, in 1990, Buffalo was the smallest market with an NFL team, but fourteen other metropolitan areas with larger populations were without teams. As a result, it is reasonable to argue that as many as forty-two NFL teams could have been supported by the 250 million people living in the United States in 1990.

Third, in 1995, the *New York Times* performed its own analysis of the number of baseball teams that could be supported in the United States. This examination focused on four criteria enumerated for each metropolitan area: the number of men between the ages of eighteen and fifty-four, per capita incomes, population growth, and the potential for the sale of luxury suites. The *Times* rated each region as either below average, average, or above average on each of these criteria. The criteria used to measure the ability to afford or

TABLE 3–1

Population and the Potential Number of
Professional Baseball and Football Teams

Year	U.S. Population (in 000s)	Actual Number of Major League Teams	Number of Metropolitan Areas without a Team but Larger in Population than Smallest Area with a Team	Potential Number of Teams
		Baseball		
1950	152,271	16	8	24
1960	180,671	16	7	23
1970	205,052	23	5	28
1980	227,757	26	6	30
1990	248,710	26	9	35
		Football		
1950	152,271	13	5	18
1960	180,671	21	11	23
1970	205,052	26	8	34
1980	227,757	28	6	34
1990	248,710	28	14	42

support a team were selected through a survey of economists who argued a region could support a team if it had a population of more than one million, a high percentage of men in the needed age category, per capita incomes above the national average, and a high proportion of businesses that could afford to purchase luxury suites. Based on these criteria, the *Times* found nine areas without MLB teams that could definitely support a team, five areas that could possibly support a team, and as many as five areas that could support at least one *additional* team. With twenty-eight teams based in the United States (including the Phoenix and St. Petersburg teams), the analysis by the *New York Times* would suggest MLB should have at least thirty-seven teams, and possibly as many as forty-seven (Ahmad-Taylor, 1995). This analysis did not include an assessment of the number of teams that could be supported in Canada or Mexico.

Fourth, consider for a moment that the Cleveland Indians are financially successful serving a metropolitan region of 2.9 million people (July 1994 population estimate). If we accept 3 million as the population base needed for a profitable team, how many teams should exist in the New York City and Los Angeles metropolitan regions? In 1994, the population of metropolitan Los Angeles was estimated to be 15.3 million. That region should be able to support five teams. New York, with a population in excess of 19 million, should have at least six teams. Between these two areas, then, there should be at least *seven additional* MLB franchises (four more teams in the New York City metropolitan area and three more in the Los Angeles region), since both areas have two teams. Currently, MLB has twenty-six teams in the United States with two new teams beginning play in 1998. Expanding the number of teams in the nation's two largest areas would mean there should be no fewer than thirty-five MLB teams. With too few teams relative to the number of cities able to support them, and with an adequate supply of talent, an *undersupply* of teams exists, increasing the competition for franchises and raising the level of subsidies cities are willing to provide.[1]

These four approaches to measuring the demand for teams illustrate how the market is failing—the demand for teams exceeds the supply—because the structure of professional sports has developed cartels not unlike that which the oil-producing nations created. MLB, the NFL, the NBA, and the NHL are the OPEC of the 1990s, at least as far as taxpayers and professional sports teams are concerned. Just as the oil-producing nations held the oil-consuming nations hostage to high prices in the 1970s, the sports leagues and their players are holding cities and their taxpayers hostage. Now that we know the major sports leagues use their power to limit the number of teams, how did they get this power? Why do sports leagues exist?

THE EVOLUTION OF SPORTS LEAGUES

One factor makes the sports business different from any other: teams require competitors. If you want to buy a loaf of bread, no baker needs another bakery to exist for you to have a loaf of bread. In fact, the baker might prefer to be the only bread maker in town. Even though you would probably suffer if there was only one baker (higher prices, less choice, lower quality—all the things that happen when monopolies exist), you could still enjoy bread in the absence of a second bakery. But, would you enjoy watching the Dallas Cowboys or Cincinnati Reds if there were no other professional teams for them to play against?

How much would you pay to see an intrasquad game among the Dolphins or Indians? Do you think you'd be a loyal and zealous fan if the Red Wings or Bulls simply went from town to town beating any odd collection of people who could be enticed to play them? Probably not. The success of professional team sports is a direct result of the existence of competitive teams that play against each other following commonly accepted rules and on similar playing fields (ninety-foot base paths, hundred-yard fields, ten-foot-high baskets, and so on). Leagues were initially developed to recruit potential competitors and to establish and maintain accepted rules of play. The success of professional team sports requires other competitors who also follow an agreed set of rules, and leagues were initially established to ensure the existence of other teams that would follow them.

Professional sports leagues, then, were needed to establish and maintain standards and to recruit investors who would establish competitive teams. The NFL, NBA, NHL, and MLB each sought a stable base of competitors who respected each other's local markets and who were willing to stage games according to an established set of rules and regulations. To succeed it was believed league members had to agree to (1) play each other, (2) refuse to play games with nonleague members, and (3) agree not to locate in an area without the permission of all concerned. In this manner team owners agreed not to compete in the same market with each other and to establish their own geographical spheres of influence. The competitive value of the league was maintained, as was the economic value of each team, by prohibiting members from playing games against teams that were not members of the league. For example, NFL teams never played games with upstart AFL teams until the merger. Similarly, in the 1970s the NBA's teams did not play games with members of the ABA, and in the 1980s the NHL's teams did not play games against teams from the World Hockey League.

Each of the professional sports leagues developed slightly differently and each had its own procedures and guidelines for success.

On balance, however, each sought to control the number of teams that would exist in each market area (generally no more than one or two teams in any market area or city) while guaranteeing the existence of a sufficient number of teams to offer regularized competition. Each league reached this point through a common beginning and a relatively similar ending; only the steps in the middle varied.

In each of the four major sports' early or formative stages two patterns of play existed: the formation of leagues of teams and the existence of individual or "barnstorming" teams. Barnstorming teams simply went from area to area playing against whatever competition could be found. Team owners quickly learned that leagues were more likely than independent groups of teams to generate profits. Fans wanted regularized competition between groups of players or teams with equal chances or opportunities to attract and retain the most skilled players. Today, just one barnstorming team remains from each league's early days. The Harlem Globetrotters entertain millions of people each year, but they are appreciated far more for their comedic prowess then their ability to win basketball championships.

The concept of a sports league, then, was initially established to ensure competitive integrity (a sufficient number of teams from different areas) and to regularize that competition and the game itself. Early entrepreneurs learned that financial success required a season of regularly scheduled games between independently owned teams that followed an agreed-upon set of rules. There also had to be an accepted set of minimum standards for playing fields, although part of baseball's allure was the variability permitted in the design of outfields. For example, Yankee Stadium, built in the 1920s, had its "death valleys" in left center field and center field, but its friendly pennant porch in right field. Fenway Park's Green Monster, Wrigley Field's ivy-covered walls, and old Crosley's Field's rising slope in the outfield are integral parts of baseball's lore. When baseball fans ask you if you ever saw "the catch," they are referring to Willie Mays's grab of Vic Wertz's blast in 1954 in the death valley of the Polo Grounds' center field. The Polo Grounds' unique dimensions and Mays's skills united to forge a moment that is cherished by most baseball fans.

But these irregularities only served to underscore the aspects of the game that had to be followed: four bases at distances of ninety feet; a pitcher's mound set sixty feet six inches from the plate; batter's boxes; four balls for a walk; three strikes for an out; a strike zone that was evaluated by independent umpires; and foul lines that delineated the area in which hits would occur. The playing field that became fair territory was identified by extending the foul lines along an agreed-upon angle from home plate that established a square for the four bases arranged in a diamond from home plate. MLB regularized this format for baseball, and the other leagues specified standards for their sports. In this manner fans could be sure the team that won did so as a result of skill and whatever luck arises from the bounce of a ball or puck, and not from the manipulation of rules or playing conditions that benefit only one team. While the Yankees might have enjoyed a short right field fence, their opponents also could and did put home runs into the right field seats. The Cleveland Browns certainly enjoyed the support provided by their rabid fans in the "Dawg Pound," but they still needed ten yards for a first down and they and their opponents received six points for a touchdown.

The early experiments with leagues and barnstorming also illustrated the need for independent team ownership. Leagues could not be successful if teams were owned by the same individual or group, or the league itself. Fans wanted each owner to have a vested interest in building the best possible team. Since winning teams generally attracted more fans, it was believed that each individual owner, if there was no interlocking ownership, would try to develop the best possible team to attract more and more fans. Fans wanted owners committed to winning who also might suffer financial losses (fewer attending fans) if the team's record declined.

The league format also provided other benefits. Early entrepreneurs found fan interest could be better maintained if a season ended with a league champion. Interest sustained across a season of games would be more likely to entice fans to see more than one game; and with a championship at stake, each game, and especially those at the end of the season, became more and more critical, further increasing fan interest. Competing leagues or divisions permitted a final set of games or a play-off to crown a champion. Baseball's championship series, the World Series, came to pass after the merger of the National and American leagues.

All the other professional sports leagues followed a similar pattern. The winner of the NHL's Stanley Cup was always determined by a play-off system even when only two of the six teams in the league failed to qualify for the postseason play-offs. The interest in league championships has now expanded to the point where the NBA finals in 1995 were televised to 164 countries (Helyar, August 1995), generating substantial revenues. To raise additional revenues, more layers have been added to the play-off formats of all leagues. MLB joined the NFL in permitting "wild card" or second-place teams to quality for its play-offs even though divisions now have just four or five teams. (After MLB's two new teams begin play, all divisions will have five teams.) In the NBA, sixteen teams qualify for the play-offs, creating the possibility that a team's play-off games could equal 25 percent of its regular-season games.

Leagues were also needed to respond aggressively to any threat to the integrity of play. When it appeared some players might have been influenced by gamblers, baseball's stern commissioner, Judge Kenesaw Landis, banished several members of the Chicago White Sox (including the legendary Shoeless Joe Jackson) from the game for life. More recently, another baseball commissioner banished Pete Rose for gambling, and that action has prevented his nomination to the sport's Hall of Fame. The NFL also suspended two members of the Green Bay Packers for one year for gambling (Paul Hornung and Jim Taylor). The NBA changed its procedures for gaining the top draft pick when it was feared fans might believe teams were trying to lose games to secure the worst record in the league. Before the lottery was established, the team with the worst record always picked first in the draft of new college players. If a team was eliminated from making the play-offs, there was clear incentive to simply lose all remaining games. To avoid this apparent conflict of interest the league established a lottery to select the team that actually gets the initial players from among all teams that do not make the play-offs. While the team with the most losses has the greatest chance of receiving the first pick in the draft of college and high school players, additional losses do not guarantee the earliest or highest pick in the draft. Maintaining the integrity of the game through the image that everyone is trying to win every game has been found to be essential for attracting and maintaining loyal and committed fans.

Most recently drug usage has been added to the list of concerns the sports leagues have with the integrity of their games (Suskind, 1995). The leagues have at least three fears from the possible use of drugs by athletes. First, if fans suspect players are using drugs to enhance their performance, the emphasis on skill development and practice might be undermined. This, in turn, would diminish the value of any athlete's accomplishments, as skill or strength might be seen to be a product of artificial means rather than hard work and skill development. Second, drug use clearly conveys an inappropriate and dangerous image to fans and provides a very poor role model for children. All teams and leagues seek to avoid any problems that would threaten the sport's marketing opportunities. Sports, as an entertainment industry, must be critically concerned with its image. Anything that tarnishes that image can reduce profits. As such, even the hint of socially undesirable activities can reduce profitable opportunities. Third, the leagues all fear that addicted players or players who use drugs will be seen as more likely to gamble or accept money from gamblers to support their addiction or drug-buying activities. As a result, all leagues have established drug-scanning procedures, counseling programs, and suspension procedures if drug use by an athlete is confirmed. Competitiveness, hard play (and even violent play) within the rules, and an absence of a hint of suspicion of gambling or "throwing" games are needed to sustain a profitable league.

Each of the four leagues or cartels has been extraordinary successful in establishing uniform rules and procedures, maintaining the integrity of its sport, and developing a structure for the designation of a champion. Each league has produced a form of entertainment valued by millions of loyal fans in several countries. There is no more viable evidence of the success of the leagues and their value than the extensive and loyal fan base enjoyed by each sport. Numerous individuals—players, owners, individuals in related businesses, owners of media companies—have made a substantial amount of money from sports. With all of this success, is it only selfish greed that sustains the desire for cartels? Before any recommendations for changing the structure of sports markets are made, it is necessary to appreciate the fear of economic collapse that convinces many people of the need to protect the existing power of the sports leagues.

FROM STRUCTURED COMPETITION TO PROTECTED MARKETS: THE EXPANDED MISSION FOR AMERICA'S SPORTS LEAGUES

Cynically, one could argue that the control over the supply of teams is a product of the selfish desire of owners and players to maximize their economic gains. While that might explain a great deal, owners and players have a real fear that the financial world of sports could collapse. Indeed, the early history of all sports leagues is replete with examples of both teams and leagues collapsing in bankruptcy. Before implementing any changes in the structure of the leagues, it is important to recognize this history, as the protectionism exhibited by teams and leagues is a direct reaction to the substantial financial problems all sports leagues encountered in their formative years.

TEAM SPORTS—THE ECONOMIC UNCERTAINTY OF THE EARLY YEARS

When more than 10 percent of all professional teams are threatening to move, when some players earn in excess of $5 million for a single season, and when new franchises sell for more than $100 million, it is hard to imagine a time when teams actually lost substantial amounts of money and ceased operations. Yet, that is exactly what did happen, and what several owners maintain may happen again. Let's leave aside, for the moment, the questions of whether or not it will happen again. Did teams go bankrupt in the past? Yes, they did.

Major League Baseball

There are several excellent histories of the early days of baseball. Harold Seymour's *Baseball the Early Years* and James Quirk and Rodney Fort's *Pay Dirt: The Business of Professional Team Sports* each chronicle an early history of teams losing money and moving from city to city seeking a supportive fan base of paying customers. Indeed, one may conclude that an early goal of the professional leagues was to recruit and attract individuals who could be persuaded to invest in a sports team. In reviewing the early years of professional sports, Scully (1995) notes:

> Most of the National League clubs lost money in the early years, and many of them folded. Some clubs were thrown out of the league and others folded for financial reasons. . . . Of the original clubs, only Chicago and Boston survived. Measured over the longer time period from 1876 to 1900, when the National League faced competition from other leagues, the failure rate of the franchises seems high. Of the twenty-nine clubs created by the National League or absorbed from the American Association, twenty-one were canceled—a business failure rate of 72 percent over the period. On an annual basis, however, about one team failed per year, a business failure rate of about three percent per year. In modern times a similar percentage of small businesses fail each year (p. 9).

The National Basketball Association

Early failure and franchise instability also characterized the founding years of professional basketball. Teams formed, reorganized, went out of business, and moved to other cities or locations in search of a stable base of fans; and this history is not that distant. The American Basketball League was formed in 1925 but collapsed in the wake of the Great Depression. In 1937, the National Basketball League was formed, but five of its thirteen member teams ceased operations in 1938 and another team folded during the World War II years. The league expanded after World War II and competed with the eleven-member Basketball Association of America. From this competition and the financial collapse of both leagues, the NBA emerged in 1949 with seventeen members. However, by the 1954–55 season there were just eight teams in the league, and just nine teams made up the NBA as late as the 1963–64 season. Table 3–2 illustrates the fate of the seventeen franchises that joined together in 1949 to form the NBA at the league's initial meeting in Fort Wayne, Indiana. From that original group, only two teams were playing in the same city fifteen years later. In total, just seven of the original franchises survived.

The NBA's financial success is really a phenomenon of the past two decades. Prior to the 1970s, the NBA was still a small organization without a national television contract. In the 1960s, for example, Chicago was unable to support a team, and until Michael Jordan's appearance, basketball in the Windy City seemed to be a risky proposition. Football's popularity and stability have existed for less than forty years, and the NHL as a transcontinental league is also a

TABLE 3–2
The Early Years of the NBA:
The Fate of the Seventeen Founding Members

Formation of the NBA

1949/50 Season	1954/55 Season	1963/64 Season
Anderson Packers (Indiana)	Defunct	Defunct
Baltimore Bullets	Baltimore Bullets	Defunct
Boston Celtics	Boston Celtics	Boston Celtics
Chicago Stags	Defunct	Defunct
Denver Nuggets	Defunct	Defunct
Fort Wayne Zollner Pistons	Fort Wayne Zollner Pistons	Detroit Pistons
Indianapolis Jets	Defunct	Defunct
Minneapolis Lakers	Minneapolis Lakers	Los Angeles Lakers
New York Knicks	New York Knicks	New York Knicks
Philadelphia Warriors	Philadelphia Warriors	Golden State Warriors
Rochester Royals	Rochester Royals	Cincinnati Royals
Sheboygan Redskins	Defunct	Defunct
St. Louis Bombers	Defunct	Defunct
Syracuse Nationals	Syracuse Nationals	Philadelphia 76ers
Tri-Cities Blackhawks	Milwaukee Hawks	St. Louis Hawks
Waterloo Hawks	Defunct	Defunct
Washington Capitols	Defunct	Baltimore Bullets*

*The Chicago Zephyrs entered the NBA in 1961 as the Chicago Packers. They were renamed the Zephyrs in 1962 and became the Baltimore Bullets for the 1963–64 season; the Chicago Bulls entered the NBA in 1966.

phenomenon of very recent vintage. Only baseball has a history of stability that spans more than fifty years.

The National Football League

Professional football's early years were also littered with failed leagues and franchises. No fewer than six different professional football leagues have actually ceased operation: the American Football League (1926); a second American Football League that tried to operate during the Depression (1937); the third American Football League, which was a victim of World War II (1941); the All-America Football Conference (1949); the World Football League (1975); and the United States Football League (1985). From the pre-1950 defunct leagues, only two franchises still exist as members of the NFL. In 1949 the Cleveland Browns and the San Francisco 49ers survived the collapse of the All-American Football Conference and became members of the NFL. When the Browns joined the NFL, their popularity helped convince the Cleveland Rams of the NFL to move to Los Angeles; the Rams had been in Cleveland since 1937.

The first stable professional football league was established by George Halas in 1920, but it would expand, contract, expand, and teams would move from area to area before the league emerged as the modern-day NFL. Halas's American Professional Football Association had as its original members the Chicago Bears, Chicago Cardinals, and the Green Bay Packers. Between 1920 and 1929 numerous struggling teams playing in thirty-three different cities tried to survive with the Bears, Cardinals, and Packers. From the teams that tried to survive in the 1920s, only one, the New York Giants, endured to become a member of the NFL with the Bears, Cardinals, and Packers (Scully, 1995; Meserole, 1995). The real growth of the NFL's popularity began in the 1960s, and many tie the increase in fan interest to the legendary overtime championship game between the New York Giants and the Baltimore Colts in 1958. The NFL added the Baltimore Colts in 1953 but did not expand again until 1960. In that year, a new American Football League appeared, and with its successful television contract, this expansion league was a real threat to the NFL. The AFL added the Miami Dolphins in 1966 and the Cincinnati Bengals in 1968. The NFL added the Minnesota Vikings in 1961 and the Atlanta Falcons in 1966. Eventually the AFL was absorbed by the NFL. The combined or merged NFL added the Tampa Bay Buccaneers and Seattle Seahawks in 1976, and then did not expand again until the mid-1990s, when the Carolina Cougars and Jacksonville Jaguars joined the league. In 1995 both the Raiders and Rams left the Los Angeles market, and it was expected the NFL would expand again to offer a team to the nation's second largest market for professional football before the end of the decade. With the move of the Cleveland franchise to Baltimore, the NFL has also agreed to place a new Browns team in Cleveland before the end of the century.

The National Hockey League

Professional hockey had its origins in Canada, and was always much smaller in scope and scale than the other professional leagues. Four teams formed the NHL in 1917, but only two, the Montreal Canadiens and the Toronto Maple Leafs (née Arenas) survived to the modern era. Numerous teams joined the league over the next decade, but only four of these still exist: the New York Rangers, the Boston Bruins, the Detroit Red Wings, and the Chicago Blackhawks. These six teams formed the NHL prior to World War II, and it would be more than four decades before the NHL would add other cities. In a battle with the expansion World Hockey League, the NHL would expand and absorb many of the more successful teams from the upstart league.

So the early history of each of the sports leagues is a tale of unstable teams developing, folding, moving, and some surviving. Leagues developed, collapsed, and then reemerged. Some owners, fearful of a possible return to an unstable past, seek to maximize their options. Harkening back to earlier unstable years, owners prefer limiting the number of teams to preserve the possibility of moving to other locations if fan support erodes.

WHERE'S THE BEEF? THE MONEY IN AND FROM PROFESSIONAL SPORTS TEAMS

To evaluate whether or not cartels are still needed to restrict the number of teams, it is critical to understand how professional sports franchises generate income for players and owners. If there is no reason to believe that there are significant financial threats to the viability of leagues, there is no justification for a cartel. This information is also critical for community leaders who seek to negotiate the best possible deal for their community (or the lowest possible subsidy). If teams can earn substantial amounts of money, there is no need for any welfare or public subsidies. Reforms designed to reduce welfare levels must be grounded in the real economics of sports, which identifies all the revenue streams available to teams.

As with any business, the way professional teams earn money has changed over time. Today there are national media contracts, cable television deals, luxury suites, club seats, permanent seat licenses (PSLs), restaurants, merchandise agreements, and naming rights. In addition, each league has always debated the extent to which revenues should be shared between large- and small-market teams. The real economics of sports is now a very complicated affair.

One subtle complexity in the real world of sports economics is the way in which each league shares, or does not share, revenue between large- and small-market teams. MLB and the NFL have always shared a portion of the revenues earned by each team. In the National League, visiting teams receive 10 percent of all ticket revenues; in the American League, the visiting team receives 15 percent of gate revenues. In addition, media revenues from the play-offs, World Series, and Game of the Week broadcasts are shared. The NFL, in contrast, has a far more extensive revenue-sharing program. Home teams retain just 60 percent of the gate or revenues from ticket sales, while the visiting team receives the balance, or 40 percent. In addition, since the 1960s, NFL teams have shared equally in the lucrative national media contracts that cover all regular-season games, all play-off games, selected pre-season games, and the Super Bowl. In neither baseball nor football, however, are other stadium- or arena-related income shared. This means income from luxury suites, clubs seats, PSLs, parking fees, naming rights, and profits from food and beverage sales are not shared. While MLB has recently amended their revenue-sharing procedures to transfer some money to small market teams from franchises in large markets with greater revenues, the NFL has not. In addition, revenues earned by teams from local media contracts are not shared. All revenues earned by NBA and NHL teams, for the most part, are not shared. In these leagues, the only revenue that is shared is the income from national media contracts, but most regular-season games are not part of these packages. Local media sales (including cable television deals) are not shared, giving some teams an extraordinarily larger profit potential. Understanding where and how teams make money helps to explain the incentives for limiting the number of teams, the fiscal stress on small-market teams, the overall profit potential of all teams, and the processes that create an environment in which subsidies from taxpayers are expected.

It is probably best to think of the sources of revenue team owners can receive in two broad categories: direct and indirect income sources. Each of these revenue streams is identified in Table 3–3.

TABLE 3–3
The Revenue Flow and Income Sources for Team Owner

Direct Income Sources	Indirect Income Sources
Ticket sales; seat licenses	Team-value appreciation
Suite and premium seating charges	Related product sales
In-stadium advertising	Associated asset value appreciation
Concessions	Advertising for related products
Parking	Media value
Other events	Salary and fringe benefits
Local media contracts	Tax advantages
National media contracts	Interest on loans
Facility and real estate rentals	Public sector incentives
Expansion franchise fees	Revenue sharing
Clothing, merchandise, souvenirs	

DIRECT SOURCES OF INCOME

When stadium or arena financing "deals" are discussed by team owners and the public sector, the direct sources of revenue are first evaluated. These are the income streams produced by fans, depending on whether they attend games or simply watch or listen to broadcasts.

Ticket Revenues

Tickets remain an important source of revenue for most franchises. In recent years, however the *relative* importance of ticket revenues has declined with the creation of other charges associated with seats and tickets. For example, in the early 1990s several teams sold PSLs. A PSL is not an admission ticket; it is a right to purchase tickets—usually season tickets—that can be sold or transferred by its owner. The value or good that fans purchase when they buy a PSL, then, is limited to the right to determine who can buy season tickets. Prior to the existence of PSLs a season ticket holder could not transfer the right to buy the tickets to anyone else. If the fan elected not to purchase the season ticket, the team decided who could purchase the tickets to future games. However, fans who purchase a PSL can assign their ticket purchase rights to any individual.

Further, PSLs can be sold without the team's permission. In certain communities where a team's popularity has increased, the value of PSLs has sharply escalated, and it is the fans who retain this new value, not the teams. The importance and revenue potential of PSLs are now so substantial that when the Los Angeles Rams sought approval from the NFL to move to St. Louis, a key element in the negotiation was how much of the new or expected PSL revenue the team would earn would be shared with the other owners. Since PSL revenues *are not ticket revenues,* they are not part of the revenue-sharing requirements of the NFL. Since the NHL and NBA do not share ticket revenue, PSL income is not shared among those teams. MLB also does not require the sharing of PSL income. PSL income, then, becomes an important component in the financing of a team. These revenues can be used to pay the team's portion of the cost of building the facility without reducing income from ticket sales, and there is no requirement to share any of this revenue with other teams in the league. This is, then, a new source of revenue for sports and a way to increase the charges paid by fans. How valuable are PSLs in terms of increasing the wealth of team owners?

The Texas Rangers, in 1991, were one of MLB's least valuable franchises, worth an estimated $101 million. In 1994, the Ballpark in Arlington opened complete with luxury suites and club seats. The team also sold PSLs, and its value increased to $157 million. The Texas Rangers went from the sixteenth most valuable baseball team to third, passing even the Los Angeles Dodgers, whose home market area, even though it is shared with the California Angels, is far larger than the market served by the Texas Rangers. The value of the Rangers increased as a result of the revenue potential created by the building of a new stadium and not as a result of the team's improved performance; the Rangers had never played a postseason game prior to the 1996 season.

Suite and Premium-Seating Charges

The value of a new stadium does not end with PSLs. Indeed, what may be far more important than PSL revenues are the annual suite and premium rental charges teams in newer facilities are able to collect for their luxury seats. Similar to PSL charges, suite and premium-seating rental charges are not ticket revenues, so they are not shared with visiting teams. These charges, however, are another cost to fans for their tickets. Revenue from suites and premium seating is now so important to the valuation of teams that the two most valued teams in the NFL have reached that pinnacle because of their stadium revenues.

Suite and club or premium-seating rental charges generally involve two different packages or forms. In suite seating, a business or individual purchases a lease for an entertainment, reception, or living-room area that also has from eight to sixteen seats for viewing games. Certain facilities lease double suites that include as many as thirty-two seats. In some facilities the lease price includes tickets to games or events and parking spaces in or near the stadium or arena.

Other teams require that tickets to games be purchased; the lease payments at these facilities are for the luxury suites but do not include event tickets. If the tickets are included in the lease price, the team and the league agree on the ticket value, which must be used in any calculation of the visiting team's share of gate receipts. The prices charged for suite leases vary from team to team, but $75,000 to $100,000 is quite common.

Club or premium seats are different from suites in that there is no private entertainment or reception area adjoining the seats; indeed, these seats are usually not in any private suite. Premium or club seats are usually more comfortable than those found elsewhere in the stadium or arena. In addition, wider aisles are common, as is food and wait service. Some of the newer stadia and arenas also provide a common area for club seat customers where refreshments can be enjoyed before and after the game. These areas lack the privacy of suites and many of the other luxuries (carpeting, plush seats), but they do provide a socialization area. Clubs seats for baseball games cost between $25 and $30 in most stadia. For basketball and football, $65 club seats are sold at several facilities.

Every facility built in the last several years has included these forms of premium seating to enhance team revenues and profits (see Table 3–4). The fiscal success of teams such as the Cleveland Indians, Texas Rangers, Cleveland Cavaliers, and Phoenix Suns means that all teams will need or want these revenue sources. However, how much of the revenue from luxury suites and premium seating is retained by the team and how much is given to the public-sector partner for the cost of constructing a new facility is negotiated as part of the lease. If the teams own their own facilities, they retain all revenues. The Ballpark in Arlington is owned by a special district unit of local government. In the first year of the new stadium's existence this entity received 115 percent of all rental revenue from the luxury suites and club seats. In years two through four the Texas Rangers received 95 percent of all lease revenues and then 100 percent in all other years. The Indianapolis Colts receive $500,000 of the luxury suite rental fees, with the public agency that built the RCA Dome receiving the balance (approximately $2.2 million). The Cleveland Indians receive all revenue from the luxury suites and

TABLE 3–4

Suite and Premium Seating in Selected New Facilities

Facility/Team	Suites	Club Seats	Total Capacity
MLB Teams			
Camden Yards (Orioles)	66	3,800	48,262
Comisky Park II (White Sox)	102	1,833	44,321
Jacobs Field (Indians)	129	2,058	42,400
Coors Field (Rockies)	56	4,400	50,000
Joe Robbie (Marlins)	215	6,750	47,662
Humphrey Metrodome (Twins)	115	0	56,144
Ballpark in Arlington (Rangers)	120	4,099	49,292
NBA Teams			
United Center (Bulls)	216	3,000	21,500
Gund Arena (Cavaliers)	92	3,000	20,562
Palace at Auburn Hills (Pistons)	180	3,000	21,454
Target Center (Timberwolves)	68	0	19,006
Madison Square Garden (Knicks)	88	2,500	19,763
America West Arena (Suns)	87	700	19,023
Rose Garden (Trail Blazers)	70	2,400	21,300
Alamodome (Spurs)	34	3,500	20,662
Delta Center (Jazz)	74	0	19,911
NFL Teams			
Georgia Dome (Falcons)	203	6,300	71,280
Carolinas Stadium (Panthers)	135	10,800	72,300
America's Center (Rams)	120	6,200	65,300

club seats at Jacobs Field even though the public sector built and owns the stadium. The Cleveland Cavaliers received the same sort of lease, and the team retains all revenue from suite and luxury seating at Gund Arena. Leases vary and every deal between a city and a team is different. Increasingly, however, luxury and premium-seating revenues are becoming a larger and larger portion of the income pie for teams.

In 1994, the Dallas Cowboys earned $37.3 million in stadium revenues, six times more than the New York Giants and the Chicago Bears, eighteen times more than the New York Jets, eight times more than the Los Angeles Rams, and thirty-seven times more than the Los Angeles Raiders. In 1995, the Cowboy's $39.8 million in stadium revenue was nine times greater than the revenue earned by the New York Giants and thirty times the amount earned by the Colts, Lions, Jets, Steelers, Broncos, and Panthers. While several of these other teams played in markets with much larger population bases, none of these teams played in facilities that could generate the kind of revenues the Dallas Cowboys could earn at Texas Stadium from their luxury suites and other sources of revenues in both 1994 and 1995. The Miami Dolphins, the second most valuable franchise in the NFL, earned less than half of what the Cowboys received in stadium revenues. Such is the value of suite and premium seating, and in no league are teams required to share these revenues with other league members. Luxury seating can and does eliminate the problem faced by small-market teams in matching the revenue received by larger market teams from local media contracts. Through luxury seating sales, a team can generate very large revenues, but this requires (1) a large enough base of fans who will pay the premium charges and (2) a guarantee that fans will continue to see the league's best teams on a regular basis. Further, if the public sector will pay for part or all of the cost of building the stadium or arena, then these rental charges can be income for the team. In addition, the ability to command high rental fees can only be secured if there are no competing teams in their region and if the best teams do not have to play games against several new teams. With more teams in a region there would be less demand for luxury seating; and, if the most popular teams made fewer appearances, demand for luxury seating could also decline. The need to generate large revenues from luxury seat sales militates against the creation of additional teams.

In-Stadium Advertising

Sporting events have always been an attractive vehicle for advertising, and none of these revenues are shared with visiting teams. With ticket prices increasing, the number and percentage of higher-income fans at sporting events has increased, making stadia and arenas even more valued advertising venues. Within the last few years stadia and arenas have also been named for their sponsors. Some communities and teams have received as much as $1 million a year for a facility named for a sponsor (RCA Dome, Indianapolis; America West Arena, Phoenix; United Center, Chicago; Coors Field, Denver; Jacobs Field, Cleveland; and others). Who retains the money from facility advertising is also part of every lease negotiation. In some instances the advertising revenues remain with the facility operators; in other leases the teams retain all advertising revenues; and in still others the advertising revenues are shared between teams and the governmental unit, with teams sometimes taking those shares that are related to their fans. In no instances do any visiting teams receive any advertising revenue.

The Cleveland Indians retain all advertising revenues at Jacobs Field, as do the Texas Rangers at the Ballpark in Arlington. The city of Indianapolis's Capital Improvements Board retains all advertising revenues for the RCA Dome, but the Indiana Pacers receive 100 percent of the advertising revenue at Indianapolis's Market Square Arena. Leases vary a great deal even within the same city. Again, advertising revenues are related to the number of fans who attend games. With fewer teams, the existing franchises have a better chance to attract more advertising revenues, as the teams that do exist control access to an attractive audience. Larger crowds made up of this attractive audience (high-income males and females) also attend when the best teams are in town. As a result, the dependency on advertising revenues creates a powerful incentive to minimize the creation of new teams that might dilute the market for advertising in an arena or stadium.

Concessions

The story is sometimes told that Walt Disney watched with disdain as hotel operators, souvenir vendors, and restaurateurs profited from locating adjacent to or near Disneyland. Vowing to capture all or most of these related business activities his theme park generated, Disney envisioned a Disney World where the entertainment giant owned the theme park, hotels, restaurants, golf courses, and even the sports teams that played in the recreational paradise built around the amusement park. Of course, what the Disney Corporation wanted was a form of vertical integration. It wanted to sell you all aspects of your recreational visit: the theme park, food, lodging, and any related recreational activities you might want to enjoy. Disney World became the model for vertical integration, encompassing multiple theme parks, numerous hotels, scores of restaurants, a shopping plaza, a series of night clubs, golf courses, water parks, and even a cruise line. In later years the corporation even added professional sports teams to its entertainment package and a sports center in Disney World.

Professional sports has learned a great deal from the Disney Corporation. Ballparks and arenas are now designed to capture more of the entire recreational experience related to attending a game by offering more elaborate and varied restaurants and other attractions within the facilities. As more and more of the food and beverage trade has been captured within the facilities, who keeps and retains these revenues has also become an important issue. While no visiting teams share in these revenues, the issue of sharing is between the teams and the public agencies that have built the stadia and arenas.

The Cleveland Indians retain all income from food and beverage sales at their new facility. The Cleveland Cavaliers retain all profits from concessions located in Gund Arena, as do the St. Louis Rams in their new indoor domed facility. The Baltimore Orioles give the Maryland Stadium Authority a small percentage of the concession revenues but retain most of the profits, and the Orlando Magic and the city of Orlando share equally in the profits from the concessions at the Orlando Arena (Orena).

Again, the income from concessions and who controls it is different in every lease and an important potential source of revenue for all teams. In addition, it is critical to understand that the emergence of food and beverage service is an important part of the income stream of teams, and facility development means less activity of this nature takes place in the areas adjacent to the stadium or arena. Sometimes the justification for developing new facilities or for attracting and retaining a team involves the anticipated development of businesses and the area around the ballpark or arena. With more and more emphasis on the need for revenues, much of this development might not occur outside of the facility as teams themselves seek to offer pregame, postgame, and during-game food, beverage, and recreation services. From museums to nightclubs to gourmet restaurants, concessions are a vital and growing segment of the stadium revenue game. Much like Walt Disney did several decades ago, when the investment in professional sports teams frequently exceeds $100 million, and when new stadia and arena cost at least $100 million, owners and facility operators cannot afford to let any revenue possibilities escape. As a result, development near or adjacent to stadia and arenas might not occur.

Concession revenues are dependent on the number of people who attend games, and the fewer the teams the greater the possibility that crowds for existing teams will be larger. With teams now relying on concession income, there is a disincentive to create new franchises that could adversely effect revenues for any team as a result of declining attendance or the decision of fans or tourists to attend games in another city.

Parking

Some communities have given teams the right to retain some or all revenues secured from fans who park their cars at stadia or arenas while attending games. The Baltimore Orioles, for example, receive 50 percent of all parking revenues, and the California Angels receive 50 percent of the profits from the parking operations at Anaheim Stadium. The Chicago White Sox receive all parking revenue at the new Comisky Park, as do the Cleveland Indians at Jacobs Field. The Colorado Rockies retain 80 percent of parking revenues, and the Yankees receive 50 percent of all parking revenues at Yankee Stadium. The city of Philadelphia, however, retains all parking revenues at Veterans Stadium, while the Texas Rangers retain all revenue at the Ballpark in Arlington. The city of Charlotte retains all parking revenues at the Charlotte Coliseum (Charlotte Hornets), as does the city of Orlando (Magic), while the Cleveland Cavaliers retain all parking revenues. The city of Denver retains all parking revenues at McNichols Arena (Denver Nuggets).

As you can see, the terms of each team's lease can and do vary as to which entity retains parking revenues. Parking can be a very important source of revenue, with fees ranging to $10 in 1995 and twenty thousand or more cars parked at some baseball and football games. While basketball and hockey games have far fewer fans and cars—five thousand to seventy-five hundred—with at least forty-three home dates, parking revenues can quickly increase even in facilities that seat twenty thousand fans. Parking revenues are also not shared with visiting teams, and the more fans that can be attracted to games, the greater the potential for parking revenues. Why create another team that could reduce the number of fans who drive to your city to a game?

Other Events

While there is probably more revenue potential for other events (for example, concerts and shows) from arenas that are home to either or both basketball and hockey teams, outdoor stadia can also be effective venues for concerts. Domed facilities have great potential for attracting shows, concerts, and large meetings or conventions. These many and varied possibilities for alternative events create opportunities with the potential for important revenue flows and profits. Who retains earnings from other uses of a facility is also part of any contract between a team and a government or authority for use of a facility. As you would expect by now, there is great variability in the agreements.

At Jacobs Field, the Indians retain any profits from other uses of the facility, but the Maryland Stadium Authority retains 100 percent of revenue for nonbaseball events at Oriole Park at Camden Yards. The Dallas Mavericks do not receive any revenue from nonbasketball events at Reunion Arena, and the Milwaukee Bucks receive only 27.5 percent of concession sales at all nonbasketball events held in the Bradley Center. The Indianapolis Colts do not receive any revenue from the RCA Dome for nonfootball events, and neither do the Detroit Lions from events at the Pontiac Silverdome. The Dallas Cowboys control all revenue at Texas Stadium for football and non-football events. The St. Louis Rams receive advertising revenue that results from the use of the new domed facility in St. Louis, but no other revenues from nonteam-related events.

Local and National Media Contracts

At the center of some of the recent revenue battles in professional sports has been the tremendous differences in the revenue various teams receive from their local media contracts. The revenue received from contracts that are negotiated between the leagues and networks for nationally or regionally televised games (individual games and play-offs) are divided among all teams.

Different aspects of each league's market changes the relative importance of local media contracts. In the NFL, for example, with games played just once a week and largely on Sundays and Mondays, all regular-season and selected pre-season games are part of the league's contracts with the networks. All playoff games and the Super Bowl are also part of the package. As a result, the national media contract is the largest source of media revenue for all NFL teams, and the revenues from these contracts with Fox, NBC, ESPN, TNT, and CBS Radio *are equally divided* by all members of the league.

Individual NFL teams retain revenues for the local radio broadcast of regular-season games and the revenue from the local radio and television broadcast of preseason games. The revenues from these broadcasts are far less than the income from the national contracts. With the vast majority of media revenues divided equally among all teams, the variations in individual team earnings from the media were quite small. Among the NFL's twenty-eight teams in 1994, the Chicago Bears reported the most media income, $41.3 million, while the Indianapolis Colts reported the least, $37.2 million—a differential of just $3.9 million. It should be noted that the NFL's newest teams were not granted an equal share of this revenue pool for their initial seasons of play.

The division of revenue from the national media contracts among all teams also explains NFL team owners' lack of interest in expansion. With most media revenues already part of a national contract, adding teams creates *no* new market revenues for other team owners. In fact, it dilutes the amount of money each owner is likely to receive. For example, in 1995, the NFL added two teams, one in Jacksonville and one in Charlotte (North Carolina). Both media markets were already served by the various television networks and received the telecast of NFL football games each week. To be sure, the presence of a team probably created some additional fan interest in these two cities. But since the cities were already served by the networks, this new level of fan interest was likely quite small.

The NFL's sixteen-game schedule with weekend contests lends itself to a neat package that can be part of a national media contract. The other sports leagues, with far more games played on all days of the week, have far fewer contests as part of a national contract. As a result, the variances in team income are far larger and in direct relationship to the size of the local market. Games that are not part of national media contracts involving MLB, NBA, and NHL teams can be marketed by each team. This gives the teams that play in New York, Los Angeles, and Chicago a decided advantage. Prior to 1995, neither MLB, the NHL, nor the NBA had developed a revenue-sharing program for media revenues that could address the imbalances between the teams. A few examples will illustrate the severity of this challenge.

Had the 1994 baseball season been played in its entirety, *Financial World* reported that the New York Yankees would have earned $54 million in media revenues while the Cleveland Indians and Minnesota Twins would have received just $11.5 million. The differential between these teams was thus more than $42 million. Interestingly enough, those extra revenues did not ensure the Yankees the ability to produce the best team in the American League in 1995, as the Cleveland Indians were able to do that. Yet, in the long run, a differential of that nature, if not offset by other sources of income or a large public subsidy not available to the Yankees, would have an impact on the access to talent.

The Boston Bruins led all NHL teams with $11.4 million in local media revenues, while the Winnipeg Jets earned just $3.2 million. The Boston Celtics and the Phoenix Suns led the NBA in media revenues, with $26 and $25.9 million, respectively, and the Indiana Pacers earned the least, $13.2 million. Differentials of this magnitude, if not offset by public subsidies or balanced by revenues from other sources, will ultimately lead to an inability of certain teams to pay the high salaries other teams are able and willing to offer. Indeed as

Scully (1995) has documented, with the differences in market sizes, the additional salary paid to "stars" by large-market teams usually translates into higher profits. The mild form of revenue sharing adopted by MLB does reduce some of the discrepancies, but large-market teams still enjoy a substantial advantage over franchises in smaller regions.

In the NHL, NBA, and in MLB, there are national media contracts for play-off and championship series games. MLB earns the most for its World Series and league championship contracts, followed by the NBA for its play-offs, league championships, and finals. The NHL still has the smallest national contracts, but its popularity is growing, and there may well be more growth in income for each team as a result of increased viewership.

Media revenues are usually not a direct part of a team's negotiations with a city or community for a stadium or arena lease. However, if a team knows it will have limited revenue as a result of local media contracts, it may well have to look for other concessions with regard to stadium or arena operations. Teams such as the Cleveland Indians might be able to partially offset some of the revenue advantage of the larger-market teams if they received more revenue from stadium operations. To accomplish that goal, however, the public sector would have to increase its commitments to the team, or fans attending games would have to spend more money at the stadium for tickets and concessions. *Indeed, one reason for the various leagues not to share revenues is to increase the pressure on cities and states to subsidize the building of new stadia and arenas.* Conversely, however, cities such as New York, Los Angeles, and Philadelphia may have no need to offer any incentives to teams in MLB, the NHL, or the NBA. Their local markets will generate substantial revenues and profits.

Facility and Real Estate Rentals

We've already addressed part of this revenue source. Each team's lease with a government or public authority addresses the share the team receives from the rental of the facility for other events (concerts, shows, conventions, and so forth). There is also one other minor source of revenue associated with the use of arena or stadium space. Several newer facilities have been developed with limited amounts of office space. Some of this space is given to the teams (generally free of cost) for their administrative offices. The other space is also leased, and an issue for negotiation is, Who receives the rental income from this office space? The Texas Rangers have been permitted to lease space at the Ballpark in Arlington. While this is a small revenue source for all teams and facilities, it is another part of the revenue package that should be considered.

Public-Sector Incentives

The incentives provided to teams and their owners generally fall into one of four categories: favored lease arrangements, loans, direct cash payments, and the construction of practice facilities. In isolated instances other incentives might also have been provided. Examples of each of these types have already been profiled, from Nashville's willingness to provide any NHL or NBA owner with $20 million if they relocate their team to St. Louis's and Denver's commitments to the Rams and Rockies, respectively, to bring football and baseball to their communities.

If fewer teams exist there will always be more incentives and subsidies given to existing franchises, as those communities without teams will offer subsidies to get one and those with teams will offer subsidies to keep the teams. As such, there is not only no incentive for existing owners to vote for expansion and if cities continue to offer subsidies, there will always be a strong incentive to existing owners to continue to vote against expansion.

The effect of any subsidy, of course, is to reduce other costs, thereby leaving greater amounts of funds to be used for player salaries or owner's profits. Revenue is, simply put, a vital factor in producing winning teams, and this permits existing owners to argue the need for their subsidies: to build a winner. Many have observed that the most successful teams, over time, have been those who play in the largest markets with greater opportunities for revenue.

There is some relationship between the size of a community and championships, especially in the NFL and NBA. In MLB, there is a mixed pattern. The Yankees, prior to 1996, had last won a pennant in 1981; the Mets won a pennant in 1986 and lost in the play-offs in 1988. Since 1980, Kansas City (two), Oakland (three), and Minnesota (two), all relatively small-market teams, have each won more than one American League pennant. Since MLB adopted division play for each league in 1969, Oakland has won six pennants and Baltimore has won five. Both of these teams play in relatively small markets, and big-market teams such as the Yankees, Red Sox, and Blue Jays have each won two pennants (through 1995). Another small-market team, Minnesota, has also won two pennants. In the National League, a large- and small-market team share the honors for the most pennants: Cincinnati and Los Angeles have both won five. The New York Mets, Philadelphia Phillies, and St. Louis Cardinals (two large- and one small-market team) have each won three pennants. Pittsburgh, another small-market team, has won two pennants. In MLB, then, more than market size accounts for or predicts pennant winners, but larger-market teams do have a decided advantage. While some of this can be compensated for in terms of stadium leases, if you are going to make the "deal" to land a team, it is hard not to acknowledge the possible disadvantages faced by small-market teams.

The disadvantages of small-market teams are quite pronounced in the NBA. Since 1980, only three teams from standard metropolitan statistical areas (SMSAs) of fewer than 2.5 million people have ever made the NBA finals. The Portland Trail Blazers have appeared twice in the NBA finals (regional population in 1990 was 1.5 million) and the Phoenix Suns and Orlando Magic have each made one unsuccessful appearance in the finals (2.1 million residents in 1990, 1.1 million residents in 1990, respectively). Interestingly enough, the America West facility built for the Suns in 1992 includes 87 suites and 2,270 club seats, and the team receives the majority of the income from the luxury seats and all revenue from advertising. The Suns are also part owners of the management company that operates the America West Arena, giving to the owners of the team additional revenues. The Portland Trail Blazers opened their new Rose Garden in 1995. As the team owns the facility—the public investment was limited to land and infrastructure—the Trail Blazers will retain all revenues from the 70 suites, 2,400 club seats, and all other attractions brought to the Rose Garden. Since these are small-market teams, these additional revenue sources may permit them to be competitive in future years.

In comparison, from 1980 to 1996, the Los Angeles Lakers have been in the NBA finals nine times, the Boston Celtics five times, the Houston Rockets and Chicago Bulls four times, the Detroit Pistons and Philadelphia 76ers three times each, and the Seattle Supersonics once. Large-market teams have clearly been more successful in the NBA, as none of these teams plays in an area with fewer than 3.4 million residents. As a result, teams such as the Indiana Pacers (regional population 1.2 million), Sacramento Kings (regional population 1.5 million), Utah Jazz (regional population 1.1 million), and Denver Nuggets (regional population 1.9 million) may continue to be challenged to produce consistent winning teams able to attract and retain star players. Conversely, these teams will likely need playing facilities with substantial potential for luxury suite and club seat revenues. It is unlikely these teams can share these revenues with any public-sector partner if they are to be competitive with teams in much larger markets.

The NFL's champions, despite the impressive revenue-sharing program that exists, have also been from the league's largest cities. Indeed, the last time a team from a region with fewer than three million residents won the Super Bowl was 1980. This team, the Pittsburgh Steelers, came close to repeating its achievment in 1996, but lost to the Dallas Cowboys. Teams from small regions, however, have made appearances in the Super Bowl. Most recently, the Buffalo Bills have made four straight losing trips to the Super Bowl, and the Denver Broncos have lost three title games to larger-market teams. In only three of the games lost by a small-market team was the team from the smaller market almost able to win the Super Bowl (Pittsburgh, 1996; Buffalo, 1991; and Cincinnati, 1989). In all other years the large-market teams that have appeared in the Super Bowl have been vastly superior to the small-market teams.

Team owners can use this argument to convince governments in smaller markets to offer subsidies to offset the disadvantage of locating in their area. And smaller markets have been very willing to accept this logic.

The Baltimore Orioles earn more from stadium revenues and ticket sales than do the Yankees despite the much larger size of the New York market. The Cleveland Indians also earn far more from stadium operations than do the Yankees, yet the Cleveland market is much smaller than the market available to the New York Yankees. In football, the Dallas Cowboys' profits from stadium revenues completely offset any of the advantages that exist for the Giants, Lions, and Bears as a result of their larger markets. These outcomes are possible because, with a restricted number of teams, Baltimore, Cleveland, and Irving (home of the Dallas Cowboys) are very willing to offer subsidies to permit their teams to compete with larger-market squads. In such an environment, why would any team owner want to see the league expand and risk losing the ability to secure a subsidy by threatening to move and being unable to say, "We need more dollars to compete with large-market teams"? If large markets had more teams, the subsidies provided by governments to smaller-market teams would no longer be needed.

Franchise Fees from Expansion Teams

When a new team is added to any of the sports leagues, the individual or group granted a franchise is required to pay an admission fee that is then divided among the existing teams, creating another source of income. While the amount specified is somewhat arbitrary, there is substantial economic logic in having such a fee.

When new teams are added to a league they become eligible to share in certain league revenues. For example, as a league member, a new team-owner would be entitled to a share of the national media contracts as well as income from the marketing of souvenirs or any other source of revenue that is shared by all teams. As the new teams now earn shares of these revenues, the shares received by the older or existing teams are decreased. These decreases occur unless the revenues in the pool increase. In many instances that pool will not increase. For example, when a new franchise begins play as the Cleveland Browns in the NFL, those owners will receive a share of the revenue earned from the contracts with Fox Television and

NBC. The networks will not increase their payments because another team exists. Both networks already broadcast games to the Cleveland region; as a result there are no new advertising revenues nor any increase in value for having a team in Cleveland. Yet, with one more member in the league, the share of media dollars received by each team is decreased.[2]

In this sense, then, the franchise fee becomes the present value of the revenues lost by the existing teams. And, when the NFL granted new franchises to Jacksonville and Carolina, those ownership groups were told they would have to wait three seasons before receiving an equal share of the NFL's lucrative television contract.

When new teams are added there is also a potential for existing teams to lose some playing dates with the most popular teams. As the length of each sport's season is now relatively stable, if a new team is added, the number of games played with opposing teams decreases. For example, if the Arizona Diamondbacks compete in the National League, the Houston Astros will have fewer home games with the Los Angeles Dodgers and the Atlanta Braves. These two teams are among the most popular and successful, and the loss of even one game to permit them to play against the Phoenix team represents a real fiscal loss for the owner of the Astros. This economic loss is offset by the portion of the franchise fee the owner of the Astros collects from the owners of the Arizona Diamondbacks. To offset the loss of games with popular teams and to increase television revenues, the NFL is now considering expanding to an 18-game season when it adds teams. With two additional games, media revenues will increase and there will be more dollars to divide with the new owners.

Lastly, when new teams are created, they are permitted to draft players from existing teams. While the more established clubs can and do protect their best players, the loss of any player represents a real economic loss of developmental expenditures made by a team. A player receives coaching and training designed to improve the quality of play. Existing teams that provide players to expansion franchises should be permitted to receive reasonable compensation for these investments. The franchise fees are also designed to offset these losses by the existing teams.

In summary, while there is a strong economic logic for franchise fees, the exact value of these fees is not determined relative to income lost. Indeed, there is some evidence to suggest that the fee levels are arbitrarily determined (Whitford, 1993). Further, the staggering amount of these fees creates substantial pressures on cities. For example, if a team's ownership group must pay more than $100 million to enter a league, they may have very few additional funds left to build their playing facility. As a result, when new teams are created and large franchise fees paid, not only is income produced for existing teams, but cities that host expansion teams may be forced to provide extensive subsidies for the development of a stadium or arena to help the owners repay their loan and begin to earn the dollars needed to pay the salaries commanded by the best athletes.

So, here's how the subsidy game works for expansion teams. The Yankees play in the largest market and receive income from the new team in Phoenix. The Yankees can then use that income together with their large local media contract to pay their players. The new team in Phoenix must pay more than $100 million to enter the league, find a stadium to play in, and then find a revenue stream to pay their players. The potential ownership group in Phoenix (or any city) says to their locally elected officials, "If we risk $100 million or more to bring baseball here, what will you invest?" Never mind that the $100 million franchise fee is creating income for wealthy owners and their players. Faced with the possibility of no team, the public sector always agrees to provide the needed funds for the stadium. That's why a new sales tax in Maricopa County was needed for Phoenix's baseball team and why a sales tax was necessary in Denver when the Rockies joined the National League.

Clothing, Merchandise, and Souvenirs

The popularity of team jerseys, hats, jackets, and other souvenirs has led to the establishment of marketing agreements among all the teams. The revenues from the sales of all of these items that are purchased outside of a stadium or arena are pooled and shared by teams in each league. Frequently, expansion teams may have to wait a few years before being granted access to this source of league revenues.

INDIRECT SOURCES OF INCOME

The issue that generates the most distrust in fans and players is the indirect income gains that can and do accrue to team owners. When players strike because they want more of the money made in, by, and through sports, and the owners cry, "We're broke," it is the gains that are realized from indirect income sources that frequently emerge as one of the real thorny issues. In terms of understanding other factors that relate to the number of teams that exist and which cities have teams, indirect sources of income are also critical factors. For cities interested in attracting or retaining a team and as civic leaders make "the deal," they need to appreciate what these indirect sources of income are and how much money may be involved. Not every owner or ownership group can or does realize income or profits from these indirect sources. Yet some do, and the profits that can result are neither small nor inconsequential.

Team Value Appreciation

One of the ways team owners realize economic gains from their teams is the change in the value of a team. In many instances the value of teams has substantially increased, and this value rises to the extent that there is a scarcity of teams. Teams are, after all, scarce resources, and only the leagues themselves can create more teams. When there is no expansion, the value of each team can increase if the sport becomes more popular. It is also interesting to note the changes in team values when a new stadium or arena is built.

In 1991 the Cleveland Indians had a market value of $75 million. The team improved and in 1993 had a market value of $81 million, an increase of 4.5 percent. In 1994, Jacobs Field opened and the team's value increased to $100 million, and by 1996 the team was estimated to be worth $125 million. From 1993 to 1996, then, the team's value increased by $44 million, or 54.3 percent. Part of this increase in value was a result of the improved play of the team, and the credit for that increase should go to the management, owners, and players. Yet a substantial portion of the increased value was also a result of the lease involved with the use of Jacobs Field, and that lease was possible only because of the public support provided by the taxpayers in the Cleveland region.

As already discussed, the owners of the Texas Rangers have also seen the value of their team increase with the opening of a new stadium. Valued at $101 million by *Financial World* in 1991, the team's value was set at $157 million in 1994. This 55.5-percent increase has made the Rangers the third most valued team in MLB. While the team is paying for a portion of the Ballpark in Arlington, a small sales tax is also assisting and providing $140 million of the financing for the new ballpark. It seems reasonable to conclude that the increased value of the Texas Rangers is a direct result of the new stadium, as the team's fortunes on the field had not substantially changed.

Increases in team values of this magnitude have not been limited to baseball. In 1992 the America West arena opened and the value of the Phoenix Suns increased from $80 million to $156 million in 1995 (a 95.8-percent increase in value) and then to $191 million in 1996 (a 139-percent increase from 1992). In 1991 the team was valued at $99 million. If this figure is used as the base, the percentage increase in 1996 is a respectable 92.9 percent. The Delta Center in Salt Lake City also seems to have had an impact on the value of the Utah Jazz. In 1991 the team's worth was estimated to be $45 million. In 1995, *Financial World* put the value of the team at $127 million, an increase of $82 million, or 182 percent. In 1996, the team's value was estimated to be $142 million. However, the Utah Jazz own the Delta Center, and there was no subsidy from or partnership with the public sector.

Beyond some individual cases, and back to the basic issue of indirect sources of wealth, the increase in average team value suggests this form of potential income is not insignificant if an owner ever decides to sell his or her team. While the value of an average major league team has decreased from $121 million in 1991 to $115 million in 1996 (a decline of 5 percent), the value of NHL teams has increased more than 68 percent from 1991, while the value of NBA teams increased by more than 81 percent over the same period. From 1991 to 1996 the average value of an NFL team increased by a more modest 31.8 percent.

To provide a complete and fair picture it is also important to recognize that the value of some teams has not increased and has even declined. The New York Yankees were believed to be worth $225 million in 1991; in 1996 *Financial World* estimated their value at $209 million. The Baltimore Orioles were purchased in 1993 for $173 million. Their estimated value in 1996 was $168 million. The decline in value of some MLB teams is related to several problems confronting baseball: declining popularity, decreased television viewership, and continuing labor unrest. While the value of most NHL teams has increased, the value of the New York Islanders remained unchanged from 1991 to 1995, but then increased by $7 million in 1996. The value of the Calgary Flames has increased by about 4 percent between 1991 and 1996. The value of the Los Angeles Lakers has declined from $200 million in 1991 to $171 million in 1996. This decrease, along with the decline in value of the Boston Celtics from $180 million to $134 million, was a result of the decline in both teams' fortunes and winning records after the retirement of Magic Johnson and Larry Bird. The value of the Detroit Pistons, however, has grown even after the loss of much of the personnel from their championship squads. In 1991 the team was worth $150 million. Its value in 1996 was placed at $186 million by *Financial World*.

Related Product Sales

Sports teams have frequently been used as marketing tools to increase the sales of various products. The ownership of a team by a brewery, for example, gives the company an excellent opportunity to market its primary product, beer, at the games and with the team's logo. One of the problems or issues in measuring a team's wealth or income flow is the value of this advertising benefit. Suppose, for example, that the Montreal Canadiens were owned by someone other than the company that also owns Molson's beer. What would the team charge for endorsing Molson's beers or making it the official or exclusive beer of the team for sale at its games? Does this profit rightly belong to the ball team? Should the players receive part of that value under a revenue-sharing plan? These have been some of the difficult questions at the heart of the labor discord in several sports.

As players are concerned with measuring the real value of the teams as part of their labor negotiations, civic leaders should also consider the possible revenue enhancement that team ownership creates for a company's other or main products. For example, if a brewery's profits increase from its ownership of the team, how much of a public subsidy is required for the building of a stadium? Beware of the possibility of related income growth if you are making the deal with a team that does generate substantial profits for a related business of the ownership group.

Realize also that breweries are really the least of your concerns relative to this issue of related product sales. The growing control of sports teams by mass media firms raises other issues related to product sales. The Atlanta Braves are owned by Turner Broadcasting, which also owns the WTBS superstation. The Turner group owns 96 percent of the Atlanta Hawks as well. The Tribune Company owns the Chicago Cubs and superstation WGN. It also owns a minor league baseball team that plays in the greater Chicago metropolitan region (Rockford Cubbies). The Walt Disney Corporation owns the Anaheim Mighty Ducks and has acquired an interest in the Angels. The Disney Corporation may well be able to build a "sports park" with games played all year as visitors also enjoy other attractions. Ackerly Communications in Seattle owns the SuperSonics. Cablevision Systems, the nation's fourth largest cable TV operator, is part of the group that owns the New York Rangers and New York Knicks; Comsat owns the Denver Nuggets and the Quebec Nordiques, which were moved to Denver for the 1995–96 season; Comcast has recently acquired a substantial interest in the Philadelphia 76ers and Flyers. Multimedia is a limited partner in the Cincinnati Reds, and Viacom has interests in the Florida Marlins, Miami Dolphins, and the Florida Panthers. When media organizations have ownership interests in teams, do the teams receive the true broadcast value of their games, or are the media companies simply able to show profits for the communications firms while the teams appear to have less money, or even lose money? As the players have tried to raise these issues, so too must civic officials as they attempt to understand how teams and their owners make money and whether or not a subsidy is needed to help the team. If media revenues are undervalued because of interlocking ownership, a team's true earning potential may never be realized.

Associated Asset Value Appreciation

As the cost of ownership of professional sports franchises has increased, a number of team owners have developed varied economic interests. We've already discussed how different ownership groups have included the teams in the marketing of other products (beer) and the interest of media and entertainment companies in using the teams as a vehicle for or an integral part of their media and entertainment holdings. Another indirect benefit that sports can have, and that civic leaders should consider, is the impact on other assets such as land.

Consider for a moment the redevelopment of downtown Cleveland, of which the Gateway project and the new facilities for the Indians and Cavs were integral components. The public sector made these investments with the hope that a renaissance of sorts would take place in downtown Cleveland. While some anecdotal evidence indicates that some redevelopment, if not a rebirth, has taken place (Peterson, 1995), there has been a renewed interest in downtown properties. One of the individuals with substantial ownership interests in the land and buildings in downtown Cleveland is also one of the owners of the sports franchises. The Gateway redevelopment effort, then, built the facilities that permitted the team owner to realize a substantial increase in wealth as the value of the team increased. Therefore, if the Gateway project were successful, this same owner and ownership group could also realize gains from the increased value of the downtown real estate they own.

This is a prime example of associated asset value appreciation that can occur when the public sector participates in financing facilities for professional sports teams. And Cleveland is not the only example. One could look at the development of sports facilities in Toronto or the Dallas/Fort Worth region and find the potential for similar outcomes. Is there anything illegal or wrong with investors making money from the enhancement of their assets? Absolutely not. In fact, it is simply good business; indeed it is very good business. These indirect gains or profits should be considered part of any partnership to retain or attract a team and must be evaluated when the responsibility for the financing of a stadium or arena is discussed. If the stadium or arena is privately owned, then any related gains should be of little or no concern to the public sector or taxpayers. However, if the taxpayers are going to invest in an arena or stadium, or if public funds are to be used to attract a team to a region, then other gains that team owners or other property owners realize should be included in the financing package for a stadium or arena.

Advertising for Related Products

Tonight, after you read this section of the book, watch a Chicago Cubs, Atlanta Braves, or Atlanta Hawks game. Count the commercials that appear for forthcoming media products (movies, upcoming shows, and so on) from Turner Broadcasting (or its affiliated companies) or from the Tribune Company (and its affiliates). Those commercials represent important marketing opportunities for the team's owners; but they are not marketing anything related to sports. They are using a sports audience to market one of their other products. That advertisement you just saw would have cost a substantial amount of money if the team and channel were owned by different firms. Since they are not, fewer revenues accrue to the team, and the owner of both the team and the media company gets free advertising for a forthcoming event or product in front of an audience attracted to sporting events. This is what I mean by advertising for related products, or products owned by the ownership group. So, when an ad for *Headline News* or CNN or *Turner Classics* appears, a real benefit is created in that the sports team becomes a marketing vehicle for these other products. How should civic officials consider these gains when reviewing proposals to finance a stadium or arena? Again, it makes excellent business sense for Turner Broadcasting to advertise a forthcoming movie or television series during an important Braves or Hawks game. Yet, the value created for the broadcast group is an important source of income for the owners of the team and something that should be included in any analysis of the public sector's need to invest in a facility.

By using the superstations for my example I do not want to limit the possibilities that could develop over the next few years. The Disney Corporation's purchase of an NHL franchise that uses a name from one of its movies is a very shrewd marketing and business decision. The team serves to underscore the company's role in family entertainment, and the entertainment serves to underscore the company's role in sports. This relationship creates income and profit potential for the owners of the team and is another source of the value of sports.

Media Value

Teams have also become very important programming elements for the super cable television stations. More than one commentator has noted that Turner Broadcasting was able to use the Braves and Hawks to build part of a media empire at a time when the various stations were struggling to exist. As more and more media firms become interested in owning sports teams, civic officials have to be aware of the related and interconnected revenue potential that exists. Substantial profits can and are created through these linkages, and these returns or gains should offset or reduce the public's investment in financing sports facilities.

Salary and Fringe Benefits

When teams report their net earnings it is critical to carefully scrutinize the office payroll involved with the team's operations. One way owners have reduced their team's earnings is to include themselves and others as employees of the team. In this manner, then, profits can be taken in the form of salary and fringe benefits. The owners receive a revenue flow, but the team reports these revenues as a cost, which reduces its profitability. Similar outcomes are possible when owners make loans to their teams. The interest on these loans becomes an expense for the team, reducing profit levels while increasing the income of the team's owners through the interest payments. When teams respond, "We're broke," look carefully at the possible indirect income generated by salaries, fringe benefits, and loan repayments to a corporation owned by the ownership group.

Tax Advantages

The tax advantages from team ownership have declined as a result of changes in the U.S. Federal Income Tax Code in 1976 and 1986. The real meaning of these changes has been to focus the financial attention of owners on the operating profits possible from their sports operations. When the ownership of sports teams provided owners with lucrative tax benefits, attention to the team's profitability could be less critical. But when tax advantages decline, owners must focus on the "bottom line," and this has had a pronounced effect on dealings with cities. Now, the revenues that can be earned from stadium operations, from the team, and as a result of incentives received from communities are far more critical than they were when the tax laws themselves established an incentive to own a team. With that incentive reduced sharply, team owners must focus on the bottom line.

The best history and analysis of the federal tax law and its implications for ownership is Quirk and Fort's *Pay Dirt: The Business of Professional Team Sports* (1992). As a result of the 1986 Tax Act and other changes that began as early as 1976, they concluded, "After 1986 it is no longer true that sports teams should be viewed as primarily tax shelters—they are tax shelters, but the tax shelter accounts for only a little more than ten percent of the value of the team" (1992, p. 120). Although 10 percent is not inconsequential, it is a far cry from what existed from 1950 to 1976, and these changes in the U.S. Tax Code have had a pronounced impact on the need for owners to focus on their team's profit margins. Let me briefly summarize what used to be the tax advantage, and how this has changed over time.

Baseball entrepreneur Bill Veeck is generally credited with finding a regulation in the U.S. Income Tax Code that allowed a team's new owner to declare player contracts as a substantial portion of the value of the team. The trick here was that the value attributed to the contracts was usually substantially greater than the amount of money paid to the players, but if a substantial portion of the team's value was the players' contracts, and the value of an individual player declined over time, the value of those contracts could be depreciated. Here's how that worked.

Suppose a team was purchased for $5 million. Under tax laws that existed through 1976, a new owner could establish a new corporation to run the ball club and declare that 90 percent of the value of the corporation was the contracted players. After all, the value of owning the Yankees, Rams, Cardinals, or Red Wings is the players the team has under contract. Players, of course, depreciate with age, so if the team's purchase price was $5 million and the players accounted for 90 percent, or $4.5 million, of this value, that figure could be "written off" over the expected life of the assets (players). If a five-year depreciation schedule was used, the new owner had a tax loss against operating profits of $900,000 per year ($4.5 million divided by 5).

The money actually paid to the players was an operating expense, as were balls, helmets, travel expenses, uniforms, paper, and so forth. As a result there was an accounting and tax difference between what was considered the value of the team and the team's obligation to pay employees. If the asset purchased is the contracts that bind certain individuals to a particular team, and the ability of these players depreciates, then the value of the asset can be depreciated. The actual salary paid to the players is an operating cost not unlike any other operating cost a team can have. These operating costs, together with the depreciation allowance, could be used to offset any income earned.

If the team purchased for $5 million I described earlier earned a profit of $900,000 after all operating costs were tabulated, this income was literally "tax free," since the $900,000 depreciation would cover the tax liability on the income. If the team earned less than $900,000 in operating profits, then a negative income or loss would exist, as the depreciation allowance would be greater than the income gained. If this took place—and here was another real benefit from owning a sports team at this time—that loss could offset other income the owner had earned from other activities (this required the team to be incorporated as a subchapter S corporation, and that was the common practice). As a result, the ownership of team sports became an effective tax shelter. As the cost of franchise acquisition increased, the value of the depreciation also increased. The greater the cost, the greater the write-off.

This tax advantage began to erode in 1976. First, the U.S. Tax Code was amended to limit the proportion of the value of any team that could be assigned to player contracts. In other words, the tax code was changed to reflect the value of a team that comes from its membership in a league and the exclusive market rights it enjoys in its home city. After 1976 owners could only declare the value of player contracts to be 50 percent of the total value of the team. The other half of the value of the team was established as its membership in a league and the exclusive market area that league membership provided. These assets, however, do not depreciate. A team purchased for $5 million now had a maximum depreciable value of $2.5 million, not the $4.5 million that would have existed prior to 1976. Second, when the tax rates for capital gains and normal income were set at or near the same level, there was far less advantage to capital income. As a result, team ownership still has a tax advantage, but it is far less than it was, which focuses the attention of owners on the profitability of the team and not its potential for generating tax savings. The change in the U.S. tax law also means that owners must look to other governments for subsidies and develop policies that will ensure that those subsidies will continue to exist. A restrained supply of teams is one way to ensure that state and local governments will be pliable when it comes to subsidies.

Interest on Loans

One way certain team owners have changed the cash flow of their teams and actually increased their own wealth has been through loans to purchase the team. When teams are sold, a great deal of cash is needed. Through creative accounting it is possible to turn the need to provide cash for the purchase into a source of income.

Everyone is familiar with the requirement for a down payment when buying an asset that is financed. When purchasing a house people generally make down payments of 5, 10, and 20 percent. The purchase of a car also frequently involves a down payment and then a loan.

When individuals or groups buy a team, a certain equity position is needed, but what sometimes happens is that owners form a separate corporation that loans the team sufficient money for the down payment. This loan has to be repaid, and it is the team that makes these payments. Since the owner of the team is the individual or group that loaned the money for the purchase, the payments for the loan are costs to the team, but income to the owners. In this manner the team's income declines and the owners are repaid for their down payment. This creative accounting then also overstates the team's expenses because there is no equity involved in the purchase. Why all this accounting double-talk? Here's the beef on this little gimmick. The team has to make payments to repay the loan given by the corporation to purchase the team. As a result, the interest on the loan and the principle repaid become costs to the team and reduce the operating profit. The owner has the advantage of using the team to repay the equity or down payment and extracting cash from the team's operation. While most of us might expect that an owner should purchase an asset or have an equity position in the team, through creative accounting team owners can extract cash flow from the team to repay themselves for their down payment and reduce the team's profitability without actually depriving themselves of profits and a cash flow.

Public-Sector Incentives

At several points I have described some of the incentives communities have provided to attract teams or to retain a club. Most of these incentives are designed to improve the fiscal position of the team. Some communities have provided incentives to the owners of teams as an inducement to attract the team. In the early 1970s, when Arlington sought the Washington Senators, the team's majority owner needed extra cash to "buy out" individuals who had a small minority interest in the team. Arlington purchased the local broadcast rights to the team's games for a sum of money that permitted the owners to gain complete ownership of the team. Arlington was never able to recover the full cost of its investment; the city, then, lost money on the investment. However, the city did become the home of the Texas Rangers. Many city leaders believe the publicity it receives from the team's presence is well worth the investment.

When the Gateway Economic Development Corporation was developing plans for a new home for the Cleveland Indians, the team's owner was not only promised offices in the new stadium, but a restaurant with a panoramic view of the playing field was built and furnished as part of the stadium. The restaurant was given to the owner to operate, and the profits from the restaurant are retained by the owner. A similar incentive was also provided to the owners of the Cleveland Cavaliers when they agreed to move their team from suburban Richfield to a downtown site adjacent to the home of the Cleveland Indians.

Nashville has made no secret of its offer of a $20 million cash award to any owner who moves an NHL or NBA team to a new arena built by the city. This incentive, crafted for the New Jersey Devils, was in addition to an offer of very favorable lease terms for use of the city-financed arena. The extra cash is being provided to offset any expenses associated with the move of the team or the termination of an existing lease. If the money is not needed for these expenses, the owner is able to retain the cash. Irwindale gave the NFL's Raiders $10 million while they were still in Los Angeles during one of the periods when Al Davis was simply looking for a new home for his team. The $10 million was a payment to keep Irwindale "in the running" as a possible home for the Raiders. In 1995 the Raiders returned to Oakland after thirteen years in Los Angeles, but Irwindale never received anything for its $10 million payment.

When Wayne Huizenga was looking for a location for the teams he owns, several local governments in Florida were willing to create a virtually independent town or city for the new entertainment/sports complex. As an independent government, the new sports and entertainment entity would not have to deal with zoning issues or resistance from community residents, as the team would

virtually own its own local government. This plan was never opera-
tionalized, but it is an example of the incentives some public officials
are willing to provide to team owners to attract teams. Other cities
that have built arenas or stadia frequently provide owners with their
own luxury suites. Each of these incentives increases the owners'
profits or their personal wealth.

Revenue Sharing

Recently, revenue sharing among large- and small-market teams
has again emerged as an important issue. In March 1995 MLB proposed to shift as much as $4 million to smaller-market teams while
reducing the income of large-market teams. This was done to permit all clubs to more equally bid for players. There is considerable
interest in expanding this program in MLB as well as extending it in
the other leagues to reduce inequities. We will return to the issue of
revenue sharing in the conclusion; as you will see, this is just the latest ploy to continue the welfare game to ensure the existence of a pli-
able public sector that will shower revenues on team owners and
players.

PROTECTIVE CARTELS AND THE SUPPLY OF TEAMS

There are very strong incentives for existing team owners to discourage expansion. More teams mean more partners sharing league
revenues and fewer cities that can be used as possible pawns in
securing subsidies and welfare. Indeed, in the extreme situation that
every city that wanted a franchise had one, no team could threaten
to move and no city would have to provide a subsidy to attract a
team. With substantial profits possible from luxury seating, especially if the public sector pays for the stadium, the only incentive to
any existing team owners to add franchises would be additional
media revenues. As this is now increasingly unlikely, unless the
power to control the number of franchises changes, owners will

likely oppose expansion, or make it difficult by establishing very high franchise fees. Indeed, given the profits possible from luxury seating, revenues are maximized if team owners and players convince cities to build the stadium or arena. Restricting the supply of teams is the best guarantee that this will occur and that public welfare will continue. Should this system be changed?

SHOULD SPORTS LEAGUES HAVE THE POWER TO LIMIT THE NUMBER OF TEAMS?

The answer to this question rests on your assessment of the profitability of team sports and the likelihood that the current economic state of professional sports is either stable or likely to improve. Those who argue that the leagues should have the power to limit the number of teams can point to the instability and frequent failure of teams in the early years of each of the professional sports leagues. Yet, the failure rates for professional sports teams are not substantially different from outcomes in other sectors of the economy, and no other business has the protective capabilities of the professional sports leagues. While the current levels of popularity and prosperity for the NBA, the NFL, and the NHL are a phenomenon of the past three decades, the review of the various ways teams earn money indicates that there are many sources of income. On balance, these sources of money have established a robust and profitable world.

Even if some teams are losing money, a point that is certainly debatable, the average value of franchises indicates the industry as a whole, in each of the four major sports leagues, is extremely healthy. A total of sixteen baseball teams are valued at more than $100 million, as are five hockey teams, all thirty NFL teams, and seventeen of the NBA's teams (Ozanian, 1995; *Financial World,* 1996). To be sure, some teams still encounter severe financial problems. The Seattle Pilots, for example, an MLB expansion team in 1969, was forced to move to Milwaukee (the Brewers) after it virtually went bankrupt at the conclusion of its first year of play. The Brewers continue to struggle financially, but a new stadium may well improve their financial future. The Seattle Mariners, created in partial response to the lawsuit by the city of Seattle against MLB as a result of the Pilots' move, have also had financial problems. A proposed new stadium to replace the aging King Dome, which has few of the revenue capabilities of newer facilities, has the potential to make this team quite profitable. The Pittsburgh Pirates are also having severe financial problems and "need" a new stadium to settle their debts.

Financial World magazine has found that several baseball, football, and hockey teams lost money in 1994 and 1995 (see Table 3–5); however, *no* NBA teams were found by *Financial World* to have lost money. Figures for MLB teams were adjusted to consider the financial outcomes had the entire 1994 season been played. It must also be remembered that many sports finance experts have questioned some of the figures used in the data reported by the teams and relied upon for this assessment. Scully (1995) best summarizes the caution with which these data must be viewed when he noted:

> It is difficult to separate fact from fancy about operational profits in professional team sports for several reasons. As privately owned entities, the clubs have no obligation to reveal their finances. Fearing political scrutiny of their business practices, the teams tend to overstate expenses and understate operating profits in public pronouncements. Stated losses from operations are often a figment of creative accounting. It is not unusual for a club, even one with a losing record located in a small market, to generate a positive cash flow while the books show red ink. This is due in part to the way clubs are purchased. A common method of purchasing a club is for investors to form a separate corporation which owns the club. The investors lend the money for the purchase and receive interest payments. These payments are a cost on the club's books, but are in fact a method of taking a cash flow from its operations. Further, an owner (managing partner) may take a large salary, a generous expense account, insurance, and other benefits. These are operational costs to a club, but may in part represent a profit withdrawal. . . . In my judgment considerable effort was made by *Financial World* to avoid some of these pitfalls . . . [but] one should be somewhat skeptical of their estimates for any particular club (pp. 116–7).

TABLE 3–5
Teams for Which *Financial World* Estimates Operating Losses
Occurred in 1994, 1995

| 1994 | | |
MLB Teams	NFL Teams	NHL Teams
San Francisco Giants	Arizona Cardinals	St. Louis Blues
Oakland Athletics	Los Angeles Rams	Buffalo Sabres
Philadelphia Phillies	Seattle Seahawks	Washington Capitals
Kansas City Royals	Washington Redskins	New York Islanders
Houston Astros	New England Patriots	Calgary Flames
California Angels	New York Jets	Hartford Whalers
Cincinnati Reds	Los Angeles Raiders	Edmonton Oilers
Detroit Tigers	Detroit Lions	Winnipeg Jets
Minnesota Twins	Indianapolis Colts	
Seattle Mariners		
Milwaukee Brewers		
Pittsburgh Pirates		

| 1995 | | |
MLB Teams	NFL Teams	NHL Teams
San Francisco Giants	Arizona Cardinals	St. Louis Blues
Oakland Athletics	Los Angeles Rams	Buffalo Sabres
Philadelphia Phillies	Seattle Seahawks	Washington Capitals
Kansas City Royals	Washington Redskins	New York Islanders
Houston Astros	New England Patriots	Calgary Flames
California Angels	New York Jets	Hartford Whalers
Cincinnati Reds	Los Angeles Raiders	Edmonton Oilers
Detroit Tigers	Detroit Lions	Winnipeg Jets
Minnesota Twins	Indianapolis Colts	
Seattle Mariners		
Milwaukee Brewers		
Pittsburgh Pirates		

Source: Reprinted from *Financial World.* Copyrighted 1995 & 1996. All rights reserved.

Operating losses were reported by *Financial World* for twenty-nine professional teams in 1994 and for nineteen in 1995. The teams that appear in bold type in Table 3–5 are those teams that had won as many games as they lost, or won more games than they lost. Of the twenty-nine teams that lost money in 1994, just eleven had winning or .500 records. It might be expected that losing teams, just as any business that did poorly in a particular year, should or would be expected to lose money. Of the 125 major league teams reviewed by *Financial World,* 23.2 percent, or slightly less than one-quarter, had operating losses in 1994. But when win and loss records are included as a small measure of success, just 8.8 percent of the successful teams lost money. Three of these teams with winning records had also recently had a considerable period of poor or mediocre performances (Houston Astros, New York Jets, and Los Angeles Raiders), so it is possible some fan support was slow in returning to these teams. If these teams are removed from the calculation, then just 6.4 percent of the successful teams in major league sports lost money in 1994. That sort of performance level would be the envy of any industry, including all of those that do not have the protections afforded to professional sports teams. Indeed, if creative accounting was involved in the estimated losses of any of the teams, the number of teams that were actually in fiscal distress could hardly be worth listing. In 1995, just six of the teams that lost money had winning records. These six represented 4.7 percent of all teams. In addition, MLB's strike may have contributed to some of the observed losses as fans were slow to return to some stadia.

When performance is considered, fewer than a handful of the members of all of the four major sports leagues were losing money. An industry this successful does not deserve special protection or the ability to decide who can have a team and who cannot. The overall picture of team sports is one of a very successful industry where protectionism is not needed; nor is tolerance of the policies that, as cartels, the leagues have followed to limit the number of teams that can play. By restricting the number of the teams, in refusing to grant franchises in certain areas, and in establishing very high entry fees for new teams, the existing team owners use the leagues to protect their markets and to earn excess profits.

THE CARTELS' SOURCES OF REVENUE: THE PEA IS UNDER EVERY SHELL

When dealing with a cartel that has the power to prohibit the creation of new outlets (teams), it is important to understand where and how it earns money. In this manner, in negotiation, one can establish what is an appropriate investment by a local government and what subsidies or incentives are simply given in response to an abusive situation. Further, if taxpayers are ever to survive sports and the financial demands made by teams, it is critical for them to understand how each cartel's membership earns money and the potential they have for paying for their own playing facilities. The myriad of revenue sources does mean that, for the owners, there is a pea under every shell. Before looking at what some cities have done to attract and retain teams, it is simply critical that you understand that sports are a healthy industry that does not need any form of protection of its status as a cartel able to choose which cities have teams and which do not.

So, who gets teams and who does not, assuming the power of the cartels is not changed? If you want an NFL team, given the sharing of media revenues, you must be willing to build a stadium with luxury suites, club seats, and other revenue options. If you do this, owners will even leave large markets, as did the Raiders, Rams, and Oilers. The unshared revenues in the NFL afford owners the ability to make additional profits and pay for the best players. No one can forgo those revenue possibilities, so the cities that will host NFL teams are those that are willing to build facilities so teams can retain most if not all revenue that is currently *not* shared with other teams and their owners. But do recognize that, if you do this, you are providing welfare to wealthy people.

If you want an MLB team, large-market areas have a distinct advantage. With so little of the media income shared, regions with several million potential cable and pay-per-view households can attract and retain teams even if the stadium does not offer the revenue potential of Jacobs Field or the Ballpark in Arlington, for example. But, if you are a small-market region such as Cleveland or even Baltimore, then, like those cities that want NFL teams, you will need to build a stadium that has enormous revenue potential for teams and their owners. Again, if you build a stadium you are providing welfare to the rich.

Securing and retaining a hockey or basketball team is similar to developing a successful relationship with an MLB team. Large-market teams have a distinct and substantial financial advantage from their ability to develop and maintain lucrative local media contracts. In the absence of any plan to share these revenues, smaller-market teams must have access to adequate revenue flows from arena operations. This means the development of facilities that have the potential to generate substantial income from luxury suites, club seats, and the sale of refreshments. With these pressures, it may well be necessary for the public sector and their partners in the different sports leagues to agree on accepted rates of return relative to any participation by a community in the financing and development of a new facility. This is the stark reality of the power of the cartels. Without changes, the welfare system will continue.

4

What Do Teams Really Mean for a City's Economy?

A new ball park represents an investment in the future. It becomes a matter of good business practice. A state-of-the-art facility reflects a community's confidence in its potential. Cities want to be regarded as big league or first class. It is a matter of pride. Major league baseball remains a significant factor in the quality-of-life equation. No community today wants to lose a franchise. It would send the wrong message to business and industry that might have an interest in it.

—GENE BUDIG,
American League president (Chass, June 1995)

WHEN PROPOSALS ARE MADE for building arenas or stadia or when cities compete to attract a team, the justifications always include the anticipated economic gains. Proponents expect direct or tangible economic benefits (more jobs, higher salaries, and additional spending from tourists and fans) and large intangible benefits from an enhanced city image. More than one mayor and civic leader have noted that without professional sports a city is not major league. Image and economic development are frequently the pillars used to support proposals for teams and their facilities. What does a city gain from a team? Why is there so much competition for teams?

As the world has been shrunk by jet planes, fax machines, and the Internet, and when things manufactured in one part of the world can easily be sold anywhere within days, cities and regions have become locked in a competitive struggle for identity and economic development. It is through their identities that cities differentiate themselves and seek to become places that attract businesses, jobs, and economic activity. Sports teams become part of and a very visible focus of this competition to establish an identity for economic development.

> There is real benefit from people in other parts of the country looking in their newspapers and seeing "Minnesota" in stories. . . . It's one of those intangibles that makes an area "major league."
> —DAVE MONA,
> public relations executive (Bennett, 1994)

> Professional sports leagues are a unique form of business. On one level they sell entertainment, but they also sell civic identity, emotion, and community involvement. The name Kansas City Chiefs says it all. The Chiefs belong to the fans and the community of Kansas City. We support the team. We share the glory of their victories. We share the bitterness of their defeats. It is because we, the citizens of Kansas City, share so much with our team that we have been willing and we will continue to be willing to make the public investments in stadia and other projects to provide the teams with the facilities which are necessary to their operation (Wilson, 1994, p. 246).
> —RICHARD BERKELEY,
> mayor of Kansas City

This competition between cities for an identity and to achieve a designation as a major league city for economic development actually occurs within groupings of urban areas. There is an economic hierarchy to cities. You could describe these different tiers of cities as a set of leagues, each having its own champions or leaders. While it is possible for cities to jump from one tier to another (Los Angeles was not a city of the importance of a New York or London in the 1940s), there is really little movement of cities between the leagues. There is, however, a considerable amount of reshuffling of the standings within each league or tier. These standings within the tiers have a pronounced impact on identities and image. Professional sports teams have been able to establish themselves as key commodities in this battle for image.

It is probably easiest to think of this ordering of cities into leagues, tiers, or categories as a sort of pyramid. At the top are the "international supercities," the truly irreplaceable centers of banking, finance, transportation, politics, and the media that, over time, have retained their dominant or central roles in societies. In this sense, New York, Los Angeles, Chicago, Washington, D.C., or San Francisco in the United States; Montreal, Vancouver, Ottawa, and Toronto in Canada; and London, Frankfurt, Rome, and Paris in Europe possess a sort of uniqueness or concentration of critical economic and political resources that establishes their image and desirability as a place to live and work. In Asia, Tokyo, Hong Kong, Shanghai, and Beijing certainly belong to this grouping of cities. If one wants to be at the center of international finance or political power, a location in the New York, Tokyo, Washington, D.C., Paris, Frankfurt, Hong Kong, Beijing, or London regions is required. Similarly, if one wants to be at the center of the mass media's world, a location in New York, London, or Los Angeles is needed.

All of these super or international cities compete with one another to be the favored location for international headquarters and for corporations that seek or need direct contact with international finance and corporate centers. Each one possesses a unique identity or competitive advantage that defines the image of a supercity. This image includes the assets that one usually expects to find in a supercity: great universities, the best orchestras and theater districts, the finest museums, the most important libraries, the most influential business and political leaders, and the best professional sports teams. Supercities, to be sure, are not without their negative characteristics that both threaten their attractiveness and require attention. For example, supercities tend to be among the most expensive in which to live or work, and many suffer from other problems (such as crime, traffic, pollution, congestion, and racial and ethnic strife). Yet the attraction and importance of supercities is not only undeniable but has been sustained over time.

Supercities do compete among themselves to be selected as key locations for leading businesses, but they do not compete, by and large, with "regional urban centers" that form the second tier of cities. Business activities that do not have to be located in the more costly supercities tend to migrate, over time, to strategic regional centers. Within this second tier of cities, critical components of a society or an economy can be found. Several regional centers have some of the characteristics of supercities and are, themselves, critical components in many societies. For example, some might not consider Boston a supercity. Yet, as home to numerous universities, including two of America's most important, Harvard and MIT, it has an image and status that surpasses that of many other large regional centers, and even some supercities. Seattle is another example of a city whose importance in the United States finds its roots in the significance of two large employers, Boeing and Microsoft. Seattle may not be a supercity, but in terms of computers and jet aircraft, no city in the world is more important. The Dallas/Fort Worth area has emerged as an important tier-two or second-level metropolitan region because of the presence of several important corporations and the transportation nexus established by the Dallas/Fort Worth International Airport. Atlanta has also achieved an important identity as a transportation, media, and banking and finance center, but it is not New York or Los Angeles.

Whenever there is a substantial change in technology—transportation or manufacturing—a reordering of the level-one regional centers in this second tier of cities can occur. In the nineteenth century, Pittsburgh and Cleveland were probably cities with more pronounced images and economic importance than Detroit, Seattle, or Dallas. The importance of the automobile in the twentieth century elevated Detroit, for a time, only to be overtaken by the "Sunbelt" cities, which increased in importance during the latter part of the twentieth century. The computer and telecommunications industries have elevated the importance of regional centers such as Houston, Dallas/Fort Worth, and San José, but these cities have not and will not challenge the supercity status of New York, Washington, London, Paris, or Rome.

In their battle for identities, these critical regional centers do try to develop many of the same assets found in supercities, and sports teams frequently become one asset for which they can successfully compete. These assets can be used in competitions for further development with other regional or second-tier centers and in efforts to become supercities. There are, to be sure, fine orchestras, museums, libraries, and universities at these regional centers. And, in some instances, these assets do meet or even surpass those found in the larger supercities. Yet, in most instances, the assets of the supercities surpass those found in the largest regional centers. With larger population bases and concentrations of wealth that can support important cultural assets, supercities seem more likely to have more extensive cultural assets. Yet, in one area, regional centers can be equal to a supercity. A regional center could have a sports team that could defeat the team from the supercity. Ever wonder why beating the Yankees is so important to so many teams? Why do the Indiana Pacers "live" to defeat the New York Knicks? These beatings or "bestings" of the teams from the supercity also occur in highly publicized settings. It is one thing for Phoenix or San Antonio to declare its symphonies are as good as or better than the Los Angeles Philharmonic. But that is a subjective value judgment. What is more decisive is a four-game sweep of the Los Angeles Lakers by the Phoenix Suns or San Antonio Spurs.

The third tier in the pyramid of cities includes somewhat smaller provincial or regional centers. It is in this league of cities that one finds communities such as Indianapolis, Cincinnati, Columbus (Ohio), Denver, Phoenix, Sacramento, Salt Lake City, Calgary, Edmonton, Winnipeg, Buffalo, Miami, Tampa, and others. Among these cities the competition for economic development is equally intense. These cities may not possess a unique or dominant business such as Microsoft or Boeing, or they may have only one such industry. Similarly, their cultural assets or mechanisms by which they can achieve an identity are typically smaller and of lower quality than those found in supercities or tier-two regional centers. However, many believe there is one way these cities can compete with one another to establish their identities, offer to their residents something special, and achieve some sense of parity with larger cities: be home to a winning sports team.

The fourth tier of cities includes still smaller regional centers and larger suburban cities. These smaller regional cities are still very important economic and cultural centers, and some are state or provincial capitals. These fourth-tier cities may also be critical transportation and distribution centers. Frequently the costs of storing goods in larger urban areas are too high, and smaller cities can become important centers. The larger suburban cities included in this grouping have either established or are seeking to establish identities independent of those they share with the center cities that led to their development. These suburban communities, while smaller than their neighboring central city, frequently have a substantial economic base that requires workers to commute to the suburban city from surrounding areas. In this fashion these suburban cities become "mini" center cities in a metropolitan region.

Many of the third- and fourth-tier or smaller regional centers frequently want to be considered "major league" or "big time" places to live and work and try to emulate the supercities and their amenities. But with smaller populations and fewer concentrations of wealth this is sometimes difficult. As a result, included in the frequent justifications used to defend the public sector's support for professional sports is the explanation that a team is needed to:

1. establish and maintain an identity for a city or region's economic development;

2. compete with larger supercities as a desirable location with the same amenities but lower costs; and,

3. stimulate economic development.

Public support and subsidies for sports teams have also been defended as needed to offset the advantage supercity teams have as a result of their larger revenue bases and local broadcast markets. However, before you agree to public support for a sports team to build an image or stimulate economic development, you need to understand just what a team means for a city's or region's economy and image.

A Competition Between Tier III and Tier IV: When Being Music City, USA, Is Not Enough

Nashville, Tennessee, an important, but small, regional center, has long been identified with country music and is an undisputed capital for that industry. In recent years, however, Nashville's prominence has been challenged by Branson, Missouri. While Nashville is also home to other important cultural assets, Vanderbilt University among them, the community's leadership has sought to enhance the region's reputation and attractiveness. In 1995, it entered into "sports wars" with another tier III or IV area, New Jersey's Meadowlands. Nashville decided to build an indoor arena to attract an NHL or NBA team. With securing a team as a result of the expansion of any of the professional leagues always uncertain (Will the league expand? When? How many teams will be added? Will an acceptable ownership group be found in our city?), Nashville decided to become a "speculator" city. It built a facility without a team and then set about attracting one from another city. In short order, at least two teams appeared willing to listen to the call of the Nashville sirens.

One of the teams, the New Jersey Devils of the NHL, played its home games at the New Jersey Meadowlands Arena. While located in the shadow of Manhattan, the Meadowlands has been able to use its own siren call to lure New York sports teams across the Hudson River. The proximity of the Meadowlands to New Jersey's wealthy commuter suburbs has attracted the New York Giants, the New York Jets, and the former New York Nets. The New Jersey Devils, formerly of Denver, Colorado, also moved to New Jersey, giving the New York City metropolitan region three NHL teams: the New York Islanders, the New York Rangers, and the New Jersey Devils. The Devils did not believe they were receiving the revenue and fan support they wanted or needed to be profitable and successful, and Nashville, eager to be home to either an NBA and/or an NHL team, beckoned with its new indoor arena.

To win this "sports war" Nashville was willing to offer the Devils or any other team: (1) a $20 million relocation fee or bonus for coming to Nashville (to be used to pay moving expenses or any other costs associated with breaking a lease or leaving another city); (2) a yearly rental for the new arena, which cost the public sector $120 million, excluding interest charges, of $750,000 per season or 5 percent of ticket sales, whichever is greater (The public sector will be responsible for maintenance and all other expenses [game day] associated with the operation of the facility. The team nets 95 percent of all ticket revenues); (3) all revenues from radio and television contracts and 97.5 percent of luxury suite rental fees; (4) 35 percent of all revenues on game days from merchandise sold, 40 percent of revenue from game day concession sales, and 75 percent of all parking revenues on game days; (5) all advertising from the scoreboard in the arena and the advertising placed on the sideboards, and 50 percent of all other advertising revenues; (6) a proposal for building a training facility for the team at no cost to the team; (7) the use of the existing Municipal Auditorium currently used by a minor league hockey team without any charge if the arena is not completed in time for the 1996–97 hockey season.

Lastly, the city of Nashville was also willing to change local laws to attract a team. The Nashville Arena is located less than a hundred feet from a church, and local ordinances do not permit the selling of alcoholic beverages within this range. In June 1995, the Nashville Metro Council approved a bill that exempted the arena from a city ordinance that prohibited beer sales within a hundred feet of a church, residence, school, or park. The mayor's press secretary, upon learning the council had made the change, noted, "Now we can go out and recruit a team" (*New York Times,* June 1995).

These commitments, combined with the city of Nashville's willingness to change local laws, produced an extremely attractive offer to any team. New Jersey made an offer to keep the Devils. In doing so the state risked changes in its relationships with and commitments to the Nets, Giants, and Jets. Such is the cost of a "sports war" between tier III or IV locations.

Once the Devils decided to stay in New Jersey, another team became interested in moving to Nashville. The ownership of the Winnipeg Jets had decided that substantially more money was to be made south of the border. Their first preference was Minneapolis, but the requirement to reimburse the province of Manitoba for previous investments and the failure of Minneapolis to offer enough cash to offset those payments made that move unlikely. Nashville's offer of a $20 million relocation fee might have made it possible to settle the team's obligations to Manitoba if the ownership would prefer to be the Nashville Jets. In the end, however, Nashville again lost its bid to be a major leaague hockey town as the Jets chose to land in Phoenix and play their games at the America West Arena. Nashville, of course, did become major league when the NFL's Oilers decided to leave Houston. The Oilers' move, however, necessitated the building of another stadium, so Nashville's arena still sits vacant.

The balance of this chapter will deal with several issues to help you evaluate whether or not any public subsidy in sports could be considered worth the likely gains in direct and indirect economic benefits or image. In this way, you can judge for yourself if competing in a sports war to achieve major league status is worth the investments and risks.

SPORTS DOLLARS: HOW BIG IS BIG?

More than a few participants in debates over a local governments' investment in professional sports have noted that for enough money you can get an academic or consulting economist to say anything you want. If you ever attend a debate or public hearing to evaluate a sports investment and its value to a city, it certainly does appear that each side can contradict any claims made by the other side. I have often mused that these "dueling consultant" battles are the misdirected responses from academics who cringed at the observation, "Those who can, do; those who can't, teach."

In their effort to assure people that those who teach can also do, dueling economists sometimes create the unfavorable impression that no one agrees on anything in the sports economics field. When experts contradict each other, elected officials are driven to do what they believe is best, or what a growth coalition or vocal electoral constituency demands. I've left several meetings hearing people mutter, "If these consultants are so well trained and teach at respected universities or work for important firms, how can they disagree so much on what the numbers mean?" The battle of the consultants sometimes alienates so many people that the contributions and arguments of advocates of either position are virtually worthless to those who have to make decisions regarding the public's investment in sports. When this occurs, "gut" feelings sometimes drive decisions, allowing the emotionalism of sports to dictate outcomes. Dueling consultants aside, there are tools that can be used.

This discussion will not become the course in economics you dreaded in high school or college. It is, however, a map to help you steer through pages of assertions, numbers, and impact analyses, and it will let you determine if all that glitters from sports brings economic gold to your community.

> Professional sports have become an important part of the entertainment business and a significant factor in the nation's economy. Not only do millions of spectators pay anywhere from five dollars to more than five hundred dollars per head to see professional sports in person, the public appetite for athletic entertainment has opened the way to multi-million dollar television contracts for promoters, lucrative personal endorsement agreements and enormous salaries for successful athletes, and the utilization of millions in tax revenues to provide new stadiums and services for owners and fans.
>
> —JAMES EDWARD MILLER,
> *The Baseball Business* (1990, p. vii)

We know that sports are both popular and an important part of our culture and life. Surprisingly, though, teams are not "big business" operations. If sports teams were classified by their gross revenues, they would be considered small to medium-sized businesses. Relying upon *Financial World*'s estimates of team revenues, it is likely that only two teams in 1994 or 1995, the New York Yankees and the Dallas Cowboys, had or would have had direct annual revenues of more than $100 million. (The baseball strike reduced the actual revenues of the Yankees.) Several baseball teams clearly had gross revenues that would have exceeded $70 million in either year: the Baltimore Orioles, the Boston Red Sox, the Chicago White Sox, the Toronto Blue Jays, the Chicago Cubs, the Atlanta Braves, the Colorado Rockies, the Los Angeles Dodgers, and the Texas Rangers. It is probable the Atlanta Braves (owned by Ted Turner, who also owns WTBS) and the Chicago Cubs (owned by the Tribune Company, which owns WGN) each had a revenue stream in excess of $100 million. Indeed, the Toronto Blue Jays may be the team with the single greatest revenue stream in 1994 when aspects of their ownership of the Toronto Skydome and the cable system that broadcasts Blue Jay games are considered. My estimate is that the gross revenues amassed by the owners of the Toronto Blue Jays in 1994, once the interlocking ownership is credited with all its revenue streams, would have exceeded $125 million had the strike not taken place.

These revenues, and the more typical figures earned by other baseball teams, generally exceed those earned by football, basketball, and hockey teams, which have shorter seasons. To be sure, some teams in these sports earn more revenue than several baseball teams located in smaller markets (for example, the Pittsburgh Pirates and Seattle Mariners). The Dallas Cowboys, for example, as a result of their stadium agreement with the city of Irving, had revenues of approximately $111 million in 1995. The Miami Dolphins also had gross revenues in excess of $70 million, and all other NFL teams, except the two expansion franchises, had revenues of more than $60 million in 1995. Basketball and hockey teams, which utilize facilities that seat far fewer fans than those used by baseball teams, generally have revenue streams below those of major league baseball teams. Only six basketball teams had revenues in excess of $60 million (Knickerbockers, Bulls, Lakers, Pistons, Cavaliers, and Suns), and only the Detroit Red Wings and New York Rangers had revenues in excess of $50 million in the NHL in 1994. In 1995, only the Rangers exceeded the $50 million plateau (Ozanian, 1995; *Financial World*, 1996).

Firms with annual budgets of $60 million or $100 million are certainly vital, vibrant, and valued in terms of the development of any region's economy. But businesses of this size are quite small when compared to other organizations in urban areas. For example, few would consider urban campuses of state universities to be engines that drive a city's economy. Yet, in budget terms, they are quite a bit larger than even the most successful sports teams. The budget for Indiana University–Purdue University Indianapolis (IUPUI), with its enrollment of more than 25,000 students and excluding its health center, is in excess of $300 million. The most successful sports franchise, then, has gross revenues that are less than half of a typical urban campus of a state university, and most teams have budgets equal to about 20 percent of the budget of an urban campus of a state university (Klacik & Rosentraub, 1993). This is your first caution light on this map of the economics of sports. If teams are relatively small businesses, how can sports be an economic engine?

There are, to be sure, a number of very well paid athletes, several of whom earn in excess of several million dollars each season. A number of the owners of teams are also quite wealthy. Regardless, the wealth of a few individuals, or even a few hundred individuals, does not make sports a "big business." The attention sports attract and the periodic discussions of the wealth of certain participants and team owners can create the impression that sports are a major industry or a critical component of our economy or of the economy of certain cities or regions. Indeed, even the historian James Edward Miller, noted author of an important book on the business of baseball, declared that professional sports are a significant part of the national economy. To the contrary, guidepost 1 on your map to the battle of the dueling consultants is that sports is really "small potatoes" in terms of the economy of the United States, the economy of any region, and the economy of virtually any city. Professional sports may be the "icing on a region's or city's economic cake," but it is not an "engine" that drives any economy.

And now you are saying, here we go again, dueling academicians. No. I am not dealing, yet, with the questions of whether (1) sports can "jump-start" a region's economy or (2) can lead the economic redevelopment of a downtown area or a specific neighborhood. We will deal with those issues in the specific analyses of sports and selected cities. I want first to examine the overall size of sports in the economy. I will demonstrate that sports are really a very small part of the economy by looking at sports as a component of the U.S. economy and the economy of all cities, counties, and regions.

The U.S. Department of Commerce each year releases its survey of employment in its *County Business Patterns* data file. Contained in this data set are the number of employees and their average salaries enumerated by the type of business in which the employer is engaged. All private-sector firms are included in the data set, with individual industries identified by a set of classifications known as standard industry codes, or SICs. There are separate SIC classifications for restaurants (eating and drinking places), hotels (and other lodging places), manufacturing, agriculture, mining, and sports clubs and managers. It is in this last category that professional sports teams and clubs are counted. A larger category, commercial sports, includes racetracks. There are many more SIC codes for other businesses.

County Business Patterns does not include information from nonprofit organizations and does not include governmental agencies and their workers. This data set also excludes certain businesses that have no employees (such as consultants and sole proprietorships). *County Business Patterns* is a measure of private-sector business activity and is produced for every county in the United States. In reviewing the size of any business as a portion of the total economy, it is therefore important to remember that with nonprofit payrolls and government payrolls excluded, any industry's share of the economy would be even less than what is reported in *County Business Patterns*. Recently, the Department of Commerce released a version of this employment information organized by zip codes. This data set permits an analysis of the size of the different private-sector business activities at the city level (or of any part of a county) by including all the zip codes that are part of a particular area or city. This refined breakdown of the U.S. economy, county by county or zip code by zip code, permits a detailed picture of the economic engines within America's private sector.

Please remember that many of the important economic benefits from professional teams are not included in the SIC category "sports clubs and managers." For example, sports teams bring fans to certain parts of a city, and that can result in new business for restaurants and hotels. There is also the possibility of increased purchases of souvenirs from new retail outlets. Part of this chapter will deal with the issue of related spending. Let's first see how big is big when we talk about sports dollars. And don't forget: We also have to deal with the issue of multiplier effects. Are we going to have fun, or what?

HOW BIG IS BIG?
SPORTS AND THE ECONOMY OF COUNTIES

> A new ballpark means security for many working men and women. It provides needed jobs and has a direct impact on the local economy. Major league baseball means millions of dollars for its member communities. Figures vary, but most clubs place their economic impact at well over $200 million a year. This, in fact, is a conservative number.
>
> —GENE BUDIG,
> American League president (Chass, June 1995)

To describe the size of the sports sector of the economy, I reviewed the total private-sector payrolls in all counties in the United States with at least three hundred thousand residents with the data available from the 1992 *County Business Patterns* survey. There were, in 1992, 161 counties across the United States with at least this many residents. Table 4–1 provides a summary of the importance of amusement and recreation services across all 161 counties. Of the 55,662,194 jobs in these 161 counties, .06 percent, or 33,397, were associated with either professional sports teams or managers. In terms of total payroll dollars, these jobs accounted for one-tenth of 1 percent of the $1.5 trillion in income reported for these 161 counties. This tiny percentage, however, still amounted to more than $1.5 billion.

The information in Table 4–2 describes employment patterns within counties of different sizes; interestingly enough, there is little difference by population size. Professional sports *never* accounted for more than .08 percent of the jobs in any group of counties. Professional sports payrolls were largest in the largest counties; even there, though, this grouping accounted for just one-half of 1 percent of the private sector's total payroll.

When I changed the focus of the analysis to each of the 161 coun-

TABLE 4–1

Private-Sector Employment and Payroll Levels in All United States Counties with 300,000 Residents, 1992

Standard Industrial Code Classification	Employment as a Percent of Total	Payroll as a Percent of Total
Eating and drinking places	6.56%	2.16%
Hotels and other lodging places	1.55%	0.82%
Amusement and recreation services	1.26%	0.94%
Commercial sports	0.12%	0.18%
Professional sports, managers	**0.06%**	**0.10%**
Remaining retail trade	13.05%	8.21%
Remaining services	32.76%	31.49%
Manufacturing	16.66%	21.42%
Wholesale trade	7.33%	9.35%
Transportation	6.34%	7.90%
Finance, insurance, & real estate	8.88%	11.59%
Agriculture	0.59%	0.39%
Mining	0.32%	0.55%
Construction	4.64%	5.12%
Unclassified	0.05%	0.07%
Total for All Counties	55,662,194	$1,502,221,516,000

TABLE 4–2

The Percentage of Employment and Private-Sector Payrolls by County Populations, 1992

Industry	Population of County			
	300,000 to 500,000 (n=66)	500,001 to 1,000,000 (n=65)	1,000,001 to 2,000,000 (n=22)	More than 2,000,000 Population (n=8)
Professional sports employment as a percent of total employment	0.03%	0.06%	0.08%	0.06%
Professional sports payrolls as a percent of private sector payrolls	0.14%	0.13%	0.24%	0.52%

ties with at least 300,000 residents, in *no* single county did the number of jobs with professional teams or sport managers account for more than four-tenths of 1 percent of all jobs. The highest proportions or concentrations of sports employment were found in Fulton County, Georgia, home to the Atlanta Falcons, Braves, and Hawks, and in Summit County, Ohio, where there is both a minor league team and a soccer team. Again, in neither of these cases did sports employment account for as much as one-half of 1 percent of all private-sector jobs. The counties with the largest concentration of sports jobs as a proportion of their local economies are identified in Table 4–3.

Table 4–3 also details the proportion of these counties' private-sector payrolls that was produced by sports firms. For some of these counties, salary data were not made available to protect the confidentiality of the employer. It is important to note, however, that in three of the counties the salaries from the professional sports sector accounted for more than one-half of 1 percent of all private-sector payrolls, but in no county did sports salaries account for more than three-quarters of 1 percent of private-sector payrolls.

As this reveals, in percentage terms sports are a very small part of any county's private-sector economy. This *does not mean* that sports payrolls are trivial or represent small numbers of dollars. In Cook County (Illinois) the payroll for professional teams was more than

TABLE 4–3

U.S. Counties with the Largest Concentrations of Direct Employment in Professional Sports: Jobs and Annual Payrolls, 1992

County (state)	Pro Sports Employment as a Percentage of All Jobs	Pro Sports Payrolls as a Percentage of All Payrolls	Total Pro Sports Jobs	Total Pro Sports Payroll (in $000s)
Fulton (GA)	0.32	*	1,727	
Cook (IL)	0.16	0.17	3,696	112,423
Marion (IN)	0.16	0.51	762	62,025
Baltimore (city)	0.26	*	760	
Suffolk (MA)	0.16	*	761	
Oakland (MI)	0.24	0.39	1,419	68,171
Hennepin (MN)	0.10	0.51	690	100,634
St. Louis (city)	0.16	0.74	422	52,574
Bronx (NY)	0.19	*	378	
Erie (NY)	0.19	*	742	
Queens (NY)	0.18	*	758	
Phila. (PA)	0.13	*	748	
Summit (OH)	0.35	*	760	
Salt Lake City (NV)	0.11	*	382	

*Data not available.

Source: *County Business Patterns,* U.S. Department of Commerce, 1992.

$112 million, and the annual payroll in Hennepin County was $100 million. In St. Louis the annual payroll was more than $52 million. Sports can generate some large payroll numbers even when those numbers represent a tiny percentage of total payroll dollars. However, as I will discuss later in this chapter, many of these salary dollars are not spent in a team's home county.

HOW BIG IS BIG?
SPORTS AND THE ECONOMY OF A CITY

One of the limitations of working with counties as the unit for analyzing economic impact—whether one is concerned with sports teams, arenas, or stadia—is that in many instances it is cities that are making the investments. As a result, any analysis of the importance of sports should not necessarily focus solely on counties, but on cities. Furthermore, many times cities are really interested in the issue of developmental impacts within a small portion of the city. That would suggest the need for a level of analysis that focuses on an area that is even smaller than a city. Can sports, an arena, or a stadium have a large impact in a small geographic area? An assessment of the impact of sports or a stadium at the county level cannot identify or indicate if these impacts have taken place. Indeed, some might suggest that looking at the county level to measure or detail the relative size of sports is far too broad a view and is designed to always illustrate that sports are both small and unable to affect growth. Perhaps within a city or within part of a city amusement and recreation firms could be a dominant portion of a local economy and an engine that drives growth. While several subsequent chapters will look carefully at what has happened in selected cities that used sports for economic development, it may be quite useful to look at one medium-sized city, Arlington, Texas, which tried to use sports and recreation to both stimulate growth and define its image.

Arlington, with 279,600 residents in 1995, is located between the cities of Dallas and Fort Worth, and to the south of the Dallas/Fort Worth International Airport. The city has tried, since the early 1970s, to develop its economic identity through sports and recreation services. In 1973, the city's leadership was able to attract the Washington Senators, which then became the Texas Rangers. The Rangers played in Arlington Stadium—a former minor league stadium—which was substantially improved in 1977 and then razed in 1994 as the city and team built "the Ballpark in Arlington." Arlington is also home to the Six Flags over Texas amusement park, the largest theme park in the southwestern United States, and to the Wet n' Wild water amusement park. The success of these three ventures, as evaluated by the city's leadership, has encouraged interest in the building of an arena that could become the home for the NBA's Dallas Mavericks and the NHL's Dallas Stars. Both teams, in 1995, played their home games at Dallas's Reunion Arena, located approximately fifteen miles east of Arlington. Arlington's existing tourist attractions, together with its convention center, have clearly established the city as a recreational center. But are sports or even the entire recreation industry the engine that drives Arlington's economy?

In 1992, the private-sector payroll for Arlington was estimated to be $1,885,222,215. More than one-quarter of this income, 26 percent, originated in businesses classified as services. The second largest industry group was manufacturing, accounting for 19.3 percent of Arlington's private-sector payroll. Retail trade was Arlington's third largest private-sector industry, accounting for 12.8 percent of all estimated payroll dollars in the city. The combined payrolls (citywide) for *all* sports-related businesses, amusement parks, recreation (theaters and so forth), hotels, and restaurants amounted to 11.4 percent of the private-sector payroll. This made the *citywide* entertainment grouping the fourth largest industry in the city. Wholesale trade was almost as large as entertainment, accounting for 10.9 percent of all private payroll dollars. Transportation and the FIRE grouping (finance, insurance, and real estate) each accounted for 6.0 percent of Arlington's private-sector payroll in 1992. All other industries and businesses accounted for 7.6 percent of the Arlington economy (see Table 4–4).

I also analyzed Arlington's economy at the zip code level, since the overwhelming effect of the sports and entertainment complexes in Arlington would likely occur in zip codes 76010, 76011, and

TABLE 4–4
Industry Size as Measured by Private-Sector Payrolls
Arlington, Texas, 1992
Total Estimated Private-Sector Payroll, $1,885,222,215

Industry Grouping	Estimated Percentage of Private-Sector Payroll Dollars
Services	26.0
Manufacturing	19.3
Retail trade	12.8
Citywide entertainment*	11.4
Wholesale trade	10.9
Other (combined)	7.6
FIRE	6.0
Transportation	6.0

*Includes all restaurant, recreation, and hotel spending throughout the city of Arlington.

Source: Center for Urban Policy and the Environment, Indiana University @ IUPUI; *County Business Patterns,* U.S. Department of Commerce, 1992.

76012. These are the areas closest to the stadium and the theme parks. To be sure, some economic impact also takes place in the other zip codes. However, there is some retail trade, hotel, and restaurant business in zip codes 76010, 76011, and 76012 that is *unrelated* to sports and the entertainment complex. For example, people who live in north Arlington would be expected to patronize restaurants in that area, and the Arlington business community and the local university access facilities in these zip codes. As a result, although this zip code analysis assumes that recreation and entertainment outside of zip codes 76010, 76011, and 76012 is not related to sports or the entertainment/convention complex, I compensated for any error by assuming *all* recreation and entertainment spending in those zip codes is related to the sports and entertainment complexes (the Ballpark in Arlington, Six Flags, Wet 'n' Wild, and the convention center).

When I separated the spending for sports, hotels, restaurants, and so forth by zip code, I found that slightly more than 7.5 percent of the total private-sector payroll dollars in Arlington were concentrated in the entertainment sector of the economy in the areas closest to the Ballpark in Arlington and the other entertainment complexes. As a result, sports and the entertainment sector would be

Arlington's *fifth largest individual industry,* smaller than the service sector, manufacturing, retail trade, wholesale trade, and the grouping of all remaining businesses in the "other" category. Sports and activities related to the entertainment complex, in terms of payroll size, were only slightly larger than transportation and the FIRE grouping. Sports and entertainment-related spending was *substantially smaller* than Arlington's two largest industries, which account for almost half of the private-sector activity in the city (see Table 4–5).

By including these data I do not want to suggest that sports and entertainment are unimportant; no city would want to lose 7.5 percent of its economic base. However, the data do underscore the observation that, even in a city the size of Arlington, and in a city with substantial sports and entertainment facilities, employment related to sports and entertainment is a small portion of the economy.

Without questioning the potential value of sports and entertainment to Arlington or any city through the establishment of a city's reputation and image—image is an issue I will address later in this chapter and in chapter 11—these data underscore that sports and

TABLE 4–5

The Entertainment Complex* Compared with Other Arlington Industries, Measured by Private Sector-Payrolls, Arlington, Texas, 1992 Total Estimated Private Sector-Payroll, $1,885,222,215

Industry Grouping	Estimated Percentage of Private-Sector Payroll Dollars
Services	26.0
Manufacturing	19.3
Retail trade	12.8
Wholesale trade	10.9
Other (combined)	7.6
ENTERTAINMENT complex*	7.5
FIRE	6.0
Transportation	6.0

*Includes all restaurant, recreation, and hotel spending taking place in zip codes 76010, 76011, and 76012.

Source: Center for Urban Policy and the Environment, Indiana University @ IUPUI; *County Business Patterns,* U.S. Department of Commerce, 1992.

entertainment are very small components of any region's economy, and even in small and medium-sized cities (similar to Arlington), sports are not the economic engine some would wish to believe they are. Sports are, simply put, too small to drive an economy. Even in Arlington, a city that would not be described as a manufacturing center or a "smokestack city," manufacturing is substantially more important than the entertainment, sports-related, and restaurant businesses combined.

How big is big when we are discussing sports dollars? Big, in dollar terms, is actually quite small in percentage terms when the entire economy of a city is considered. Sports teams are small to medium-sized businesses, and even in areas with several teams, the professional team sports component of an economy never accounts for as much as 1 percent of the jobs or 1 percent of the payrolls in that county.

SPORTS AND RELATED SPENDING

Okay, so now you're saying, "Yeah, sports itself may be small, but what of the *related* spending. You know, people go to a game, they eat dinner, buy souvenirs, and maybe they even stay in a hotel if they come from outside the city." To get a fair or balanced picture of the economic importance of sports, those impacts must be calculated; if not, it creates a biased picture. But how big is the spending (hotels, restaurants, souvenirs, and so forth) associated with sports?

If you read some of the justifications of public support for teams or playing facilities, the expected growth in spending at hotels and restaurants is enormous. Indeed, many justifications for tax support for stadia or arenas frequently include the expectation of increased restaurant and hotel activity. For example, an economic impact assessment of the Target Center in Minneapolis reported that "22 new eating and restaurant places have opened resulting in new construction in excess of $10 million" (Arthur Anderson and Company, 1994). A study of the impact of Oriole Park at Camden Yards concluded that fans spent $38 million at downtown restaurants, hotels, and souvenir stores (Ahmadi, 1992). In Arlington, the hotel and restaurant activity in the city produced an annual private-sector payroll of $214.9 million. The development of Jacobs Field and Gund Arena in Cleveland also led to the opening of more than twenty new restaurants and a new hotel near these projects. But just *how big is this benefit* to an economy? Restaurant and hotel spending related to sports does represent a large amount of money, right? In percentage terms, no. In dollar terms, maybe yes, but maybe no.

First, back to the issue of the relative size of this portion of any county's economy. For example, Maricopa County (Phoenix), Arizona, is home to the NBA's Suns, the NFL's Cardinals, and is also the spring training home for several baseball teams. All restaurant and hotel payrolls in 1992 amounted to 3.9 percent of that county's private-sector payroll. This proportion included all hotel and restaurant payrolls, including those produced by the convention and winter tourist trade in Phoenix, Scottsdale, and Mesa that was completely unrelated to sports. This figure also reflects the activity of households in the Phoenix metropolitan region who eat out as part of their usual schedule. Los Angeles County, in 1992, was home to several sports teams: the Dodgers, the Lakers, the Clippers, the Kings, and the Raiders (the Rams played in Orange County). That county also hosts a large convention center and several important tourist and shopping facilities. Payrolls at hotels and restaurants in this area amounted to 2.7 percent of the private sector's payroll. In Fulton County (Atlanta), home to the Braves, Falcons, and Hawks, hotels and restaurants accounted for 3.2 percent of the private-sector payroll. From coast to coast, and in counties of various sizes, even if we include *all* hotel and restaurant payrolls, *not just the portion* that could or should be attributed to sports, this segment of the economy is also too small to be an engine that drives any local economy. The level of dollars reported is high; but in proportion to other industries in almost every area, restaurants and hotels are small parts of the economy. Only in selected tourist regions—Las Vegas, Nevada, and Orlando, Florida—are the proportions substantially different and in those communities, the spending at retaurants is not dependent upon professional sports.

Okay, so now you're saying that these are just percentage games. Restaurants and hotels may be a small proportion, but it is still an important segment of the economy involving a large number of dollars. So what if the percentages are small. If the level of dollars is high, isn't that the key issue? Maybe not.

Consider this, the second point I want you to keep in mind when you deal with sports and related spending. How much more food do people eat because of the presence of a team? In other words, if a family eats dinner near the stadium or arena before a game, where did they *not* eat their dinner that night? If they would have eaten at a restaurant near their home, then the consumption of food as part of the sporting event is merely a transfer of expenditures from a restaurant near their home to one near the stadium or arena. This change of location for the expenditure certainly creates an impact in both areas—more spending near the facility and less in the neighborhood. But from the economy's perspective there is no growth or increase in spending levels, merely a transfer. Further, if the family would have eaten at home instead of at a restaurant, then the transfer of expenditures takes place between the supermarket and the restaurant, with consumption declining at the supermarket while restaurant sales increase. Again, there is economic impact in the sense that the restaurant may gain while the supermarket suffers, but the overall change in the community or city is not one of growth, but merely a transfer of activity from one vendor to another.

It may well be true that the presence of the Target Center in Minneapolis led to the building of twenty-two new restaurants adjacent to the arena. Cleveland's new facilities also likely led to the development of new restaurants. But if other restaurants closed across the city or in certain neighborhoods because people chose to frequent those facilities near the stadium or arena, there was *no growth* or economic gain that should be reported. Furthermore, how much public money should be invested to merely transfer some portion of restaurant and hotel spending?

Let's forget all these points for a moment. While restaurant and hotel employment and salaries are a small portion of most region's economies, how much of this activity is really sports related? Can that be estimated? Perhaps it can. Relying, again, on information from *County Business Patterns* (refer to Table 4–1), 6.6 percent of all private-sector jobs in counties with more than three hundred thousand residents were found in eating and drinking places. These jobs are relatively low-wage positions, as they accounted for just 2.2 percent of all private-sector payrolls. However, this still means that the aggregate or overall payroll in restaurants and drinking places exceeded $30 billion. Hotels and other lodging places accounted for 1.6 percent of all jobs, but less than 1 percent of the total payroll. Of these jobs and payrolls, how many jobs and how many payroll dollars are related to sports? Well, no one knows for sure, but I can develop some proportions to give you an idea.

Assume, for the moment, that there is a direct relationship between all amusement and recreation services and purchases at restaurants and hotels. In other words, let's argue for the moment that if you ever go out for any form of recreation that you will use a restaurant and a hotel. In other words, we are going to establish a "high-end estimate."

Amusement and recreation spending accounted for 1.26 percent of all private-sector jobs in counties with more than three hundred thousand residents (refer to Table 4–1) and .94 percent of all private-sector payrolls. If that represented the portion of restaurant and hotel jobs and payrolls associated with amusements and recreation services, then 701,334 jobs with an annual payroll of $14.1 billion were created in hotels and restaurants from all recreational activities in all counties. Now, commercial (which includes racing) and professional sports account for .18 percent of all jobs, or 14.3 percent of the amusement and recreational service jobs. This would mean that of the 701,344 jobs created by amusement and recreational jobs in restaurants and hotels, 100,192 were created in restaurants and hotels in the United States as a result of sports. In payroll terms this would amount to $4.2 billion for all counties with more than three hundred thousand residents. But that was for all sports, not just professional sports. If we looked at just professional sports, the corresponding numbers are 233,781 jobs with an average annual payroll of $1.5 billion across the United States. Since the total private-sector payroll reported in *County Business Patterns* was $1.5 trillion, the figure of $1.5 billion amounts to one-tenth of 1 percent of the private-sector payroll reported for counties with more than three hundred thousand residents in 1992. Again, this is not a small number, but in percentage terms it is virtually negligible. Others have also found that the amount of restaurant and hotel trade related to sports facilities is quite small in percentage terms.

Be wary of the predictions that the presence of sports teams, arenas, and stadia will result in the growth of robust restaurant and hotel structures (Baade, 1994, 1995; Greco, 1993). Will there be some level of job creation? Yes!! Will more people come to downtown? Yes!! Will there be increased restaurant and hotel activity? Yes!! But there will also be decreases in spending at restaurants further from the stadium and less spending on other forms of recreation. A large proportion of the spending on sports, or that which results from sports, is merely a transfer of activity from one area to another. Sports are not only small potatoes, but those potatoes may have been someone else's before the team or stadium existed. We need to discuss in greater detail the transfer of spending when teams exist.

ECONOMIC ACTIVITY AND ECONOMIC IMPACT

Maryland's Department of Economic and Employment Development determined that "during the 1992 baseball season, fan expenditures on such items as tickets, concessions, souvenirs, gifts, parking, transportation, lodging and other travel-related incidentals, as well as visiting team expenditures, directly supported $117 million in gross sales, $44 million in employee income, and over 1,500 full-time equivalent jobs" (Ahmadi, 1992). The Target Center study for Minneapolis's Timberwolves noted "annual spending of approximately $57.5 million. This spending level supports an estimated 693 jobs in full-time equivalent terms" (Arthur Anderson, 1994). When Arlington sought to convince its voters to support an increase in a local sales tax to fund the Ballpark in Arlington, an information sheet distributed by the city manager's office noted: "The Texas

Rangers currently have an annual economic impact on Arlington's economy of approximately $98 million. This figure is based on a study conducted four years ago by a team of economists at the University of Texas at Arlington. According to Dr. John M. Trapini, who headed the study team, the Texas Rangers ball club in 1986 generated approximately $65.7 million for the Arlington economy. Using the same methodology, adjusted for the rate of inflation and 1990 attendance figures, the annual economic impact of the Texas Rangers on the Arlington economy is currently $97,797,000" (city of Arlington, undated). Jacksonville and its taxpayers were told that their new NFL team would generate $130 million and create three thousand jobs (Norton, 1993).

Well, this is getting a bit complicated. Some people use numbers; others use percentages. There is also one additional matter that I have to raise that is going to complicate the situation a bit more. When you review studies of the economic importance of sports facilities and teams, in addition to the differences created when one focuses on percentages instead of raw numbers, there is also a difference between *economic activity* and *economic impact*. There are also positive and negative impacts that people sometimes forget cancel each other. Consider the following examples.

Suppose you do go to a Texas Ranger, Baltimore Oriole, or Jacksonville Jaguar game. In addition to your ticket, what else are you likely to buy? Well, you might have lunch or dinner or buy some refreshments at the game. You might pay for parking at the game, and you might even buy a souvenir. Now, suppose you don't go to the game. What are you likely to do instead? You will probably still eat lunch or dinner, so that expenditure of a meal purchased before or after the game still takes place. Suppose you also decided to go to the movies instead of the ball game, or to see a show. There would still be a ticket purchase, so that spending on your Oriole, or Ranger, or Jaguar ticket is not additional spending. What about those souvenirs? Well, that might be additional spending, but if you buy an Oriole shirt instead of a shirt at a mall later that week, then your souvenir is not new spending either. What economic impact was created if you attended the game instead of a movie? Maybe what you did was simply transfer money from the movie theater owner to the team owner. Is it fair, then, to count your spending and "activity" as the "impact" of the team when you would have spent the money in any event? *If the economic activity would have taken place if the team did not exist, then there is NO overall economic impact, just a transfer of economic activity.*

So, economic impact is not the same as economic activity. Now let's think a bit about a *positive economic impact*, which is actually completely offset by a *negative economic impact*. Suppose a young kid throws a rock through your window and it costs you $50 to replace the glass. The repair creates work for someone (indeed, if there is extensive vandalism new jobs might even be created). As a result, the act of vandalism generates positive economic impact for the people who are hired to replace the glass. The impact is the *transfer* of $50 from your pocket to the worker who replaced the glass. The $50 could even be seen as growth for the individual who did the repair, but for you there is no real growth, just negative economic impact since you had a perfectly good window before the act of vandalism. Indeed, since you just spent $50 to repair the glass, perhaps you cannot afford to buy a shirt or attend a professional sporting event. In this instance, then, the negative economic impact offsets the positive gain, and there is *no net impact* for the economy or real development, only a sort of transfer from one part of the economy (you) to another (the glass repair person) with no increase or change in your quality of life. In the case of the broken glass, you transfer funds from recreational spending or savings to maintenance. There is no positive impact because you would have spent the money in any event. Impact, then, does not mean economic growth. If a stadium or arena is built and it creates one hundred new jobs in restaurants near the facility, but one hundred jobs are lost in other parts of the city because people now eat near the stadium or arena, there is no positive impact, just a reshuffling of economic activity with all winners balanced by losers.

What, then, is positive economic impact? Positive economic impact is new spending or economic activity brought to a neighborhood, community, city or county in which the stadium or arena is located. This occurs in two ways: (1) people from outside the area, city, or county come to attend a game and spend money they would not have spent in the area, city, or county or (2) people in the area, city or county decide to spend money there instead of going elsewhere for their recreation. In terms of this second point, we usually refer to this growth as deflection. It is *deflected impact or growth* in the sense that instead of going to Atlanta for a game, people in Jacksonville spend their recreation dollars in Jacksonville. Arlington residents can attend events in Dallas or Fort Worth, but if they stay in Arlington, then there is deflected growth. Likewise, because Indianapolis has the Colts, maybe some residents do not take a trip to Chicago or Cincinnati to see an NFL game but stay home and attend a Colts game. That is another example of deflected growth.

Another way people sometimes think about economic impact is through what is called the *substitution effect*. Attendance at a sporting event is just one of the ways in which people can spend their recreation dollars. If someone attends a baseball or basketball game, what did he or she not do with those recreation dollars? In other words, what spending takes place in the absence of attendance at sporting events? Or, how much of what is spent for or through attendance at a ball game is just a substitution for some other type of spending that would have taken place? If the spending would have taken place anyway, then there is no economic growth.

Counting the growth from deflection or the people who come to a city or county for a game is also not a simple task. Neither is measuring the substitution effects that take place when people spend their recreational dollars for something other than baseball, basketball, football, or hockey. For example, suppose that in a region the vast majority of recreational venues are in the center city or county. Now suppose that the same city or county adds a new stadium or arena. If everyone was already coming to the city or county for recreation, is there any new growth? If they attend a game instead of a movie in the same county, then the spending on baseball or basketball is a transfer or substitution for spending already in the area.

Fort Wayne, Indiana, was considering an investment to attract a minor league baseball team to the city. Fort Wayne is a medium-sized city and the recreational hub for a region of about 675,000 people. Within this region, all movie theaters, theaters for live shows, and concert facilities are located in the city of Fort Wayne. As a result, the city already attracts, or is the location for, a substantial portion of the region's recreational trade. If a team existed, how much more recreational trade would it attract, or would the team simply take spending away from the theaters? Similarly, the Indianapolis region serves a population base of more than 1.4 million people. Today, 95 percent of all movie theaters in the region are located in the consolidated city-county of Indianapolis, and all professional sports teams play their home games in the city. How much economic growth should or could the city have expected when its new stadium for the AAA Indianapolis Indians opened in 1996?

Several cities that have built new facilities have found that the teams attracted record numbers of fans when their new facilities opened. For example, the Baltimore Orioles drew one million more fans to Camden Yards than they had drawn to Memorial Stadium in their last year at the older facility. The Cleveland Indians would likely have drawn one million more fans their first year in Jacobs Field than in their last year in Municipal Stadium had there been no baseball strike in 1994. Both cities also reported higher than expected or usual occupancy rates at nearby or downtown hotels. Did these higher attendance levels and occupancy rates bring economic growth or simply reshuffle existing economic activity from other recreational venues or activities? Was there economic growth or simply a substitution of activities?

There is also the issue that economic gain from one community to another generates a loss for the other community. In that sense, is there ever economic growth, or just a transfer of economic activity from one area to another? For now, let's just focus on impact and growth in spending levels and how we can measure that and get back to figuring out how much activity takes place at a stadium or arena.

There are two sources of real increases in economic activity that can generate growth from sports and related recreation activities: (1) people who come to the community from other cities and counties and spend their discretionary dollars in the city or county where the stadium or arena is located and (2) the retention of recreational spending from city or county residents who would have gone to other cities and counties. Clearly, if a city or county has a team that plays in an attractive facility, some people might not take trips to other regions to see sporting events or for other reasons. If they do stay "home" with their recreational dollars, this deflection away from other regions becomes a real increase in spending levels. How much deflection can one expect? Four assessments of the spending habits of fans offer some answers to this question.

In 1987, a random survey of 786 households in the Fort Wayne (Indiana) region found that 39.9 percent had made a trip to another city to attend a sporting event. These respondents were then asked if they would reduce the number of trips they made to other cities if a minor league baseball team was in Fort Wayne. A total of forty respondents, 12.7 percent, indicated they would cancel some of their trips. These respondents also indicated they would likely attend seven games in Fort Wayne. From the model developed to predict attendance it could then be argued that these fans would account for 11.9 percent of the revenues generated by the presence of the team in this community. This 11.9 percent of the revenues resulting from the stadium and team would be an increase in the spending that takes place in the Fort Wayne economy (Rosentraub & Swindell, 1993).

A similar survey was conducted in 1988 among people who attended Cincinnati's celebration of "Tall Stacks" and those individuals who attended Cincinnati's 1990 Travel, Sports, and Boat Show. "Tall Stacks" is an annual celebration along the Ohio River commemorating Cincinnati's riverboat heritage. The festival is an annual event. The Travel, Sports, and Boat Show includes four hundred exhibitors for which an admission charge is made. When asked if the Tall Stacks event had substituted for another trip to another location, 23 percent of the sample said it had. For the travel and sport show, 19 percent of the people indicated the existence of the show deflected their spending into the Cincinnati area (Cobb & Weinberg, 1993). These people, while less likely to rent hotel rooms, still would consume meals and purchase souvenirs using money that would have been spent in another city's economy. As a result, their spending also means real growth for a city or community.

In 1996, the city of Indianapolis was considering a new arena for the Indiana Pacers and the revenue needs of the Indianapolis Colts.

A survey was conducted to determine how much revenue was generated by both teams. Respondents from across the region were asked if they would attend basketball and football games in other cities if the teams left. Slightly less than one-quarter of the people who attended Pacer games, 23.3 percent, said they would go to another city for a game. Slightly more than one-third of the respondents who had gone to a Colts game indicated it was "likely" that they would go to another city to see an NFL game if the team was no longer present. These percentages, then, represent the proportion of fan spending at Pacers and Colts games that is deflected spending that occurs in the Indianapolis regional economy.

A study of the cost and possible revenue sources of a new stadium for the Pittsburgh Pirates also estimated the growth effects of the team on the city's economy. The city of Pittsburgh collects an amusement tax on all recreational activities within the city. The research team compared tax revenues in the year of the baseball strike, 1994, with revenues in previous years. Their analysis indicated that 41 percent of the fan attendance at Pirate games was real growth (positive impact) for the city. This analysis, however, did not focus on the entire Pittsburgh region. For example, it is likely that some people who live in suburban areas, rather than attending Pirate games, stayed in their cities for their recreation. If that did indeed take place, more substitution may take place than recorded in this study. There are more than two million people in the Pittsburgh metropolitan region, but fewer than 20 percent of the region's residents live in the city of Pittsburgh. As such, while it is likely that the presence of Pirate games does substantially enhance revenues for the city of Pittsburgh, much of that spending comes from people in other cities in the region. When the Pirates do not play, some recreational dollars spent on Pirate games stay in the Pittsburgh metropolitan region (Applebaum et al., 1995).

So, what does deflection or substitution mean for any city or region? Based on the surveys performed, you can anticipate that between 12 percent and 34 percent of the attendance at a sporting event represents deflected activity or an increase in spending levels in a community. However, you must remember that these figures are based on the fact that prior to the existence of the team or new facility in Fort Wayne, there was no team or any facility. Furthermore, if there was no sports show in Cincinnati, it is likely people would go elsewhere. The survey in Indianapolis focused on a hypothetical outcome—the absence of either team, and not the real number of trips taken to other cities to see games. You must also remember that these figures are for a region or metropolitan area. Individual cities might have an experience very different from that of the revenues forecast for Pittsburgh or for Colts fans in Indianapolis. The deflection or substitution depends on the extent to which the center city is already a recreational hub for its region. You may well find the figure found for fans in Fort Wayne and for Pacer fans, 24 percent, represents the real deflected activity.

If the center city or county is not a recreational hub, outcomes similar to those expected in Pittsburgh might be anticipated and the real increase in spending levels could be as much as 40 percent of the activity that occurs. Conversely, if you build a new facility for an existing team—Camden Yards (Baltimore), Jacobs Field (Cleveland), the United Center (Chicago), Gund Arena (Cleveland), or the Delta Center (Salt Lake City)—the deflected growth might be a lower percentage, since some fans would have attended games at the older venues. In that situation, it might be more appropriate to apply the 12-to-34 percent deflection figure to the projected increase in spending levels.

In other words, in 1993, with a vastly improved team, the Cleveland Indians drew more than two million fans to antiquated Cleveland Stadium but would have drawn three million to Jacobs Field in 1994. The new growth from deflection would amount to between 12 and 34 percent of the increase in attendance (900,000) or between 108,000 (12-percent deflection) to 306,000 (34-percent deflection). The remaining fans would have still spent their recreational dollars in the Cleveland region, but at some other venue in another part of the city or county. Of course, if the team's record also improved it is likely some of this increase in attendance levels would have taken place even if the team had stayed at the old facility. Furthermore, the activity now takes place downtown at Jacobs Field, and that might have an important political and social value. But, for purposes of anticipating new revenues, certainly planning for an increase of at least 12-percent growth, and perhaps as much as 34 percent, for the region is both reasonable and appropriate. But it is unlikely that there will be any more than that in terms of the entire region. The rest will simply be the transfer of activity from other forms of recreation in the area to sports. However, if Cleveland had lost its role as a recreation provider in the region, then the city of Cleveland might have had a growth in recreational activity that was closer to what was projected for Pittsburgh, 41 percent. Just remember, a portion of this growth, probably 7 of the 41 percent, was a loss to some other city in the metropolitan region, based on the expectation of 34-percent deflection from sports in any region.

So, what does all this mean for communities considering investments in sports? Well, for starters, projections of overall economic impact are going to include a great deal of money that is already circulating in your economy. The team or arena will take recreation dollars from other activities. Any restaurants included or developed in the arena or stadium, or near the new facility, will take business away from other existing outlets. *But, there will also be positive economic impact or growth.* How much? The answer will depend on recreational patterns within any city. If the city or county is already the site of much of the recreational activity in the region, real increases in spending levels may not exceed 24 percent. If the city has lost its role in entertainment and recreation, the increase may be closer to 34 percent. However, some of that increase will come at the expense of other cities in the region.

SPORTS AND THE ECONOMY: MULTIPLIERS—AN ECONOMY'S MAGICAL MYSTERY TOUR

You probably have noticed that I constantly use payrolls to measure the importance or size of sports and other components of a local economy, and right about now you're thinking, *Well he's really stack-*

*ing the deck. There are many other impacts to consider, and by focusing
on that he is trying to build a case that sports are small. He is fixing the
outcome.* Let me explain to you why I focus on payrolls and do not
include other items to measure the size of sports, restaurants, hotels,
factories, and so forth.

Think about this example. I live in Indianapolis. Suppose that I
attend an Indiana Pacers basketball game, as I often do. Before the
game I decide to eat dinner with a friend who does not live in Indianapolis but who came to stay with me because he wanted to attend
a game. The restaurant where we decided to eat our meal purchased
the vegetables for our salads from farms in Illinois or Texas. The
chickens we ate came from Michigan, or perhaps Arkansas. The beer
and wine we drank was from processing plants, breweries, or vine-
yards in Milwaukee, St. Louis, or Napa Valley. What proportion of
our food expenditures took place in Indianapolis? I know where we
paid the bill for dinner, but where did our dollars end up? Where did
our dollars create new jobs or new waves of spending and respending? Our consumption took place in Indianapolis, but the products
we consumed were brought to Indianapolis from other economies
for our consumption. The impact of our consumption affected several economies, not just the one in Indianapolis.

Suppose, in addition, the restaurant was financed with investment dollars from Chicago (First Chicago is a very large bank in
Indianapolis), Columbus, Ohio (Bank One is another large bank in
Indianapolis), or New York (investment bankers), and that the
restaurant is owned by individuals who live in New York, Atlanta, or
Dallas. Also, consider the table we ate at and the dinnerware used. If
those materials are from North Carolina, California, England, or
China, what proportion of our dinner dollars remained in Indianapolis? What does the source of those materials mean for Indianapolis's economy or the impact of the meals my friend and I are
eating before the game?

When we pay $40 for our meal, how much of that money
remains in Indianapolis? Let's try to trace it out a bit. Some of the
money from our dinner bill is used to pay (1) the businesses that
supplied the food served, (2) the interest charged on the loan for the
restaurant, (3) the restaurant's overhead (dinnerware, tables, equip-

ment, and so on), (4) the employees of the restaurant, (5) all other suppliers, and (6) the owners in terms of their profits. How much of our $40 payment actually stays in Indianapolis, and how do we count only those dollars when measuring the economic impact of spending and respending that resulted from our sports-related spending?

Economists have long used multipliers to accurately and fairly record economic effects. All dollars spent are respent and respent. When you purchased this book, some of the money was respent by the publisher on salaries and for profit. I also get a share of the revenue, and I respend those dollars on my children's college tuition, a new car, and maybe a new computer. Each dollar you spend— whether for a ticket to a baseball game or a dinner—is respent several times. Part of the money you spent for a ticket to the ball game becomes part of the salary of players, managers, and others who work at the stadium or arena. They in turn spend their salary, and on it goes. In this manner we refer to the recirculation of dollars spent as having a "multiplier effect." Each dollar is spent and respent, and by studying spending patterns, economists have developed numbers to indicate how many times a dollar recirculates. Obviously if you want to inflate the total economic impact of an arena or team you could use a higher multiplier, say 3, 4, or 5, making $100 million in direct spending become a half-billion dollars or more in secondary effects. If you want to deflate the economic impact, use a low multiplier, say 1 or 1.1.

A multiplier might appear to some to be the magical mystery tour of any economy. If abused or misrepresented, the multiplier can produce estimates of impact that are nothing more than a mythical expectation of growth. How do you select the right multiplier? Will we have to rely on the "dueling economists"? Probably. Choosing an appropriate multiplier can indeed become a world of dueling consultants. Let me help establish some benchmarks for you as you choose the right multiplier. First, do remember that all multipliers people use or develop can and should be actually developed through careful research. The U.S. Department of Commerce does produce a set of multipliers for the nation, each state, and every region based on average expenditure patterns by "average" wage earners and professionals. Numerous prominent researchers have also developed their own multipliers through empirical research. A multiplier is not a contrived number. If someone uses a multiplier in any analysis you review, ask them where they got it and why they decided it was both appropriate and valid. Second, also realize the multipliers are valid only for specific geographic areas. They are not interchangeable, nor can they be shared like a sweater or coat. Think of it this way. If you buy something in New York City, a city with more than twelve million workers, it is more likely that a part of what you bought was manufactured or developed in New York City than if you bought the same item in a small town in southern Indiana with 250 residents. As a result, the multipliers in a small town will be much smaller than those in a larger city. Third, the larger an area is geographically and by population, the more likely it is to capture more of the spending and respending that happens. For this reason, the multiplier for any good or service will be larger if the region or state is the unit of analysis instead of the county, city, or zip code area. If we calculated the multiplier effect of sports spending, the figure for Ohio should be larger than the figure for Cuyahoga County. But that figure would likely be larger than the figure for the city of Cleveland (whose population is less than two-fifths of its county, Cuyahoga). The multipliers for Cleveland might be larger than the figure for downtown Cleveland or for a neighborhood. As a result, the multipliers for many goods and services consumed by residents of New York City are likely to be larger than the multiplier for the same good or service initially consumed in Richmond, Indiana.

Fourth, multipliers are also based on the usual spending patterns by the proverbial "average person." As approximately half of the money earned by all sports teams is paid to athletes, one has to consider whether or not the spending by these people is similar to that of the "average person" in the city or county where the team is located. For example, with most athletes earning hundreds of thousands, if not millions, of dollars each season, what proportion of these dollars are spent in the local economy? Some athletes might prefer to maintain their permanent home in another area; some may also elect to save more money than the average person since the life-span of their ability to earn high wages is quite short. The consumption patterns of athletes might also be different than those of the average person. They might buy more luxury items that are not produced in the local economy than the typical person. Outcomes of this nature might mean that a substantial portion of the economic activity associated with a team (the dollars collected to pay players) immediately leaves a local area's economy. As such, they would have to be subtracted before any multiplier is applied. Furthemore, if the players do take the money from the economy, then the spending on tickets that occurs can represent a real loss to the economy (Noll and Zimbalist, 1997).

Let's get back to my dinner in Indianapolis before a Pacers game. If all or most of the materials used and the food eaten in the restaurant were from outside Indianapolis, then many of our dollars would leave the city to pay for those materials. If the ownership group is in New York or Dallas, the profits that are part of my bill also leave Indianapolis (just like the dollars paid to the players) and accrue to the owners of the restaurant where they live. The respending of these dollars occurs in other economies. Similarly, if the dishes, furniture, fixtures, and utensils I used were imported into Indianapolis, the money that must be used to pay for this overhead also leaves the city. To be sure, these dollars do have multiplier or ripple impacts, but where do these ripples or impacts surface? They surface throughout the national economy, and if imported products (from outside the United States) are also part of the meal (foreign wine or china, for example) the primary and secondary economic impacts do not occur in Indianapolis but in another country. Indianapolis, in this example, becomes a transfer point, processing dollars that have a reduced or diminished effect on the local economy. Similar economic flows occur if the clothing and souvenir materials sold at Market Square Arena, home of the Pacers, are manufactured in other cities.

Which dollars spent by me and my friend are most likely to remain in Indianapolis or any city that hosts a sports team or any business? Typically, those dollars spent on employees who live in the area are most likely to remain in a small geographic area such as a city or county and are the dollars most likely to be recirculated in a local economy. From these dollars and the spending habits of employees who live in Indianapolis—the ripple effect of the wages paid by me through my meal—what proportion is most likely to remain in Indianapolis? Those dollars that are also spent on other employees who live in the area. My interest in looking at salaries to gauge economic activity within small geographic areas such as cities is a reflection of the integration of any city's economy with the economy of the nation and the world. It is this integration that makes the use of aggregate spending to measure local economic impacts very difficult.

Let me give you an example of an overestimation of the economic impact created by sports or recreation spending and something you should be careful to avoid. In 1994, a private marketing research firm was retained by Arlington, Texas, to measure the economic value of tourism to the city. In their Executive Digest, the consultants noted the following points and then made an important conclusion for the city's leadership:

> Tourism spending has increased 13 percent since 1991. The direct economic impact on the Arlington economy in 1994 was $310,022,030, for an average of $45.40 per visitor per day. Estimated additional spending from visitors who do not attend any of the three major attractions or stay at a hotel/motel in Arlington brings the total to a projected $341,054,630.
>
> Tourists who visit the three major attractions spend a projected $252,562,270 a year. This increase comes despite the baseball strike which lead to the cancellation of twenty-one Texas Rangers home games in 1994, for an estimated loss of $42 million.
>
> Tourists who stay in an Arlington hotel or motel but do not visit one of the three major attractions spend an additional $57,459,760 for a total of $310,022,030 attributable directly to tourism.
>
> Thousands of other travelers pass through Arlington and buy gasoline, food, or other items but do not stay in an Arlington hotel or motel or visit any of the major attractions. In addition, others attend conventions or similar events in the city but do not stay in an Arlington hotel or motel or visit any of the major attractions, and their economic impact is not included in the measured projections.
>
> Thus, $310,022,030 is a very conservative estimate of the total economic impact of visitors to Arlington in 1994. If this unmea-

sured visitor spending amounts to only ten percent of the total measured spending, the actual economic impact could be as high as $341,024,233. Using the industry standard multiplier of 3, this brings the combined economic impact of tourism in Arlington to more than a billion dollars a year.

First of all, the *regional* or *statewide* multiplier for each of the components of the tourism industry is not 3. The Bureau of Economic Analysis at the Department of Commerce does develop regional and statewide multipliers. In terms of the hotel, restaurant, and amusement sector of the Texas economy, the highest multiplier effect for the *entire* state of Texas was 2.51. That would mean each dollar of output produced $2.51 in Texas, not in any one particular city within the state. Within any city, it is likely the multiplier effects would be less, as employees might live in other areas or spend their money in more than one city.

Indeed, as my example of a meal illustrates, the economy of the entire nation is entwined. Within any metropolitan area the linkages are quite pronounced. People work in one city, live in another, and sometimes shop or pursue recreational opportunities elsewhere. People travel to other parts of the country and other countries, spending their dollars as they tour. With all of these linkages, what dollars do stay in a city? The dollars spent on salaries are the dollars most likely to stay in a small geographic unit such as a city.

What multiplier should be used if one looks only at salaries? Again, multiplier figures are not subjective numbers, but the product of extensive analyses of any economy. Let me show you some examples of multipliers that have been developed for some states and cities. Professional sports fit into the category established for hotels, amusement services, and recreation by the Department of Commerce. As the information in Table 4–6 indicates, it would seem prudent to use a multiplier of 2.0 or less for spending related to tourism, sports, and amusements. Indianapolis, a city with a population of approximately eight hundred thousand, had an earnings multiplier of 1.9487 for these kinds of businesses. Fort Wayne, at the center of a county of approximately three hundred thousand residents, had an earnings multiplier of 1.7 for these services. For Texas as a whole, the earnings multiplier was 2.06, not the 3.0 indicated in the consultant's report (see Table 4–6). The forecasted economic impact, therefore, was overstated by at least one-third in that report. In addition, as the multiplier of 2.06 was for the state of Texas and not the city of Arlington, it is quite likely that an even smaller multiplier would have been appropriate.[1]

Should you use a multiplier when you are trying to estimate the economic impact of a team, arena, or stadium? Yes. But what multiplier, and against what figure or number should it be applied? Here are some steps for you to follow the next time you review an assessment of a team's worth to a region or the economic value of a new stadium or arena. *First*, as a rule of thumb, for a region of more than one million people, do not use a multiplier of more than 2. In smaller regions, slightly smaller multipliers must be used. *Second*, to determine the number against which the multiplier should be applied, review the consultant's report to find the estimate of the total wages to be paid to employees (players, restaurant workers, etc.). REDUCE this figure by an amount equal to 50 percent of what the players receive. This will ensure that the dollars players save or spend in other economies are not counted as part of the impact in your region. *Third*, remember that the vast majority of the dollars used by employers to pay these salaries came from the fans, and those fans would have spent many of those dollars in your economy if the team were not there or if the arena had not been built. In the

TABLE 4–6
Earnings Multipliers for Services in Selected Areas

Service	State or City			
	Texas	Indiana	Indianapolis	Ft. Wayne
Hotels, recreation	2.0635	1.8850	1.9487	1.7043
Personal services	1.7806	1.7039	1.7003	1.5147
Business services	1.7747	1.6186	1.6605	1.4904
Restaurants	2.2061	2.0304	1.9336	1.8198
Health services	1.6553	1.5727	1.5764	1.4457
Other services	2.0744	2.0591	2.0556	1.9143

Source: U.S. Department of Commerce, Economics and Statistics Administration, Bureau of Economic Analysis.

absence of sports, as discussed earlier, people do spend money on other forms of recreation. As I've noted, no more than 34 percent OF THE TOTAL DOLLARS SPENT FOR SALARIES (less the 50 percent removed for players' spending habits) should be considered new economic activity, and it is likely that no more than 24 percent of the spending represents a real increase in economic activity in your city or region. The dollars spent for salaries should then be multiplied by the fraction you believe is real new activity (no more than 34 percent but no less than 24 percent) after you remove 50 percent for the players' salaries. For the example here, I am going to use 24 percent as the amount of revenue that is new to a city or county's economy. *Fourth*, I am not forgetting that a large portion of the salary received by players also comes from the national media and merchandise contracts that also exist. Obviously if a team was not in your community, these dollars could not be spent in your area. However, by assuming that 50 percent of what the players earn is spent in your area, I am including those dollars in the analysis. Now, let's apply these numbers to a real example.

In 1995, the Cleveland Indians paid their players $36.3 million. In terms of wages paid, let's assume half of this amount was spent in the Cleveland economy. Let's also expect that the wages paid to all other employees hired as a result of games played was $5 million (*a very generous* estimate given the wages paid to most workers in the service sector). Added together, the total wages paid that could be part of the local economy is ($36.3 million [players' salaries], divided by 2, plus $5 million, or) $23.15 million. The revenue used to pay the players and other workers came from the expenditures of fans. To eliminate the spending that would have taken place had people not gone to a game, this figure is multiplied by 24 percent (.24). (Remember, I could have used a figure of 11.9 percent to produce a low-end estimate.) The total figure representing new economic activity is $5.6 million. If a multiplier of 2 is used, the total economic growth would be $11.2 million. While this is not an insignificant number, I believe you will find it to be a figure substantially lower than what you might find some advocates for teams and new facilities present to fax you. It is also useful to compare this number to the money spent or proposed for the stadium or arena.

SPORTS, IMAGE, AND ECONOMIC DEVELOPMENT

> Five "hard determinants" are, in our experience and analysis related to successful entrepreneurship. They are: (1) Universities, (2) Interstate Highways, (3) Airports, (4) Advanced Telecommunications, and (5) A Nice Place to Live.
> —DAVID BIRCH et al. (1993)

> At bottom, the practice of selling places entails the various ways in which public and private agencies—local authorities and local entrepreneurs, often working collaboratively—strive to sell the image of a particular geographically defined place, usually a town or city, so as to make it attractive to economic enterprises, to tourists, and even to inhabitants of that place. The chief ambitions are to encourage economic enterprises (and notably footloose high-technology industries) to locate themselves in this place and to entice tourists to visit the place in large numbers, and both of these ambitions obviously tie in with the attempts that all sorts of localities in Britain, North America, and elsewhere are making to secure inward capital investment, a degree of local job creation and hence local economic (re)generation.
> —GERRY KEARNS and CHRIS PHILO (1993, p. 3)

At a minimum, sports clearly help a city become "a nice place to live." No, they don't ease pollution, reduce crime, improve learning, or make people better workers, parents, or spouses, but they do create entertainment. In that sense, sports do help define the quality of life in any city. Other things also define the quality of life: schools that produce highly educated children, safe streets, museums and the performing arts, libraries, and colleges and universities. Corporations carefully evaluate the quality of life in a community when making locational decisions, and as professional team sports make an important contribution to the definition of that quality, the level and quality of professional sports can contribute to or help define a city's or region's image and its attractiveness. But can sports or any single factor affect locational decisions or economic development? Probably not!!

I know that many people believe sports can and do transform an identity of a city. It is frequently argued that without professional sports teams a city cannot be "truly big league." Indeed, in a society where sports are so important, doesn't the absence of a team mean a city is "third or fourth tier"? While all of those feelings may well exist, sports teams are never the defining factors that attract economic development. Indeed, many other investments can be made that can transform a city's image. However, let's accept for the moment that sports do transform a city's image. Will that new image mean that businesses and people will relocate to your city? Little information has ever been published that would support the view that sports affect locational decisions by businesses or anyone.

PHH Fantus is a consulting and management firm that annually assists more than a hundred corporate clients in finding new locations for their business activities. Robert Ady, president of PHH Fantus, probably best summarized the importance of the image sports convey to a city. In June 1993, while speaking to a group of business and community leaders at Arrowhead Stadium in Kansas City, he noted:

> In fact, the single most important location criterion today is grouped under operating conditions. No, I must tell you now that it is not the presence of a professional sports team—it is in fact the availability of a qualified workforce. In today's competitive and ever-changing environment, companies are locating where they feel assured of securing such a workforce. Not only the availability of managerial talent but, more importantly, the availability of skilled and technical talent. Other typical operating condition criteria might include: proximity to an international airport, tranquil labor-management relations, sophisticated telecommunications availability, and dual-feed utility systems.

Let me also fairly report—to give a balanced view of Mr. Ady's remarks—some of the positive points he made about the importance of sports for economic development. He noted that sporting events represent a great opportunity to bring prospective companies to a city and to highlight things the city has accomplished with the private sector. Since bringing a prospect to town is essential to any relocation process, sports can be a great tool when making the deal. Furthermore, sports do seem to be a force that generates tremendous civic pride, and that pride can set one community apart from another.

WHAT FACTORS AFFECT
CORPORATE LOCATION DECISIONS?

So, why do companies choose certain areas? Why does economic development take place in some areas and not in others? A "mini" industry of sorts has developed to both understand and predict corporate location decisions. The interest in this work is related to the ability to "sell" marketing programs and formulae for success to cities and regions seeking to attract businesses to their community. At least two perspectives have been developed with regard to the importance of the arts, professional sports, and other amenities in the decision process businesses use to select sites for their operations. Within the first perspective—which might be labeled the factor cost view—a tiered framework is said to guide locational choices. At the first level or tier in this decision tree it is assumed that firms seek to maximize their profits or market shares. As a result, businesses select locations where their aggregate costs for production, transportation, energy, taxes, and labor are minimized. (The quality and level of public goods also enter the decision process at this stage, since taxes are payments for the quality of services received from the government.) On a secondary level, or at the second tier in the decision tree, the quality of life and the presence or absence of cultural assets such as the arts, professional sports, museums, universities, libraries, and civic pride, culture, and image enter into the decision framework.

People who use the factor-cost view of locational decisions likely underestimate the value of second-tier items or amenities in corporate location decisions. This results from the observation that it is

quite rare for only one area or region to meet a corporation's particular cost constraints. More often, several areas can offer a business a
competitive factor-cost environment (Bartik, 1991). When several
areas satisfy a corporation's cost constraints, second-tier issues frequently determine location decisions.

Underscoring this point, some students of business location have
noted that other factors, such as quality of life, affect a corporation's
"choice between two otherwise equally profitable locations" (Weber,
1984, p. 77). Traditional location research that stresses the first-tier
value of factor costs, then, also clearly suggests that quality-of-life
features such as the arts might not be initially considered, but these
factors do have profound effects on the final locational choice of any
business. When several areas satisfy a corporation's cost calculus, the
professional sports teams and other quality-of-life features may well
be the factors that ultimately determine a final locational choice.

A second perspective has also developed concerning the importance of community assets and the quality of life in the locational
choices of businesses. Within this second view, quality-of-life issues
are now seen as "first-tier" determinants of locational choices. This
elevation of the quality of life and community assets such as professional sports teams has resulted from changes in the characteristics
of the workforce and the sensitivity of employers to workers' concerns.

> A nice place to live is perhaps the most profound of the hard deter-
> minants (of locational choice). It is, at least, somewhat measurable.
> It has to do with climate, density of living (low being better), qual-
> ity of education, recreational and cultural opportunities, etc. It's
> important because, perhaps for the first time in a long time, it can
> be acted upon freely. Workers in the 1990s can choose to live where
> they want, and demand that employers follow them. Why? Because
> they are in short supply (Birch et al., 1993, p. 15).

Birch, among others, has recently argued that high-quality workers are in short supply. As a result, firms that require workers whose
productivity is high must meet their needs, which include a demand
for areas where the quality of life is viewed as favorable for housing,

education, professional sports, and the arts. In support of Birch's view, one can also note the higher number of two-career households in the workforce. With less time and more money available for amenities, these households want more direct access to professional sports, the arts, culture, and higher-quality communities.

Whether one selects the factor-cost approach to locational decision making, or the view that quality of life is now a first-tier factor for businesses, professional sports, the arts, culture, and the quality of life are clearly important determinants of the economic viability of a community and in the creation of jobs for any city. A series of surveys conducted over the past two decades demonstrate the increasing awareness of the quality of life as an important locational factor. Shanahan (1980) found that quality of life appeared to be more important to firms that employed highly trained, salaried, and mobile personnel. Furthermore, he found that, in the view of respondents, the presence of varied and high-quality programs (and teams) defined the general level of a community's civility. The scale and scope of the programs available were also found to be associated with views that the community was progressive, resourceful, energetic, and concerned with its culture.

A 1979 study of ten major SMSAs conducted by the Joint Economic Committee asked business leaders to "identify characteristics of the city that influenced their decision to expand or stay at a present location" (Shanahan, 1980, p. 12). The results showed that out of a total twenty-six possible criteria, the leaders ranked quality-of-life issues as six of the seven most important, with cultural attractions ranked seventh. The Joint Economic Committee concluded that "improving the quality of life in cities where it is poor and maintaining it where it is good, can have an important impact on decisions of firms to relocate, alter the size of their workforce, and reduce or expand their operations" (Shanahan, 1980, p. 13). In another survey conducted in 1984 for a large corporation, the quality of life was ranked "third overall (among criteria for industrial location) carrying the same weight as utility costs" (Penne, 1986, p. I–1). The Real Estate Research Corporation noted that these findings represented "a major shift in corporate thinking over the last 15 years and reflects the change in employee mix in many of America's giants" (Penne, 1986, p. I–2).

Two 1987 surveys presented the most compelling evidence indicating quality of life as a major factor in corporate location decisions. One survey asked economic development directors from the United States, Canada, and other countries to rank the quality of life as a factor in attracting new investment to their service areas (O'Connor, 1987, p. 778). More than 84 percent of the respondents believed that quality of life ranked as one of the top five factors, and 9 percent thought it was the most important factor. This survey also found that many communities across the nation were undertaking large projects to improve the quality of life.

The second survey asked corporate facility planners to rank quality of life as a location factor. The results showed that 83 percent believed quality of life was "either very important or critically important in locating headquarters" (O'Connor, 1987, p. 779). Furthermore, 81 percent believed that quality of life was important for selecting locations for research and development facilities. *Rating Places* concluded: "There is increasing empirical evidence, however, that quality of life is also important, especially when two places are equally attractive from an economic standpoint. . . . Those metropolitan areas with a good quality of life had a significant competitive edge over others in attracting residents despite small differentials in economic opportunity" (Radich, 1993, p. 47).

Making cities exciting, maintaining a sense of a high-quality environment with varied cultural activities in cities, and establishing and maintaining a highly visible image for cities are real and important concerns for all community leaders. Professional team sports can and do contribute to each of these objectives, but so do quality schools, safe and clean neighborhoods, sidewalks, bicycle paths, orchestras, museums, and activities for children. Each of these assets can and does have substantial economic impacts that generate growth and that, when the appropriate multipliers are used, would show substantial economic growth. Which asset should your community develop? And how much should you spend for it? Those are the questions you must answer when you consider an investment in sports to improve a community's image and its quality of life. How much quality can you buy for the money you are being asked to spend? Which assets need public support? These questions should also be answered, and the other chapters in this book will help you see how other communities have answered them.

SPORTS AND A CITY'S ECONOMY: CONCLUSIONS

Okay, where has this journey through sports and its economic impact on cities taken us? What lessons or guideposts has this sometimes confusing review of cities, their economies, and professional sports provided? Eight general points or principles have been established.

1. Sports teams themselves are small to medium-sized firms. They are clearly vibrant, vital, and important components of any city or county's economy, but no more so in economic terms than many, many other firms. By themselves, sports teams are not economic engines; they have too few employees and involve too few direct dollars to be a driving force in any city or county's economy.

2. The professional sports sector, even in urban areas with multiple teams, is a very small portion of any region's economy. In no county do professional team sports account for as much as 1 percent of the county's private sector payroll or 1 percent of all of the private sector's jobs.

3: When the spending that sports frequently generates at hotels and restaurants is added to the impact from the teams themselves, the total number of private-sector jobs created is still quite small. The overall payroll dollars associated with the sports sector and with the related spending at hotels and restaurants amount to a very small proportion of any county's private sector economy.

4. A substantial portion of the spending that takes places at arenas and ballparks, and at the restaurants and retail outlets near or in these facilities, is merely a transfer of economic activity within your

community. As a result, the actual benefit of the team's presence is a fraction of the spending that takes place at the stadium or arena. In the absence of a team or new facility, people will still spend money on recreation and at restaurants. They will even continue to buy clothes and hats regardless of the presence, or absence, of a team. If people eat a meal at or near a stadium or arena, they likely did not eat a meal at another restaurant located elsewhere. Increases in economic activity from sports facilities and teams result from people making additional trips into your community for recreation and from your own residents staying home for their recreation. Several surveys have been conducted to estimate the amount of economic activity that is real or net growth, and not merely a transfer between different forms of recreation. The estimates of growth range from 11.9 percent of the spending by fans to 34 percent. As a result, whatever gross figure is used to estimate the economic activity generated by a team or the facility that is used, no less than 66 percent would exist in your community even if the team did not. Furthermore, it is possible that as much as four-fifths of spending would occur in the absence of the team.

5. The majority of the revenue collected by teams is used to pay players. However, players tend to save more money than do other people, their productive lives are shorter, and they also tend to spend money in their "home" communities, which often are not in your county. Their purchase of luxury items may also generate very little economic activity in your community. As a result, when analyzing the total revenue generated by a team or a facility, remember that with more than half of all funds spent by fans being used to pay players, one-half of that total will not be respent in your economy.

6. The new net dollars that are spent for sports and related activities do recirculate in your economy. As such, a multiplier should be used to measure the recirculation of these dollars. The highest multiplier that should be used is 2, and smaller communities should use a smaller multiplier. In the example used to illustrate the economic gains from the Cleveland Indians, my gross estimate was that the gain for Cleveland was in the $11 million range each year, substantially below what many consulting reports will predict.

7. Sports are an important part of any community's quality of life. Can teams themselves attract other businesses and bring economic development to a community? Probably not; too many other factors affect a corporation's decisions regarding where it needs to be located. However, quality of life is an important factor in any locational choice, and professional sports teams do add to any community's quality of life. You have to decide if your community's investment in professional sports is worth the enhancements to the quality of life. Could you invest in other things that would also enhance the community's quality of life and thus increase its attractiveness as a place to live and work? Yes. Are sports a better investment? No one knows for sure, so you will have to decide if the investment is worth the perception of an enhanced quality of life more so than any other investment.

8. Real economic gains can accrue to a city if a team moves from another community. However, this gain is likely to be no more than $10 or $15 million in new economic activity. This increment needs to be evaluated relative to the investment made by the public sector.

5

How Do Governments Make Money from Sports?

THE FOCUS OF CHAPTER 4 was on the relationship of sports to local economies. Now we turn to the financial returns earned by governments from sports. There are essentially two ways governments can earn revenues from the presence of teams or through the building of facilities. First, tax levels may increase as a result of economic activity that takes place within a government's boundaries. Second, the governmental entity could share in the revenues generated by the stadium, arena, or team. For the most part, governments rely on tax revenues as their primary source of revenue from sports. The question that must be answered, then, is: Do state and local governments receive sufficient new tax revenues from the existence of sports teams to offset their investments? Does even the small economic impact of sports translate into sufficient new tax revenues to cover the public sector's subsidies of professional sports teams? Later sections of this chapter will also discuss various ways governments can share in the revenues produced by teams and the facilities they use.

Many people believe that if an economy grows, even by a small amount, the public sector will receive more tax dollars. As funny or strange as this is going to seem, a sports team or facility could be quite successful and could even generate positive economic impact but *fail to produce* the tax dollars a city, county, or state needs to pay for its investments in sports. How can this happen? Well, the next part of our journey through the real economics of sports is to understand the *fiscal impact* of sports, or the increment in tax revenues that results from the presence of a team and its facilities.

FISCAL AND ECONOMIC IMPACT: VIVE LA DIFFÉRENCE!!!

I know this is beginning to sound like a public finance or economics class, but, in truth, to survive in the real economics of sports there are some ideas or concepts that have to become second nature for you. Understanding the economic impact and fiscal impact of a team or facility is critical to surviving sports.

Fiscal gains refer to the increased tax revenues a community receives as a result of positive economic impact. Governments collect money through taxes and charges. The ability of any local government to capture a portion of the benefits of any team or sports facility is related to the taxes it administers or user charges it implements. For example, suppose you attend a game and buy a $15 hat. If the state administers a 4-percent sales tax, it receives 60 cents from your transaction. If the local government charges a 1-percent sales tax, it receives 15 cents. However, if there is no local sales tax, then the *fiscal* impact of your transaction may be limited to the state government through its sales tax. It is also possible that both the state and local governments administer an income tax. If so, the purchase of the hat may also generate income tax revenues.

Part of the problem or challenge for local governments in terms of securing a return on their investments in sports facilities is their excessive reliance on property taxes. Most sports arenas and stadia are exempt from local property taxes, since they are frequently owned by the government, a special district or quasi-government agency, or a nonprofit organization. Each of these entities is usually exempt from local property taxes (except in Ontario Province). The Gateway Corporation in Cleveland also makes a small property tax payment to the city of Cleveland. When stadia and arenas are privately owned, local governments are often asked to either exempt the facility from local property taxes as part of the incentives to attract a team or abate any local property tax responsibilities. In these situations, increased property tax revenues will result only from increases in the value of property near the stadium or arena. As a result, there may well be few new property tax dollars for the public sector. You must also remember that seventeen states have state-mandated ceilings on property taxes, and these controls limit the fiscal gains from property development even if there is a substantial economic impact from the presence of a team or a new arena or stadium. It is very possible, even likely, that positive economic impact can occur without any additional fiscal or tax gains for local government dependent on property taxes. In such a situation, a local government's investment might produce returns for the private sector and economic growth, but no fiscal gains. It remains to be determined if that small increase will support the public's commitments to the facility.

Some states have passed legislation that allows local governments to use a small sales tax or income tax to help support their investments in sports facilities. In other areas special taxes can be used to help support sports facilities (Indianapolis's food-and-beverage tax, Cleveland's "sin" tax on alcohol and tobacco products, Pittsburgh's regional assets tax), and, in other areas, local governments can pass an economic development income tax (Indiana), some of which can be used for stadia and arenas. Amusement taxes have also been used in several areas (Indianapolis, Pittsburgh, Arlington), and these charges are nothing more than a per ticket or sales tax. It might be best to think of these charges as "user fees," charges for the use of a facility generally set at $1 or $2 per ticket.

State and local governments, then, frequently receive money or a return on their investments in sports when taxes are paid or when consumers are charged for admission to a facility or arena. If an economy expands, there is positive economic impact. But if the impact does not produce any additional taxes, then it is possible to have economic growth (positive economic impact) but no change in a community's *fiscal status.*

Positive economic impact or growth refers to new spending or activity that occurs in a city or county as a result of a team or new facility. Fiscal growth or gains refer to the additional tax dollars or charges a government receives as a result of the presence of a team or a new stadium. The terms are quite different, and in practice can produce very different outcomes and very different views of the impact and growth that result from a team's presence or the development of a new stadium or arena.

It might seem like a complicated task to project fiscal gains relative to the investments being made, but through two examples I hope to show you that you can easily project what your community can expect in revenues for the public sector from a new stadium or if a team begins to play in your city. I want to accomplish this by performing a fiscal analysis for two different cities that have invested or considered investing in professional sports. From these case studies we can then develop a work sheet that any community can use to estimate its fiscal gains. These gains could then be compared to any commitments or investments the city might expect to make for the team or the new facility.

FORT WAYNE CONSIDERS MINOR LEAGUE BASEBALL

Fort Wayne, Indiana, is a medium-sized city that, in 1989, considered a small investment, approximately $2 million, in a stadium for a Class A minor league team. Fort Wayne had had a long and impressive history as a sports city prior to the 1950s. Fort Wayne's Zollner Pistons was one of the charter members of the NBA, and the NBA was actually founded in Fort Wayne. The Zollner Pistons (the Zollner Company actually does manufacture pistons) moved to Detroit in 1957 despite receiving a new arena (which the team had demanded) from Allen County (Fort Wayne). In fact, the movement of the Zollner Pistons to Detroit was one of the first moves by a team from a city with a history of supporting its franchise to a larger community in anticipation of greater financial success. Interestingly, that success was not immediate for the Detroit Pistons, as the final season attendance at Zollner Piston games in Fort Wayne exceeded attendance for the team's first and second years in Detroit.

Fort Wayne was also home to one of the most successful women's baseball teams, the Fort Wayne Daisies. The success and history of the Daisies were part of the inspiration for the movie *A League of Their Own*. However, after the collapse of the women's baseball league and the move of the Pistons, Fort Wayne's stake in the world of sports was limited to a minor league hockey team. An indoor soccer team began play in 1986 but went bankrupt in 1990. A minor league basketball team began play in Fort Wayne in 1991. The possibility of attracting a minor league baseball team to the city was quite appealing to several different groups (investors, city officials, the chamber of commerce, and sports fans). In 1988, the ownership of the Wausau Timbers came calling on Fort Wayne. Fort Wayne and its market area are much larger than Wausau, Wisconsin. Indeed, in 1988, Fort Wayne was probably the largest community in America without any professional baseball team in its region. While Fort Wayne's population is only 170,000, Allen County has 300,000 residents, and the region is home to 675,000 people.

The owners of the Timbers wanted their team to play in an existing facility in Fort Wayne that would have required about $2 million in modifications to make it appropriate for minor league baseball. The city offered the team's owners a fifteen-year loan for $1.2 million (the interest rate on the loan was to be 6.48 percent). The team would be completely responsible for repaying the loan, and the renovations would still require an additional $750,000. While the team would also be responsible for these funds, the city's leadership would join with the team owners to raise the funds from fans, the private sector, and the nonprofit sector. If the team was unable to make the payments on the loan, the city would accept responsibility for the loan. When the needed support from the private and non-profit sectors could not be found for the $750,000 cash investment, the owners ended their discussions with the city and Fort Wayne lost the opportunity to have minor league baseball.

Should Fort Wayne have provided more incentives to encourage the relocation of the team? Would the city have recouped its investment if it had expanded its commitment to include complete responsibility for the stadium's renovations? Time for a fiscal analysis.

Fort Wayne and Allen County's main source of tax revenues is the local property tax. There is a small local-option income tax, and the majority of these revenues accrue to Fort Wayne. This tax, in 1989, was just two-tenths of 1 percent. A 1-percent food-and-beverage tax is also collected in the county for all consumption at restaurants and bars. These revenues are dedicated to the Allen County Coliseum Commission, which operates the facilities in which the hockey team plays its home games. There is also a 5-percent innkeepers' tax on all hotel room charges. While some of these revenues accrue to Allen County and not the city of Fort Wayne, all local taxes were combined in the fiscal analysis. Although only the city of Fort Wayne was initially involved in the effort to recruit a team, when the region was finally successful in attracting a team, both units of government worked together to bring professional baseball to northeast Indiana. As such, I tabulated the combined local government fiscal impact in my example.

To measure the fiscal gains to local governments I calculated the anticipated positive economic impact or growth from the team's operation and expected that 27.3 percent of the total impact would be positive or real growth (high-end estimate). The worst-case estimate was that 11.9 percent of the economic impact would be new activity in the city of Fort Wayne. These estimates were developed through household surveys that asked people about their interest in both attending games and changing their recreational patterns (staying in Fort Wayne as opposed to going elsewhere if a team were in the city). An estimate of the expected influx of people from other counties was also included based on a survey of attendees at other Fort Wayne recreational sites (Swindell & Rosentraub, 1992).

Based on attendance levels for other Class A teams, and adjusting those market penetration rates for the size of the Fort Wayne region, I projected that a Fort Wayne team would attract 235,000 fans in 1989. To that figure was added a "honeymoon" or first-year effect of an additional 23,500 fans; thus, expecting 258,500 fans. (In 1994, during the Major League Baseball strike and their second season in Indiana, the Fort Wayne Wizards drew 254,503 fans.) The league average for ticket prices, adjusted to include the cost of promotions, was $0.81 per fan (Peck, 1985). This figure was then adjusted and incorporated in the projections for Fort Wayne. In the Fort Wayne fiscal impact analysis an average ticket price of $1.00 to $1.25 was used, resulting in an estimated ticket revenue of between $235,000 and $293,750. I then used the midpoint of this range, $265,000, to estimate local tax dollars.

The city's consultant and team owners estimated spending by fans at the stadium for food and souvenirs to be $1.58 per fan. Therefore, if 235,000 fans attended games, approximately $371,300 would be spent inside the stadium. Peck (1985) performed a survey of fans at Class A minor league baseball games to estimate spending outside the stadium and found the average to be approximately $8.00 per fan. This figure was then adjusted for inflation to 1989 levels, meaning that the city could anticipate $1.9 million of spending by fans outside the stadium (including parking fees). An estimate of players' salaries was made based on league averages, and I anticipated that half of the $316,000 payroll would be spent outside of Fort Wayne since few of the players made their permanent homes in northeast Indiana. I utilized estimates of spending by visiting teams drawn from analyses done by several minor league teams (Swindell & Rosentraub, 1992) and produced an estimate of $178,500 in spending for the Fort Wayne area. I also expected that the presence of the team would create a few seasonal jobs with salaries of $200,000, and the team's office staff would have salaries of about $100,000, based on estimates produced by surveying all other Class A teams in the same league.

Finally, I multiplied the average number of jobs created by the expected salary level, based on salaries paid in Fort Wayne for similar tasks. Local governments would also collect all parking fees, which were estimated to be $100,000 per year. Applying all the relevant taxes possible, and using a multiplier of 2, a high-end number for a city of Fort Wayne's size, local governments would receive $135,532 in new revenues per year. The low-end estimate was $121,036 per year. The information in Table 5–1 includes estimates of growth in the local economy and in local taxes, assuming an increase of either 11.9 or 27.3 percent in economic activity. As these are the low- and high-end estimates, the real outcomes are probably somewhere in between these levels.

If the city had decided to assume all of the costs for renovating the stadium, to recoup its investment of approximately $2 million would have taken at least fourteen years. And that would not have included the costs associated with any other renovations or maintenance at the stadium. The economic gain or growth in the private sector would have been in excess of $7 million *per year,* but no one was willing to provide the team with even $750,000 to help support the renovations to the stadium. With the city unwilling to improve upon its efforts, the Timbers were eventually sold to another group and never moved to Fort Wayne. Fort Wayne will not receive any new property-tax dollars as the area where the team would play was already a center for retail sales and recreation.

In 1992, another Class A team, the Kenosha Twins, indicated that they were prepared to move to Fort Wayne. However, under the Professional Baseball Agreement passed by Major League Baseball in December 1990, certain new guidelines had to be followed for all minor league baseball parks (Johnson, 1993). The effect of these new guidelines raised the cost of the renovations at Fort Wayne's facility from slightly less than $2 million to more than $5 million (Swindell & Rosentraub, 1993). Based on the continued success of the minor league hockey team and of the new minor league basketball team (Continental Basketball League), Fort Wayne and Allen County decided to jointly fund the entire cost of the renovation, subject to a lease that protects the exposure of the city and county.

TABLE 5–1

A Fiscal Impact Summary for Fort Wayne and Allen County

Revenue	Total Impact	Economic Activity New Economic Growth Estimate		Local Tax Revenues New Economic Growth Estimate	
		11.9 Percentage	27.3 Percentage	11.9 Percentage	27.3 Percentage
Fans Spending					
Ticket sales	$ 265,000	$ 31,535	$ 72,345	$ 315	$ 726
In stadium[1]	371,300	44,185	$101,365	442	1,017
Outside[2]	1,880,000	223,720	513,240	4,027[3]	9,273
First year	241,450	28,733	65,916	591	1514
Subtotal	2,519,250	328,173	752,866	5,375	12,530
Team Spending					
Salaries	316,000[4]	158,000[5]	158,000[5]	316	316
Jobs created	200,000	200,000	200,000	400	400
Operations	100,000	11,900	27,300	71	164
Subtotal	616,000	369,900	385,300	787	880
Visiting teams	178,500	178,500	178,500	4,356[6]	4,356[6]
Parking				100,000	100,000
SUBTOTAL	3,313,750	876,573	1,316,666	110,518	117,766
Multiplier	2.0	2.0	2.0	2.0	2.0
Total	$6,627,500	$1,753,146	$2,633,332	$121,036[7]	$135,532[7]

[1]Includes advertising revenues.
[2]Includes parking fees.
[3]Assumes 20 percent of expenses subject to 5-percent hotel tax; 80 percent of expenditures subject to 1-percent food-and-beverage tax.
[4]Players' salaries, while paid by the Major League affiliate, do have a direct impact on the Fort Wayne economy and local government tax revenues.
[5]While all of the players' salaries are new economic gains, a portion of their income will be spent at their permanent homes. A portion, however, will be spent in Fort Wayne.
[6]Assumes half of the expenditures subject to 5-percent hotel tax; half of the expenditures subject to 1-percent food-and-beverage tax.
[7]The multiplier was not applied to the direct expense of $100,000 for parking but was applied to all other figures.

The Kenosha Twins, now the Fort Wayne Wizards, agreed to pay rent of $222,000 per year, but receive all advertising revenues. All parking revenues and concession profits are placed in a pool for stadium operations, and if all costs are met, any profits belong to the Wizards. If all costs are not met, the team is responsible for any shortfalls. Additionally, the maintenance of the physical plant is the responsibility of the city and county. How has this arrangement worked? So far, no tax dollars have been used to pay for any of the costs of renovations or operations. The team is a financial success; both partners in this arrangement are satisfied, but the city and county receive no real profits from the investment they made. They likely will never lose tax dollars unless fan interest wanes. However, if the team is successful, the profits belong to the team's owners.

How did the fiscal analysis help in this process? Well, for some of the public officials it clearly identified that the new or additional tax revenues the team would generate would not be sufficient to offset a large public investment. The city, then, would have to use other tax revenues if it were to subsidize the stadium, or wait fourteen years to earn enough money to offset its investment had it accepted full responsibility for the stadium's renovations. Furthermore, with substantial private-sector activity from the team (refer to Table 5–1), there was enough revenue to return a profit for the team while building an acceptable facility that was not subsidized by the public sector.

SAVE THE PIRATES!
PITTSBURGH CONSIDERS ITS OPTIONS

The Pittsburgh Pirates have been losing money for several years, and in the early 1990s, the team needed a loan of $8 million from the city of Pittsburgh (Applebaum et al., 1995). To "Save the Pirates," many believe a new stadium is needed. Currently, the Pirates play in Three Rivers Stadium, a circular doughnut built in the tradition of the 1970s, when cities sought facilities that could serve both football and baseball teams. The Steelers and Pirates have played at Three Rivers since it opened. The Pirates left "cozy" Forbes Field for the artificial surface of Three Rivers, and the older park was razed in the early 1970s. Many of the team's supporters believe that a playing facility similar to Jacobs Field, the Ballpark in Arlington, or Oriole Park at Camden Yards would substantially improve attendance levels. If a stadium that was as much a part of the attraction of a baseball game as the teams playing were built with luxury suites and club seats, perhaps the team's finances could be reversed. Outcomes in Cleveland, Arlington, and Baltimore clearly suggest this is indeed possible, as those new facilities are extremely popular and part of the reason fans are attending games in record numbers. In each of these cities attendance levels have significantly increased and the financial value of two of these teams has improved substantially as well.

The challenge for Pittsburgh is to determine if a new facility built for the Pirates could generate sufficient revenues to (1) meet the obligations still required for Three Rivers Stadium, (2) fund the new stadium, and (3) leave enough revenues for the Pirates to be competitive in terms of paying players' salaries. A fiscal analysis can help address these questions, and students and faculty from Carnegie Mellon University tried to illustrate the outcomes from a new, baseball-only stadium. I used some of the data they developed to build a separate analysis of the fiscal impacts resulting from a public-sector effort to "Save the Pirates."

Pittsburgh receives revenues from an amusement tax, a business privilege tax, a mercantile tax, an occupation tax, a parking tax, and a wage tax. There is also a 1-percent countywide sales tax for the support of regional assets, and there are state sales and income taxes. If the city built a new stadium, increased attendance would affect each of these revenue sources. In addition, the construction of a new stadium would offer several new revenue options, including possibly naming the facility for a corporation, leases and premium ticket prices for luxury boxes and club seats, and expanded food and beverage services. A new facility could also be designed to capitalize on opportunities for advertising inside and outside of the stadium. In looking at each of these potential revenue sources, however, it is important to remember that the Pirates will also need some portion of these in-stadium revenues to remain competitive in terms of players' salaries and to address their current fiscal problems and debt. As such, Pittsburgh needs to consider how much new tax revenue will be generated and what its obligations would be for the new stadium and for Three Rivers Stadium. It is also possible to estimate the other revenue sources, then determine what share of revenues the public sector might need to meet its obligations and what share it could agree to give to the ownership of the Pirates to stabilize the team's finances and enhance its competitiveness in attracting and retaining the best players.

Okay, so let's start with the tax revenues. How much will the public sector realize in new revenues? Attendance levels at the new stadium must be projected. The Carnegie Mellon University research team looked at the percentage increases in attendance at all new baseball facilities built since 1960 and then applied the annual average increases to the base of the attendance at Pirates' games in 1993. In other words, the average annual increase at new ballparks in their first year of operations was multiplied against the Pirates' attendance levels in 1993 to estimate the attendance expected in the new stadium's first year. To project attendance levels in subsequent years, the averages from all other new ballparks for their second year of operation was multiplied against the first-year figure. This same process was followed for years 2 through 15. After year 15, it was assumed that the attendance level in 2014 would be the attendance the Pirates could expect through 2040. While estimating expected attendance is always a risk, the process followed by the Carnegie Mellon University team is the best possible approach. It is possible the team could be as successful as the Cleveland Indians, who sold more than 90 percent of all tickets for games in 1995 and 100 percent of all tickets for 1996. The Toronto Blue Jays also sold more than 95 percent of their seats for several years. If the Pirates were able to sell 95 percent of their tickets at the new stadium, their annual attendance would be 2,885,625. The plan upon which this fiscal analysis is based was for a facility with 37,500 seats. Such a stadium is smaller than any of the most recently built facilities (Oriole Park at Camden Yards, Jacobs Field, the Ballpark in Arlington, Coors Field, and Comiskey Park II), but given the population size of the Pirates' market, civic and team leaders in Pittsburgh believed the size of the facility should be reduced to enhance the intimacy of the stadium and the sight lines for fans.

Most facilities have a useful life of about forty years; the fiscal impact analysis was performed for the years 2000 to 2040 (forty-one years). It was anticipated that the interest rate negotiated for the bonds would be the rate that Allegheny County or the state of Pennsylvania could secure.[1] The county's bond rating is stronger (higher) than the rating given to the city of Pittsburgh; the state's rating is even stronger. The difference is not surprising given the wealth of the county and Pittsburgh's suburbs compared to that of the population in the city of Pittsburgh. With stronger ratings from the county or state the bonds used to finance the stadium would have lower interest rates and thus cost less in financing charges.

The total fiscal impact analysis is presented in Tables 5–2, 5–3, and 5–4. Table 5–2 describes the anticipated revenues *after* meeting the costs associated with Three Rivers Stadium. Table 5–3 identifies the expected costs of developing, building, and maintaining the new stadium. Construction costs were calculated based on the average costs of developing other recent facilities for major league teams. The city is considering three different sites for a new stadium. The acquisition costs and site preparation costs were averaged, and that average was added to the construction costs (see Table 5–3).

The Carnegie Mellon University research team also used an input-output model of the Pittsburgh economy to estimate the multiplier effects or the indirect spending that would result from the new stadium and the increased attendance it generated. From this estimate the economic impact of the Pirates could be measured, as could the economic growth created and the tax revenues that would be produced by this economic activity. I adjusted the outcomes expected by the Carnegie Mellon University research team to reflect the likely substitution effects that would occur if the Pirates did leave the region. In other words, a good proportion of the recreation spending at the new stadium would still occur even if the Pirates moved to another region. People would attend other events and engage in other activities if they did not attend a Pirates game. From this adjusted figure the indirect taxes that all state and local governments would collect if the Pirates played in the new stadium were tabulated and included. A further adjustment was made to remove half of the players' salaries from the estimate of spending in the region.

Okay, so what's the bottom line? If the public sector built the stadium by itself, and if the Pirates paid rent that eventually grew to $4.1 million in 2040, the public sector's loss, according to the

Carnegie Mellon study, would average $5,820,397 per year from 2000 to 2040. The Carnegie Mellon University team estimated the total direct and indirect economic benefit of the Pirates to be $93,546,802 per year. My work suggests that between 12 and 24 percent of this figure is the real economic growth created by the team. That means, at a minimum, the loss of the Pirates would cost the economy more than $11 million each year. The loss could be as great as $22 million. The indirect taxes received by all state and local governments from this spending would be $1,878,180 per year. However, removing the players' salaries would reduce this figure to $1.4 million per year. This is an annualized figure (per year estimate), removing any economic and tax growth from the construction of the stadium. Why not count the impact of the construction of the stadium? Because even if the Pirates leave there is nothing to stop the city of Pittsburgh from spending this money on other construction projects. As a result, it is still possible for the construction impact to occur. And, if the construction of a new stadium did not take place, then the city would not collect additional taxes and families and businesses could then spend those tax dollars for other things. In summary, then, the construction dollars would be spent whether or not the stadium is built.

The "bottom line" is contained in Table 5–4. Even with the indirect taxes, the public sector would need to invest, on average, $5,820,397 each year from 2000 to 2040 before subtracting the impact of removing 50 percent of the players' salaries. So, after adjusting for the removal of 50 percent of the players' salaries from the economy, expecting a loss of at least $6 million per year and perhaps as much as $10 million per year, should the public sector make the investment? Should some other private-sector entities agree to support the team through a payment to ensure that the public sector does not lose any money?

Let's see what else is on the table, so to speak, to support the stadium and avoid a subsidy by the public sector. A fee could be charged to name the stadium; there will be fees for the luxury suites and clubs seats. There will be in-stadium and outside-stadium advertising. There will also be concession income. Lastly, there are also cable television, local television, and local radio broadcast

TABLE 5–2

A New Stadium for the Pittsburgh Pirates: Anticipated Tax Revenues after Meeting Obligations for Three Rivers Stadium

Year	Tickets Sold	Amuse-ment Tax	Mercan-tile Tax	Business Privi-lege Tax	Parking Tax	Con-cession Income	Rental Payment	Total Marginal Revenue
2000	$2,805,400	$624,992	$37,992	$4,065	$440,710	$743,168	$1,187,486	$3,038,413
2001	2,672,700	563,581	34,259	3,665	397,406	670,145	1,070,803	2,739,859
2002	2,659,269	576,001	35,014	3,746	406,164	684,914	1,094,402	2,800,241
2003	2,885,625	703,074	42,739	4,572	495,769	836,014	1,335,840	3,418,008
2004	2,885,625	731,197	44,448	4,755	515,599	869,455	1,389,274	3,554,728
2005	2,885,625	760,445	46,226	4,946	536,223	904,233	1,444,845	3,696,917
2006	2,885,625	790,862	48,075	5,143	557,672	940,402	1,502,639	3,844,794
2007	2,885,625	822,497	49,998	5,349	579,979	978,018	1,562,744	3,998,586
2008	2,842,188	872,234	53,021	5,673	615,051	1,037,160	1,657,245	4,240,384
2009	2,885,625	889,613	54,078	5,786	627,306	1,057,825	1,690,264	4,324,871
2010	2,687,243	800,726	48,674	5,208	564,627	952,130	1,521,379	3,892,744
2011	2,510,561	666,713	40,528	4,336	470,129	792,777	1,266,754	3,241,237
2012	2,801,604	972,989	59,146	6,328	686,098	1,156,965	1,848,678	4,730,204
2013	2,791,480	999,720	60,771	6,502	704,947	1,188,751	1,899,469	4,860,160
2014	2,582,531	820,283	49,863	5,335	578,418	975,385	1,558,537	3,987,821
2015	2,582,531	851,371	51,753	5,537	600,340	1,012,352	1,617,605	4,138,958
2016	2,582,531	883,638	53,714	5,747	623,093	1,050,720	1,678,913	4,295,825
2017	2,582,531	917,128	55,750	5,965	646,708	1,090,542	1,742,543	4,458,636
2018	2,582,531	951,887	57,863	6,191	671,218	1,131,874	1,808,586	4,627,619
2019	2,582,531	987,964	60,056	6,425	696,657	1,174,772	1,877,131	4,803,005
2020	2,582,531	1,025,408	62,332	6,669	723,061	1,219,296	1,948,274	4,985,040
2021	2,582,531	1,064,271	64,694	6,922	750,465	1,265,507	2,022,114	5,173,973
2022	2,582,531	1,104,606	67,146	7,184	778,907	1,313,470	2,098,752	5,370,065
2023	2,582,531	1,146,471	69,691	7,456	808,428	1,363,250	2,178,295	5,573,591
2024	2,582,531	1,189,922	72,332	7,739	839,067	1,414,917	2,260,852	5,784,829
2025	2,582,531	1,235,020	75,074	8,032	870,868	1,468,543	2,346,538	6,004,075
2026	2,582,531	1,281,828	77,919	8,337	903,874	1,524,200	2,435,472	6,231,630
2027	2,582,531	1,330,409	80,872	8,652	938,130	1,581,968	2,527,777	6,467,808
2028	2,582,531	1,380,831	83,937	8,980	973,686	1,641,924	2,623,579	6,712,937
2029	2,582,531	1,433,165	87,119	9,321	1,010,588	1,704,153	2,723,013	6,967,359
2030	2,582,531	1,487,482	90,420	9,674	1,048,890	1,768,740	2,826,215	7,231,421
2031	2,582,531	1,543,857	93,847	10,041	1,088,642	1,835,776	2,933,329	7,505,492
2032	2,582,531	1,602,369	97,404	10,421	1,129,902	1,905,352	3,044,502	7,789,950
2033	2,582,531	1,663,099	101,096	10,816	1,172,725	1,977,564	3,159,889	8,085,189
2034	2,582,531	1,726,131	104,927	11,226	1,217,172	2,052,514	3,279,648	8,391,618
2035	2,582,531	1,791,551	108,904	11,652	1,263,302	2,130,304	3,403,947	8,709,660
2036	2,582,531	1,859,451	113,031	12,093	1,311,182	2,211,043	3,532,957	9,039,757
2037	2,582,531	1,929,924	117,315	12,552	1,360,875	2,294,841	3,666,856	9,382,363
2038	2,582,531	2,003,068	121,762	13,027	1,412,453	2,381,816	3,805,830	9,737,956
2039	2,582,531	2,078,984	126,376	13,521	1,465,984	2,472,087	3,950,071	10,107,023
2040	2,582,531	2,157,778	131,166	14,033	1,521,545	2,565,779	4,099,778	10,490,079
Total 2000–2040		$48,222,539	$2,931,331	$313,622	$34,003,861	$57,340,647	$91,622,825	$234,434,824
Annual Average		$1,176,159	$71,496	$7,649	$829,362	$1,398,552	$2,234,703	$5,717,923

TABLE 5–3
A New Stadium for the Pittsburgh Pirates: Anticipated Costs

Year	Operating Costs	Capital Cost	Annual Debt	Total Costs
2000	$1,446,370	$620,945	$9,213,406	$11,280,721
2001	1,304,250	644,479	9,213,406	11,162,135
2002	1,332,994	668,904	9,213,406	11,215,304
2003	1,818,079	694,256	9,213,406	11,725,741
2004	1,846,047	720,568	9,213,406	11,780,021
2005	2,141,752	747,878	9,213,406	12,103,036
2006	2,222,924	776,222	9,213,406	12,212,552
2007	2,307,173	805,641	9,213,406	12,326,220
2008	2,018,542	836,175	9,213,406	12,068,123
2009	2,349,450	867,866	9,213,406	12,430,722
2010	1,853,056	900,758	9,213,406	11,967,220
2011	1,542,920	934,897	9,213,406	11,691,223
2012	2,251,710	970,329	9,213,406	12,435,445
2013	2,313,573	1,007,105	9,213,406	12,534,084
2014	1,898,314	1,045,274	9,213,406	12,156,994
2015	1,970,260	1,084,890	9,213,406	12,268,556
2016	2,044,933	1,126,007	9,213,406	12,384,346
2017	2,122,436	1,168,683	9,213,406	12,504,525
2018	2,202,877	1,212,976	9,213,406	12,629,259
2019	2,286,366	1,258,948	9,213,406	12,758,720
2020	2,373,019	1,306,662	9,213,406	12,893,087
2021	2,462,956	1,356,185	9,213,406	13,032,547
2022	2,556,302	1,407,584	9,213,406	13,177,292
2023	2,653,186	1,460,931	9,213,406	13,327,523
2024	2,753,742	1,516,301	9,213,406	13,483,449
2025	2,858,109	1,573,768	9,213,406	13,645,283
2026	2,966,431	1,633,414	9,213,406	13,813,251
2027	3,078,859	1,695,321	9,213,406	13,987,586
2028	3,195,548	1,759,573	9,213,406	14,168,527
2029	3,316,659	1,826,261	9,213,406	14,356,326
2030	3,442,360	1,895,476	9,213,406	14,551,242
2031	3,572,826	1,967,315	9,213,406	14,753,547
2032	3,708,236	2,041,876	9,213,406	14,963,518
2033	3,848,778	2,119,263	9,213,406	15,181,447
2034	3,994,647	2,199,583	9,213,406	15,407,636
2035	4,146,044	2,282,948	9,213,406	15,642,398
2036	4,303,179	2,369,471	9,213,406	15,886,056
2037	4,466,269	2,459,274	9,213,406	16,138,949
2038	4,635,541	2,552,481	9,213,406	16,401,428
2039	4,811,228	2,649,220	9,213,406	16,673,854
2040	4,993,574	2,749,625	9,213,406	16,956,605
Totals	$113,411,519	$58,915,333	$377,749,646	$550,076,498
Annualized	$2,766,135	$1,436,959	$9,213,406	$13,416,500

TABLE 5–4

The Public Sector's Fiscal Position for a New Stadium for the Pittsburgh Pirates (All Players' Salaries Included)

Year	Anticipated Revenues-Expected Costs	Indirect Taxes	Net Position
2000	$-8,242,308	$1,878,180	$-6,364,128
2001	-8,422,276	1,878,180	-6,544,096
2002	-8,415,063	1,878,180	-6,536,883
2003	-8,307,733	1,878,180	-6,429,553
2004	-8,225,293	1,878,180	-6,347,113
2005	-8,406,119	1,878,180	-6,527,939
2006	-8,367,758	1,878,180	-6,489,578
2007	-8,327,634	1,878,180	-6,449,454
2008	-7,827,739	1,878,180	-5,949,559
2009	-8,105,852	1,878,180	-6,227,672
2010	-8,074,476	1,878,180	-6,196,296
2011	-8,449,986	1,878,180	-6,571,806
2012	-7,705,241	1,878,180	-5,827,061
2013	-7,673,924	1,878,180	-5,795,744
2014	-8,169,173	1,878,180	-6,290,993
2015	-8,129,598	1,878,180	-6,251,418
2016	-8,088,521	1,878,180	-6,210,341
2017	-8,045,889	1,878,180	-6,167,709
2018	-8,001,640	1,878,180	-6,123,460
2019	-7,955,715	1,878,180	-6,077,535
2020	-7,908,047	1,878,180	-6,029,867
2021	-7,858,574	1,878,180	-5,980,394
2022	-7,807,227	1,878,180	-5,929,047
2023	-7,753,932	1,878,180	-5,875,752
2024	-7,698,620	1,878,180	-5,820,440
2025	-7,641,208	1,878,180	-5,763,028
2026	-7,581,621	1,878,180	-5,703,441
2027	-7,519,778	1,878,180	-5,641,598
2028	-7,455,590	1,878,180	-5,577,410
2029	-7,388,967	1,878,180	-5,510,787
2030	-7,319,821	1,878,180	-5,441,641
2031	-7,248,055	1,878,180	-5,369,875
2032	-7,173,568	1,878,180	-5,295,388
2033	-7,096,258	1,878,180	-5,218,078
2034	-7,016,018	1,878,180	-5,137,838
2035	-6,932,738	1,878,180	-5,054,558
2036	-6,846,299	1,878,180	-4,968,119
2037	-6,756,586	1,878,180	-4,878,406
2038	-6,663,472	1,878,180	-4,785,292
2039	-6,566,831	1,878,180	-4,688,651
2040	-6,466,526	1,878,180	-4,588,346
Totals	$-315,641,674	$77,005,380	$-238,636,294
Yearly Expense	$-7,698,577	$1,878,180	$-5,820,397

income. The team, too, needs money to support its operations. Let's estimate those income possibilities and see what options they afford for the fiscal analysis.

Without considering these other sources of income, at least two options could be considered. First, if the civic and community leaders agree that the Pirates are needed, the public sector could agree to absorb the annual loss through higher taxes or reduced service. If that were seen as desirable, the public sector could plan to include the $5.8 to $10 million annual loss in its budget. Second, if the city and team agree that it is mutually beneficial for the team to remain, the public sector could give to the Pirates all other revenues associated with the operation of the stadium in exchange for an agreement that the team be responsible for giving the public sector $5.82 to $10 million each year to support "the shortfall." An arrangement to support any shortfalls in this manner has been reached by the city of Fort Wayne and the minor league franchises that use its facilities. Such an arrangement has still permitted the teams to earn profits while the public sector does not subsidize the facilities with taxes.

Well, let's suppose neither of these options is acceptable. They should not be. How much revenue is likely from the other sources? First consider concessions. Price Waterhouse (1994) found the average fan spent $5.41 for food and beverages when attending MLB games in 1992. Inflated to 1995 levels, the Pirates could expect $6.09 per fan (4-percent inflation rate). That would mean at least $17 million in annual sales inside the stadium. It is likely the Pirates would even sell more to their fans, as newer stadia include a far larger array of vendors and products than older facilities. According to the Price Waterhouse survey, one team averaged $9.36 of concession spending per fan. If the Pirates simply achieved a midpoint between the league average and the high figure in 1992, the team could expect revenues in excess of $21 million from food and beverage sales. Adjusted to 1995 levels, this figure becomes $22.7 million. By the year 2000, when a new facility might open in Pittsburgh, this figure could be as high as $27.7 million, at an inflation rate of 4 percent.

The Baltimore Orioles pay the Maryland Stadium Authority 7.5 percent of concession revenues outside of those revenues earned in the luxury box and suite area (a different percentage is used there).

For the sake of this example, however, assume that the 7.5 percent were applied to the anticipated $27.7 million in revenues that would likely occur at the new facility in Pittsburgh. If this were an acceptable arrangement, more than $2 million would be available to support the annual shortfall for the stadium. The Orioles also give the Maryland State Authority 10 percent of revenues earned from suite leases. There are seventy-two suites with an annual revenue of $5.4 million. The stadium authority's share is $540,000 each year. This is another potential source of money for the financing of the stadium.

Naming rights—the fee charged for granting a corporation the right to use its name for a facility—vary but are usually about $1 million a year. Indianapolis's Capital Improvements Board receives $1 million each year for twenty years from RCA in exchange for renaming the Hoosier Dome the RCA Dome. Richard Jacobs, owner of the Cleveland Indians, pays $400,000 a year for ten years and $986,930 a year in years 11 through 20 to have the stadium where the Indians play named Jacobs Field (Bartimole, 1994). A similar amount of money was secured from the Gund family when Cleveland named the new home of the Cavaliers Gund Arena (Coopers & Lybrand, 1992; Cuyahoga County Auditor, 1995). For the naming rights for the new home of the Colorado Rockies, the Coors Brewing Company paid $15 million divided over ten years at $1.5 million per year (Whitford, 1993). Certainly a new facility for the Pirates has the potential to generate as much income through naming rights as Indianapolis's RCA Dome or Denver's Coors Field.

The Texas Rangers contribute to the cost of their new home through rental payments. The team's base rent is $2 million, and it pays an additional $1.5 million per year until the city retires its debt obligations. The Rangers also earn approximately $13.8 million in leasing fees for luxury suites, and the city of Arlington received 115 percent of this money in year 1 and 5 percent in years 2 through 4. The city received a total of $14,467,000 from suite income, and these dollars were used to help pay for the stadium. Arlington estimates that its stadium project cost approximately $200 million, with the team paying $65 million (Greene, 1995). The city will also continue to collect rent of $2 million annually from the team after the stadium bonds are retired.

With these examples in mind, an option for Pittsburgh might be to follow the lease arrangements used for the Baltimore Orioles. In that case, the city could expect to receive $2.54 million, while the team retained all broadcast revenues. If another $1 million was secured for naming rights—and the team retained all other advertising revenues—a total of $3.54 million each year could be dedicated to the stadium's construction costs. This amount is between one half and one quarter of the annual shortfall of between $5.82 and $10 million needed to build and operate the new stadium and Three Rivers Stadium.

Other possibilities exist as well, including payments from media sources and cable television. For example, a $1 or $2 per game charge could be assessed against those who watch games on cable television. Given the profitability of the team's presence for the print media, it might be expected that a contribution to offset the public sector's loss could be made by Pittsburgh's newspapers.

With these projected numbers, should the city of Pittsburgh move forward with the investment? Should the city organize meetings to convince those who benefit from the stadium to support the anticipated shortfall? These are the questions civic officials must answer, but the fiscal analysis discussed here clearly identifies the costs and possible revenue sources to support the investment in a new stadium. It might well be possible to reduce the annual public-sector subsidy to between $3 and $6 million. Is that investment worth the benefits the Pirates generate? That is the question the citizens of Pittsburgh and Allegheny County must answer.

THE ROLE OF A FISCAL ANALYSIS IN EVALUATING A PUBLIC-PRIVATE PARTNERSHIP

A fiscal analysis should be only one deciding factor in answering the question, "Should we build a stadium?" The fiscal analysis can help you understand how much the stadium will cost, how much the city or county or state will likely receive or earn if the stadium or arena is built, and what tax subsidies might be required. It then remains for voters and civic leaders to decide if any shortfall is worth the other advantages that might occur if the new stadium is built.

So, if you're going to do a fiscal analysis, here is a step-by-step guide to follow in building the totals.

1. Estimate the Cost of the Proposed Stadium. First, decide if you need to build an indoor or outdoor facility. Specify the kind of scoreboard, restaurants, and other amenities you want included. This is not a difficult task given the number of stadia and arenas that have been built in the last few years. If you like Camden Yards, or Jacobs Field, or the Ballpark in Arlington, simply consult these governments or the local media to find out how much the facility cost. If the facility was built several years ago, inflate the cost of construction by the construction or consumer price index for your community. Those numbers can be secured from any library, the U.S. Department of Commerce, or most states' departments of commerce.

2. Estimate Site Acquisition and Preparation Costs (roads and other infrastructure). The cost of the land and its preparation needs to be tabulated and added to the stadium or arena price. Be sure that this estimate or calculation includes the costs associated with needed infrastructure, including roads, freeway exits and entrances, parking facilities, mass transit stations, pedestrian walkways, common areas, and the changes needed in existing streets and roads. If the land for a planned facility is owned by government, estimate its market value through an independent appraisal just as a bank or mortgage company would do if you were applying for a loan. The cost of the land that the government already owns represents an "opportunity cost." In other words, the government has a cost in the sense that the land used for the stadium or arena cannot be used for something else or even sold. It has value and should be included in the fiscal analysis.

3. Identify the Interest Rate on Debt Instruments. Once the capital costs are identified, it is necessary to determine the financing costs associated with any bonds that will have to be secured. This is essentially the same step a potential homeowner takes in trying to estimate mortgage payments by examining the various interest rates available. Some cities may find that the interest rates available to a county or the state would mean lower financing costs. For example, the city of Pittsburgh's finances are more strained than those of either Allegheny County or the state of Pennsylvania. As a result, if either of those two governments were willing to guarantee the bonds or "co-sign" for the stadium loan, the cost of the facility would be less because the financing charges would be less. Similarly, Cuyahoga County and the state of Ohio can receive more favorable terms than the city of Cleveland. If those governments would co-sign for loans, Cleveland saves money. It is important that public officials investigate the various financing options available through different levels of government.

4. Estimate Operating Costs. While it is possible to develop a lease that makes the team responsible for the operating costs of a new stadium or arena, it is a good idea for the public sector to estimate these costs as part of its fiscal analysis. Operating costs include the permanent staff that must be hired to operate and maintain the facility (setup costs associated with events) and the event-day staff needed to ensure the safe use of the facility. For example, extra security personnel will be needed inside the arena, and it might also be necessary for extra or special traffic control officers to be available for each game or event at the new facility.

Maintenance costs must also be planned and included in the fiscal analysis. Again, it may well be that the lease could assign these costs and responsibilities to the teams and other users. But it is important for the fiscal analysis to include this cost, as maintenance will be an increasing cost issue as a facility ages and new technology affords opportunities to enhance the arena or stadium (new scoreboards, video display, sound systems, and so forth).

5. Identify All Sources of Tax Revenues. Once the costs have been identified, it is time to turn the analysis to an estimation of the revenues that will accrue as a result of the stadium or arena's operations. List each of the sources of revenues or taxes and user charges that the government levies. These revenue sources include income taxes, sales taxes, property taxes, business taxes, amusement taxes, parking taxes and fees, food-and-beverage taxes, hotel taxes, tolls, cable television charges (if games or events are to be telecast), and any ticket charges that are assessed. Different governments have used different combinations of fees and taxes. Using this checklist will ensure that all possible sources of income are included. If some of these sources are not used or available, it may be appropriate to add a tax or user charge to offset the cost of the stadium or arena. Be sure that the estimates of tax revenues reflect any negative economic impact that could take place for other recreational facilities that might offset the gains that result from the presence of the team and stadium.

The failure to carefully project tax revenues can lead to very difficult choices or situations. For example, Cleveland and Cuyahoga County relied on "sin taxes" (taxes on alcohol and cigarettes) to support their investments in two sports facilities built by the Gateway Economic Development Corporation. The corporation was created by local governments to build the new home for the Indians and to attract the Cavaliers back to downtown Cleveland. The taxes raised were not sufficient to cover the costs for even one of the facilities, and the economic growth generated by both the Indians and the Cavaliers could not generate enough new taxes to cover the shortfall. As a result, the county had to guarantee more than $120 million in construction bonds through property taxes.

6. Estimate Attendance and Spending Patterns. Numerous methods are used to project attendance at a new stadium or arena and the spending likely to take place. Price Waterhouse, as mentioned earlier, does an annual survey of facility operators. From this survey one can estimate fan spending inside the ballpark or arena. Various governments have also surveyed fans or spectators attending different events and can estimate consumption inside and outside of the facility. To project anticipated attendance one can look at the patterns of attendance for teams that built new facilities or the attendance levels at new arenas. These can be used to project or estimate likely attendance at any new ballpark or facility if the size of the market area is controlled. In other words, a region with five million residents will likely have higher attendance levels than a region with two million residents. However, the smaller region can estimate future attendance levels by determining the percentage increase in the larger region when the new facility was developed. This percentage increase could then be applied against the attendance level before a new facility was built to estimate what the new attendance level will be.

Why should you anticipate a higher level of attendance just because a new facility is built? Attending any game or event has become more than just an opportunity to see a contest or concert. Stadia and arenas are now "part of the show." When the Astrodome was built in Houston, people came to see the "Eighth Wonder of the World" as well as major league baseball. Toronto's Skydome with its retractable roof is as much a part of the experience of attending a ball game as is seeing the Blue Jays. Jacobs Field and the Ballpark in Arlington are also fine examples of the creation of a venue that makes attending a game an event in and of itself. Yankee Stadium, Fenway Park, and Wrigley Field are each landmarks people want to see regardless of who is playing or what is being played. As such, when a new "landmark" is built, it may well attract far more fans even if the team does not improve.

Once attendance levels have been projected, anticipated revenues from tickets purchased can be determined, as can the total amount of food, beverages, and souvenirs that will be purchased. The appropriate sales and other taxes can be calculated as well.

7. *Calculate Indirect Spending.* The last step in the estimation of revenues is to calculate the multiplier or indirect income likely to be produced as a result of the stadium or arena's operation. The positive economic impact created by the team, stadium, or arena will mean more or additional tax revenue for the public sector. These gains should be included in the analysis as part of the "return" to the public sector for the investment made in the stadium or arena. Many consultants can perform the input-output analysis for you. Several cities and states also have this capability, as do many universities and research centers.

8. While the cartel structure of sports makes it difficult for cities to enter into partnerships with teams and receive a share of the revenues generated at the arenas and ballparks that are subsidized by

taxpayers, this option should not be abandoned. If governments are to assume a level of fiscal risk in the building of facilities, there should be a discussion of a revenue sharing program with the team. In a true public/private partnership both partners would assume some level of risk for building the stadium and arena, and each would share in the profits. Teams usually want all the revenues, and cities have to be far more aggressive in seeking revenue-sharing programs with their private-sector sports partners. As the case studies that follow will illustrate, some cities have been successful in this regard, while others only "hope" to receive additional tax revenues. In some cities, the public sector retains parking revenues, luxury seat payments, revenue from the sale of food and beverages, and advertising income. In other cities, the teams take all of the revenue while the public sector pays for a large portion of the stadium or arena.

PLANS, OTHER REVENUES, AND THE INTANGIBLE BENEFITS OF SPORTS

So, when the fiscal analysis is done, does that mean you have your answer as to whether or not the public sector should support a stadium or arena? Not quite, but you are very close in terms of understanding what "the deal" will cost you. Now comes the most difficult part of all: asking yourself and answering the question, what do we get for this investment?

For example, let's return to the situation involving Pittsburgh's decision to build (or not to build) a new stadium for the Pirates. The estimate I produced together with the group from Carnegie Mellon University suggested that the shortfall for publicly developed facilities might be as much as $6 million if certain stadium revenues were assigned to the city. Suppose, just for fun, that the city and team agreed to the lease I suggested, whereby the public sector's annual loss was reduced from almost $6 million to about $3 million. All of the other revenues at the stadium were given to the Pirates. What else would Pittsburgh get for its $3 million each year?

Let me give you another way of thinking about what a city might get for its $3 million or even for a $10 million annual investment in the world of sports. In the early spring of 1995 Michael Jordan "unretired" from professional basketball. The first game he appeared in after his "I'm Back" announcement was against the Indiana Pacers in Indianapolis. NBC seized the game for its Game of the Week and broadcast the return of his "Airness" to numerous countries. During various breaks in the action NBC displayed aerial and ground-level shots of Indianapolis's skyline, civic fountains and monuments, and downtown parks. On a glorious spring afternoon, Indianapolis received worldwide attention and publicity. That night each of the network news programs highlighted Michael Jordan's return, as did the following morning's breakfast news shows. In each of these newscasts Indianapolis was mentioned and was sometimes even highlighted. Did anyone move to Indianapolis because of that coverage? No, but what would Indianapolis have had to pay to get that kind of attention to help identify and market itself? Indianapolis received that attention because it is part of the cultural icon known as sports as a result of the presence of the Indiana Pacers basketball team. The city has also made an investment to keep and retain the Pacers. Was that investment worth the publicity received when Jordan returned to basketball?

Suppose the strategy of building a new stadium for the Pirates was linked to an effort to rebuild a section of the downtown area or to attract a large number of people to the downtown area. Can the stadium revitalize a small section of downtown? Possibly yes; some of the case studies in the chapters that follow will detail the success and failure of development associated with a new stadium or arena. Would that development—if it did occur—be worth the $3 to $10 million each year the new stadium will cost the citizens of Pittsburgh? Are there better ways to develop downtown regions? Is it worth several million dollars a year to have more than two million people use or visit the downtown section of Pittsburgh?

Those are the sort of questions the citizens of Pittsburgh would have to answer. However, it also matters if the city has developed a

plan for integrating the stadium in its overall strategy for the downtown area or for the region. Too often there is virtually no planning
but a good deal of hoping that the stadium or arena will "jump-
start" the economy or region. By itself, a stadium or arena cannot
jump-start even the small economy of a part of downtown. But as
part of an overall plan or strategy, a stadium could be helpful and
useful. Does such a plan exist, and what is expected or anticipated
from the development of the stadium or arena? Is the support and
implementation of the plan worth $3 or $10 million? Can the stadium or arena generate benefits in terms of the plan's success that
would be worth the $3 to $10 million annual investment?

Those are the difficult questions cities and their leaders have to
ask and answer as they play "sports wars." If no plan for economic
development or revitalization exists, estimating the importance of
the stadium or arena is very difficult. The community must also
decide if a cross subsidy—the transfer of property or other taxes to
the stadium—is worth the possible gains from future economic
development or the revitalization of a portion of the community. As
several of the case studies will illustrate, several cities used sports as
a development theme. The fiscal analysis helps pinpoint exactly
what is being committed to sports, and if a development plan exists,
a community can evaluate whether the investment is worth the
return or contribution to the plan's success.

The final step or issue that should be debated when a fiscal analysis is completed is the "image" benefits that might result from the
presence of the team and a new stadium, as well as the negative consequences that might result if the team leaves for another city. I'm
reminded of a talk show I did on teams and their movement in the
Minneapolis–St. Paul area. After I had detailed the very small effects
teams have on local economies, a caller wanted me to discuss the
decline of St. Louis that took place after the Cardinals left for Arizona. Even though the economy of St. Louis had not suffered—
indeed had improved—after the Cardinals left, this caller had the
distinct impression that the city was in decline.

It was not only the caller who believed St. Louis's image had
declined. When we interviewed civic officials in St. Louis regarding
the investments they made to attract the Rams from Los Angeles to

the new domed stadium, each told us they supported the concept because most people in America believed that "St. Louis's best days were behind her." So, image matters to people even if those of us who study the economic effects of stadia and teams conclude there is no real benefit from the presence of a team.

What does the fiscal analysis add to this discussion of the image benefits? At least a price tag is placed on the benefit through the fiscal analysis. Returning to the examples of Pittsburgh and Fort Wayne, the city of Pittsburgh and its taxpayers and the residents of Allegheny County will likely have to contribute between $3 and $10 million each year to keep the team in the region (in the absence of any revenue sharing by MLB). If they accept this public-private partnership, the Pittsburgh Pirates will likely continue to play in the city. Each day when baseball fans across America read their sports pages, Pittsburgh will be in the standings. The city will likely host an All-Star game once in the next twenty-five years and enjoy all of that national attention. The Pirates will likely make the play-offs and even appear in a World Series. Those events will also increase the city's exposure. Pittsburgh will be one of a select group of cities home to at least three major league sports teams: the Pirates, Steelers, and Penguins. In this regard the city is more similar to other larger centers such as Detroit, Chicago, and New York, which have at least four teams, and less similar to Indianapolis, Columbus, Louisville, and San Antonio. Is that benefit worth $3 million a year? Is it worth more than $10 million? Fort Wayne now has minor league baseball and its investment may total less than $5 million over the life of the team. Is the image benefit worth the investment? These questions can be answered only by those cities' taxpayers and leaders, but through the fiscal analysis they will at least know what they are paying and what they are likely to receive. It remains for each citizen to debate whether the value is worth the investment or subsidy at a time when franchises are bought and sold for tens and hundreds of millions of dollars and several players earn in excess of $1 million each season.

6

Sports and Downtown Development

Indianapolis's Effort to Go from Indiana*NO*place to Indiana*SPORTS*place

EVERAL CITIES IN BOTH the Rust Belt and the Sun Belt have used and justified their partnerships or deals with sports teams to build playing facilities as efforts to revitalize downtown areas. The incentives provided to teams when downtown rehabilitation is an objective of the "deal" should be seen as an investment to change development patterns. Cities have frequently used incentives to encourage development in particular areas, and if teams or sports facilities do help to energize a downtown region, any public money dedicated to the project might be a very wise investment. Success for these cities from their investments in sports, however, must be measured in terms of the extent to which downtown areas became or remained vital as employment, housing, or recreation centers.

In the Rust Belt, Cleveland and Indianapolis are probably the best known examples of cities that used sports as an important part of their redefinition of downtown. In the Sun Belt, Phoenix and Dallas have also used sports facilities and the public sector's partnerships with teams as a tool for reconstructing or reestablishing the importance of downtown areas within their regional economies. What makes each of these efforts important for taxpayers and their leaders is that the public sector's investment was tied to the accomplishment of a very specific set of objectives. What the communities were buying through their investment in sports facilities or teams was a program to jump-start a downtown development or redevelopment effort. Did these cities get what they wanted? Can sports facilities be a cornerstone for preserving downtown areas?

Maintaining vibrant downtown areas is not a new challenge for America's cities. The rush to suburban locations first led by residents in the nineteenth century expanded to include businesses in the last half of the twentieth century. A substantial portion of America's urban population has always sought homes a bit removed from the hustle and bustle of city centers. New York's early middle class moved to the northern part of Manhattan and then to Brooklyn, Queens, and the Bronx. Their children moved to Long Island, Westchester, and New Jersey as the metropolitan region expanded to more than fourteen million residents. Los Angeles's early residents moved to the San Fernando Valley and then to San Pedro, the San Gabriel Valley, and then Orange County. From Boston to Dallas and from Atlanta to Seattle, residential development has always pushed out from the center.

For most of the twentieth century those who moved to the suburban parts of a metropolitan region found themselves commuting to downtown jobs, but that pattern changed as businesses were also able to decentralize from the downtown locations so integral to firms in the early part of the century. With more and more companies finding lower costs (cheaper land, lower tax rates, and lower transportation costs) in the suburbs and higher levels of worker satisfaction from the shorter commutes these suburban locations provided, the importance and even the need for a downtown area in many regions began to disappear. Many regions are now dominated by large suburban or edge cities or even a series of small exurban cities that often surround a shrinking core or center city.

In the 1970s many professional teams followed their fans to the suburbs. The Boston (New England) Patriots, Dallas Cowboys, Kansas

City Royals, Kansas City Chiefs, Texas Rangers (from Washington, D.C., to suburban Arlington, Texas), Detroit Lions, Detroit Pistons, Los Angeles Rams (now the St. Louis Rams), Miami Dolphins, New York Giants, New York Jets, Cleveland Cavaliers, Arizona Cardinals (moved from downtown St. Louis in the 1980s), New Jersey Devils (moved from Denver), and Buffalo Bills each moved from downtown or center city locations to suburban venues. The New Jersey Nets moved from one suburban area, Uniondale, to another several times. Some other expansion teams (California Angels and the Charlotte Hornets) were created and placed in suburban locations among the throngs leaving the cities. The New Jersey Nets came from Long Island; as such this team has always played in suburban locations. The Hornets play within the city of Charlotte, but not in its downtown area.

To be sure, there were some exceptions to the flight to the suburbs. The Cincinnati Reds and Bengals, the Pittsburgh Pirates and Steelers, and the Minnesota Vikings and Twins each moved to a center city location or stayed within a center city in the 1970s and 1980s. The Toronto Blue Jays and Montreal Expos have always played within their respective center cities, with the Blue Jays having a decidedly downtown location. The Expos play within the city of Montreal at the site of the Olympic Park a few short kilometers from downtown Montreal. The Indianapolis Colts moved from a suburban location within the city of Baltimore to downtown Indianapolis's RCA Dome (née Hoosier Dome).

The 1990s, however, saw a new trend led by the construction of a downtown ball park in Baltimore that was reminiscent of the smaller fields of decades past. Oriole Park at Camden Yards was followed by Jacobs Field, Comiskey Park II, and Coors Field, and each of these facilities was located in a downtown or inner-city area. The St. Louis Rams moved from a suburban city, Anaheim, to a new downtown facility in St. Louis in 1995. Even the suburban Ballpark in Arlington was designed to evoke memories of the downtown ball parks of the early twentieth century. Currently, several other cities, including Milwaukee, Phoenix, Boston, Chicago, Nashville, Cincinnati, Detroit, Seattle, and New York are considering or have built new sports facilities designed to facilitate or complement downtown redevelopment efforts. With these many efforts contemplated it seems fair to ask, Can sports facilities or teams save America's downtown areas? To answer that question, probably no city is more important to study than Indianapolis. No city has as clearly targeted sports as the cornerstone of its downtown development policies and programs as Indianapolis.

INDIANAPOLIS AND THE SPORTS AND DOWNTOWN DEVELOPMENT STRATEGY

Indianapolis found itself considering economic development policies and programs at the same time many cities in North America were dealing with the Rust Belt's decline and recession. In the 1970s Indianapolis was a city with a declining job base, a deteriorating downtown core, and a very limited image in the national and international economic landscape. Indianapolis was also shrinking in size. Between 1970 and 1980 the consolidated city of Indianapolis lost population while the metropolitan area enjoyed a 17.6-percent growth rate (see Table 6–1). When Indianapolis and its county consolidated in the early 1970s to form "UniGov" (unified government), a considerable amount of suburban land was joined with Indianapolis's older neighborhoods and downtown area. When this annexation did not lead to a period of substantial growth for the city, Indianapolis's leadership realized that drastic policies and changes were required. Indeed, in 1970, Indianapolis's population accounted for 66.3 percent of the metropolitan region. By 1980, the consolidated city would account for just 53.7 percent of the region's population. In this environment it was relatively easy for the city's leadership to conclude that something dramatic was needed to improve the image and attractiveness of the city and to reverse the deteriorating and declining importance of Indianapolis's downtown core.

Fearing a continuing loss of Indianapolis's economic importance, redeveloping downtown, as a tool for enhancing the city's role

TABLE 6–1
Population Growth in Indianapolis, 1970–1992

Area	Year				Percentage Change 1970 to 1992
	1970	1980	1990	1992	
Consolidated Indianapolis	737,000	701,000	731000	747000	1.4%
Percentage change		-4.9%	4.3%	2.2%	
As a percentage of the region	66.3%	53.7%	53.0%	52.5%	
Metropolitan Indianapolis	1,111,000	1,306,000	1,380,000	1,424,000	28.2%
Percentage change		17.6%	5.7%	3.2%	

in the region, emerged as the central policy issue or concern for community leaders in the 1970s. A coalition of leaders from the public, private, and nonprofit sectors responded to Indianapolis's malaise by developing a program that focused on two objectives: (1) establishing a market niche for Indianapolis in (amateur) sports and (2) using this sports strategy to redevelop the downtown core as the cultural and economic center of the city and region.

Many people in Indianapolis believe its image problems were best summarized on a late-night talk show when favorite son Kurt Vonnegut described the city as a cemetery with lights that came to life one day a year for the Indianapolis 500. A survey commissioned by the Greater Indianapolis Progress Committee in the mid-1970s found the city to have a "non-image"—neither positive nor favorable—in the national media and among convention planners. A finding of no image was actually a substantial improvement over earlier assessments of Indiana's capital city. Indianapolis had been called "Naptown" by some and IndianaNOplace by others. John Gunther, in 1947, almost ended the city's future when he described Indianapolis as "an unkempt city, unswept, raw, a terrific place for basketball and auto racing, a former pivot of the Ku-Kluxers" (Hudnut, 1995). No image or a non-image was probably a substantial improvement upon Vonnegut's characterization and the view that Gunther distributed in his works. Yet, for a city with aspirations for regional and national leadership, a very different image was desired by Indianapolis's business and political elite.

When Indianapolis initiated its redevelopment program in the 1970s and 1980s, several organizations or partnerships were formed to rebuild the city's image and downtown center. An economic development corporation was created to assist companies considering a move to Indianapolis or to help local corporations that might want to expand their operations within the city. The overriding mission for this organization was to encourage businesses to locate in downtown Indianapolis. Another group was created to market the city as a venue for sports events and as the headquarters location for amateur sports organizations. A third organization focused on the image of Indianapolis in the national media and on increasing the positive exposure of the city in national and international publications.

At first glance a focus on sports as a tool for economic development might seem to be a poor choice. As already discussed, sports are a very small component of any economy; could sports have an impact that would substantially influence overall development patterns? The direct (and indirect) spending associated with restaurants and hotels is also too small to change economic patterns (Johnson, 1993; Swindell & Rosentraub, 1992; Baade & Dye, 1988; Rosentraub & Nunn, 1978). These important limitations, however, might be addressed by the Indianapolis program. First, Indianapolis's approach was quite unique and different from redevelopment efforts that focused on one team or a single facility. Indianapolis targeted amateur sports as an industry, two professional sports teams (the Pacers and then the Colts), and a collection of individual sporting events (NCAA Final Four, NCAA championships, and others). Together, these three sets of sports-related activities, events, and organizations became the focal point of its development efforts. Second, this focus on numerous events was coupled with the development of several sports facilities, including a home for the Indiana Pacers, Market Square Arena, and a home for a potential NFL team (the Hoosier Dome, which the Colts moved to in the 1980s). Did Indianapolis's sports strategy have the potential for a larger impact than efforts that focused on one team or a single new sports facility?

Third, Indianapolis's leaders proposed to use sports and its cultural importance to attract a wide range of business activities to the downtown area. While the economic impacts of any single team or event and the amateur sports industry itself are unlikely to create a large change in any area, the cultural importance of sports might provide it with the potential to solidify a wide range of economic interests or firms that would consider locating in the center of a sports capital. Indianapolis's leadership hoped that the cultural significance of sports would convince many legal, banking, and insurance companies to stay in a downtown area known for its vibrancy as a center for athletic events. The city was determined to show its faith in its downtown through substantial investments to develop the facilities to attract these events. It was also hoped that these tangible signs of the city's commitment to the downtown area would convince the private sector of the city's commitment to maintaining and enhancing the central core of Indianapolis.

Indianapolis's plan for economic development, then, was not shortsighted in its focus on sports but quite provocative and actually tailored to meet the suggestions frequently made by economic development experts. First, there was a clear geographic focus. The downtown area was to be targeted and this bias was designed to capitalize on existing assets and several public investments. These existing assets included a government center employing thousands of people (state and local government), a large private-sector employer (Lilly), a developing state university campus (Indiana University–Purdue University Indianapolis, 1995 enrollment twenty-seven thousand), and a hospital and health services center (Indiana University Medical Center). Second, to further establish the center, public investments were made to enhance the downtown area (convention center, stadium, indoor sports arena, retail and commercial centers, and cultural centers). Third, to maintain a coalition of development interests, not only was a specific industry targeted to become a market niche for Indianapolis, but this industry had substantial value to society and the potential to attract substantial support. Fourth, Indianapolis's leadership was committed to this sports development strategy for more than twenty years. Aspects of the programs were initiated early in the 1970s during the second term of

Mayor Richard Lugar, and were refined, continued, and under-scored during each of the four (four-year) terms of Mayor William Hudnut. As a result, this was not an example of a policy program given a brief time period to succeed. If sports could contribute to or redevelop a downtown area, it would most likely occur through Indianapolis's prolonged policy focus and substantial level of investment.

REBUILDING DOWNTOWN INDIANAPOLIS

A central component to Indianapolis's strategy was building several facilities that would be the new anchors for the revitalized down-town and the core of the Indianapolis region. In 1974, Market Square Arena opened as the new 16,950-seat home for the Indiana Pacers. Market Square Arena also became the city's premier indoor arena, a designation it held for a decade until the Hoosier Dome opened. Today, for events that cannot attract at least thirty thousand spectators, Market Square Arena remains a viable facility. From 1974 through 1990 more than thirty major development projects for the downtown area were initiated. The state of Indiana also developed its new Government Center at a cost of $264 million, and Indiana University's investment in its Indianapolis campus totaled more than $231 million.

Seven of these projects were completely related to the sports identity Indianapolis tried to establish. In 1984, Indianapolis opened the 61,000-seat RCA Dome (née Hoosier Dome; RCA pur-chased the naming rights to the Dome in 1994), which became the home for the Indianapolis Colts and has hosted the NCAA men's basketball Final Four twice (this event will return to Indianapolis for the fourth time in 2000; the first Final Four held in Indianapolis was played at Market Square Arena). Other facilities developed included the Sports Center, a tennis stadium for the annual hard-court tennis championships (now sponsored by RCA), the Indiana University Natatorium, the Indiana University Track and Field Stadium, the

Velodrome (bicycle racing), and the National Institute for Fitness and Sports. By 1989, a total of seven national organizations (Athletics Congress of the USA, U.S. Canoe and Kayak Team, U.S. Diving, Inc., U.S. Gymnastics Federation, U.S. Rowing, U.S. Synchronized Swimming, and U.S. Water Polo) and two international organizations (International Baseball Association, International Hockey League) had moved their governing offices to Indianapolis.

The projects identified in Table 6–2 do not include all development that took place in the downtown area during this time period. Some developments (the city's monuments, a large park area, the state's refurbishing of the capitol building, new fire stations, and others) were not appropriate for consideration here given that they would have taken place even if a sports strategy had not been specified. To be sure, there is a subjective element to this classification process. However, through interviews, we did try to ascertain which projects were specifically intended to be part of the strategy.

Several important points emerge from a review of Table 6–2. First, a total of $2.76 billion for capital development was invested in downtown Indianapolis. This clearly represents a substantial commitment of funds targeted to a specific area and in support of a tightly designed policy program. Second, there was extensive commitment of private funds to the strategy. Indeed, more than half of the funds invested, 55.7 percent, were from the private sector. Third, the nonprofit sector was also an active participant, although responsible for slightly less than one of every ten dollars invested, 8.5 percent. Taken together, then, the private and nonprofit sectors were responsible for approximately two-thirds of the funds invested in the amateur sports and downtown redevelopment strategies. Fourth, the city of Indianapolis's investment amounted to less than one-fifth of the total investment, 15.8 percent. Fifth, the investment by the state of Indiana and Indiana University was actually more than the expenditure made by the city of Indianapolis.

In spite of the criticisms made regarding certain sports development, Indianapolis was quite successful in leveraging funds for its sports strategy. Basically, a $2.76 billion investment for an economic development program required $436.1 million from the city of Indianapolis. For every dollar invested by the city, it was able to

Table 6–2

Sources of Funds for Economic Development Projects (in $0,000,000)

Projects	Year	Federal	State	City	Private	Philan-thropic	Total
Market Square Arena	1974	0	0	16	0	0	16
Children's Museum	1976	0	0	0	0	25	25
Hyatt Hotel/Bank	1977	0	0	0	55	0	55
Sports Center	1979	0	0	4	1.5	1.5	7
Indiana Theater	1980	1.5	0	0	4.5	0	6
Capitol Tunnel	1982	1.4	0	0	0	0	1.4
IU Track and Field Stadium	1982	0	1.9	0	0	4	5.9
IU Natatorium	1982	1.5	7	0	0	13	21.5
Velodrome	1982	0.48	0	1.1	0	1.1	2.68
2 W. Washington Offices	1982	1.2	0	0	11.8	0	13
1 N. Capitol Offices	1982	3.2	0	0	10.41	0	13.61
Hoosier Dome	1984	0	0	48	0	30	78
Lower Canal Apartments	1985	7.9	0	10.3	0	2	20.2
Heliport	1985	2.5	0.12	0.6	2.36	0	5.58
Walker Building	1985	2	0	0	0	1.4	3.4
Embassy Suite Hotel	1985	6.45	0	0	25.05	0	31.5
Lockerbie Market	1986	1.8	0	0	14	0	15.8
Union Station	1986	16.3	0	1	36.01	0	53.31
City Market	1986	0	0	0	0	4.7	4.7
Pan Am Plaza	1987	0	0	5.7	25	4.5	35.2
Lockfield Apartments	1987	0	0	0.62	24.6	0	25.22
Canal Overlook Apartments	1988	0	0	0	11	0	11
Zoo	1988	0	0	0	0	37.5	37.5
Nat'l Institute of Sports	1988	0	3	3	0	3	9
Eiteljorg Museum	1989	0	0	0	0	60	60
Westin Hotel	1989	0.5	0	0	65	0	65.5
Indiana University	1990	0	231	0	0	0	231
Farm Bureau	1992	0	0	0	0	36	36
State Office Center	1992	0	264	0	0	0	264
Lilly Corporate Expansion	1992	0	0	0	242	0	242
Circle Centre Mall	1995	0	0	290	0	10	300
Other projects	74–92	0	0	0	1008.53	0	1008.53
Property tax abatements	74–92	0	0	55.8	0	0	55.8
TOTAL		46.7	507.0	436.1	1536.8	233.7	2760.33
PERCENT		1.7	18.4	15.8	55.7	8.5	100

Source: Department of Metropolitan Development, city of Indianapolis.

leverage $5.33. If the investments by the state in its office center and Indiana University in its Indianapolis campus are removed—based on the argument that these investments would have been made without an economic development plan—for each dollar spent by the city, it was able to leverage $4.20. However, it should be noted that the state of Indiana and Indiana University's components of the redevelopment of downtown were something city officials and leaders worked to secure through a variety of political avenues. Put another way, had the city not focused on a downtown economic development plan, would the state and university have invested as much as they did? It is possible that the state and Indiana University could have selected different sites for their expansions, or decided a declining downtown was not where additional resources should be invested. With no possible way to answer such a question, it is best to report the leverage ratios with and without the involvement of the state and the university.

THE ECONOMIC IMPACT OF INDIANAPOLIS'S INVESTMENTS

There are many ways the impacts from an investment strategy as pronounced as Indianapolis's should be measured. It would be unfair to simply ask the question, Did the sports and downtown strategy succeed?, then provide a simple yes or no. As with any program as extensive as Indianapolis's effort, there were important successes as well as outcomes that were not as positive as hoped. A balanced review of Indianapolis's efforts requires several different perspectives to answer the question, Did it work? To provide as complete a view of the outcomes from Indianapolis's twenty-plus-year strategy, several different views of development outcomes were used. First, I considered the growth in sports-related employment. If the amateur sports strategy was successful, and if professional teams were attracted to Indianapolis, one would expect to see job growth in this area in Indianapolis to be more substantial than growth in other cities. Second, I evaluated the effects of a pronounced economic development strategy on economic growth by looking at growth rates in Indianapolis compared with those of other Midwestern cities. These communities encountered most if not all of the same pressures and constraints (cost factors) regarding economic development as did Indianapolis. Did Indianapolis's sports strategy change the city's relative standing among competitor cities? Did Indianapolis have more growth? Third, I analyzed the relationship between sports and the city's overall economic development. Did sports "jump-start" other investments? Fourth, using anecdotal evidence, we also considered the impact of sports and downtown development on Indianapolis's image.

THE GROWTH IN SPORTS-RELATED EMPLOYMENT

It was possible to compare the growth in sports-related employment in Indianapolis to that of twenty-nine other central-city counties for which comparable data were available. Indianapolis's growth of 49.3 percent in sports-related employment opportunities ranked the city ninth (see Figure 6–1). Sports-related job growth was greater in Prince George's County (Maryland), Columbus (Ohio), Dallas, Houston, San Diego, Pittsburgh, and Boston.

When the analysis focuses only on changes from 1983 to 1989, Indianapolis's increase of almost 60 percent placed it second among all twenty-nine cities (see Figure 6–2). This second time period may be more appropriate, for it allows some time for the impact of Indianapolis's programs and policies to have taken place.

This spurt at the end of the development period could be a result of job growth generated after relocations were realized and new organizations were in place. In addition, the sports-related economic growth of Columbus, Ohio, surpassed that of Indianapolis even though that area did not have a sports strategy for economic development. The growth in Indianapolis still trailed the 79.2 percent increase for Columbus, Ohio.

FIGURE 6–1
Growth in Sports-Related Employees, 1977–1989

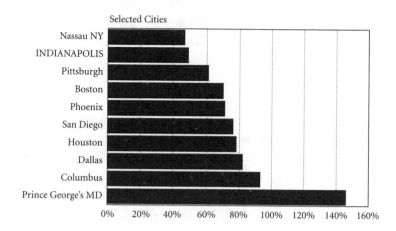

FIGURE 6–2
Growth in Sports-Related Employees, 1983–1989

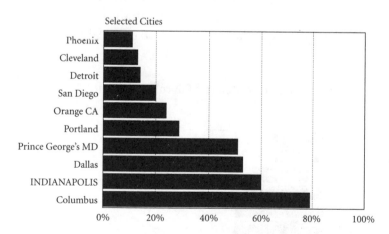

Many analysts prefer to focus their attention not on changes in the proportion of jobs available but on the relative changes in the size of payrolls. Such an analysis addresses the relative value of creating a larger number of low-paying jobs or a fewer number of high-paying opportunities. Figure 6–3 focuses on changes in the level of sports-related payrolls, and the changes for Indianapolis certainly indicate the attraction of a large number of high-paying jobs. Not only was payroll growth in Indianapolis the highest of all the areas in the study for the 1983 to 1989 period, but the percentage increase in sports-related payrolls in Indianapolis was more than 100 percentage points larger than the second ranked area, Orange County, California.

There seems to be little doubt that the sports development strategy was successful in terms of attracting sports-related employment opportunities that substantially increased sports-related payrolls in the Indianapolis area for such employment. However, these impressive gains notwithstanding, sports-related employment and sports-related payrolls remained a relatively inconsequential component of the Indianapolis economy. In 1989, all sports-related jobs accounted for .32 percent—one-third of 1 percent—of all jobs in the Indianapolis economy, and the sports-related payroll accounted for less than one-half of 1 percent of the total payrolls of all Indianapolis businesses. While the growth in this component of the Indianapolis economy was clearly substantial, its presence in the total economy of Indianapolis remained so small as to be almost invisible in terms of

FIGURE 6–3
Growth in Sports-Related Payrolls, 1983–1989

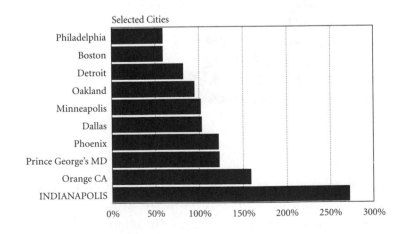

overall impact and importance. In 1977, for example, sports-related employment accounted for .29 percent of all jobs, less than one-third of 1 percent. The sports strategy itself, then, increased the proportion of sports-related jobs in the Indianapolis economy by .03 percentage points. The growth in payrolls from 1977 was larger, but still inconsequential. In 1977, sports-related payrolls accounted for .24 percent—one-quarter of 1 percent—of the Indianapolis payroll; in 1989, this proportion had doubled, but was still less than one-half of 1 percent of all payrolls.

OVERALL ECONOMIC GROWTH IN INDIANAPOLIS

One way to measure success is to compare growth and changes in employment patterns with those observed for other areas with which Indianapolis regularly competes for firms and jobs. As a small regional center, Indianapolis does not compete with Tier I cities for development, but it does compete with other regional centers. Discussions with economic development and municipal leaders in Indianapolis identified Columbus (Ohio), Minneapolis, St. Paul, St. Louis, Dayton, Cincinnati, Louisville, Milwaukee, and Fort Wayne (Indiana) as cities with similar cost and asset levels with which Indianapolis finds itself in regular competition. The analysis in this section focused on the counties in which central cities were located and their metropolitan areas.

From 1977 to 1989, the number of jobs in Indianapolis increased by 32.9 percent, exceeded only by growth in Columbus and Minneapolis. In each of the counties where these central cities are located, the number of jobs increased by more than 50 percent. As illustrated in Figure 6–4, the increase in the number of jobs in Indianapolis was similar to the increases in Fort Wayne (29.8 percent), St. Paul (28.9 percent), and St. Louis (28.8 percent).

In addition to looking at overall changes in the number of jobs, the changes in the number of jobs for different industries—services, finances, and manufacturing—were also examined. Generally, service-sector jobs pay less than jobs in either the manufacturing or finance sectors. From 1977 to 1989, Indianapolis enjoyed a 121-percent

FIGURE 6–4
Central Counties 1977–1989 Total Employee Growth

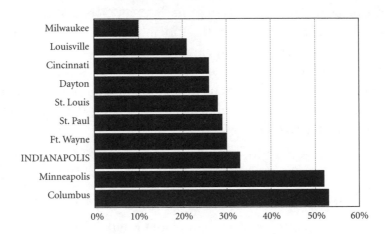

increase in service-sector jobs; Columbus had the second largest gain in this category with a 109-percent increase, and Minneapolis was third (see Figure 6–5).

In the manufacturing sector, the number of jobs available declined in all areas, with the exception of Minneapolis and St. Paul; Indianapolis's decline was the third largest. In the finance sector, the

FIGURE 6–5
Central Counties 1977–1989 Service-Sector Employee Growth

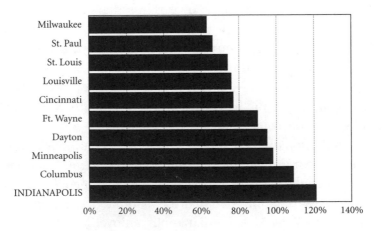

largest increases occurred in Columbus, Minneapolis, and Fort Wayne; the increase of 25.3 percent in Indianapolis was larger only than the increase reported for Dayton (see Figure 6–6).

Another way to assess the performance of the Indianapolis economy is to compare the proportion of jobs in the region defined by the comparison communities as those located in the county. This is illustrated in Figure 6–7.

FIGURE 6–6

Central Counties 1977–1989 Finance-Sector Employee Growth

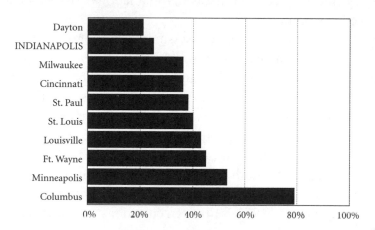

FIGURE 6–7

Regional Shares 1977–1989 Total Employees

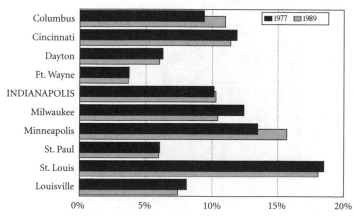

1977 Regional Total = 3,382,432
1989 Regional Total = 4,427,834

In 1977, 10.1 percent of the jobs in the ten counties studied were located in Indianapolis; in 1989, this share had increased .2 percentage points to 10.3 percent. In contrast, Columbus's share of jobs increased by 1.6 percentage points, and Minneapolis's share increased by 2.2 percentage points. Fort Wayne's share of the job market was unchanged, while the proportion of jobs declined for Cincinnati, Dayton, Milwaukee, St. Paul, St. Louis, and Louisville. By industry, Indianapolis's share of finance jobs declined by 1.6 percentage points, and its share of manufacturing jobs declined by .9 percentage points. In the service area, Indianapolis's share increased 1.6 percentage points.

The "bottom line" for many assessments of economic development may well be changes in payroll. If more disposable income is generated in an area, its economy and tax base expand. The increase in total payroll in Indianapolis was surpassed by those of Minneapolis, Columbus, St. Louis, and St. Paul. Indianapolis's gains were 6 percent larger than the increase found for Fort Wayne and 10 percent larger than the percentage increase in Cincinnati (see Figure 6–8).

Indianapolis's share of the total payroll for the ten counties, from 1977 to 1989, actually decreased by .2 percentage points (see Figure 6–9). Furthermore, in 1977, for the ten counties studied, Indianapo-

FIGURE 6–8
Central Counties 1977–1989 Total Payroll Growth.

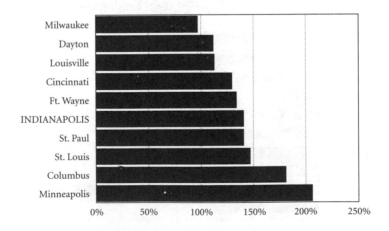

FIGURE 6–9
Regional Shares 1977–1989 Total Payroll

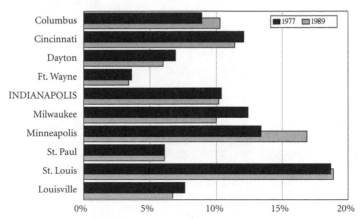

1977 Regional Total = $41,644,234
1989 Regional Total = $101,260

lis had the second highest average income, exceeded only by Dayton's. In 1989, Indianapolis's average income of $22,794 was ranked fifth behind those of Minneapolis, St. Louis, St. Paul, and Cincinnati.

In 1977, average salaries in Indianapolis ranked the county second among the ten comparison areas; in 1989, Indianapolis's rank had declined to fifth. Dayton was the only area that had a higher average salary than Indianapolis in 1977, but by 1989, Minneapolis, St. Louis, St. Paul, and Cincinnati each had average incomes above Indianapolis's at the county level. Indianapolis's increase from 1977 to 1989 was sixth among the ten county areas. At the metropolitan statistical area (MSA) level, the Indianapolis region faired somewhat better; ranked second in 1977, the region was fourth in 1989, with the seventh largest percentage increase. In terms of overall salary levels, then, Marion County slipped further than the Indianapolis region (see Table 6–3).

Changing the focus of the analysis from the counties in which the central cities are located to the metropolitan regions offers a slightly different view of outcomes. At the MSA level, the 41 percent increase in the number of employees for the Indianapolis region was surpassed only by Minneapolis–St. Paul, 52.2 percent, and Columbus, 49.7 percent (see Figure 6–10).

TABLE 6–3

Average Salary Levels, Indianapolis and Comparison Areas

Area	Avg. Salary 1977	Rank	Avg. Salary 1989	Rank	Percentage Increase 1977 to 1989	Rank
	COUNTY					
Minneapolis	12,233	6	24,617	1	101	1
St. Louis	12,401	5	23,949	2	93	2
St. Paul	12,471	4	23,318	3	87	3
Cincinnati	12,546	3	22,959	4	83	5
Indianapolis	**12,593**	**2**	**22,794**	**5**	**81**	**6**
Dayton	13,445	1	22,711	6	69	10
Milwaukee	12,226	7	21,958	7	80	8
Columbus	11,661	9	21,351	8	83	4
Ft. Wayne	11,836	8	21,292	9	80	7
Louisville	11,645	10	20,580	10	77	9
	MSA					
Minn./St. Paul	12,081	6	23,506	1	95	1
St. Louis	12,088	5	22,651	2	87	2
Cincinnati	12,098	4	21,870	3	81	4
Indianapolis	**12,152**	**2**	**21,849**	**4**	**80**	**7**
Milwaukee	12,131	3	21,843	5	80	6
Dayton	12,633	1	21,539	6	71	9
Columbus	11,530	8	21,088	7	83	3
Ft. Wayne	11,650	7	20,992	8	80	5
Louisville	11,344	9	19,845	9	75	8

FIGURE 6–10

MSA's 1977–1989 Total Employee Growth

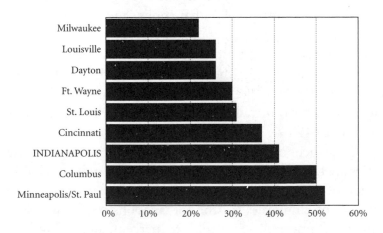

In terms of total employee growth, Indianapolis ranked third (see Figure 6–10). The Indianapolis MSA also had the largest increase in service-sector jobs, 128 percent, more than 18 percentage points larger than the increase reported by the region with the next largest growth (see Figure 6–11).

In the manufacturing sector, only the Minneapolis–St. Paul region had an increase in jobs, and the loss of jobs in the Indianapolis region was larger than the losses in the Fort Wayne, Cincinnati, St. Louis, and Dayton regions. The proportional increase in finance jobs in Indianapolis was also the second smallest, exceeding only the Dayton region (see Figures 6–12 and 6–13).

There was also a decline in the Indianapolis MSA's rank in terms of average income. In 1977, the Indianapolis MSA had the second highest average income; in 1989, the region was fourth behind the Minneapolis–St. Paul, St. Louis, and Cincinnati regions.

To compare and contrast changes for the Indianapolis MSA and the county within which Indianapolis is located (Marion), I generated a set of figures to assess outcomes for the United States, the state of Indiana, and the Midwest region (Kentucky, Illinois, Ohio, Michigan, Indiana, Wisconsin, and Minnesota). Looking first at the number of jobs created, the growth rate from 1977 to 1989 in the Indi-

FIGURE 6–11
MSA's 1977–1989 Service-Sector Employee Growth

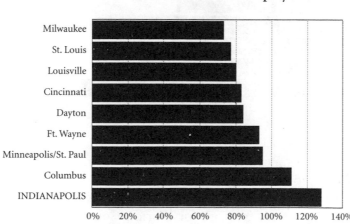

FIGURE 6–12

MSA's 1977–1989 Manufacturing-Sector Employee Growth

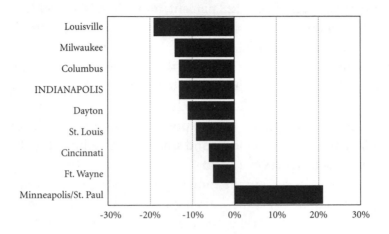

FIGURE 6–13

MSA's 1977–1989 Finance-Sector Employee Growth

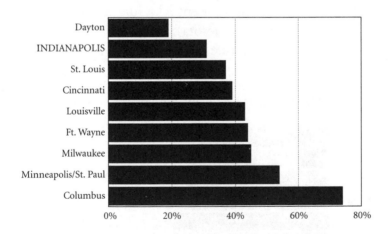

anapolis MSA was 41.1 percent. This rate of job creation was equal to the rate for the nation as a whole, and 8.2 percentage points greater than the rate of increase for Marion County. The job creation rate for Marion County, however, exceeded the rate for the state of Indiana. In terms of the jobs created, then, the Indianapolis

MSA grew at the same rate as the nation, which exceeded the growth rate in Marion County, in the state of Indiana, and in the seven-state area (see Figure 6–14).

Figure 6–15 compares the changes in job levels for the service, manufacturing, and financial sectors. Marion County's increase in jobs was driven by the service sector, with a percentage increase larger than the changes in Indiana, the Midwest region, or in the United States. The Indianapolis MSA's percentage increase in service jobs was larger than the growth in Marion County. Marion County's growth in jobs in the financial sector trailed that of the region, the MSA, the state of Indiana, and the United States. In addition, Marion County's percentage loss in manufacturing jobs was larger than the loss for all other geographic regions.

Payroll growth in the Indianapolis MSA was less than the growth observed for the country as a whole, but larger than the increase reported for Marion County. Marion County's increase was also larger than the increase for the seven-state region and for the state of Indiana (see Figure 6–15).

In summary, Indianapolis's focus on its downtown area and sports as a development strategy was associated with substantial growth. However, *Indianapolis's strategy did not result in more*

FIGURE 6–14
Geographic Areas, 1977–1989 Total Employee Growth

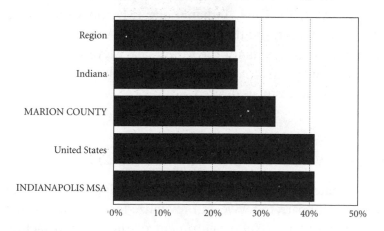

FIGURE 6–15
Geographic Areas, 1977–1989 Total Payroll Growth

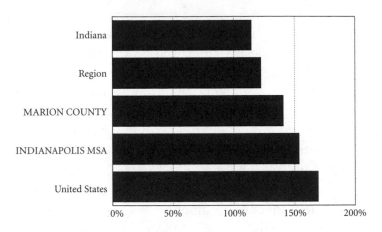

growth or the concentration of higher paying jobs. Indianapolis's share of the ten counties' employees increased from 10.1 percent in 1977 to 10.3 percent in 1989, but this growth was concentrated in the service sector. Indianapolis's share of finance and manufacturing jobs decreased, as did its share of payroll dollars. The large number of lower paying service-sector jobs might also be responsible for Indianapolis's declining rank in average salary levels. In 1977, the average salary in Indianapolis was the second highest of the ten areas selected for study. By 1989, Indianapolis (Marion County) had slipped to fifth highest, and the Indianapolis MSA was fourth highest. The slightly higher rank for the MSA's salary levels also suggests that the ability of the city to concentrate jobs in the downtown area has not been as successful as desired.

SAVING DOWNTOWN: CAN SPORTS DO IT? NO!!

Both the (amateur) sports and downtown development strategies were designed, in part, to revive and revitalize Indianapolis's downtown business district. The development of the physical facilities within which events would be hosted did shift the focus of the region's entertainment and culture from suburban areas to downtown. Employment opportunities, however, did not follow. In 1970, the 95,562 people working downtown represented 30 percent of all workers in the county and 22.8 percent of workers in the MSA. In 1980, the 111,400 downtown workers accounted for 26.8 percent of the county's jobs and 20.9 percent of the region's employees. By 1990, there was actually a net decline in downtown jobs from 1980, and the 105,500 downtown workers represented 21.2 percent of the county's jobs and 15.8 percent of those in the MSA. By 1990, then, downtown employment opportunities, while fewer in number when compared to 1980, were still greater than the number in 1970 (see Figure 6–16).

It is important to note, however, that although Indianapolis's strategies for economic development were unable to stop the trend toward job development in areas outside of the downtown center, progress has been made in at least stabilizing, to a limited extent, the job situation in downtown. If a city is able to maintain a vital downtown core while its regional economy expands, then a program for development would achieve an important level of success.

There are at least two other ways of examining the influence of

FIGURE 6–16
Job Location in the Indianapolis Region

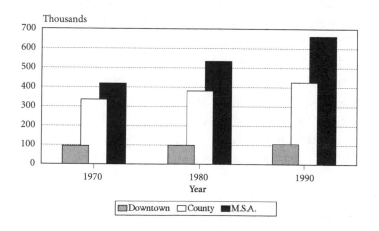

the downtown development and (amateur) sports strategy on the concentration of employment opportunities in Indianapolis (Marion County). First, it is possible to compare the spread of job opportunities to Indianapolis's suburbs with the diffusion in the comparison areas. This is done in Table 6–4 for both the number of jobs and total payroll. Second, it also possible to determine whether the jobs that remain in the downtown area are higher paying than those in other areas of the city, county, and metropolitan area.

Table 6–4 presents the proportion of jobs and payrolls in 1977 and 1989 concentrated in each central county. In Indianapolis, for example, in 1977, 85.4 percent of all jobs and 88.5 percent of all payroll dollars were concentrated in Marion County. By 1989, these proportions had declined to 80.5 percent and 84.0 percent, respectively. Cincinnati and Milwaukee each had proportional losses greater than Indianapolis's; all other areas had less diffusion than Indianapolis, with two experiencing some degree of concentration. In Louisville, the proportion of jobs was unchanged, but the proportion of the MSA's total payroll in the central county had increased; in the Minneapolis–St. Paul region, the proportion of jobs and payrolls was more concentrated in the central counties in 1989.

By this measure, then, Indianapolis did not do as well as some other areas in holding jobs and total payroll in the central area. However, in 1977, average salaries in Marion County (Indianapolis) were 3.7 percent higher than average salaries in the Indianapolis MSA. This differential increased by .7 percentage points, to 4.4 percent, in 1989. Indianapolis's increase in higher paying jobs was surpassed by Minneapolis (+3.4 percentage points), St. Louis (+3.1 percentage points), Louisville (+1.0 percentage points), and Cincinnati (+2.7 percentage points), but was greater than the changes in St. Paul (–4.0 percentage points), Dayton (–2.4 percentage points), Milwaukee (–.3 percentage points), and Fort Wayne (–.2 percentage points).

Using the 1987 Census of Retail and Service Establishments, I also was able to compare average salaries for these two sectors of the economy by zip code areas. In this way, the average salary levels in downtown Indianapolis could be compared with the near down-

TABLE 6–4

Changes in the Concentration of Employment Opportunities and Payroll: Central City (County) Jobs and Payroll as a Proportion of the MSA

Area	Employment			Payroll		
	1977 Ratio	1989 Ratio	Percent-age Change	1977 Ratio	1989 Ratio	Percent-age Change
Indianapolis	85.4	80.5	-4.9	88.5	84.0	-4.5
Cincinnati	83.7	76.5	-7.2	86.8	80.3	-6.5
Columbus	83.1	79.2	-3.9	84.7	81.8	-2.9
Dayton	77.4	75.4	-2.0	79.4	79.7	+0.3
Fort Wayne	86.3	82.4	-3.9	88.6	85.4	-3.2
Louisville	88.9	88.9	0.0	88.9	90.1	+1.2
Milwaukee	77.1	69.1	-8.0	77.7	69.4	-8.3
Minn./St. Paul	80.2	82.1	+1.9	81.1	83.1	+2.0
St. Louis	71.3	70.9	-0.4	75.9	74.8	-1.1

town, outer city, and other county areas. Retail jobs in the downtown area were higher paid than in any other area of the region, although the differences were small (less than 5 percent). Service-sector employees in the downtown area, however, had annual salaries that were 14 percent higher than the salaries of service workers in the suburban sections of the county.

CAN SPORTS UNIFY A COMMUNITY'S EFFORTS FOR REDEVELOPMENT? NOT REALLY!!

Recognizing that sports are a very small part of any area's economy, if there is any expectation that sports can contribute to development, it is that sports, by nature of their importance in and for society, can create a sort of "glue" that holds together important economic interests. In this manner, sports could foster growth through their importance to society, as people might consider a city "big time" or "major league" if it is a sports center. Having already considered the extent to which the sports and downtown development strategies were unable to focus development in the downtown center, we next considered whether the growth in sports-related employment or payrolls was correlated with growth in any particular sectors of the economy. A correlation analysis was performed for all twenty-nine counties in the United States for which sports employment data were available. This analysis reviewed the relationship between the sports sector, the total economy, and all broad sectors of the economy. In addition, specific, more narrow sectors that might have been correlated with the sports sector were analyzed. In summary, sports growth was not associated with overall growth for the period 1977 through 1989, but it was correlated with growth in other service-sector jobs (.51), and with the hotel and lodging sector (.49). For none of the other industrial groups or broad sectors of the economy was there a statistically significant correlation for employment growth in the 1977 to 1989 period.

When I shifted the focus of the analysis to 1983 through 1989, the period of largest growth in sports-related employment, modest correlations with the service sector (.54), hotels (.41), and with business services (.44) still existed. There was no strong evidence that sports created a growth coalition that stimulated the economy or created a large number of jobs even in the shorter time period. The associations that were present were also in employment areas that do not have a large concentration of high-paying jobs.

SPORTS, DOWNTOWN DEVELOPMENT, AND IMAGERY

While there is little doubt that the image of Indianapolis has substantially changed during the twenty years of the sports and downtown development effort, it is quite difficult to point to any specific measure of economic development and declare that the sports strategy worked. Indianapolis's hosting of national and international events changed its image; but so too did the growth that took place in the Midwest's economy and the vitality in the Indiana economy as a result of the recovery of the U.S. automobile industry, Indiana's largest single employer. There is, however, one example that might best illustrate what Indianapolis's redevelopment program meant for the city's image.

As discussed earlier when Michael Jordan "unretired" from professional basketball, NBC televised the game and aired numerous views of Indianapolis's skyline to all parts of the country. No one moved to Indianapolis because of that coverage, but was the exposure worth Indiana*No*Place's investment?

CONCLUSIONS: DID THE SPORTS STRATEGY WORK, AND WHAT LESSONS WERE LEARNED?

Indianapolis, more so than any other city, developed an articulated economic development strategy for its downtown that emphasized amateur and professional sports. This policy was designed to rebuild the core area and avoid a "doughnut" pattern of prospering areas along an outer beltway surrounding a deteriorating center. It was also hoped that the sports strategy would generate substantial economic development in the entire region. In relying on sports, Indianapolis's efforts were probably not unlike Louisville's emphasis on the arts to anchor downtown development (Whitt, 1988) and Baltimore's emphasis on tourism and the location of the home of the Baltimore Orioles. Cleveland's development of new downtown playing facilities for its basketball and baseball teams was not only similar but supporters there pointed to Indianapolis as a model. When Cleveland's leaders developed the Gateway complex plans, they made repeated trips to Indianapolis to survey the success the former "cemetery with lights" had achieved. Many other cities have also initiated "sports strategies" as a cornerstone for economic development, pointing to the success of Indianapolis, Cleveland, and Baltimore. So Indianapolis's efforts encouraged Cleveland and Baltimore. The experiences of these three cities encouraged Jacksonville, Memphis, and Charlotte to emphasize sports for downtown and economic development. With many communities basing their investments and policies on Indianapolis's success, it seems critical to determine if Indianapolis's program was successful (Norton, 1993).

While there were important achievements that should be attributed to Indianapolis's sports strategy, on balance, it seems fair to conclude there were no significant or substantial shifts in economic development. Simply put, the sports strategy did not achieve its objectives. In 1992, as described in Table 6–5, sports accounted for approximately 1.1 percent of the private-sector payroll in downtown Indianapolis and about 3.1 percent of all jobs. In addition, even if all hotel and restaurant jobs are assumed to be a direct result of sports, just 4.3 percent of the private-sector payroll was produced by these parts of the private-sector economy. As such, other communities' leaders should be quite cautious with regard to the possible "pay-offs" from a sports development program.

The sports and downtown development policy in Indianapolis was part of a series of outcomes that contributed to a partial stabilization of the number of jobs in the downtown area. Although the downtown core's share of regional employment opportunities declined, the absolute number of people working downtown remained relatively unchanged from 1980 to 1990, and above 1970 levels. While this is clearly an important achievement, a portion of

TABLE 6–5

Employment in the Indianapolis City Center, 1992

Industry	Employment as a Percentage of Total for Indpls. CBD	Annual Payroll as a Percentage of Total for Indpls. CBD
Total estimate for city center	84,750	$1,792,971,687
Sports-related industries combined	10.3%	4.3%
Eating & drinking places total	5.5%	2.9%
Hotels & other lodging places	1.7%	0.3%
Sports, amusement, & recreation	3.1%	1.1%
Remaining retail trade	4.7%	3.5%
Remaining services	35.2%	33.2%
Manufacturing	10.4%	28.9%
Wholesale trade	6.9%	6.7%
Transportation	11.0%	9.7%
Finance, insurance, & real estate	17.3%	10.9%
Agriculture	0.1%	0.0%
Mining	0.2%	0.3%
Construction	3.9%	2.6%
Unclassified	0.1%	0.0%

Source: U.S. Department of Commerce, 1992.

the success was a result of the expansion of Indiana University, the presence of large public-sector employers (state, county, and city), and the continued growth of downtown Indianapolis's largest employer, the Lilly Corporation. With substantial geographic decentralization pressures within the American economy, Indianapolis's accomplishment is still clearly enviable, but this stabilization of jobs and the downtown area was not directly related to sports. The Indianapolis region's growth did not differ substantially from the growth in other midwestern areas.

With these points in mind, the best that can be said for Indianapolis's sports strategy is that it was marginally successful in creating a small number of jobs. Attendance at sporting events did generate a number of service-sector and hotel jobs. The growth in service-sector jobs may have been related to the relatively high proportion of attendees at sporting events in Indianapolis from outside the region. While most sporting events are usually attended by local residents, Indianapolis's connection with amateur sports and the NCAA has made it a site for a number of national and international championship events (Schaffer et al., 1993).

This important outcome must be contrasted with other stark realities. The Indianapolis metropolitan area grew faster than the city in terms of new jobs created and total payroll growth. Overall, average salaries in Indianapolis declined in comparison to salaries with many of those cities with which Indianapolis's leadership believes it competes. Indianapolis slipped from having the second highest average salaries among these ten communities in the 1970s to fourth or fifth, depending on whether the basis of comparison is the city or the metropolitan region. In addition, the entire impact of sports, under the best of circumstances, would amount to only 1.1 percent of the Indianapolis economy.

Without minimizing the success and publicity Indianapolis has enjoyed, outcomes of this magnitude are so small that it is plausible to consider that, had the city focused on other factors, a larger economic impact would have been possible. Indianapolis was successful with its amateur sports strategy if success is measured by the return on the investment. If success is measured by growth in jobs and payrolls, then Indianapolis was not as successful as other cities with which it competes for economic development. The sports strategy tied to downtown development was not able to attract a substantial level of other forms of economic activity. This outcome has to be considered somewhat disappointing given the success the city had in fostering a public-private partnership that secured substantial investments from the private sector. These observations do not preclude the possibility that, had no sports strategy been developed, Indianapolis's economic fortunes might have precipitously declined and that other initiatives would have been far less likely to secure the kind of partnerships Indianapolis established with the private sector. However, proponents of a sports strategy who would then wish to argue that the image benefits were critical would need to address the levels of economic success in the other cities with which Indianapolis competes and that did not have a sports strategy. Again, the argument could continue that, without the sports strategy, Indianapolis's economy would have declined even more and the public-private partnerships that leveraged private capital would have been more similar to patterns elsewhere (Squires, 1989).

In terms of overall development, including the benefits of the image of being a major league city (the Colts and the Pacers) and an amateur sports and NCAA capital city, Indianapolis's experience indicates that sports will not generate the growth or overall impacts its boosters and supporters frequently claim. An overall sports strategy that involves large numbers of attendees at events who do not live in the region can be a successful investment strategy only if that success is evaluated solely in terms of the growth in sports-related employment. Given how small sports are as an industry and the low pay associated with the numerous service-sector jobs created by sports activities, sports do not seem to be a prudent vehicle around which a development or redevelopment effort should be organized. A sports strategy—even one as pronounced as Indianapolis's and connected to a downtown development emphasis—has little potential to be an economic stimulus for a community or region.

The sports strategy, however, did have an impact on the city's image and identity. A new skyline can be portrayed as a backdrop to sports events, and this does create a favorable impression. Sports, then, can redefine an image, but a sports strategy for economic development does not seem to have the promise for success that its many advocates claim, even when a program is as concentrated and as long term as the one Indianapolis pursued. So, what lessons do we learn from Indianapolis's experiences?

1. Small Cannot Become Big. Since no city emphasized sports as part of its development strategy to the extent that Indianapolis did, it should be fairly obvious that sports, by themselves, cannot become a substantial or large component of any city's economy. Large increases in the number of jobs in the sports sectors will not substantially change the overall job and salary levels in a community. Sports are relatively "small potatoes" when their importance to a region or city's economy is considered. No matter what emphasis and faith is placed on sports, do not expect them to become a major part of an economy or even to lead an economic recovery or the redevelopment of any area. Sports can help; sports can create excitement, but sports are too small a component of any economy to lead economic changes or propel large-scale redevelopment efforts. Sports are small and will remain so relative to any other sector of a city's economy or inventory of jobs.

2. Sports Do Generate Excitement and Imagery. Rebuilding a downtown core area, or reestablishing a city's image and reputation, requires the cooperation of a number of people and firms. Coalitions have to be built and maintained. Indianapolis's partnership for sports and downtown redevelopment lasted for almost two decades. The excitement created from the attraction of numerous sporting events (e.g., the Pan American Games, the men's Final Four basketball championships, and others) to the attraction and retention of the Indianapolis Colts and the Indiana Pacers clearly helped to maintain the coalition and attract new members. The image of a successful city attracting events and teams created an impression or an illusion of economic success and vitality that certainly contributed to and helped maintain the focus on downtown development in Indianapolis. Although this impact had no direct economic benefits, its political and social value should not be discounted.

Sports may help maintain a coalition of groups, but it cannot bring economic development to a region as large as a typical downtown or city center.

3. *An Economy's Engines Are Still Its Engines.* If sports cannot be an engine and do not drive an economy, what does? In Indianapolis's case the engines of its downtown economy are the health-related industries (Lilly and Indiana University Hospitals), education, the public sector (state center), insurance companies, banks and financial institutions, retail development (one of the nation's largest shopping mall developers has its headquarters in Indianapolis), and the legal community. Further from the center, heavy manufacturing, the automobile industry, and transportation create the wealth people need to purchase the sports industry's tickets. The engines that drive Indianapolis are similar to those that helped the city establish itself in the post–World War II era. Indeed, if there is an economic miracle in Indianapolis it is not sports but the reengineering of its manufacturing sector.

4. *Build Community Partnerships That Are Financial Partnerships.* The limitations of the economic impact from sports in no way minimizes the substantial success Indianapolis had in building a set of real partnerships to pursue its economic development strategy. Indianapolis's investment or tax exposure was far less than the investments or subsidies provided by other cities. In this regard, an important lesson to be learned is that successful partnerships can be built that minimize the investment of the city's resources. Indeed, Indianapolis's ability to leverage noncity funds for its economic development program was quite impressive. The lesson for other communities is that real partnerships exist when each side takes risks and earns returns. Indianapolis's return was a decidedly different image and shape for its city. Indianapolis's leaders wanted a new downtown and a new image. They invested more than $436 million in this effort, but those funds accounted for just 15 percent of the total investment. The private sector, in contrast, spent more than $1.54 billion, or almost four times as much. It would seem Indianapolis received a fair return on its money relative to image and reputation issues as well as an enormous private-sector investment in downtown Indianapolis. Indianapolis's downtown has enormous private-sector commitments that keep that sector and the public sector unified in an effort to keep the downtown area vital and robust.

5. *Plan Your Work and Work Your Plan.* When Indianapolis committed itself to sports and downtown development, it had a detailed plan for rebuilding and redesigning the central core. From this perspective Indianapolis's leadership knew exactly what they wanted to achieve and had a set of plans to be followed as museums, an arena, and a domed-stadium were built. There was no "hoped for" development or "future plans" that were or would be developed. The city prepared a downtown redevelopment plan, and it followed this plan. While some did criticize the rather elite nature of the planning process (to be sure, there could have been more public discussion), Indianapolis was not an example of "build it and maybe development will come."

The last piece, or capstone, of the plan, a large downtown shopping center, opened in September 1995. When Circle Centre Mall welcomed its first customers, Indianapolis had finished a plan conceived in the 1970s that included a university, a new state center, a new convention center, numerous private-sector buildings, two theaters, and three different venues for professional sports (tennis, basketball, and football). Indianapolis planned its work, worked its plan, and now has a rebuilt downtown area.

7

Sports and Downtown Development II

Cleveland, the Mistake by the Lake, and the Burning of the Cuyahoga

I T IS PROBABLY SAFE to conclude that Cleveland has spent more for and on professional sports teams and their playing facilities than any other community in the United States. The building of Jacobs Field, Gund Arena, and the surrounding garages by the Gateway Redevelopment Corporation cost approximately $462 million.[1] Cleveland's commitments to professional sports did not end with these new facilities for the Indians and Cavaliers. Once cities build facilities for one team they frequently have to provide similar offers or inducements for other teams in their community. After watching the public sector lead efforts to build a new stadium and arena for the area's baseball and basketball teams, the owner of the Browns, Art Modell, threatened to leave Cleveland unless a similar effort to enhance the revenue potential of his NFL franchise was made. The community responded with a $175 million proposal to renovate aging Cleveland Stadium (née Municipal Stadium), but that was not sufficient to convince Mr. Modell to stay in Cleveland.[2] Three days before the election to approve the final piece of the $175 million redevelopment package, stories circulated that Mr. Modell was actively discussing the relocation of the Browns to Baltimore. Mr. Modell himself did nothing to dispel these stories; indeed, he encouraged them.

> Citing a source close to Modell, the *Baltimore Sun* reported in today's editions that Modell intends to announce Monday in Baltimore that he is moving his franchise there. Details were still sketchy Friday, but *The Sun* reported that Modell is expected to be accompanied at the 12:30 P.M. news conference by Maryland Governor Parris N. Glendening, Baltimore Mayor Kurt Schmoke, and Maryland Stadium Authority Chairman John Moag.
>
> "I've got to do what I have to to protect my family, my franchise, and my employees," Modell said in a lengthy telephone interview with several of the reporters who cover the team regularly. "We'll see what develops in the next few days, and I wouldn't jump to any conclusions. At the same time I don't want to hold out any false hopes either" (Associated Press, 1995).

It might be possible to describe Mr. Modell's statement as typical for owners who like to dangle franchises in front of elected officials, taxpayers, and fans. Baltimore was an especially vulnerable pawn, having lost the Colts to Indianapolis. Cleveland too was quite vulnerable, having faced the potential loss of the Indians. The Browns had played in Cleveland for fifty years and rarely failed to draw fewer than sixty-five thousand fans to their games. Indeed, throughout the 1990s, average home attendance for Browns games exceeded seventy thousand. This gave the team one of the largest average home attendance figures in the NFL and clearly demonstrated that the fans supported the franchise through winning and losing years (*New York Times*, November 1995). The Browns last won a league championship in 1964 and last appeared in a league championship game in 1967. They are one of the teams that have never appeared in a Super Bowl despite winning several division titles in the 1980s. Despite this mixed record of success on the field, the Browns were steadfastly supported by the rabid "Dawg Pound" fans for decades.

This support from loyal fans while the team failed to win a championship for more than thirty years did not stop Mr. Modell from playing one city against another in a game of "sports wars." Indeed, one day before the public referendum to provide more than $175 million to remodel Cleveland's aging stadium, Mr. Modell accepted an offer from Baltimore and the state of Maryland. The offer included $75 million in incentives and rent-free use of a new $200 million publicly financed stadium. After fifty years in Cleveland and average fan attendance in excess of seventy thousand per game, the Cleveland Browns would be known as the Baltimore Ravens. As Art Modell summarized it himself, "I leave my heart and part of my soul in Cleveland. But frankly, it came down to a simple proposition: I had no choice. . . . What is required is beyond the capacity of Cleveland. I didn't want to be known as a shakedown artist" (Ginsburg, 1995). Mr. Modell continued to underscore that he was losing money and could not earn a profit in Cleveland. Yet in May 1995 *Financial World* reported that the Browns had earned a profit of $6 million in 1994 and $5.8 million in 1995.

Even after the announcement of the Browns' move, the voters still approved the extension of the "sin tax" to complete the financing for the $175 million renovation package. If the proposed package for a football team or stadium is added to the investments in Jacobs Field and Gund Arena, the $637 million in investments for facilities for professional sports teams, financed over a period of twenty-five years, will cost the community more than $1 billion. While there is substantial debate and disagreement over the exact proportion of the bill that will be paid by the public through taxes, the total figure or investment by *both the public and private sectors* is still larger than any other U.S. community's investment in sports. Indianapolis's sports and downtown development strategy cost $2.7 billion, but those funds also supported numerous nonsports facilities. In contrast, the proposed investment of $637 million (excluding interest charges) by the Cleveland region was solely for sports facilities and teams. St. Louis's and Missouri's investments to attract the Rams, while clearly substantial and in the $300 million range (without interest), was a bit less, and the new Trans World Dome is also part of a convention center. In contrast, the facilities built in

Cleveland were primarily for the use of professional sports teams. When these facilities are used for other activities, the profits from those events mostly accrue to the individual teams, not the public sector that invested in the sports facilities for Cleveland's teams.[3]

CLEVELAND AS A SHRINKING GIANT

Why was this much money spent on sports? What did the community get? Was the investment a wise one? While this chapter will answer these questions and identify several important lessons for other cities considering sports investments, the investments themselves, no matter how large or small, need to be placed in the context of Cleveland's recent history. That history has been both dispirited and turbulent.

In terms of the dispirited elements of Cleveland's recent history, of paramount importance has been the decline of the city of Cleveland. Cleveland is a shrinking giant in terms of its population and the wealth of its residents. The population of the city has declined relative to both the region and its home county, Cuyahoga. In 1970, the city's 750,897 residents made up 57 percent of Cuyahoga County and 25 percent of the region's population. By 1990, Cleveland's 505,616 residents made up 51 percent of Cuyahoga County and 18 percent of the region (see Table 7–1). During this same period, 1970 to 1990, the state of Ohio's population increased slightly from 10,657,000 in 1970 to 11,021,419. In 1970, then, 7 percent of Ohio's residents lived in Cleveland. By 1990, the city accounted for 4.6 percent of Ohio's population.

Not only has the population of Cleveland declined, but so has the population of Cuyahoga County and the population of the greater Cleveland metropolitan region. In 1970 the region had 3,000,276 residents; by 1990 the population had shrunk to 2,768,823 (a decline of 7.7 percent). Across the same two decades, Cuyahoga County's population declined from 1,721,300 to 1,421,140 (17.4 percent); and the population of the city of Cleveland dropped by almost one-third from 1970 to 1990 (see Table 7–1). As Cleveland and Cuyahoga County considered a new home for the Cleveland Indians, the community was confronted with the very real possibility that its best days were behind it. Both the city and county were losing residents and becoming a smaller part of the region.

The shrinking of Cleveland has involved more than just a loss of population. Cleveland's residents are far less wealthy than they once were. While it is not surprising to find that as communities decline in population there is also a loss of wealth, as Cleveland's population shrank, its residents were becoming *far less wealthy*. Indeed, Cleveland had become a tale of two cities with a growing concentration of low-income households in a decaying center city surrounded by far wealthier suburban communities. In 1970, most households in Cleveland had incomes equal to between three-quarters and four-fifths of the income of residents of suburban communities. By 1990, most Cleveland households had incomes that were about one-half that of their suburban counterparts (see Table 7–2).

Indeed, the pattern common to most of America's metropolitan regions is that households in center cities have incomes that are lower than those of suburban residents. However, the rapidity with which this has changed and the magnitude of its shift has been quite dramatic in the Cleveland metropolitan region. From 1970 to 1980

TABLE 7–1
Population Changes in Metropolitan Cleveland, 1970 to 1990

Census Area	City/ County	1970 Pop.	1980 Pop.	% Chg. '70 to '80	1990 Pop.	% Chg. '70 to '90
	Cleveland	750,897	573,822	-23.6	505,616	-32.7
Akron PMSA	Portage	125,868	135,856	+7.9	142,585	+13.3
	Summit	553,371	524,472	-5.2	514,990	-6.9
Cleveland PMSA	Cuyahoga	1,720,835	1,498,400	-12.9	1,412,140	-17.9
	Geauga	62,977	74,474	+18.3	81,129	+28.8
	Lake	197,200	212,801	+7.6	215,499	+9.3
	Medina	82,717	113,150	+36.8	122,354	+47.9
Lorain-Elyria PMSA	Lorain	256,843	274,909	+7.0	271,126	+5.6
Region		3,000,276	2,834,062	-5.5	2,768,823	-7.7
Percentage Cleveland		25.0	20.3	-4.7	18.3	-6.7

Source: U.S. Bureau of the Census.

there was at least a 15 percent decline in the ratio of household incomes in the city of Cleveland to household incomes in *every* suburban community. The difference in income between the residents of some suburban communities and Cleveland's residents was more than 20 percent, and in one instance was nearly 30 percent. The trend continued from 1980 to 1990, creating a virtual two-world society with regard to income and wealth. By 1990, in two suburban communities, the average income of residents was twice that of the residents of the city of Cleveland, and every suburban community's residents had incomes that were at least 37 percent larger than those of Cleveland's residents. What had been the largest differential in income between residents of Cleveland and suburbanites in 1980 had become the smallest differential in wealth by 1990. Simply put, the residents of Cleveland are substantially poorer than the residents of suburban Cleveland. Cleveland is an example of an urban area that became, in a short period of twenty years, two cities or regions, one reasonably wealthy, one quite impoverished (see Tables 7–2 and 7–3).

Income is not the only factor that divides the residents of the Cleveland metropolitan region; metropolitan Cleveland is also a tale of two cities in terms of race. The region's African-American community is concentrated in the city and its adjacent suburbs while other suburbs are largely home to the region's ethnic white population. African-American migration to Cleveland began when there was a substantial need for workers in the growing smokestack economy of the late nineteenth and early twentieth centuries. As Cleveland's economy and factories boomed, migration from the southern states brought large numbers of African Americans to the city. While this community was devastated by the Depression, as the economy recovered, more African Americans were attracted to the city, and the African-American population had increased from 8,400 in 1910 to 84,000 in 1940 (Grabowski, 1992). Propelled by the postwar expansion, Cleveland's overall population swelled to more than 950,000, and the city and county regained its robust, smokestack reputation. The African-American population climbed to more than 147,000, accounting for approximately 16 percent of the city's population.

TABLE 7–2

Median Household Income of Cleveland Residents as a Percentage of the Median Household Income of Suburban Residents, 1970 to 1990

Census Area	City/ County	1970	1980	1990	Percentage Change 1970 to 1990
Akron PMSA	Portage	82.8	65.3	58.9	-23.9
	Summit	82.3	66.8	61.5	-20.8
Cleveland PMSA	Cuyahoga	80.4	68.2	62.3	-18.1
	Geauga	73.3	50.4	43.3	-30.0
	Lake	76.0	54.9	50.1	-25.9
	Medina	81.4	53.8	46.8	-34.6
Lorain-Elyria PMSA	Lorain	84.4	60.3	57.3	-27.1

Source: U.S. Bureau of the Census.

TABLE 7–3

Median Household Income of Cleveland Region Residents, 1970 to 1990

Census Area	City/ County	1970	1980	1990	Percentage Change 1970 to 1990
	Cleveland	$9,098	$12,277	$17,822	
Akron PMSA	Portage	$10,989	$18,788	$30,253	-23.9
	Summit	$11,057	$18,381	$28,996	-20.8
Cleveland PMSA	Cuyahoga	$11,309	$18,009	$28,595	-18.1
	Geauga	$12,411	$24,351	$41,113	-30.0
	Lake	$11,964	$22,369	$35,605	-25.9
	Medina	$11,178	$22,804	$38,083	-34.6
Lorain-Elyria PMSA	Lorain	$10,786	$20,371	$31,098	-27.1

Cleveland's minority community supported some of the Negro League's best baseball teams, which shared League Field with the Cleveland Indians. The existence of two baseball teams—one black, one white—mirrored the segregated structure of the city and life in Cleveland. The African-American community, however, was severely affected by the decline of Cleveland's economy. As factories moved to the Sun Belt and smokestack jobs were lost to other nations, unemployment in Cleveland began to increase. Cleveland began to be defined by joblessness, failing schools, deteriorating neighborhoods, and high levels of racial and economic segregation. These problems disproportionately affected the African-American community. It was perhaps not unreasonable to expect a violent reaction to the segregation and economic hopelessness that had become part of Cleveland's everyday life.

CONFLICTS AND CONFRONTATIONS

The seeds for a social explosion involving racial and income issues in Cleveland had been sown for more than half a century. Separation and isolation of a largely minority underclass created an explosive situation not unlike that found in many American cities. A riot began on July 18, 1966, during a summer of nationwide racial conflicts, and the Cleveland disturbance lasted for almost one week. The immediate cause of the riot was an inflammatory sign in the Hough section of inner Cleveland. When the police responded to a gathering of African Americans, violence erupted and continued as sections of the city were destroyed.

If there were any positive outcomes from this destruction it was the election, in 1967, of Carl Stokes as the first African-American mayor of a large U.S. city. The clear hope was that Stokes would forge a peaceful relationship between the city's racial groups (Swanstrom, 1985) and invigorate downtown development as well as economic expansion throughout the city. Political leaders understood that if the city's existing economic and social situation was left unchanged, the charged and destructive atmosphere of 1966 would do nothing but accelerate the cascading decline of Cleveland's economy and population base. Cleveland needed leadership and economic development to generate excitement and hope for the future. Unfortunately, neither leadership nor sustained economic development took place during the Stokes years.

Stokes, with the financial support of Cleveland's business establishment, did launch the "Cleveland: Now!!" campaign. However, this effort was unable to offset the long-standing problems and, in 1968, the city was again the site of severe racial riots. In 1971 Stokes decided not to seek reelection, and a division within the Democratic Party enabled Republican Ralph Perk to become mayor. Perk attempted to stabilize the city's deteriorating finances by eliminating city jobs and reducing the salaries of retained employees. Mayor Perk's efforts were not successful, and the city's debt actually increased. Mayor Perk also was a vocal supporter of several proposals for downtown redevelopment and supported subsidies to businesses if they would stay in downtown Cleveland. This perspective eventually cost him electoral support as neighborhood leaders in Cleveland began to question whether or not their communities would benefit from a redesigned and redeveloped downtown. There was widespread fear that the proposed downtown redevelopment effort would create more jobs for suburbanites and fail to address the problems plaguing inner-city Cleveland.

As Cleveland continued to decline economically, a series of plans for rebuilding downtown and other large-scale projects were proposed by various groups. The proposed initiatives included a new airport, a downtown people-mover, and a pedestrian mall. Some of these plans did little to dispel the fear that downtown development was being emphasized at the expense of redevelopment of neighborhoods. Proposals to build a downtown of corporate headquarters and shopping facilities at a time when numerous inner-city neighborhoods needed redevelopment of their own deteriorating infrastructure, better schools, and increased police protection did little to bridge any schisms in the community. With substantial conflict over the path for a new Cleveland, an advocate for neighborhood development, Dennis Kucinich, was elected mayor in 1977. However, the turbulent character of Cleveland politics did not dissipate during the Kucinich years; it escalated as the region's business interests and the new mayor seemed to be in a perpetual state of conflict.

An excellent history of the Kucinich years is contained in Swanstrom's *The Crisis of Growth Politics*. While Kucinich had held local offices before, he was still, at the time of his election as mayor, a relatively unknown personality and a political outsider in terms of relationships with the community's business leaders. Conflicts arose almost immediately with the business community over development issues; Cleveland's two daily newspapers became pointed critics, and the city eventually defaulted on loans rather than sell its municipally owned power plant. Kucinich survived a recall election in his second year in office, but his victory did nothing to quell the conflict. Furthermore, in the mayor's 1979 race he choose to use racial issues and politics as a cornerstone of his campaign. While race was not an unknown factor in Cleveland's politics, Mayor Kucinich's tactics seemed to underscore what was wrong with Cleveland, not what was possible (Swanstrom, 1985).

Each of these conflicts—racial segregation, job loss, identity problems, bitter local politics—became critical to the entire sports and downtown development effort in Cleveland. Dennis Kucinich's successor, strongly supported by Cleveland's business community, was committed to the identification of a redevelopment program that would minimize, if not avoid, the kind of tensions that had dominated Cleveland's local politics for more than two decades. George Voinovich, a Republican, was able to defeat Mayor Kucinich, a Democrat, in a city with a disproportionately Democratic voting base based on the sentiment that someone was needed who could bridge schisms and rebuild Cleveland.

With the support of the business community, Voinovich was able to reverse some of Cleveland's fortunes. The financial community of Cleveland that was so opposed to Mayor Kucinich now helped to design a plan to reverse the city's bankruptcy. Such a plan could have been developed with the Kucinich administration, but there was no common ground between the financial community and the mayor on which to develop such a plan. With the city's finances stabilized, Mayor Voinovich turned his attention to the "Flats." The Flats, the former site of numerous factories, had become a derelict and decaying portion of Cleveland located on the banks of the Cuyahoga River. During the Voinovich years the Flats became an upscale restaurant and entertainment area. Cleveland, whose Cuyahoga River had burned in 1969, establishing it and the city as the source of endless jokes, was now a center for restaurants and entertainment. The attention this and other projects received helped Cleveland become known as a comeback city. To be sure, however, this "comeback" did not include everyone.

The comeback did not stem the tide of unemployment or population losses; Swanstrom reported that the region lost 262,000 jobs between 1978 and 1982, and Mayor Voinovich conceded that in 1983 the downtown area alone had lost 15,000 jobs during his administration (Swanstrom, 1985, p. 248). Declines of this magnitude seemed to sustain the point that an even more concerted effort would be required to save Cleveland. With Indianapolis receiving considerable attention for its "sports strategy," perhaps sports could also help downtown Cleveland. Many of Cleveland's leaders made repeated trips to Indianapolis to understand what sports had accomplished for that city and to determine if a similar approach could not only "save" Cleveland's teams but generate additional jobs and downtown development. In an effort to find a development strategy that could attract support from the entire community and generate more economic activity in downtown Cleveland, the city's leadership launched the "Central Market Gateway Development" project. However, before we review the Gateway saga, let's return to the real "Mistake by the Lake" and Cleveland's history with professional sports teams.

CLEVELAND AND PROFESSIONAL SPORTS: THE MISTAKE BY THE LAKE AND ADVENTURES IN SUBURBIA

A negative image of Cleveland existed in the national media and in the national consciousness as a result of race riots and the state of race relations; the local political battles between neighborhoods, the mayor, and the city's corporate leadership; and the environmental problems of the Cuyahoga River. It became common to refer to the city of Cleveland by the nickname long assigned to Municipal Stadium, "the Mistake by the Lake." While Cleveland was never a mistake by the lake, its Municipal Stadium may well have richly deserved that nickname.

Municipal Stadium was built in 1931 as part of Cleveland's efforts to attract the 1932 Olympics. Seeking to build a stadium that could be a home for professional sports teams, the site for the opening and closing ceremonies for an Olympics, and the venue for the Olympic track and field events, the stadium was built as a giant circle or oval. It was also very large to both impress the International Olympic Committee and serve as a distinctive architectural statement for Cleveland. When completed, Municipal Stadium's seating capacity was 71,189, and in 1932 "it possessed the largest seating capacity of any outdoor arena in the world" (Grabowski, 1992, p. 48). While a facility this large was certainly an asset for any community's bid to host the Olympics, as a venue for baseball or football it left many fans distant from the action on the field. In addition, the new facility was located adjacent to Lake Erie and was susceptible to cold north winds. While this would not be much of a problem for the summer Olympic games, the winds from the lake created a damp and drafty atmosphere for baseball and football games played at other times of the year. The cold, and the distance from the field, underscored much of the public's sentiment that the building was a mistake. Built to satisfy many users, Municipal Stadium was a compromise that did not meet the needs of a football team, a baseball team, or the fans of either sport.

The Cleveland Indians as a team and business were also not particularly impressed with Municipal Stadium. When the facility was completed, the team did play its 1932, 1933, and 1934 seasons there. However, in 1935 the Indians returned to League Park, a nineteenth-century venue remodeled to seat 27,000 people in 1909. There were apparently two reasons for the move back to the smaller and older facility. First, Cleveland's fans, accustomed to the intimate confines of League Park, were not enamored of the world's largest outdoor stadium. The Indians, simply put, were not drawing crowds large enough to support the costs associated with the new park. Second, the team was playing poorly and there was some hope that returning to the old park might bring a return of the team's winning ways.

From 1935 through 1946 the team used League Park for most games, only playing holiday and Saturday games at the larger Municipal Stadium. An interesting footnote to the Indians' "two-home" policy was that Joe DiMaggio's fifty-six-game hitting streak reached its zenith on a Friday night at League Park. On the following Saturday night the streak ended at Municipal Stadium. Even Joltin' Joe was stopped by the Mistake by the Lake.

The Cleveland Indians became full-time residents of Municipal Stadium in 1947 when Bill Veeck took over ownership of the team. Veeck was able to attract larger crowds to Indians games through several promotions (including the first ever Ladies' Day) and, more important, the recruitment of star players from the Negro Leagues. Veeck recruited Minnie Minoso, Larry Doby, and Satchel Paige, and while these three stars helped the Indians to a pennant and World Series championship in 1948, the absence of the three key players from the Negro Leagues accelerated the collapse of that league.

When the Indians moved to Municipal Stadium, they were joined by the Cleveland Browns. These two teams continued to use the facility into the 1990s. By the 1980s, however, there were frequent requests from the Indians for a new stadium. Cleveland politics and the Indians' lackluster performance seemed to push the idea of a new stadium to the back burner. When the NBA's Cleveland Cavaliers moved to the suburbs, interest in a new home for the Cleveland Indians was renewed. But even that interest would have to wait at least ten years before a new stadium proposal was developed and funded.

Cleveland's NBA franchise began play in 1970 in the Cleveland Arena, an aging downtown facility. The team elected to build its own arena in the suburbs, and in 1974 the Cavs moved to Richfield Coliseum, an entertainment venue that hosted concerts, the circus, and the Cavs. The Cavs' move to a suburban location in the 1970s was part of a nationwide trend; many teams sought to follow their wealthier fans to the suburbs to avoid the conflicts and tensions that were dominating so many of America's urban centers. Richfield Coliseum also provided the Cavs and the struggling NBA with direct access to a larger market. Richfield is closer to Akron, so the team could draw fans from both Cleveland and the Akron-Canton metropolitan areas. Fans from both areas would now be able to attend games and events at a location closer to their homes.[4]

The move of the Cavs to the suburbs, as well as the relocation of one of the region's prime sites for hosting entertainment and regional recreation events, did little to dispel the view that Cleveland was becoming two cities, one black and one white. The move to the largely white suburbs underscored a sense that the region's future was not in the city of Cleveland, seemed to underscore the isolation of the two racial groups from each other, and helped create an environment that had an aging Municipal Stadium in the inner city and a new facility in the suburbs. What was new and good was (in) the suburbs; what was old and inadequate was (in) Cleveland.

SPORTS FOR IMAGE AND REDEVELOPMENT, CLEVELAND STYLE

Against this backdrop of a declining image, political conflict, and a shrinking economic and population base, planning for a new stadium for the Cleveland Indians began. The first proposal, in 1983, was to build a domed stadium in downtown Cleveland. A county-wide property tax was proposed to pay for the stadium, but this proposal was rejected by the voters in 1984. With numerous states passing laws and voter initiatives to limit or cap property taxes, selecting the property tax as the vehicle for financing a new stadium may have been a classic miscalculation. It should not have been a shock to learn that voters in Cuyahoga County did not want to increase their property taxes.[5]

The unpopular choice of a property tax to finance the new stadium was not the only factor that led to this proposal's defeat. Domed facilities are very expensive, and the cost might have exceeded the needs of the community and of the team. The proposal that was submitted to the voters was also poorly defined. The exact scope and placement of the facility was not specified. Indeed, the exact cost of the stadium was not known. There was also a lack of agreement among the community's leadership that a domed stadium, or any stadium for that matter, was needed. While in latter years there would be strong unity within the city's leadership for two new facilities, one for the Indians and one for the Cavaliers, in the early 1980s there was no such accord. Lastly, the Indians had played extremely poorly for a number of years and fan support had eroded. As a result, there was concern that fans just did not want to spend any more money for an unsuccessful franchise. Considering all these factors, the timing of the referendum and the formulation of the proposal could not have been more poorly planned.

When the domed stadium was presented to voters, it was also unclear if there was a viable threat that the team might move to another city if a new facility was not developed. Frequently, the threat of a move is seen by team owners as necessary to secure the public's participation in the building of the stadium. While the threat may not have been made in 1984 when the domed stadium proposal was on the ballot, the possibility that the team might leave Cleveland clearly became an issue after David and Richard Jacobs bought the team. The Jacobs brothers purchased the team from the estate of Steve O'Neill. Ironically, a condition of the sale was that the team remain in Cleveland and the Jacobses, with their substantial investments in the redevelopment of downtown Cleveland, seemed to be the ideal owners to respect this commitment. They were wealthy; Richard Jacobs's wealth made him one of the nation's four hundred richest people (Keating, 1995). His company was interested in developing a shopping center, office buildings, and a hotel in downtown Cleveland. While there may have not been a direct linkage between the purchase of the team and these other developments—the Jacobses did receive property tax abatements worth $225 million for their proposed developments—Richard Jacobs was adding the Cleveland Indians to a redevelopment effort in which his company played a very large role (Keating, Krumholz, & Metzger, 1989).

Although the Jacobs family seemed to be the ideal owners for a sports franchise—wealthy, long-term linkages to the area, and substantial real estate interests in downtown Cleveland—they clearly wanted a new stadium for the Indians in downtown Cleveland to complement their other investments. One factor that made Richard Jacobs a desirable owner from Cleveland's perspective—his economic commitments and interest in downtown Cleveland—also made him a strong advocate for a new downtown stadium to improve the value of his other holdings and investments.

It was apparent to all that the age and condition of Cleveland (née Municipal) Stadium together with its poor sight lines for baseball made it an unacceptable venue. That was readily apparent to the Indians in the 1930s. Add to this the fact that the Cleveland Indians were tenants in a facility managed, indirectly, by the Browns, and Mr. Jacobs faced an untenable situation. He also believed, as did many other baseball fans, that Cleveland Stadium was simply too big for baseball and left fans too removed from the field of play. Another problem created by the size of the facility plagued the Indians. With very few season ticket holders and a very large stadium, fans in Cleveland had grown accustomed to buying their tickets on the day of the game. However, this meant that the owners never knew how many people might actually attend. As a result, on some game days there were insufficient staff to handle the crowd, and this further alienated fans. On other game days there were too many staff, increasing the costs of operating the team.

The possibility that a new stadium might enhance the value of other real estate holdings coupled with the ability to threaten to leave if a new stadium with a favorable lease was not forthcoming placed the Indians' new owners in a very favorable position to argue for and demand a new stadium. A new stadium with luxury boxes and club seating would not only increase the value of downtown real estate but also give the team the potential for revenue levels that could not be generated in a fifty-year-old stadium designed for neither baseball nor football.

The city and the business community's interest in a new stadium was also tied to the need for a large development anchor on the southern edge of downtown. Cleveland needed an anchor for redevelopment to accomplish what the RCA Dome (née Hoosier Dome) and Market Square Arena had accomplished for Indianapolis: establish brackets or physical borders for the downtown redevelopment effort. Building a new baseball stadium would also serve to underscore the "comeback" image of Cleveland, an image that was receiving considerable attention and coverage in numerous magazines. If a stadium similar to Baltimore's Oriole Park at Camden Yards could be built, then the renaissance of downtown Cleveland could continue and the images of conflicts, race riots, burning rivers, mistakes by the lakes, and feuds between elected officials and the business community could be laid to rest. When the Gateway Project was proposed, the owners indicated the new stadium would secure Cleveland as the Indians' home.

THE GATEWAY PROJECT

Cleveland's big leap into financial support for professional sports was the Central Market Gateway Project (popularly known as the Gateway Project). Michael White was elected mayor in 1989, succeeding George Voinovich, who decided (in the spring of 1989) to seek the governorship of Ohio (and won in 1990). Mayor White joined several other elected officials and Richard Jacobs in supporting the building of two facilities, one for the Indians and an indoor arena that would attract the Cavaliers back from the suburbs. The Browns, playing before sellout crowds in Cleveland Stadium, were not interested in being part of the Gateway Project. (However, the design of the facility for the Indians would permit expansion to accommodate the football team. That option was never pursued, as Art Modell had other ideas in terms of a home stadium for his Browns.)

On March 21, 1990, the Cuyahoga County commissioners

approved a public/private partnership to develop the Central Market Gateway Project, an economic development zone that includes a new publicly owned stadium and arena. The 50/50 partnership included a $174 million commitment of private sector funds for the Gateway Project. To finance the public portion of the $344 million development, the Commissioners today placed an initiative on the

May 8 ballot seeking voter approval of a small excise tax on the purchase of alcoholic beverages and cigarettes (Cuyahoga County,
March 21, 1990).

It is important to note what was in the original documents prepared for the public vote because soon after the release of the press
announcement problems began to emerge in terms of the cost and
scope of the project. These problems are representative of some of
the issues or procedures that other communities should avoid when
"making the deal" for professional sports.

The $174 million in private funds was to come from several
sources (see Table 7–4). The press announcement from the Cuyahoga County commissioners indicated that the majority of the private funds, 56.9 percent, or $99 million, would come from the teams
or the sale of luxury boxes (loges) or club seats. Cleveland Tomorrow, a nonprofit organization supported by the city's leading businesses, was prepared to commit from $18 to $20 million, and $38.5
million in property loans was expected from banks. The loans
would be repaid by Gateway from income that the nonprofit corporation would earn from facility leases and other activities. The commissioners estimated that Gateway's earnings from interest would
be $16.5 million. The commissioners also declared that the facility
for the Indians would cost $128 million to build and that a facility
for the Cavs would cost $75 million. A total of $22 million was budgeted to secure the land for the sports facilities and another $36 to
$51 million was set aside to acquire other lands for continued devel-
opment. A budget line of $67.5 million for financing and working
capital was also included in the public announcement, and the
material circulated by the committee was designed to secure the
public's approval of a "sin tax" referendum, a tax on alcoholic beverages and cigarette and tobacco products.

EARLY UNCERTAINTIES

It did not take long for it to become apparent that potential problems existed with the financing plan endorsed by the County Com-

TABLE 7–4

The Original Financial Plan for the Gateway Project:
A Proposed Baseball Stadium and Arena for Basketball

Anticipated Costs

Stadium construction	$128 million
Arena construction	$75 million
Land acquisition	$22 million
Land for future development	$36 to $51 million
Financing and working capital	$67.5 million
Total Cost	$343.5 million

Anticipated Revenues

Income from luxury seats	$99 million
Cleveland tomorrow	$20 million
Property loans[1]	$38.5 million
Interest earnings	$16.5 million
Total private investment	$174 million
"Sin tax commitment[2]"	$169.5 million
Total Anticipated Revenue	$343.5 million

[1]Property loans were to be repaid by income earned by the Gateway Corporation.
[2]The "sin tax" revenues would be used to pay for the bonds sold to generate $169.5 million.

Source: Gateway To The Future Committee.

mission. On April 15, 1990, three weeks after the county commissioners issued their press release, it was reported that a lease with each of the teams was unlikely before the May 8, 1990, referendum on the sin tax. The individual responsible for negotiating the leases expected an agreement by election day (Kissling, 1990). As a result, it became widely known that the expected commitment of $99 million from the teams or the facilities (sale of luxury seating) was not something that either team had accepted. Not only was this investment by the teams unspecified but it was not even clear if both teams were coming to the new facilities. The Indians had indicated they would play in the new stadium, but the Cavs had yet to agree that they would leave Richfield Coliseum.

It was also clear that no one knew how much the two facilities would cost. No architectural plans had been approved or accepted by the public sector; nor had either team been asked what they would like to have in a facility. Prior to the election, then, it appeared no one knew what would be built, how much it would cost, and how much the teams had agreed to contribute to the total cost. Without signed leases it was even impossible to tell if the teams would play in the proposed facilities.

The lack of specificity continued into April. Three weeks before the election there were still no architectural drawings of the proposed facilities, and it became clear the cost estimates included in the Cuyahoga commissioners' announcement were based on average construction costs of facilities built elsewhere. What may have made the situation even more precarious was that the redevelopment corporation that was to oversee the operation of the facilities would not be formed until *after* the election. The last piece of uncertainty involved the failure to produce a redevelopment plan for the area. The city of Cleveland's planners had not even begun to propose a plan for the redevelopment of the land adjacent to the sports facilities, yet a targeted amount had been budgeted for this redevelopment. Predictions and projections of anticipated economic activity were being presented without anyone knowing what the redevelopment was to be. A vote was scheduled for May 8 for a substantial public investment in a public/private partnership for two facilities that had yet to be designed, and no agreement with the private partners had been established

Despite all of these uncertainties, the expectation that the combined cost for both facilities would be only slightly more than $200 million was underscored in the weeks preceding the election. On April 29, 1990, nine days before the referendum, the *Cleveland Plain Dealer* again reported that the new stadium for the Indians would cost $128 million and the new facility for the Cavs would cost $75 million (DeLater, April 29, 1990). The uncertainty about what the public's investment would be did not deter the owners of the Indians from threatening to leave the city if the public did not support the partnership and the sin tax. Mr. Jacobs claimed his fate was no longer in his hands but in the hands of voters (Larkin, 1990, p. 1D). If the voters rejected the proposal the team would leave Cleveland. Larkin, a columnist for the *Cleveland Plain Dealer,* noted after his interview with team owner Richard Jacobs: "Anyone who thinks the Indians will still be playing in the (Cleveland) Stadium at the end of the century is nuts. They'll either be in a new stadium here or a new stadium elsewhere. Period." No plans existed for the stadium, no leases specified the private sector's obligations, but threats by the Indians to leave Cleveland were being made and widely reported. Cleveland and Cuyahoga County voters were being asked to support a plan that had yet to be finalized, and if the voters did not accept this deal, the Indians' owner was making it clear that the team would leave Cleveland. The sin tax vote had become a tool in a classic sports war battle. If the public did not agree to build a facility on terms acceptable to the owner, the team would leave. It did not matter that no one knew what was to be built, how much it would cost, or what amount the teams would contribute. Vote yes or lose the Indians was the clear and distinct message.

The ownership of the Cleveland Cavaliers also entered the fray, copying the hardball sports wars tactics of the Indians. The Cavs' owners did not agree to play at the proposed arena until May 2, less than a week before the referendum. Polls showed the vote was going to be very close, and without a commitment from the Cavs it is likely the vote would have failed. Using these political currents, the Cavs' ownership negotiated a very favorable deal. In the announcement that the Cavs would play in the new arena it was also reported that they would provide $43.6 million "up front" for the project (DeLater, May 3, 1990). This was to be their share of the proposed $99 million from the teams and the sale of luxury seating. However, the money was not to be paid up front but over a period of thirty years, and, as was learned later, this money was contingent on numerous factors, but more on this later in the saga.

To increase the pressure on the voters, on the same day that it was reported that the Cavs would leave their suburban home for a downtown arena, MLB's commissioner Fay Vincent declared, "Should this facility [for the Indians] not be available in Cleveland, should the vote be a negative one, we may be finding ourselves confronting a subject that we want to avoid" (Becker & Mio, 1990). Furthermore, in comments before the Cleveland City Council, Vincent made it clear that the Indians satisfied three of the criteria MLB used when reviewing requests to move: (1) the team was losing money; (2) the team played in a poor facility; and (3) the Indians would have lost the community's support if the tax referendum was defeated. Ironically, the team's poor on-the-field performance for more than a decade was not one of the factors MLB considered when reviewing attendance levels and financial support for a team. The Cavs, the Indians, and MLB were playing with Cleveland and winning.

While there were no plans for the new facilities; no accurate cost estimates for the new facilities; and no lease agreements with either team, both the Indians and the Cavs contributed almost $300,000 to support the campaign for a "sin tax" to build the facilities. A total of $1 million was raised from a number of private interests to convince the public to support the tax for a new stadium, a new arena, and the redevelopment of land adjacent to the facilities (Keating, 1995).

CUYAHOGA COUNTY APPROVES THE "SIN TAX"

It's probably appropriate that a vote on the public financing of sports facilities went "right down to the wire," into "extra innings," or "overtime." That's not to suggest that a run-off election was needed, but the vote was extraordinarily close and proponents of the Gateway concept were not assured of victory until the very last votes were counted early in the morning of May 9, 1990. Approximately 383,000 votes were cast, and the measure supporting the sin tax passed with 51.7 percent of the vote. Ironically, within the city of Cleveland, the measure actually failed, as a majority of the voters in twenty of the city's twenty-one wards voted against the proposed tax. Within the city of Cleveland, 56 percent of the voters cast their ballots against the tax. In the suburban areas, 55 percent of the voters supported the tax plan. As more suburban residents voted, their support overcame the opposition from city residents.

The voting pattern in Cleveland was quite similar to the one that took place in Denver when that area considered a new tax for a baseball stadium (the new home of the Colorado Rockies). In Denver, voters who lived outside the city of Denver supported a tax for a new stadium while a majority of the voters in the city of Denver voted against the plan. Ironically, in both Denver and Cleveland, each city's mayor was a strong advocate for the new facilities, but neither could convince his own electorate to support his concept. In both areas suburban voters made the difference in terms of securing passage of the proposals for the public's support of sports facilities.

DEFINING "THE DEAL":
THE INDIANS GET A SHOWPLACE

Shortly after the passage of the sin tax the real business of developing a lease for each team and designing the new facilities began. With both teams' owners knowing that the stadium and arena would be built and that the public had already voted to supply tax dollars, there was a clear set of incentives for them to adopt very aggressive negotiating positions. The Indians already had the implied and tacit support of MLB to move if a satisfactory deal was not developed. The Cavs could always remain at Richfield Coliseum if they found the terms of the lease or the design of the proposed arena unacceptable. Both owners also had the region's political and corporate leadership in the uncomfortable position of having secured the public's support to build the facilities to retain and attract the teams. If either the Indians or Cavs now chose not to play at the new facilities, there would be considerable political embarrassment. Given all these factors, the owners of the Indians and Cavs were in a strong position to negotiate for a very favorable lease in a very profitable facility.

The Indians and Gateway agreed to lease terms on December 8, 1990, six months after the sin tax vote. At a press conference to describe the agreement, it was reported that Gateway would receive $12.5 million from the sale of premium seats for the development of the stadium (Stainer, 1990). However, when the lease was signed, the parties agreed that $20 million would be provided for the development of the baseball stadium (Gateway Economic Development Corporation, 1991a). While this was a substantial improvement from the figure originally suggested in December 1990, it still left Gateway with considerably less funds than was originally estimated. The campaign literature used during the sin tax election suggested that as much as $99 million would be forthcoming from the teams and the luxury seating sales. In addition to the $20 million from the luxury seating, the team also agreed to underwrite $2.9 million of the annual debt service. (This annual payment has a present value of $31 million, as that was the specific bond that the Indians agreed to repay. However, the "up-front" payment required from the Indians was $2.9 million.) An initial agreement with the Cavs had discussed an investment of $43 million spread across thirty years. Combined, these totals would be about two-thirds of what was initially anticipated and publicized.

The Indians also agreed to pay rent for use of the facility based on the number of fans who attended games; Table 7–5 describes the terms of the lease relative to required rental payments for different attendance levels. A large incentive provided to the team was that no rental payments would be required until at least 1,850,000 tickets had been sold.

Rental payments began after that with seventy-five cents paid to Gateway for the 400,000 tickets sold in excess of 1,850,000. The sliding scale led to payments of $1.25 per ticket if more than 2.5 million tickets were sold. If the team sold three million tickets Gateway would receive $1,175,000 in rental income. When the Indians sold virtually all of their tickets for the 1996 season, Gateway was guaranteed a payment of $1,718,000, as it was expected that 3,434,400 fans would attend Indians games in 1996. The amounts paid to Gateway were to be adjusted in the eleventh and sixteenth years of the twenty-year lease. The per-ticket fee or rental charge paid to Gateway would be adjusted by 40 percent of the average percentage increase in ticket prices from year 1 to year 11 and by a similar percentage reflecting increases in ticket prices between the eleventh and sixteenth years.

TABLE 7–5

Rental Charges for the Cleveland Indians' Use of Jacobs Field

Attendance Levels	Amount Paid to Gateway Per Ticket Sold	Total Paid if Three Million Tickets Sold
0 to 1,850,000	$0.00	$0.00
1,850,001 to 2,250,000	0.75 per ticket sold	300,000
2,250,001 to 2,500,000	1.00 per ticket sold	250,000
2,500,001 or more	1.25 per ticket sold	625,000

The lease negotiated by the Indians' ownership also contained other important incentives or monetary rewards. The team was given the right to use the facility for nonbaseball events (such as concerts and meetings), and a substantial portion of the profits from these events would be retained by the team. The owner was also given use of two private stadium suites and a couple of office complexes for the team; no rent or fee was to be paid for either of these facilities. Gateway also built, as part of the stadium, a restaurant for the team's owner and agreed to completely furnish the restaurant, all offices, and the suites given to the owners. Although the Indians' owner was not charged any rental fees for the restaurant and did not pay for any of the furnishings placed in the restaurant, he received all the income from the operation of the restaurant through his stadium management company. For all of these assets, then, the team paid $22.9 million (luxury seating and debt underwriting) and agreed to pay rent for use of the facility if more than 1,850,000 tickets were sold.

Maintaining the facility and paying for capital repairs involved the creation of another company, the Ballpark Management Company. This company, owned by Mr. Jacobs, was assigned responsibility for maintenance and repairs. However, as the manager of the ballpark, this company was permitted to retain *all* revenues from advertising and the sale of food and beverages. Gateway receives one-third of any new scoreboard advertising revenue in excess of $1.5 million (adjusted in later years relative to the consumer price index) and one-quarter of all net nonbaseball event revenue. Revenue from (1) all regular season games, (2) play-off games that are part of the American League's championship series, (3) any other postseason games, (4) all World Series games, and (5) any All-Star games played at the stadium belonged to the facility's management company. The team, then, and not Gateway, was responsible for maintaining the stadium, but as the sole operator of the facility, sharing very little of its income with Gateway, the team was well protected in assuming this responsibility. Indeed, the team stood to realize substantial profits through its operation of the stadium.

The stadium designed by Gateway and the Indians did not cost the $128 million indicated in the original announcements of the campaign literature used to convince voters to support the sin tax. The final cost of the stadium, as tabulated by Gateway, was $176 million, or $48 million more than the estimated cost. The corporation's final cost figure represents an increase of 37 percent in the construction costs from what was forecast during the campaign for the sin tax and when the county commissioners announced their support for the project.

YOU CAN GO HOME AGAIN IF THE MONEY IS RIGHT: THE COST OF BRINGING THE CAVS BACK TO CLEVELAND

In many ways the owners of the Cavs were in the best possible position to negotiate a very favorable lease with Gateway. First, the team owned its own arena in a suburban area that provided access to basketball fans from Cleveland, Cuyahoga County, and Akron. The team controlled all revenue sources at their arena, including parking. As there was no mass transportation to the facility, fans had to have private transportation to reach it. The team charged $6 to park a car at all events (during the last three years that the team played at the arena). With control over all revenues at the Richfield Coliseum, a substantial incentive package would be needed to attract the Cavs back to downtown Cleveland. Second, the Cavs owners were well aware of the incentives provided to the Indians. They would settle for nothing less.

What did the Cavs get in their lease? First, the team's owners received a restaurant to match one of the incentives provided to the Indians' owner. Second, the Cavs were also given the right to collect parking fees of $1.5 million before sharing any revenues with Gateway. After collecting $1.5 million in revenues the Cavs agreed to pay to Gateway 67 percent of the excess, subject to a set of conditions which could reduce the share given to Gateway. The ability to earn $1.5 million from parking was necessary to offset the parking revenues the owners were receiving at the Richfield Coliseum.

Third, the Cavs also agreed to pay "the sum of twenty-seven and one-half percent (27.5 percent) of the Executive Suite Revenue, and forty-eight percent (48 percent) of the Club Seat Revenue" (Gateway Economic Development Corporation, 1991b, p. 52). This money was not paid "up front" but in each of the thirty years of the lease.[6] As the Cavs' owners only committed funds from their anticipated sale of suites and club seats, there was little, if any, investment of their own money in the new arena. The Cavs were investing the money they were going to charge their fans. The Cavs also agreed to a rental schedule somewhat similar to the one used for the Indians. However, since it was highly unlikely that the attendance levels would ever reach the 1,850,000 threshold, the effective rental liability for the team was the payments from leasing luxury seating (see Table 7–6).

As with the lease with the Indians, Gateway was ultimately responsible for capital repairs, but the Cavs were responsible for routine maintenance. Gateway's responsibility for capital repairs was to be met through its financial contributions to the Arena Improvement Fund, which the Cavs access for repairs. A maintenance and repair agreement similar to the one developed for the Indians was also given to the Cavs. The company operating the facility was responsible for the repairs, but it also retained most of the revenue from the operation of the facility (advertising, profits from sale of food, beverages, and so on).

While it was originally thought the arena would cost $75 million, the actual cost was substantially higher. In May 1994 the estimated cost of the arena was placed at $130 million. This was an update on a previous estimate of $118 million, which, itself, was $43 million more than original proposal. In reporting the increase in cost to $130 million, Thomas V. Chema, executive director of the Gateway Economic Development Corporation, noted that the final cost

TABLE 7–6

Rental Charges for the Cleveland Cavaliers Use of Gund Arena

Attendance Levels	Amount Paid to Gateway Per Ticket Sold	Total Paid if Three Million Tickets Sold
0 to 1,850,000	$0.00	$0.00
1,850,001 to 2,500,000	$0.75 per ticket sold	$412,500
$2,500,001 or more	$1.00 per ticket sold	$499,999

would be "somewhat north of $130 million" (Kissling, 1994, p. 1). On December 15, 1994, the *Cleveland Plain Dealer* reported the total cost of the arena would be $148 million (Koff, 1994). Earlier in 1994 the Cuyahoga County auditor had estimated the arena was to cost $124,250,000, but additional cost overruns were found. With a $148 million price tag, the cost overrun was 97.3 percent of the original figure presented to voters by the Cuyahoga commissioners. If the auditor's estimate of $124,250,000 is used, the cost overrun is a more modest 65.7 percent.

WHAT DID THE GATEWAY PROJECT COST?

As recently as August 1995 there was still considerable debate over the actual cost of the Gateway project. The Cavs had already completed their first season in their new home and the Indians were in the middle of their second season and a successful run for the American League pennant, but the debates over what was spent continued. One source reported that the total cost of the Gateway project was approximately $462 million, or 34 percent more than the original forecast of $344 million (Bartimole, 1995a). In the spring of 1995 the Cuyahoga County auditor had already placed the cost of the project at $435 million, and that was before an additional $28 million in excess costs for Gund Arena had been included.

WHY DID THE GATEWAY PROJECT COST SO MUCH MORE THAN FIRST ANTICIPATED?

Why did the Gateway project cost so much more than anticipated? Several factors contributed to the large overruns. First, and of paramount importance, no designs, plans, or leases for the two facilities had been accepted and approved by the teams and the city of Cleveland and Cuyahoga County prior to the public vote on the sin tax to support the Gateway project. As a result, no one knew what the facilities were going to cost and how much revenue the teams were to contribute. Expectations were that the contributions from the teams would amount to almost $100 million and that the final cost would be a roughly even split between the public and private sector, but those were goals or aspirations as opposed to agreed-to principles or stipulations. When the sin tax was narrowly supported, the political leaders who had supported the measure were under a great deal of pressure to make sure the project took place and that both teams would agree to play at the new facilities. This created a very favorable bargaining position for the teams and a very weak bargaining position for the public sector. Both the Cavs and the Indians took advantage of this situation as the facilities were designed and leases were developed.

Second, in each of the documents developed by the city to secure the participation of the teams, especially those used prior to the sin tax vote, the phrases used to describe the planned facilities included such vague concepts as "state of the art" or "similar to facilities built in Baltimore [Oriole Park at Camden Yards] and Arlington, Texas [The Ballpark in Arlington]." Recent indoor arenas also mentioned as models for Gund Arena included facilities built or planned for Chicago (United Center) and Salt Lake City (Delta Center). In short, there were references to specific facilities but no proposals, plans, or contracts. Prior to the sin tax vote, no one knew what the facilities would cost and who would pay for what portions of the cost or be responsible for what proportion of any overruns. Indeed, voters were not even assured that there was a ceiling or "cap" of $344 million as the total cost of the project.

Third, part of the cost overruns has to be attributed to the inducements built in for both teams in their facilities. Luxury restaurants were added as inducements in each. Gateway completely furnished these restaurants and gave the team owners the right to operate the restaurants and retain all profits. This is a very profitable inducement, since all of the overhead normally associated with a restaurant was paid for by Gateway and given to the owners at no charge. The cost of the restaurant in Jacobs Field was placed at $5.1 million; the cost of the restaurant at Gund Arena was estimated to be $2.4 million (Bartimole, 1995b).

The inducements did not end with subsidized restaurants. The Gunds were given 30,000 square feet of office space within the arena;

the Jacobses received 57,500 square feet of office space in a building. Both sets of offices were fully equipped, but there is some uncertainty over who paid for the furnishings. One respected critic of the Gateway project is confident the public sector absorbed these expenses. "The office of the Gund brothers cost $1,443,800 to furnish; the Jacobs's office building had some $900,000 in furnishings and cost $6 million plus to construct" (Bartimole, 1995b, p. 2). A Gateway official contends that Mr. Jacobs paid for his office and that the Gund brothers paid for a $330,000 upgrade to their office complex. However, both owners did receive luxury boxes in their respective facilities, at no cost, and they are free to entertain guests for all events in these suites (Bartimole, 1995b).

HOW MUCH DID THE TEAMS PAY FOR GATEWAY?

One of the advertisements used by the Gateway to the Future Committee to secure passage of the sin tax featured a sports fan with the caption:

> I said: Let the team owners and big shots pay. Then I found out they are paying. Big time. $174 million up front and all the costs to run it once it's done. If they finally got the big boys to put up their millions here's my two cents. I'm voting YES on Issue 2 [sin tax].

The advertisement went on to note "Big Corporations and sports teams will pay $174 million for Gateway. That's half of the cost, but the public will own and control the whole project. The tenants, not the public, will pay ALL the operating costs." In addition, the ad noted,

What will the public pay?
No property tax
No sales tax
No tax abatement
Just a few pennies on alcohol and cigarettes

The ad also noted that "Cleveland's Mayor White, Ohio's Governor Celeste, Congressman Feighan, County Commissioners Boyle, Brown, and Hagan, the Cuyahoga County Mayors and Managers Association, and Cleveland Council President Westbrook all back Gateway as the next step in a bright future for all of Greater Cleveland."

Truth in advertising? Well, in the absence of leases and designs for the facilities a number of commitments were made. What happened when the contracts, agreements, and plans were finally developed? Unfortunately for taxpayers, several things changed. First, as already noted the project cost considerably more than the original forecast of $344 million. Second, it is true that the public sector is not responsible for either operating or maintaining the facilities. Yet, both owners will receive virtually all profits from the operation of the facilities, and this will yield more than sufficient funds to maintain the facilities. Third, in terms of "up-front money," Gateway did receive $20 million from the sale of luxury seating at Jacobs Field, and the team also assumed $2.9 million of the stadium's debt. The initial investment by the Indians, then, was $22.9 million.

To calculate what the teams paid, I performed an analysis of their commitments in terms of the leases that were eventually signed. Let's start with the Indians. The baseball team made two up-front commitments: $20 million from the sale of luxury suites and the assumption of $31 million in debt. There was then an up-front investment from the Indians of $20.0 million for the project and a commitment to invest $51 million in the facility. In their first year at Jacobs Field the Indians drew 1,995,174 fans in the strike-shortened season. For the 1996 season, every ticket was sold. This meant 3,434,000 fans attended Indians games. (Gateway receives its payment even if there are fans who do not attend the game. Gateway's revenues are based on tickets sold, not the actual attendance.) I assumed the team would attract at least three million fans in each subsequent season for the balance of their twenty-year lease.

With these attendance levels, the Indians would pay $12,501,586 to Gateway in rental fees. (The $12.5 million payment is the present value of the annual rental payments using a discount rate of 8.75 percent for all years after 1995. An adjustment was made in the eleventh and sixteenth years to reflect the potential for higher rents due Gateway as specified in the lease. The discount rate selected was based on the prime rate in effect in 1995.) The total commitment of the Cleveland Indians to Gateway, then, could be as high as $63,501,586 (rental charges, bond payments, and up-front payments), but this total is dependent on an annual attendance level of three million. If attendance declines in any year, the rental fees collected by Gateway would be less. These calculations are summarized in Table 7–7. The lease signed by the Indians was for twenty years, although Gateway had wanted a thirty-year agreement. The team did indicate that it too was interested in a thirty-year agreement, but legal obstacles prohibited an agreement for more than twenty years. Thirty-year totals are also contained in Table 7–7.

I also performed a similar present value analysis of the payments the Cleveland Cavaliers will make to Gateway. The results of this analysis are contained in Table 7–8. It is unlikely that attendance at Gund Arena would be high enough to trigger the rental charges specified in Table 7–6. The rental income Gateway will receive from the Cavs will be related to the sale of luxury suites and club seats. For the team's inaugural season, eighty-eight suites were sold, generating $10.5 million in revenue. Gateway was to receive $2,887,500 from this sale, less any of the agreed deductions. A total of 1,930 full-season club seat packages were also sold for the inaugural season, as were thirty partial-season seats. It is estimated that these sales produced $6,079,500 for the team, and the share due Gateway was $2,918,160 less any agreed-to deductions. In the first year, according to documents filed with Gateway by the Cavs and agreed to by both parties, the deductions permitted were equal to the payments due in the team's first season. As a result, Gateway received *no rental income* from the Cavs in the team's first year at Gund Arena. An official conceded to me that they did not expect to receive any revenues from the Cavs "in the first few years" that the team played in Gund Arena. The ongoing negotiations with regard to the cost overruns could also mean the team will increase its overall investment. These uncertainties make it difficult to produce a firm estimate of what the Cavs will spend or contribute for the development of Gund Arena. The "high-end" and "low-end" estimates are provided in Table 7–8.

If the Cavs received the same level of income in each year of their lease as they did in the first year from the sale of suites and club seats, their maximum obligation to Gateway would be $66,39,733 (in present value terms). As already noted, no payment was required for the 1994–95 season, so the "high-end" estimate of rental payments by the Cavs is $60,524,073. If Gateway were not to receive any

TABLE 7–7
The Estimated Payments of the Cleveland Indians to Gateway

Year	Attendance	Total Paid to Gateway	Present Value
1994	1,995,174	$ 108,881	$ 108,881
1995	3,000,000	1,175,000	1,175,000
1996	3,434,400	1,718,000	1,579,770
1997	3,000,000	1,175,000	993,526
1998	3,000,000	1,175,000	913,587
1999	3,000,000	1,175,000	840,080
2000	3,000,000	1,175,000	772,488
2001	3,000,000	1,175,000	710,333
2002	3,000,000	1,175,000	653,180
2003	3,000,000	1,175,000	600,625
2004	3,000,000	1,175,000	552,299
2005	3,000,000	1,233,750	533,254
2006	3,000,000	1,233,750	490,349
2007	3,000,000	1,233,750	450,896
2008	3,000,000	1,233,750	414,617
2009	3,000,000	1,233,750	381,257
2010	3,000,000	1,233,750	350,581
2011	3,000,000	1,295,438	338,492
2012	3,000,000	1,360,209	326,820
2013	3,000,000	1,428,220	315,550
2014	3,000,000	1,499,631	304,669
2015	3,000,000	1,574,612	294,163
2016	3,000,000	1,653,343	284,020
2017	3,000,000	1,736,010	274,226
2018	3,000,000	1,822,811	264,770
2019	3,000,000	1,913,951	255,640
2020	3,000,000	2,009,649	246,825
2021	3,000,000	2,110,131	238,313
2022	3,000,000	2,215,638	230,096
2023	3,000,000	2,326,420	222,161
2024	3,000,000	2,442,741	214,501
30-year lease total (percent value)			$15,222,088
20-year lease total (percent value)			$12,501,586
Suite payment			20,000,000
Bond assumption			31,000,000
20-year total			$63,501,586

income for additional years— suppose a worst-case scenario of four years—a low-end estimate of the revenue or rental income that Gateway would receive would be $41.6 million (see Table 7–8).

If the "best-case" figure is added to the high-end estimate of the payments to be received from the Indians, both teams would pay $95,426,348 for the facilities (in present value terms). This figure is certainly reasonably close to the initial estimate of $99 million pub-

TABLE 7–8

Estimated Payments of the Cleveland Cavaliers to Gateway

Year	Suite Sales	Gateway Share	Club Seat Sales	Gateway Share	Total Paid to Gateway	Present Value
1995	$10,500,000	$2,887500	$6,079,500	$2,918,160	$5,805,660	$5,805,660
1996	10,500,000	2,887500	6,079,500	2,918,160	5,805,660	5,338,538
1997	10,500,000	2,887500	6,079,500	2,918,160	5,805,660	4,909,000
1998	10,500,000	2,887500	6,079,500	2,918,160	5,805,660	4,514,023
1999	10,500,000	2,887500	6,079,500	2,918,160	5,805,660	4,150,826
2000	10,500,000	2,887500	6,079,500	2,918,160	5,805,660	3,816,852
2001	10,500,000	2,887500	6,079,500	2,918,160	5,805,660	3,509,749
2002	10,500,000	2,887500	6,079,500	2,918,160	5,805,660	3,227,355
2003	10,500,000	2,887500	6,079,500	2,918,160	5,805,660	2,967,683
2004	10,500,000	2,887500	6,079,500	2,918,160	5,805,660	2,728,904
2005	10,500,000	2,887500	6,079,500	2,918,160	5,805,660	2,509,337
2006	10,500,000	2,887500	6,079,500	2,918,160	5,805,660	2,307,436
2007	10,500,000	2,887500	6,079,500	2,918,160	5,805,660	2,121,780
2008	10,500,000	2,887500	6,079,500	2,918,160	5,805,660	1,951,062
2009	10,500,000	2,887500	6,079,500	2,918,160	5,805,660	1,794,080
2010	10,500,000	2,887500	6,079,500	2,918,160	5,805,660	1,649,729
2011	10,500,000	2,887500	6,079,500	2,918,160	5,805,660	1,516,992
2012	10,500,000	2,887500	6,079,500	2,918,160	5,805,660	1,394,935
2013	10,500,000	2,887500	6,079,500	2,918,160	5,805,660	1,282,699
2014	10,500,000	2,887500	6,079,500	2,918,160	5,805,660	1,179,493
2015	10,500,000	2,887500	6,079,500	2,918,160	5,805,660	1,084,592
2016	10,500,000	2,887500	6,079,500	2,918,160	5,805,660	997,326
2017	10,500,000	2,887500	6,079,500	2,918,160	5,805,660	917,081
2018	10,500,000	2,887500	6,079,500	2,918,160	5,805,660	843,293
2019	10,500,000	2,887500	6,079,500	2,918,160	5,805,660	775,442
2020	10,500,000	2,887500	6,079,500	2,918,160	5,805,660	713,050
2021	10,500,000	2,887500	6,079,500	2,918,160	5,805,660	655,678
2022	10,500,000	2,887500	6,079,500	2,918,160	5,805,660	602,922
2023	10,500,000	2,887500	6,079,500	2,918,160	5,805,660	554,411
2024	10,500,000	2,887500	6,079,500	2,918,160	5,805,660	509,804

Lease total		$66,329,733
"Worst-case" total		$41,611,685
"Best-case" total		$60,524,073

licized during the sin tax election. If the worst-case scenario is used, the total payments by the teams to Gateway would be $76,513,960, or 77.3 percent of the anticipated amount.

Whether one uses the best- or worst-case scenario to arrive at these projections, several assumptions built into these numbers should be remembered. First, the Indians must continue to attract three million fans each season and the popularity of the Cavs and NBA basketball must be sufficient to sell the number of suites and club seats sold in Gund Arena's initial year. The Indians exceeded the three million total in their pennant-winning season of 1995, and that does provide Gateway with some protection against attendance declines in future years. Maintaining an average of three million fans for twenty years is a feat unattained by any other MLB baseball team. As such the revenues projected for the Indians and their contributions to Gateway are a "high-level" estimate.

The popularity of the Cavs and NBA basketball must also continue for thirty years at the levels that supported first-year luxury seat sales of $10.5 million. The league's popularity levels have never been sustained for thirty years, so there is some risk involved with this projection. Revenues from the Cavs could be less than Table 7–8 projects. Second, to fulfill the best-case scenario, the allowances subtracted from the payment expected in the Cavs' first season must not continue. If the official I interviewed was correct, and the reductions will continue for the first few years, the payments from the Cavs might be closer to the worst-case scenario.

WHITHER GOES THE PUBLIC/PRIVATE PARTNERSHIP? WHAT DID EACH SECTOR PAY FOR GATEWAY?

The Gateway concept was presented to the voters as a public/private partnership with as much as $174 million coming from the private sector. The teams themselves invested between $76.5 and $95.4 million. There were also other private-sector contributions, which are detailed in Table 7–9.

There appear to have been five other sources of private-sector funds for the Gateway project. First, Gateway sold the naming rights for both the baseball stadium and the arena. Many cities have renamed facilities in exchange for an advertising fee. Both families that own the teams purchased the right to name the facilities for $400,000 for the years 1994 through 2003. From 2004 through 2013, the fee increases to $986,930. It should be noted that these fees are well below those that other cities have been able to negotiate from firms that want to advertise their name as part of a sports venue. Nevertheless, when combined (the payment for Gund Arena and the payment for Jacobs Field), Gateway will receive $800,000 each year from 1994 through 2003 and $1,973,860 from 2004 through 2013. The present value of these payments is $11,665,700.

TABLE 7–9
Other Private-Sector Contributions to Gateway

Year	Naming Rights		Parking Fees	
	Annual Fees	Present Value	Annual Fees	Present Value
1994	$ 800,000	$ 800,000	$ 1,200,000	$ 1,200,000
1995	800,000	735,632	1,200,000	1,103,448
1996	800,000	676,443	1,200,000	1,014,665
1997	800,000	622,017	1,200,000	933,025
1998	800,000	571,970	1,200,000	857,954
1999	800,000	525,949	1,200,000	788,924
2000	800,000	483,631	1,200,000	725,447
2001	800,000	444,718	1,200,000	667,078
2002	800,000	408,936	1,200,000	613,405
2003	800,000	376,034	1,200,000	564,050
2004	1,973,860	853,147	1,200,000	518,667
2005	1,973,860	784,503	1,200,000	476,935
2006	1,973,860	721,382	1,200,000	438,561
2007	1,973,860	663,340	1,200,000	403,275
2008	1,973,860	609,967	1,200,000	370,827
2009	1,973,860	560,890	1,200,000	340,990
2010	1,973,860	515,761	1,200,000	313,554
2011	1,973,860	474,263	1,200,000	288,326
2012	1,973,860	436,103	1,200,000	265,127
2013	1,973,860	401,015	1,200,000	243,795
Total		$ 11,665,700		$ 12,128,055

Other Private-Sector Contributions	
Source	Amount
Cleveland Tomorrow	$28,000,000
Interest income	9,300,000
Foundation	2,000,000
Total	$39,300,000

The Cuyahoga County auditor's office also expected Gateway to be able to earn $1.2 million per year in parking revenues; the present value of these payments from 1994 through 2013 is $12,128,055. The Cleveland Tomorrow nonprofit organization (foundation) and one other foundation contributed a total of $30 million to the Gateway project, and interest income earned by Gateway was estimated by the county auditor's office to be $9.3 million. When all these private-sector investments are added together, the private sector's investment totals $63,093,755.

This $63.1 million has to be added to the investments by the teams themselves to arrive at the total private-sector share. The investment by the teams can range from $105.1 million to $129.8. This brings the entire private-sector investment to between $168.2 million and $192.9 million. The original campaign material prepared for the sin tax election indicated that the "big boys" were going to pay $174 million in up-front money. While that did not occur, the *present value* of the twenty-year investment by the private sector will, at a minimum, reach $168 million and could exceed the anticipated $174 million in up-front dollars.

To estimate each sector's share of the total cost of Gateway, I used the total cost figure of $462 million for the project, the latest figure cited by Cleveland's news media when this chapter was written. Using that figure, and, if Gateway does receive the maximum payments from the teams, the public sector will be responsible for at least 58 percent of the cost of the project and perhaps as much as 64 percent. This level of the public sector's responsibility *assumes* attendance levels for the Indians will remain at three million tickets sold per year and that the popularity of the NBA and the Cavs does not wane. In other words, I expect the same number of club seats and suites to be sold for thirty years.

In reviewing these percentages, readers are reminded that they do not include interest charges for the bonds sold. I only tabulated the present value of the revenue streams anticipated from the teams and divided all private-sector revenue contributions by the total construction cost for the Gateway project. If the interest on the bonds were also included, the public sector's share of the cost for the project would be *much higher*. The information provided, however, clearly indicates that the private sector's contribution never amounted to as much as voters and the county commissioners were promised. It is also highly unlikely that public/private partnership will amount to the fifty-fifty split or equal partnership that was initially discussed. Private-sector money was invested in the project, but not only was more public-sector money invested, but the public sector's responsibilities could increase if the popularity of either team declines. In this manner, then, the public sector's investment is related to the popularity of sports, but the returns on the popularity of teams—the increased value of the teams themselves and the profits earned by the owners—are not shared with the public sector.

GATEWAY, REBUILDING CLEVELAND'S IMAGE, AND SPORTS WARS: BENEFITS AND LESSONS LEARNED

What did Cleveland "get" for its investment in sports? Elsewhere in this book we'll discuss the value of some of the intangible and image benefits, and Cleveland's image in the national press has been elevated. It is no longer a city with a burning river, racial riots, a depressed and decaying downtown, and conflict between its political and economic leadership. Cleveland is seen as a "winner" with a downtown area that attracts residents, people from across the region, and tourists. Cleveland is now attracting more than five million people to its downtown areas for baseball and basketball games and other forms of entertainment. These five million people who attend events are coming to a downtown that just one decade ago was avoided. In the vicinity of the Gateway complex, more than twenty new restaurants have opened and a new hotel and other building projects have been initiated. The city's Playhouse Square complements the entertainment provided at the Gateway complex, and the Rock 'n' Roll Hall of Fame has also added luster to Cleveland's renaissance. What did it cost to build the attractions that bring people to downtown Cleveland? The public investment, not counting interest and the incentive package that will be provided to some football team, was more than $320 million. Is that worth what Cleveland received?

While that is a question for the people of Cuyahoga County to answer, there are some points to remember. What's the value of bringing people to downtown? If a trip downtown underscores the vitality and potential that exists for and in American cities, is an investment of $320 million excessive to permit people to see and participate in that vitality and the excitement of urban life? Likewise, if an investment of this sort creates an atmosphere in which there is some degree of mixing between racial groups, is that worth the investment, given the racial polarization that exists in Cleveland and throughout American society? These are the questions that have to be answered by voters and leaders when they consider whether or not a sports investment is worth the commitments made. And these benefits should not be considered trivial and inconsequential. In a similar vein, however, $320 million in public funds to create twenty or so restaurants, a hotel, and even an office building cannot be considered an example of extensive urban redevelopment. Gateway did not create hundreds of jobs or address the poverty, unemployment, and infrastructure issues that plague Cleveland's inner-city neighborhoods

Beyond the conclusions that two facilities were built, that five million people now come to downtown Cleveland, and that the team owners received very lucrative inducements, the Gateway saga identifies several lessons every community should learn before participating in a sports war or before using sports for development. First, before any election is held, define what it is that is to be built and have a set of agreements specifying who is responsible for what. The Gateway plans did not exist before the election to vote on the sin tax, and there were no firm agreements concerning who would pay for what. There were no leases for the facilities, and the commitments made to the public were virtually meaningless. As a result, the redevelopment funds were quickly swallowed in cost overruns for the facilities, and the private sector's share never amounted to what was anticipated. As the cost for the facilities escalated—in part because the owners of both teams had very favorable bargaining positions—the public's share of the investment increased. A fifty-fifty partnership quickly became something quite different. And if the teams do not remain as popular as they currently are, the public's portion of the partnership will only increase. The Gateway deal established a cap for the private-sector investment, but no such protection existed for the public sector.

Second, if the facilities are to be part of a redevelopment effort, a plan for that redesign should exist. Indianapolis's sports and downtown development strategy had such a plan. For better or worse, the Indianapolis plan, initiated in 1974, was completed in 1995, and voters, the public sector, and the private sector can "see" what was accomplished and determine if the benefits were worth the commitments. No such plan existed when Cuyahoga County's voters were asked to vote for the sin tax, and while efforts of other groups before and since left some with a view that a plan existed or exists, that perspective is not agreed to by all. As already noted, sports themselves are too small a component of any community's economy to sustain or create economic growth. But as part of an overall strategy sports facilities can potentially contribute to economic growth. If no plan exists or if there is not widespread support for the plan, there will be little or no real economic growth.

The Gateway saga also begs a third question or lesson for cities engaging in a sports war with professional teams. Could a better deal have been negotiated? Hindsight is always more accurate. It is also a luxury to be able to second-guess decision makers who may not be able to analyze options when teams threaten to move and elected officials demand signed contracts that mean teams do not leave town during their administration. Even with these caveats, some things can still be learned from the Gateway experience.

The Richfield Coliseum was built in 1974 and lacked many of the revenue-generating amenities of more modern arenas. The Gund family would have eventually needed those amenities to survive and to keep the team competitive, given the changes in basketball economics. What were those amenities that they would have desired?

Extensive luxury suites and club seating. Who buys most of these suites and club seats? Business firms, and the Gateway complex could have offered something to the Gunds they could not get in suburban Ohio: a downtown location near those firms and business executives who buy premium seats and a downtown location with mass transportation access to the suburbs. Assets of this nature create an attractive venue for an arena, as business executives can either return to their cars parked in downtown lots after a game or take the train to the suburbs. Further, their families can take the train downtown and ride home in the car Dad or Mom conveniently parked in a downtown facility when they commuted to work. These locational advantages and the need of all NBA owners to earn as much revenue as they can from facility operations would have eventually forced the Gunds to downtown Cleveland. Remember, NBA teams do not share arena revenues or gate (admission) revenues, and Cleveland does not have a media size that permits it to match the revenue potential of the New York Knicks, the Detroit Pistons, or the Los Angeles Lakers. As a result, the Gunds needed to generate more money from their arena than they could from Richfield Coliseum. The Gunds needed a downtown location as much as Cleveland needed the Gunds downtown. Cleveland and Gateway could have afforded to wait for the Gunds to realize that their existing arena no longer gave them the revenue potential a new downtown facility could generate. At that time a more favorable lease might have been possible.

Would Cleveland have risked losing the Cavs to another market? After all, they did lose the Browns. If Cleveland did not give the Cavs everything they wanted, why wouldn't the team have moved to Nashville or some other city willing to build them an arena? How many cities without NBA teams have as many *Fortune* 500 firms and other businesses that can afford to buy luxury suites and club seats? Not sure of that answer? Before negotiating with any professional sports team, before you submit a referendum to the public, be sure of the assets you have that teams need to survive and owners need to realize a profit. Cleveland's position might have been far stronger than it imagined, as the city is home to several *Fortune* 500 firms and numerous firms critical to the economy of the Midwest.

It is also hard not to criticize aspects of the negotiations with the Indians. The potential existed for substantial gains for the Jacobs family from the continued successful redevelopment of downtown Cleveland. Corporations involving the Jacobs family own substantial tracts of land in downtown Cleveland. If Gateway is successful, the value of those assets will increase. Put another way, what was it worth to the corporations and the Jacobs family to have the Gateway project developed? Before Gateway and the city of Cleveland initiated or completed its negotiations with Mr. Jacobs, it would have been valuable to predict or model the anticipated gains in real estate values he would realize from the presence of the new stadium. The individuals who supported the Gateway concept were eager to point out the anticipated economic benefits for the region. A similar analysis was needed to understand how much all existing landowners and developers would gain from the anticipated renaissance in downtown Cleveland. If those gains were estimated and known to Gateway and the city of Cleveland, a different lease arrangement with the Indians might have been possible. Perhaps a portion of the incremental growth in real estate values could have been pledged to pay for the cost of Jacobs Field and for Gund Arena.

Cities must understand all of the potential economic changes a sports facility can cause and who is likely to benefit from increased property values. With those data in hand, the public's representatives might be able to secure a very different lease or contract from team owners, especially if substantial real estate gains are possible. When you enter into a sports war to retain or attract a team, be sure you understand all the revenue gains that can accrue to a team's owner.

Cleveland has its Gateway complex and long-term commitment from the Indians and the Cavs to stay in Cleveland. The Indians are bound to the city for at least twenty years. The Cavs' lease is for thirty years. These are impressive and valuable commitments in a time when teams are moving from city to city with increasing regularity. Yet, important lessons from Cleveland's experience should be remembered, and mistakes were made that should not be repeated. All communities, including Cleveland, can benefit from this case study.

1. Never Buy a "Pig in a Poke." No community should ever vote for a plan or facility that does not exist. This almost sounds too simple or obvious, yet Cuyahoga County's voters were asked to support two facilities and a complex financing scheme when plans and models did not exist and when no one had agreed to the private sector's share of the expense. Cleveland bought a beautiful "pig in a poke." Both Jacobs Field and Gund Arena are impressive and beautiful structures. But with no firm prices or contracts, and no leases or firm private-sector commitments, the public sector was asked for a blank check that cost the community millions more than anyone ever wanted to spend. Don't repeat this error. When you begin your encounter with professional sports teams, know what you are buying, what it will cost, and who will pay for what.

2. Always Know What's in the Deal for All Sides. When all firms negotiate with cities and states for economic incentives or choose a new location from among competing venues, their staff or managers know what the anticipated benefits and liabilities are for each site. Firms know where their profits will be maximized and their costs minimized. They can then balance these gains against intangible factors such as the quality of life. It is imperative for communities to know the assets and benefits they can create or generate for businesses and sports teams when they begin negotiations. Cleveland's failure to do this in terms of the economic gains Mr. Jacobs might realize from the development of Gateway might have led the city to overestimate the need to provide incentives. Similarly, the financing of professional basketball had changed so dramatically since the Richfield Coliseum was built in 1974 that the Gunds would have needed either a new building or to have substantially remodeled the Coliseum. Furthermore, a remodeled Richfield Coliseum would not have brought the facility any closer to the market that NBA teams must have to sell luxury seating: corporations and individuals who can afford luxury suites and club seats. That market is in many of America's downtown areas, and Gateway controlled that access. Perhaps fewer incentives were needed to bring the Gunds back to Cleveland. The changing market conditions in the NBA might have been Gateway's and Cleveland's strongest undervalued asset.

To maximize the value of that asset, however, Gateway and Cleveland would have had to perform market analyses indicating the likely sale of luxury and club seats. Market information of that type is critical to every negotiation, and cities that enter sports wars have to commit themselves to know their market and its assets and liabilities at least as well as teams and other private firms know their markets and the benefits and liabilities of each venue they are reviewing as a possible site.

3. *Plan Your Work and Work Your Plan.* While different groups in Cleveland clearly thought a plan for the redevelopment of downtown and for the Gateway area existed, others did not. The *Cleveland Plain Dealer* reported that prior to the sin tax vote the city's planners had not formed a redevelopment plan or program, but that $30 to $50 million was committed for redevelopment. As demonstrated earlier, sports are too small a portion of any economy to cause economic development. Sports can contribute to development, but that development has to be planned. Before committing the public to investments of hundreds of millions of dollars, have a plan, and plan to follow it.

8

Reviving the Glory of Days Past

St. Louis's Blitz to Save
Its Image, Identity, and Teams

Why do the deal for the Rams? Because some people around the nation think St. Louis's best days are behind us. We needed to do something dramatic.
——Sen. Thomas Eagleton, June 1995

ST. LOUIS'S RECENT HISTORY has themes that are strikingly similar to the issues that have confronted older cities across the United States: a declining population base, a declining economic base, an increasing separation of the races with minorities concentrated in the central city and whites fleeing to the suburbs, urban unrest, declining public school achievement levels, and the bankruptcy of a leading and highly visible employer (Trans World Airlines). In 1960, the residents of the city of St. Louis accounted for 51.6 percent of the population of St. Louis County and more than one-third of the residents of the St. Louis metropolitan region. By 1970 the city's residents accounted for one-quarter of the metropolitan region, and by 1990 the city's residents were just 16.2 percent of the region's population. Table 8–1 illustrates not only the shrinking proportion of St. Louis City's population as a component of the region, but the sheer number of people who had left the community. In 1960 the city had three-quarters of a million residents; the 1996 population estimate indicates the city has lost more than half of its 1960 population base.

The increasing concentration of the nonwhite population inside the shrinking city of St. Louis is illustrated in Table 8–2. In 1960, slightly more than one-quarter of the city of St. Louis's population was classified as nonwhite; by 1990, virtually half of the city's population was classified as nonwhite. In the metropolitan region, the nonwhite population increased less than 5 percentage points during the thirty-year period from 1960 to 1990 (see Table 8–2).

TABLE 8–1

The City of St. Louis's Population and Its Percentage of All Residents of Missouri, St. Louis County, and the St. Louis Metropolitan Area

(Percentages Refer to the City of St. Louis's Population as a Proportion of the State, County, and Metropolitan Area)

Area	1960	1970	1980	1990	1996
Missouri	4,319,813	4,676,501	4,916,766	5,190,719	5,306,000
	17.4%	13.3%	9.2%	7.6%	6.9%
City	750,026	622,236	453,085	396,685	366,000
County	703,532	951,353	973,896	993,529	1,005,200
	51.6%	39.5%	31.8%	28.5%	26.7%
Metro area	2,161,228	2,429,246	2,377,043	2,444,099	2,552,400
	34.7%	25.6%	19.1%	16.2%	14.3%

Source: Bureau of the Census, U.S. Department of Commerce; State of Missouri.

TABLE 8–2

The Percentage of the Population That Is Nonwhite: Missouri, St. Louis City, St. Louis County, and the St. Louis Metropolitan Area

Area	1960	1970	1980	1990
Missouri	9.2	10.6	10.0	13.6
City	28.8	41.2	47.0	49.0
County	2.8	5.2	13.0	15.8
Metro area	13.8	16.0	18.7	18.7

Source: Bureau of the Census, U.S. Department of Commerce; State of Missouri.

St. Louis also had an important negative distinction separating it from some other midwestern cities. Downtown St. Louis lost two sports teams to Sun Belt cities, and there was some uncertainty over the future of other franchises. In 1968, the NBA's Hawks left for Atlanta; twenty years later the NFL's Cardinals moved to Phoenix. In the 1980s the city's leaders worried that the NHL's Blues might also leave, and then, in the 1990s, the city's beloved baseball Cardinals were suddenly sold. When one considers all of these factors, Senator Eagleton's impressions seem almost prophetic. Maybe too many people were thinking St. Louis's past was its glory; many leaders agreed with Senator Eagleton that dramatic actions were needed to enhance its image and keep downtown vital.

St. Louis's experiment with "doing something dramatic" emphasized sports. There were certainly efforts to rebuild neighborhoods, improve schools, and make the city safe. But St. Louis sought pizzazz, and it turned to sports to achieve a favorable national image in an effort to make people believe it was a "can-do" city and not a "has-been" place. It's too early to determine if St. Louis's ventures have been successful or if the return on its investments will net just a few days of headlines. After all, the Blues and Rams each have finished one complete season in their new homes. However, it is possible to review St. Louis's extensive relationships with the Blues and Rams and learn some very important lessons from the two very different approaches involving the use of sports facilities and teams to build and maintain a city's identity. A public/private partnership with a substantial private-sector investment helped to save the Blues and lead to the building of a first-class arena. Then, in a move that established a new plateau for public subsidies, the city joined with St. Louis County and the state of Missouri to lure the Rams from Anaheim. The unprecedented—for that time—public subsidies provided to the Rams fundamentally altered the bargaining position of all cities and may have ushered in an era of corporate welfare for teams that taxpayers from Maryland to California will long support.

Drastic times demand drastic actions, and St. Louis took drastic steps. Since 1979 there has been more than $2 billion in completed development; far more than $1 billion worth of construction is in progress (Land Clearance for Redevelopment Authority, 1992).

Much of this development is tied to sports, tourism, and recreation. These developments have become linked with the image of St. Louis or, better put, the new image of St. Louis; no longer a city in decline, St. Louis's leaders see their city as one with an image of a community "on the move" (East-West Gateway Coordinating Council, 1992a). At least that's how some leaders rationalize the dramatic actions that were taken that redefined the real economics of cities and sports.

THE LEGENDARY HISTORY OF ST. LOUIS'S PROFESSIONAL TEAMS

At a time when nostalgia has become a growth industry for sports through the building of intimate ballparks that evoke memories of yesteryear, it is not hard to imagine why the leadership of St. Louis rallied to support a program designed to change the city's image based on the community's sports icons. St. Louis has a rich professional sports history that was a consistent part of its past glory, and that history and its glowing memories were used to build extensive political support for several initiatives. The city has been home to every major type of professional sport and several "also-ran" or much smaller sports: indoor soccer, arena football, and roller hockey. Currently the Cardinals, Rams, Blues, Ambush (indoor soccer), Stampede (arena football), and Vipers (roller hockey) call St. Louis home. The city's legendary sports status is tied to its beloved Cardinals and its long history with the St. Louis Browns (Baltimore Orioles).

BASEBALL

For more than fifty years St. Louis was home to two baseball teams: the American League Browns and the National League Cardinals. Between 1902 and 1953 the Browns played in St. Louis and shared the same stadium, the second Sportsman's Park, with the Cardinals. The apex of St. Louis's love affair with baseball was the 1944 World Series when the Cardinals defeated the Browns in the "streetcar" World Series. The first dent in St. Louis's sports armor took place in 1953 when the Browns, plagued by declining performance and attendance, left Sportsman's Park for Baltimore and a new life as the Orioles.

Founded in 1892, the Cardinals have total attendance figures that rank second in baseball annals to those of the New York Yankees. This is a remarkable achievement given the far smaller size of the St. Louis region and its market. However, the Cardinals are an icon similar to the Brooklyn Dodgers and the Chicago Cubs. St. Louis is the Cardinals, and the Cardinals have always been St. Louis. In 1996 the Cardinals welcomed the 100 millionth fan to see one of their games. The Cardinals have also been one of MLB's most successful on-the-field teams. They have appeared in fifteen World Series, winning nine. The Cardinals' World Series success ranks them fourth among all MLB teams and second among teams that have stayed in one city for the vast majority of their existence.

The Cardinals' history also includes a forty-year period when the team was owned by one entity. In 1953 the team was purchased by August "Gussie" Busch through his brewery. Publicly, Gussie proclaimed that he purchased the team largely to ensure that it would not follow the example of the Browns and leave St. Louis. To his board of directors, however, he declared, "The development of the Cardinals will have untold value for our company. This is one of the finest moves in the history of Anheuser-Busch" (Helyar, 1994, p. 103). Gussie would underscore and enhance St. Louis's association with baseball and beer. Fans still fondly remember Gussie riding around the stadium on a Budweiser wagon being pulled by a team of his world-famous Clydesdale horses. The Cardinals' home, Sportsman's Park, was renamed Busch Stadium, and the Cardinals fourteen-station radio network carried Harry Carey's play-by-play and beer commercials throughout the Midwest (Helyar, November 1994). Gussie was also instrumental in the building of a new stadium in downtown St. Louis. Busch Memorial Stadium (renamed Busch Stadium in 1982) opened in 1966 and is the team's current home.

The Cardinals have given baseball some of its greatest memories and stars, including Rogers Hornsby, Joe Medwick, Johnny Mize, Stan Musial, Enos Slaughter, the Dean brothers, the legendary Gas House Gang, Red Schoendienst, Bob Gibson, Lou Brock, and Vince Coleman. Roger Maris also ended his playing days as a Cardinal. The Cardinals and Gussie Busch also gave something more lasting to baseball. Many point to the confrontation between Curt Flood and the Cardinals as the beginning of the changes in MLB's structure that have led to the current salary levels. While the Busch family loved baseball, Gussie and the brewery did not love paying high salaries to players.

In March 1969, before sportswriters and the board of Anheuser-Busch, Gussie lectured his players on their excessive demands for additional pension funds. This lecture, on the heels of a testy salary fight with Curt Flood, soured both men on each other. At the end of the season Flood was traded to Philadelphia, and his subsequent lawsuit challenging the reserve clause unleashed a series of changes that have altered the financing of sports. It is somehow a bit ironic that two strains of the real world of sports economics—escalating player salaries and excessive public-sector subsidies of sports—are both to be found in St. Louis. Such is this city's storied and romanticized history in sports and sports economics.

HOCKEY

Professional hockey has been played in St. Louis for almost thirty years and is also a stalwart portion of the city's identity. In 1967 Sidney Solomon purchased the financially troubled St. Louis Arena as part of a deal to bring NHL hockey to the city. The St. Louis Blues joined the NHL in 1967. He retained ownership of the Blues until 1977 when the St. Louis–based Ralston Purina Company purchased the team. Corporate ownership did not bring success, and the Blues skated on thin financial ice. Claiming losses of several million dollars, the company tried to sell the team to a local group of corporate leaders, Civic Progress. When the sale could not be arranged, the team was nearly forced to declare bankruptcy. Finally, the Blues and the St. Louis Arena were bought by a nonlocal investor, Harry Ornest, for a "fire sale" price. After failing to move the team to Canada, Ornest sold the Blues, in 1986, to a local group. The aging St. Louis Arena was bought by the city, splitting ownership of the two assets for the first time. The Blues continued to play at the arena until 1994, when the new Kiel Center opened. This state-of-the-art facility was developed by the Blues' owners, the Kiel Center Partners, as part of a public/private partnership with the city. The Blues now seem financially secure and well anchored in the St. Louis community. The event that probably provides the best signal of their fiscal stability was the signing of the "Great One." On Tuesday March 5, 1996, the largest crowd ever to see a hockey game in St. Louis (20,725) welcomed Wayne Gretzky. Not only was hockey back on solid ice with the Kiel Center as a home and stable ownership, but the Blues players had a much needed unifying force with Gretzky as team captain. Of course, nothing in the modern age of sports is permanent. Just as the Rams left Anaheim for St. Louis, Gretzky left St. Louis for the New York Rangers in 1996. The impact of the loss of the "Great One" on the financial stability of the Blues remains to be seen.

BASKETBALL

St. Louis's history with basketball and football have not been as pleasant. The NBA's Hawks stayed but thirteen years (1955 to 1968). The Hawks were never well supported by St. Louis's sports fans, and the old Kiel Center was not attractive enough to offset the general "ho-hum" attitude toward basketball. Attendance levels of only a few thousand visibly underscored the lack of community support for the team. In 1968 the Hawks moved to Atlanta. From 1974 through 1976 the Spirits of St. Louis of the American Basketball Association (ABA) played at the St. Louis Arena, but they did not survive the merger of the ABA with the NBA.

FOOTBALL

The football Cardinals moved from Chicago to St. Louis in 1960. The team was originally owned by the Bidwill family, but eventually was taken over by Bill Bidwill, a son of the original owner.. Between 1960 and 1965 the team used the old Busch Stadium (Sportsman's Park) as tenants of the baseball Cardinals. This relationship continued at the new Busch Stadium, where the team played until it left for Phoenix in 1988. The football Cardinals left after years of threats to move in an attempt to get a new stadium for the team. In 1988, antagonism between the team and the St. Louis community was so high that a new stadium was not politically feasible. Football would eventually return to St. Louis in 1995, but not before the public sector agreed to an extraordinary investment that may well have redefined sports economics.

THE FIGHT FOR A CITY'S IMAGE:
SAVING THE BLUES AND GRABBING THE RAMS

St. Louis's journey to restore its image, in the minds of its own residents, in the region, and in the nation, has involved the battle to save the Blues and bring NFL football back. While there is renewed concern with the future of the Cardinals since Anheuser-Busch decided to sell the team, the real sports story within St. Louis has been its efforts to preserve its identity with and through sports. The city's attempts to save the Blues and grab the Rams as part of their image-building process are a story of partnership, success, and subsidies. In the course of its journey into the real economics of cities and sports to enhance its image and do something dramatic, St. Louis, in one instance, built an effective public/private partnership that included substantial private-sector fiscal investments. Commitments and investments were made by both the public and private sectors, and each was able to meets its objectives. Problems and challenges remain for this partnership, even after the Blues have been saved and a new playing facility has been built, but saving the team and building the new Kiel Center did not involve excessive subsidies. Indeed, the building of the new Kiel Center and the retention of the Blues is probably as close to a success story as any city can get in the world of sports. The "deal" that brought the Rams to St. Louis, on the other hand, may well have undermined the ability of other cities' leaders to reduce the welfare paid to professional sports teams. This transfer of wealth to the rich and protection of the cartel structure of sports have the potential to set new records.

SAVING THE BLUES: DOING SPORTS RIGHT!!

When the Blues were purchased in 1986, the new owners knew a new facility was needed to help make the team financially successful. A modern facility with state-of-the-art sound and video systems was required. Luxury seating was also needed to provide the revenues required to keep the team competitive. The new Kiel Center opened in 1995 and is the home for several St. Louis–based teams including the Blues, the St. Louis University Billikens (basketball), the Ambush (soccer), the Stampede (arena football), and the Vipers (roller hockey). The new arena replaced the sixty-five-year-old St. Louis Arena, now closed and owned by the city, and the Henry W. Kiel Memorial Auditorium, which was opened in 1934 and built with $6 million of the proceeds from a 1923 city bond issue. The publicly built, owned, and operated Kiel Auditorium was razed for construction of the Kiel Center. The Center has 18,500 seats (for hockey; more for other events) and an attached 1,240 space parking garage. In addition to sports events, the Kiel Center is the St. Louis region's primary indoor facility for the circus, concerts, ice skating shows, and small conventions.

The partnership for building the Kiel Center was forged by Mayor Vincent Schoemehl Jr. after an earlier effort to build a new arena failed. In the late 1980s Anheuser-Busch wanted to build a new arena complex just south of Busch Stadium. Busch's plan entailed the demolition of the historic Cupples warehouse buildings to provide for the parking that would be lost by building the new arena facility. Many preservationists and Mayor Schoemehl did not want these buildings torn down, and the public attention and disagreement convinced Mr. Busch to cancel his project. Mr. Busch decided not to get involved with the arena development process, and the mayor sought investors for a new downtown facility to avoid the possibility of a venue being located in suburban St. Louis County. Suburban areas of the region were interested in building both a home for the Blues and a facility that could host concerts and other events. Mayor Schoemehl chose to negotiate with one of St. Louis's corporate leadership groups, Civic Progress. An ordinance permitting the use of a sunset provision in the federal tax code for issuing tax-exempt bonds for sports-related facilities was rushed through the city's board of aldermen on December 17, 1990.

Lease arrangements for the Kiel Center are quite complex. The city owns the Kiel property and leases it to a city agency, the Land Clearance for Redevelopment Authority (LCRA). LCRA then entered into a lease and development arrangement with Kiel Center Redevelopment Corporation (KCRC), which is a subsidiary of Kiel Center Partners. The Partners have subleased Kiel from the KCRC. The Partners group involves the participation of twenty of the twenty-six Civic Progress corporate giants in St. Louis, such as Anheuser-Busch, Monsanto, Wetterau, and General American Life.

Financing for the center also was complex. The Partners invested $135 million from five sources: (1) $62.5 million from city-issued bonds that are *privately guaranteed* by the Kiel Partners; (2) $30 million invested by the Partners themselves; (3) $36.9 million in loans from banks that are members of Civic Progress, guaranteed by the Partners; (4) $3.8 million in deposits on suites and club seating; and (5) $1.8 million in investment earnings. In addition, $34.5 million was invested by the city of St. Louis from two bond issues, $10 million for demolishing the old Kiel Auditorium, and $24.5 million for construction of the parking garage. The $10 million bond issue was financed using approximately $1 million of city revenue previously used to operate the arena and the city's income from parking revenues. The bonds for the parking facility are paid from fees collected from users. Partial operating support for the center comes from the commitment made by corporations to lease sixty-five luxury boxes for ten years at $50,000 per year, thus raising some $3.2 million annually.

To finance the public sector's share of the Kiel Center, the St. Louis Industrial Development Authority sold $62.4 million in tax-exempt bonds. (These are the bonds guaranteed by the Kiel Center Partners.) The Kiel Center also received financial protection by a deed restriction on the city-owned venue, the arena. This restriction bars the arena from ever holding any event that charges an admission price. In this manner, the Kiel Center is the region's primary indoor arena for events seating less than 21,000 people. In addition, Kiel Partners has a noncompete agreement with the publicly owned Trans World Dome that, in essence, gives Kiel the right of first refusal for any shows that can be accommodated at the center. Concerts with the potential for more than 21,000 attendees play "the Dome"; attractions with smaller gate potential play "the Center." The city's actual commitment to Kiel has gone beyond the $35 million for demolition and garage construction, but there is still substantial private-sector support in this partnership. In addition, the city has been able to use tax receipts collected as a result of the presence of the arena and the events it hosts to support its investment.

The tax revenues represent real income for the city; had the Kiel Center not been built in St. Louis these revenues would have accrued to other communities. As there was real interest in building a modern arena in suburban St. Louis, the presence of the new Kiel Center within the city does generate new tax revenues, and these tax receipts support the overwhelming majority of St. Louis's financial responsibilities for the Blues' home. The partners' guarantee of other city bonds, together with the ability of the city to use luxury suite revenue to cover the facilities' operating expenses, reduces the public's subsidy of this playing facility. The city's investment that is tied to general taxes may well be limited to the $10 million demolition of the aging Kiel Auditorium, the building of the parking garage, and the expense of maintaining or destroying the old St. Louis Arena. There is also a level of public investment in the sense that the new Kiel Center pays no local property taxes and the city retains title to the building.

The Kiel Center's grand opening was Saturday, October 8, 1994. The planned twenty-one-month construction phase was completed on schedule, but the opening itself was a bit disappointing in that a gala event scheduled to coincide with a Blues vs. Chicago Blackhawks game was not possible because the NHL and its players had not ended their lockout/strike. The opening of the new Kiel Center was thus shrouded in the battle between the players and owners for the profits of professional sports. The facility has been very well received by the community, but some financial events have been troublesome. In 1995 several companies filed suits claiming a total of $5.5 million in unpaid expenses in excess of their contract totals. Local lawyers have noted that the magnitude of the claims is unusually high for a project of this size. In addition, Kiel Partners had to invest an additional $17 million to cover losses of the Center and the Blues.

The Kiel Center has also been the subject of recent attention from the St. Louis City Board of Aldermen as a result of the failure to complete the Kiel Opera House attached to the new complex. The Opera House is the only remaining portion of the old 1930s Kiel complex and was to have been renovated for events seating approximately 3,500 people. Work on the Kiel Opera House, as a part of the Kiel Center complex, has not been completed even though the Center itself opened in October 1994. Kiel Center Partners are balking at investing another $5 to $7 million to complete its restoration, arguing that the original cost estimates for the renovations were $2.5 million and that amount has already been spent. The Opera House remains unfinished, with the city claiming that since it fulfilled its obligations, the Kiel Partners must now honor each of their guarantees regardless of the final cost. The debate continues despite an impressive list of public-sector investments that includes:

- Spending $10 million for demolition of Kiel Auditorium, asbestos removal in the Opera House, and $24.5 million for a parking garage;

- Providing a lease to Kiel Center Partners for seventy years at $1 per year and, since the city retains ownership, removing any property tax liability for the partners;

- Tearing down the historic Children's Building to provide more Kiel parking;

- Refusing to book any events at the city-owned arena to avoid competition with Kiel, thus eliminating the city's main source of revenue to pay off the outstanding debt on the arena;

- Reducing construction costs by issuing bonds backed by city assets; and

- Agreeing to tear down the city jail located across from Kiel.

The city's leadership maintains that the Opera House must be finished. Kiel Partners has not agreed and is studying the cost and economic feasibility of completing the project. Angered over the delay, the board of aldermen approved a resolution to review the entire Kiel Center deal, including the lease agreement. Associate City Councillor Fran Oates wrote a memo, not a formal legal opinion, stating that nothing in the master lease between LCRA and Kiel Partners authorized LCRA to excuse themselves from completion of the renovations. The city's financial commitments to this project could then increase if the Kiel Partners argue that their current losses preclude completion of the Opera House without additional investments from the public sector.

Kiel Partners is a subtenant of the LCRA under a master lease from the landlord, the city. The terms of the master lease state simply that the Opera House must be renovated and opened and Kiel Partners, as subtenants, are legally bound to these terms. City Alderman Dan McGuire headed a review of these arrangements as chair of the Ways and Means Committee and then turned to the city's comptroller, Darlene Green, who under city charter is responsible for enforcing all agreements and leases relating to city property. Green has, in turn, turned the issue over to the city's attorney. Mayor Freeman Bosley Jr. has made no formal statement and says simply that the legal machinery is at work and he hopes the Opera House can be satisfactorily renovated. In basketball parlance, we have Kiel Partners to LCRA to city to McGuire to Green to Taborn to . . . The play is still in motion. The mayor appears to be waiting on the sidelines.

CHASING THE DREAM OF AN NFL TEAM:
A FIVE-ACT MELODRAMA WITH EPILOGUES

Act I: St. Louis Builds a Stadium and Creates the Potential for a New Standard for Corporate Welfare

The story behind the provision of one of the largest welfare payments to a professional sports team to encourage its move from one city to another begins with St. Louis's loss of the football Cardinals. In 1987, Bill Bidwill threatened, again, to move his team unless he received a new stadium. The city was not interested in building a new football-only facility, believing Busch Stadium was sufficient for both the football and baseball Cardinals. After all, the football Cardinals seldom sold all the tickets to the games they played in the 55,000-seat doughnut stadium. The refusal to build a new stadium was perceived by Mr. Bidwill as a de facto declaration by the city of its lack of interest in his needs (or wants) and a virtual declaration that he and the team should "take a hike." He did. A new stadium was a nonnegotiable condition for his remaining in St. Louis. As the city was unwilling to meet his demand, Mr. Bidwill accepted an offer to use Arizona State University's Sun Devil Stadium in Tempe (a suburb of Phoenix). While Mr. Bidwill was promised a new stadium in the Phoenix metropolitan area when he left St. Louis, to date, he still waits for a facility promised him almost a decade ago with all of the revenue potential of other new parks.

After the loss of the Cardinals there was almost instant interest in getting another team. Ironically, while St. Louis's civic and political leadership wanted to bring NFL football back to the community, no one quite knew how to do it. The political or leadership void was eventually filled by the NFL Partnership (NFLP), a group of community business leaders with the single-minded goal of attracting a new team. The Partnership was headed by Jerry Clinton, the president of Grey Eagle Distributors, Inc., of St. Louis, the Anheuser-Busch distributor for all of St. Louis County with market coverage of about one-fifth of Missouri's population. Also in the Partnership were Fran Murray, who at the time owned 49 percent of the New England Patriots, and Walter Payton, the legendary former star of the Chicago Bears. NFLP had a two-part game plan for attracting an expansion franchise, as it appeared the NFL would add two additional teams in the early 1990s. First, the NFLP would accept responsibility for securing the funds to pay the steep franchise fee expected to be demanded by the NFL. Second, the NFLP would turn to the public sector to build the stadium the NFL would want to see before reentering the St. Louis market.

There was little doubt in anyone's mind that the only way St. Louis would succeed in winning an NFL expansion team or attracting a team from another city was if a new stadium existed. As a result, St. Louis's NFL Partnership soon became the major proponents of a plan to build a domed stadium as part of the Cervantes Convention Center. Just as Indianapolis had built its Hoosier Dome as part of the Indiana Convention Center and attracted the Colts, St. Louis's leadership wanted a state-of-the-art football stadium that would also provide the Convention Center with thousands of square feet of exhibition space to help elevate the city's image as a premier convention site. The existing Cervantes Center complex did not have adequate exhibit space, especially on one level, to allow St. Louis to compete with the top-tier cities in the burgeoning national convention market. The stadium proponents also argued that having major league football would add a publicity dimension to the overall attractiveness of St. Louis as a place to visit, meet, and recreate. It was hoped that the new domed stadium, if joined to a convention center, would be fiscally profitable.

These ideas and sentiments were later expressed at the groundbreaking ceremonies for the new domed stadium on July 13, 1992, when then-mayor Vincent Schoemehl Jr. labeled the project "an economic engine for the entire St. Louis region." The domed stadium would be the third piece in the America's Center complex consisting of the new stadium, the Cervantes Convention Center, and an executive conference center. The America's Center would become the second largest single-level convention center in the United States (McCormick Place in Chicago is first) and the seventh largest in overall square footage.

At one point during the planning process it was claimed that the expansion of the Cervantes Convention Center and the attraction of an NFL team would add an estimated $580 million per year to the region's economy. While clearly an overstated claim, during this maelstrom of football frenzy, no one really questioned the dollar figures being used to build support for the project. All attention and zeal were focused on getting a new team—at some cost, at any cost—and since a stadium was required, the project moved forward. The city and county adopted the original stadium lease in 1990 and assigned the pro football rights to the NFLP. For its efforts the NFLP was designated as St. Louis's lead in any effort to secure an expansion franchise. It was decided to build a new state-of-the art stadium and fill it later, a "build it and they will come" strategy that already had been used by other cities in their attempts to lure professional sports.

The NFLP signed a thirty-year lease with the St. Louis Convention and Visitors Commission (CVC), which operates the Convention Center complex, for use of the new stadium and were granted an impressive array of income flows and other concessions if they could bring a team to St. Louis. The NFLP's team would receive all income from food, beverages, and concessions sold on game days and two-thirds of the profit from the sale of food and beverages in the luxury suites and from club seat attendees on all other days the dome was used; all income from the sale or rental of luxury boxes; most income from advertising; all income from club seats; and the CVC even agreed to manage, operate, and maintain the stadium on game days. All of these revenues from a stadium built with public funds were granted for a thirty-year period for an annual lease cost of $250,000. The CVC did not plan to increase the yearly payments even to adjust for inflation across three decades. Clearly this represented one of the best sports lease deals ever created if the NFLP could secure a team. The NFLP was thus receiving an impressive set of subsidies to help it be selected as an ownership group for an NFL expansion team. As the city's leadership expected the Partnership to have to pay a substantial franchise fee to the NFL, the lease provided to the Partnership was designed to illustrate St. Louis's public-sector commitment to the NFL. Such a statement was needed after the city had refused to work with Mr. Bidwill, and the generous lease established an extraordinary set of subsidies. Essentially the public sector was promising to build the stadium and permit the team to retain virtually all of the revenues generated from football games and some revenues generated from other events. The expectation was that the public sector would recoup its investment from the use of the football stadium as exhibition space for newly attracted conventions. While this plan obviously was filled with financial risks for the public sector—would the city indeed attract a sufficient number of conventions to offset its investments?—few were inclined to oppose the plan and strategy.

As a sideline event, during the initial planning phase of the stadium, a suit was filed by Rev. Larry Rice of the New Life Evangelistic Center to halt the project and prohibit the use of tax money to support the building of a new stadium. He argued, as do many critics of public subsidies for professional sports teams, that the funds spent for playing facilities were needed for things such as houses for the homeless, job retraining, and low- and moderate-income housing for inner-city residents. Reverend Rice managed to place in sharp focus the question of alternative uses for public funds and the economic returns (human from his perspective) compared to the stadium investment. Reverend Rice fasted in protest when the stadium project continued.

Reverend Rice was not the only voice of opposition. The standing city comptroller, Virvus Jones, raised concerns with the validity of the economic projections of benefits from the stadium. If the projections were in error, he too could not support the use of scarce public funds to subsidize professional sports. Both Rice and Jones were concerned with the $720 million lifetime cost (construction plus interest and the maintenance of the facility) for the project. With the specter raised of a lower payoff from the investment, alternative uses for the money seemed justified. Both men asked, Were sports worth the cost? What would the city get for its investment? What would it pay?

During 1990–91, the financing of the new domed stadium became a major political football not only locally but also in the Missouri state capitol. State Representative Tony Ribaudo, who had lost his bid for Speaker of the House, disputed the then-speaker's endorsement of the stadium project and the $12 million per year in state funds that would be needed to pay for the facility. In sharp contrast, then-mayor Vincent Schoemehl's bid to become governor of Missouri brought to the surface his vigorous support for the project and the use of public tax dollars to attract NFL football back to St. Louis despite the city's pressing social and economic needs. In St. Louis, the race for president of the board of aldermen also made the stadium a campaign issue. Across Missouri, everyone was debating the use of public funds to subsidize wealthy team owners and economically privileged players. But, alas, the subsidies did not end.

In an attempt to dispel the controversy over the economic and fiscal impact, two reports were issued in March 1991 by a prominent accounting firm. With the city of St. Louis and the state of Missouri proposing to support their responsibilities for the stadium with taxes drawn from their general funds, there was a need to demonstrate the "returns" from the commitment of public funds to a sports palace. Both units of government needed an analysis of the "new net public fiscal benefits" from funding the stadium project. These studies estimated the combined benefits from all facets of the new convention/sports complex and did not focus on the benefits generated by any one element such as the sports component. The benefits tabulated were compared with the public investment by the city and state.

These analyses were performed for NFLP and the state's Office of Administration and specifically enumerated the economic importance of the entire project for the city of St. Louis and the state of Missouri (Coopers & Lybrand, 1991a, 1991b). The reports sought to document the new net public fiscal benefits that would result from the new taxes needed to support the public's investment. No study was done for the county since it did not require general higher tax collections as a condition for its support. An integral component of the overall financing plan for the new stadium was an increased tax on hotel and motel rooms that was submitted to St. Louis County voters. The proposal was approved by a two-thirds majority on April 4, 1990, and almost doubled this tax from 3.75 percent to 7.25 percent. The campaign was very well financed and strongly supported by local businesses and the NFL Partnership. The key argument leading to the success of the vote was that this tax would not be paid by county (or city) residents but rather by visitors to the area as a "user fee" for public services and amenities such as the stadium. The tax would thus be exported from the region. County voters were happy to tax others to pay for their share of the cost of the new stadium. Proceeds from the county hotel/motel tax were earmarked to pay for its share of the stadium's construction and maintenance, $6 million per year. Any collections above this amount, however, would not go to support the stadium but would go into the county's general fund. In addition, the new hotel tax rate had the potential to generate far more money than was needed for the county's share of the stadium. Since residents of St. Louis County were unlikely to pay a hotel and motel tax, few disagreed with taxing others to help build the stadium, and there was no real discussion of the implications of higher taxes on overall tourist spending in the region.[1]

The reports illustrated, to the satisfaction of elected officials, the fiscal returns from the entire project. With these reports in hand, it was now possible to guarantee that the remaining funding for the stadium would come from the city of St. Louis ($6 million) and the state of Missouri ($12 million). The total public-sector investment would be $24 million *per year* for thirty years to pay for construction ($20 million annually) and establish a preservation fund ($4 million) for maintenance, operations, and future renovations and enhancement. For this investment, St. Louis was able to build a domed stadium for a total cost of $301 million. The stadium itself cost $202 million and contains 65,300 seats. Land and site preparation costs, as well as all legal and architectural fees, amounted to $99 million. The dome has 113 luxury/club suites and 6,500 club seats. As the entire financing package involved public funds, the facility would exist without any investment from the NFLP. Their commitment was limited to a small rental fee if and when a team arrived.

With all of the public-sector partners in agreement, the financing plan for the stadium was completed. The domed stadium would be paid for by taxpayers until the year 2022; the city and county each agreed to pay $6 million per year, and the state of Missouri committed itself to pay $12 million per year. The full cost of paying off the bond indebtedness plus annual maintenance will be approximately $720 million. Only a small amount of private funds went for actual stadium construction, about $4.2 million from the proceeds of personal seat licenses (PSLs).

The bonds were issued with tax-exempt governmental status rather than as private-activity bonds as originally planned. This was made possible, in large part, by an exemption granted to St. Louis (and some other cities) from the federal Tax Reform Act of 1986 prohibiting tax-exempt activity bonds being used to finance stadiums that benefit private interests. By classifying the bonds as governmental, the federal deadline for issuing the bonds was met, and using up all of the state of Missouri's allotment of $258 million for private-activity bonds for the issue year was avoided. St. Louis was among the few cities grandfathered for special tax status when the federal tax laws changed. The tax-exempt status saved considerable interest costs compared to a taxable private issue.

The stadium project and its funding were actually a political milestone in St. Louis's history. They represented the first time the city was able to join with the county and the state to build a project for St. Louis's regional development. This outcome assumes even greater significance in an area in which regional cooperation is scarce and state involvement in such a clearly regional and urban endeavor is practically unknown. Some argued that it set a precedent for greater state involvement in regional projects, although most remain skeptical about future reliance on state financial involvement in similar local projects. Both the city and the state will rely on general revenue growth in their sales, income, restaurant, and hotel tax receipts from the convention and sports complex to pay for their share. Only the county would use earmarked funds for this project. Concerning the state's participation, it is interesting to note that in the 1996 Missouri legislative session several bills had been introduced to eliminate any future state support for convention or sports projects.

Act II: Who's on First? No, Who's on Second!!
Who Is St. Louis's Ownership Group?!

When "wooing" the NFL in an expansion derby, two things are needed. First, a community needs to have a unified public sector and a plan for the building of a stadium. Second, an ownership group with the cash to pay a franchise fee and still operate is required. Ironically, the St. Louis public sector had its act together; it was the divided private sector and its infighting and flailing that cost St. Louis an expansion franchise.

The events that led to the demise of St. Louis's hopes to be awarded an expansion franchise are succinctly summarized in Table 8–3 and briefly reviewed in this explanation of the second and third acts of this melodrama.

With everything seemingly in place for the building of a first-class football stadium, St. Louis was poised to enter the NFL's expansion sweepstakes. But alas, who was in charge of getting a new football team? While the public sector had completed a minor miracle and coordinated funding for the new stadium between the city, county, and state, the private-sector solidarity began to crack. Disputes within the NFLP, exacerbated by the strains created to secure the financing needed to meet the NFL's steep franchise fee, led to disunity and the emergence or formation of a second partnership, the Gateway Football Partnership, headed by Wal-Mart-family-linked E. Stanley Kroenke.

Now, there were two groups standing on first base, each thinking the other was on second in terms of raising the needed dollars for an NFL franchise and both representing and leading St. Louis's bid to attract an expansion team. More important, both believed if they received the nod from the NFL they would be able to access the very favorable lease NFLP had received for use of the dome. To put it mildly, NFLP did not see it that way. In a nutshell, here is the problem. Gateway may have had more potential and financial ability to pay the NFL's franchise fee, but the NFLP still controlled the original stadium lease. St. Louis was in the enviable position of having two potential ownership groups for a new team, but the city had already given the lease for the use of its new domed stadium to one of these partnership groups. What would happen if the NFL wanted the Gateway group? With peace negotiations between the two groups under way, Jerry Clinton announced in October 1993 that he would not pursue the application for an expansion team from the NFLP. Another NFLP partner, Fran Murray, however, would not agree to follow Mr. Clinton's example. Fran Murray continued as an active "player" seeking an NFL franchise, and this raised the possibility that if Gateway received the franchise it could not use the domed stadium. While there was some confidence within the Gateway group that if they were awarded an NFL franchise they could be successful in a legal challenge to the existing lease arrangement, the NFL was clearly unimpressed with the fractious situation. Why expand in a community where legal action might await the NFL? NFLP had the lease, Gateway wanted the team, and the NFL did not want a lawsuit. This love triangle seemed destined for failure.

Act III: The NFL Really Wants to Come to St. Louis, but No One Can Agree on Who (Would Own the Team) and Where He Is

Originally scheduled for October, the NFL delayed its final decision to award the second of two expansion teams until November 30, 1993. The NFL wanted to place a team in St. Louis, but the confusion over who would own the St. Louis franchise and who controlled the lease for use of the dome required additional time to permit a resolution to develop. The price for an expansion franchise was set at about $140 million, with $70 million up front and $16 million in interest charges on the balance. In addition, potential ownership groups were informed that they would also suffer $48 million in lost income from league revenues. From 1995 through 1997 the two expansion teams would receive only 50 percent of the shares other teams would receive from the national television package. Joining the NFL was going to cost a small fortune, and this was a staggering investment for any ownership group. The NFLP formally named their anticipated team the St. Louis Stallions. The NFL, committed to adding two teams, awarded one franchise to Charlotte in October 1993, then agreed to wait to see if St. Louis could resolve its franchise ownership lease problems. When that could not be

TABLE 8–3

Losing an NFL Expansion Franchise:
The Collapse of Private-Sector Unity

Date	Event
Spring, 1988	After twenty-eight seasons, the Cardinals move to Phoenix.
5/12/89	The Missouri legislature passes a bill for the state-city-county financing of a new stadium in St. Louis.
5/23/91	The NFL announces it will add two expansion teams in time for the 1995 season.
9/27/91	Mr. Clinton and Mr. Murray bring Mr. Orthwein into the NFLP as Chair and CEO; he owns a share of the New England Patriots, which is perceived to be a "back up" to getting an expansion team.
5/19/92	Five finalists are chosen for the two NFL expansion teams: St. Louis, Baltimore, Charlotte, Jacksonville, and Memphis. Many believed St. Louis is destined to receive a team.
7/13/92	Ground is broken for a new stadium to be completed in 1995.
11/5/92	Mr. Orthwein becomes the sole owner of the Patriots, which reinforces the view it is a backup team. If St. Louis loses its expansion team bid, Mr. Orthwein's hopes to move the Patriots to St. Louis.
9/9/93	Mr. Clinton and Mr. Orthwein part ways, and Mr. Clinton assumes control of NFLP. However, he lacks adequate resources to finance a new team.
10/26/93	Lacking cash, Mr. Clinton steps aside for wealthy Missouri businessman Stan Kroenke, who then becomes the financial support for Gateway.
10/26/93	The NFL awards the first franchise to Charlotte, but the second franchise award is put off to allow St. Louis to "get its financial act together." Control over the stadium lease looms as the major deterrent to approval.
11/30/93	The second franchise is awarded to Jacksonville and St. Louis's expansion team, the Stallions, "drops dead in the gate."

done to the league's satisfaction, Jacksonville received the second franchise in November 1993.

Act IV: The Emergence of a New Knight

Done in by the lease problems, St. Louis lost its bid for an expansion franchise, a struggle in which many believed St. Louis was the odds-on favorite. After all, St. Louis had agreed to build a premier stadium and give the new team virtually all of the revenues from the facility. The NFLP also had included the legendary Walter Payton as part of their ownership group. These three factors seemed to make St. Louis the NFL's logical choice. The lease battle ended the city's dreams. However, the public sector was still building its football palace. Now, a large number of people found themselves in the very embarrassing situation of having "built it" only to find "they did not come." A new group was needed to build bridges where feuds existed among the private-sector partners in an effort to lure an existing team to the dome. The events in Act IV, St. Louis's successful grab of the Los Angeles Rams, are summarized in Table 8–4.

After the failure of the expansion team bid, FANS Inc. was

TABLE 8–4
A Chronology of Events in the Rams' Odyssey

Date	Event
1/6/94	The Rams warn Anaheim that they want out of their stadium lease.
1/21/94	Mr. Orthwein sells the Patriots to a Massachusetts buyer and St. Louis loses its fallback team.
5/3/94	The Rams give Anaheim a lease-termination notice.
8/7/94	The Rams give FANS Inc. a "wish" list for their move to St. Louis.
8/10/94	The Rams await the solving of St. Louis's lease problems.
8/11/94	FANS recruits Senator Thomas Eagleton who masterminds a settlement of the maze of legal, financial, and political issues surrounding the stadium lease.
9/15/94	FANS purchases Mr. Clinton's control of the lease and secures its right to award the lease arrangements to the Rams.
1/17/95	Rams owner Georgia Frontiere announces the Rams move to St. Louis for the 1995 season. The team will play at Busch Stadium until the new stadium is completed.
3/15/95	The NFL owners vote overwhelmingly to block the Rams' move. Eyeing the millions in St. Louis's PSL money, they want a multimillion-dollar payment before approving a relocation.
4/12/95	After rumblings of litigation from the Rams and Missouri Attorney General Jay Nixon, the NFL owners settle for a lower sum and vote 23–6–1 to approve the Rams move to St. Louis; the Raiders abstain and the Cardinals' owner, Mr. Bidwell, voted no. Ironically, Rams owner Ms. Frontiere casts the deciding vote since twenty-three were required for approval.

formed to bring an NFL team to St. Louis. FANS Inc., the third private-sector group formed to work with the public sector in an effort to bring NFL football back to St. Louis, was prepared to pay $3.5 million to Jerry Clinton for his 30 percent share of the stadium lease he had purchased from James Busch Orthwein in September 1993. Eventually Mr. Orthwein relinquished his 65 percent share of the stadium lease to FANS Inc. for $1 to help facilitate the deal to bring the Rams to St. Louis. Civic pride sometimes counts for something.

Mr. Clinton negotiated and finally received an $8 million payment for his expenses plus the long-term use of a luxury box in the new stadium. With this accomplished, Mr. Clinton's rights of first refusal of Mr. Orthwein's share of the lease were eliminated and Mr. Orthwein had removed himself from the NFLP and its lease claims. Control of the lease for the new stadium had remained in the hands of Mr. Clinton and Mr. Orthwein until FANS Inc. cleared the playing field. This had to be done before St. Louis could approach any NFL team and convince them to move to St. Louis. FANS purchased the lease rights to the stadium from Mr. Clinton and received written commitments from the other members of the NFLP to relinquish their shares in the old lease agreement. With considerable efforts led by local legend Sen. Thomas Eagleton, FANS Inc. was able to resolve all of the lease and side agreement issues surrounding the use of the new domed stadium. Senator Eagleton became St. Louis's knight in shining armor and, having helped establish order within the private-sector ownership groups, now turned his attention to the difficult task of convincing a team to move to St. Louis.

The Rams were one of the NFL's teams dissatisfied with their existing home and thus a potential candidate for relocation. Having left the Los Angeles Coliseum for suburban Anaheim, the team still desired a stadium with more of the revenue sources available in newer facilities. When Los Angeles, Anaheim, and Orange County seemed unwilling to build a new facility, the Rams cast a roving eye toward their original midwestern roots (the team had been founded in Cleveland). FANS was only too eager to respond.

With a stadium built and an extremely generous lease already available as a "lure," Senator Eagleton set his sights on the Rams. He could offer them a lease that would permit them to retain control of the revenues produced by the stadium, and there would be no need for the Rams to contribute to the building of the stadium. The Rams, however, had other "needs." There was the matter of their lease obligations to the city of Anaheim. There was also the cost of moving the team and its possessions across the country. The St. Louis Rams, if they were to exist, would also need a new practice facility. With the team controlling most revenues from the stadium, an additional new revenue source was needed to meet these new "needs" or demands from the Rams. After all, these costs were small in comparison to the $700+ million already spent on or committed (including interest charges) to the new stadium. What's a few more million dollars among friends?

The revenues to meet many of these additional needs did not come from the public sector; they came from the fans themselves. FANS sold PSLs and used the vast majority of these revenues to support the demands made by the Rams. With all of the commitments in place, Rams president John Shaw orchestrated the move for the Rams, and in January 1995 the Sports Complex Authority entered into a relocation agreement with CVC, FANS Inc., and the Rams to move them to St. Louis.

The total cost of moving the Rams was estimated to be $191 million. This included, as part of the original $120 million deal, $60 million obtained from Stan Kroenke's purchase of 30 percent of the Rams team. In addition, another $71 million included a $46 million payment to the NFL ($20 million up front and $1.7 million per year for fifteen years); $12.5 million to the Fox TV network if ratings slipped after the Rams' transfer from Los Angeles, the nation's second largest TV market; and $13 million in the waived Rams' share of money from the league's sale of expansion team franchises.

St. Louis's football fans did not balk at the thought of paying for the right to buy season tickets, or to provide these funds to the team to help with their move from Los Angeles. FANS received 70,000 requests for PSLs, far exceeding the supply. In the end, more than 52,000 PSLs were sold and 5,300 club seats and 90 luxury boxes were leased to local fans and businesses. Suites with a seating capacity of ten to sixteen were leased for five, ten, or fifteen years and ranged in price from $47,500 to $75,000. Club seat leases ranged in price from

$700 to $2,200. Unlike the PSLs, suite and club seat rental payments include tickets, special parking, and upgraded food service. Any refreshments that are purchased involve separate fees, of course. The PSLs and leased luxury seating raised some $74 million for St. Louis, and without them the Rams' move would not have taken place; St. Louis's football fans, it has to be fairly reported, thought their taxes, PSL payments, and season ticket payments were fair prices to be paid to have ten football games played in St. Louis in each year.

The $74 million received through the sale of PSLs was distributed for the following expenses: $26 million for the debt at the city of Anaheim; $13 million in relocation costs for the Rams; $10 million as part of the relocation cost the Rams had to pay to the NFL; $5 million to be used for the Rams' new practice facility; slightly less than $5 million for stadium improvements; $8 million to settle Mr. Clinton's claims; and $6.5 million for legal and advertising fees. The other revenues the Rams had to pay to the NFL to move and the share of the PSL income demanded by the NFL were the responsibility of the Rams and not FANS.

Act V: The Dangling Threads

The incentives to attract the Rams also included building a practice facility whose final cost is estimated to be $15 million. The city of St. Louis is considering extending its amusement tax to fund its share of this facility. However financed, local taxpayers will support approximately $12.5 million of the facility's cost. FANS Inc. will be responsible for $2.5 million. As a part of the planning for this facility its ownership will not vest with the Rams, but will be transferred to the county. It will then be leased back to the Rams for thirty years, the duration of the stadium lease. This ownership arrangement will eliminate the Rams' property tax liability, but also will keep ownership of the practice facility in local hands if the team were to relocate before the end of its stadium lease.

As the dome was completed, a new controversy involving its external advertising emerged. Some believed that the advertising was "tacky" for a public facility. The problem is that revenues from this advertising provided much-needed funds for the CVC and the Rams (of course). Advertising is estimated to raise about $6 million during the first year; CVC gets 25 percent of the first $6 million and 10 percent of all remaining funds. The Rams receive the rest of the money. In addition, Trans World Airlines (TWA) will pay $1.3 million per year, increased by an inflation factor of 3.5 percent per year, for twenty years, to paint its logo on the top of the dome; it is the fifth airline to name a sports stadium. TWA gets valuable advertising and name recognition on national TV during any broadcast of a Rams games. The CVC receives $325,000 from the TWA deal; $975,000 goes to the Rams. Other companies have also considered advertising inside the new dome. Anheuser-Busch and Coca-Cola are the dome's "official beverages." Advertising revenue has become yet another dimension of the controversy over the extensive public support for the Rams and the lack of financial returns to the community from its $720 million investment. Only about one-quarter of all advertising revenues comes to the city (of course).

TABLE 8–5
The Final Tally for the Rams: Who Receives and Who Pays

Amount	Purpose	Revenue Source(s)
The Rams receive		
$26 million	To meet financial obligations in Anaheim	PSL income
$13 million	Relocation fee, moving expenses	PSL income
$15 million	Practice facility	Fans Inc., city, county
$5 to $10 million	Stadium improvements	PSL income
Other expenses		
$8 million	For Mr. Clinton's lease rights	PSL income
$6.5 million	Legal and marketing expenses	PSL income
Rams expenses		
$29 million	NFL relocation fee	$2 million PSL income; Rams
$17 million	NFL share of PSL income	PSL income
$13 million	Share of future NFL expansion fees	Foregone income
0 to $12.5 million	Potential fee to Fox Television	Foregone income

Epilogue I: St. Louis and the Rams as Victims

The drama surrounding the Rams' move to St. Louis has not ended; indeed, the final act has not been completed. The CVC filed suit against the NFL and twenty-four of its member teams claiming that the $29 million relocation fee assessed against the Rams (and paid by FANS Inc.) was unfair. The initial $20 million payment of this fee came directly from the proceeds of the PSLs; the remaining $9 million will be paid by the Rams over several years, but not with PSL money. The payment for this relocation assessment was made after an unsuccessful attempt by FANS Inc. to renegotiate the fee. While FANS believed the fee was unfair, they were afraid that their refusal to make the payment would lead to another lost franchise. This was a risk St. Louis was not willing to take. The Rams issued a statement of support for the suit, noting that the Raiders were not charged for their recent move from Los Angeles to Oakland. Curiously, the Raiders did not pay a relocation fee after the NFL approved their move to Oakland in 1995, but the Cardinals did pay $7.5 million in 1987 to move from St. Louis to Phoenix and the Rams did pay $29 million in 1996 to move to St. Louis. FANS Inc. has argued that the NFL should have a consistent fee assessment policy for relocation. De facto, it is believed, St. Louis had been discriminated against for both football moves, one out and one in. Teams excluded from the CVC suit against the NFL were the Rams, Cincinnati, Raiders, Carolina, Jacksonville, and Tampa Bay. Carolina and Jacksonville are expansion teams; Cincinnati and Tampa Bay voted in favor of the Rams' move; the Raiders are involved in litigation at present with the NFL.

The suit filed in U.S. District Court argues that the NFL extorted the $29 million fee as well as other monetary concessions. The basis of the suit is that the NFL and its member clubs acted in an anticompetitive manner and in so doing violated both federal and Missouri antitrust laws. If this view is sustained, the award would be staggering; treble actual damages plus punitive damages, interest, and litigation costs. Factoring in the estimated return to the Rams of at least $25 million per year, this is $750 million over the thirty-year life of the lease. Treble damages would bring this to over $2.25 billion.

Epilogue II: An Escape Hatch for the Rams

As if the continued turbulence was not enough, there is more to the Rams' saga. A recent analysis of the voluminous lease with the Rams revealed that they are free to move as early as 2005 after giving one year's notice; they are able to break their lease at ten-year intervals as a result of a clause in the agreement that requires the Trans World Dome to be in the top 25 percent of all football facilities in the country. As the lease specifies, the stadium or any of its components must be in the "First Tier" by March 1, 2005, or March 1, 2015, or the thirty-year lease becomes a one-year lease. Another section goes even farther and states that the stadium must also be operated, managed, maintained, or repaired to a "First Tier" standard. Apparently, however, nowhere is it specified exactly how such a ranking will be determined. Annex 1 of the lease states that to be "First Tier" on those dates, quoting directly, "the facilities, taken as a whole, and each component of the facilities, respectively taken as a whole, must be among the 'top' twenty-five percent of all NFL football stadia and football facilities, if such stadia and facilities were to be rated or ranked according to the matter sought to be measured."

One might legitimately ask several questions about these provisions: What do they mean? Who ranks the stadiums? By what criteria are they ranked? St. Louis wanted a thirty-year lease, and the Rams wanted to make certain the stadium remained first class and that their profits were maximized as a result of its features. Thus this provision. If not met, they can leave as early as 2005.

This provision of the lease strongly implies that additional public funds, in addition to its original cost, will need to be spent on the stadium on a "regular" basis to keep up its standing. The question is how willing and able the financiers will be to keep up with advances in stadium technology and design in what is likely to be a rapidly evolving and highly competitive environment. The "evolving" sports markets that might well have new or remodeled stadia and thus compete with the Trans World Dome's top 25 percent rating could include Charlotte, Nashville, Baltimore, Chicago, Detroit, Denver, Houston, Cincinnati, Arizona, Seattle, and Tampa Bay.

The threat of a Rams' departure, with them barely settled in, has added dramatically to the stadium frenzy. While St. Louis's CVC has set up a preservation fund with $4 million per year to maintain the dome's ranking among all facilities, will this suffice to keep it in the "top 25 percent" of all NFL football stadia? No one knows. This is one more facet to the precedent-setting nature of the Rams' arrangement and the expectations that it places on St. Louis as well as other cities.

THE LESSONS LEARNED FROM ANOTHER CITY'S USE OF SPORTS TO ENHANCE ITS IMAGE AND DO SOMETHING WITH PIZZAZZ

There are two completely different components to the St. Louis story. An indoor arena that may well have been built in the suburbs became a cornerstone of an effort to revitalize downtown St. Louis. This facility was also instrumental in saving an NHL franchise, and its construction was accomplished as part of a public/private partnership. However, the city's relative success in developing the new Kiel Center was completely dwarfed by the public subsidies provided to encourage the Rams to move to downtown St. Louis. After losing an NFL team, St. Louis found itself virtually held hostage by the cartel that is the NFL and the public sector forced to pay a king's ransom to secure another team. In one sense St. Louis's payment was designed to be a lesson for other cities that might refuse to deal with the demands for a new stadium from an existing team. The costs of attracting a new franchise might be far more than the cost of dealing with teams already part of your city. While Cleveland's success in receiving some compensation for the loss of its NFL team may give some cities the courage to reduce their subsidies, Cleveland was willing to invest $175 million to keep Art Modell's team. St. Louis, on the other hand, had refused to meet Mr. Bidwill's demands in 1987. The cost for failing to work with him was more than $200 million (plus interest) financed across thirty years. Sometimes winning a battle with a professional team by refusing to meet its demands leads to much larger financial investments or subsidies in the future. Such is the power of the sports cartel; they indeed do have the ability to teach cities lessons regarding the costs of failing to capitulate to the structure of their welfare system.

In reviewing St. Louis's history with subsidizing sports, some have argued that the city has really been quite fortunate and prudent. Bernie Miklasz, a well-known local sportswriter, noted that the old arena facility was used from 1929 to 1994 and housed the Blues for most of their twenty-seven years in St. Louis. When they left the arena in 1994 they moved into the Kiel Center, which was substantially financed with private funds. The Cardinals used old Busch Stadium (Sportsman's Park) until Anheuser-Busch helped pay for the construction of a new baseball park. In this sense, then, St. Louis hosted teams without a large public-sector investment until it lured the Rams from California. The subsidies given to the Rams, if averaged across the years 1929 to 1995, would represent a small investment in sports.

How's that for justifying the provision of welfare to wealthy owners and players?

In the 1980s it probably would have cost St. Louis less than $100 million for a stadium to retain the football Cardinals. That proposal was virtually "shouted down" by people from across the community. It was apparent, then, that St. Louis was fed up with the team's owner, and maybe with the team itself. As Miklasz notes, "For decades, St. Louis lagged behind the rest of the nation in sports investment. That inflated the cost of the Rams' contract. St. Louis had to catch up. If anything, the ledger is even" (Miklasz, 1995). This logic, to sustain the provision of welfare to professional sports, insures the existence of cartels who, with the cooperation of governments and a supportive media, extract welfare and demand the transfer of wealth from taxpayers to the super rich.

LESSONS LEARNED

St. Louis's efforts to rebuild parts of its downtown area and to restore its image through sports created two very different sets of lessons for other communities. In one instance, St. Louis's political leadership forged an effective partnership with its economic elite to (1) jointly develop a much-needed arena, (2) ensure that the arena would be in downtown St. Louis, and (3) keep the Blues from migrating elsewhere. In the other instance, St. Louis may well have set a new standard for subsidizing professional sports.

1. PARTNERSHIPS ARE POSSIBLE

Indoor arenas, with their potential for hosting concerts, the circus, shows, and conventions, can be profitable for private investors. It is also possible for a city to support its share of any investments through user charges or entertainment taxes. As team owners secure the revenue for their contributions to a building's cost from the sale of luxury seating, the public sector can follow the same process. Even in the cartel world of sports it is not necessary to subsidize an arena.

The Kiel Center will cost the city of St. Louis approximately $50 million. A total of $35 million was contributed to the construction of the facility (land, demolition of the old structure), and the city also spent $15 million to purchase the old arena. Other public concessions included a deed restriction on its own property and a non-compete clause with another piece of city property. The only specifically identifiable return to the city for this is the dedicated parking revenues. The other returns to the city are related to direct general revenues associated with the events at Kiel and secondary revenues from associated activities. Packaging Kiel, a nominally private venture, required $50 million in outlays plus a variety of other concessions. What appears to be a simple deal can actually have many strings attached to bring the project to fruition. St. Louis illustrates this and provides a caveat for other cities: Beware the strings attached—each one has a cost. However, even with these twists in mind, it is still likely that the city will be able to support all of its investments by collecting taxes that result from events and sales at the new arena.

This, then, is the lesson for cities contemplating an indoor arena. You can build and develop a "state-of-the-art" facility and not have to subsidize it into existence. A city may not realize any profits other than the benefits it enjoys from having the facility present, but it can develop the facility without having taxpayers who do not attend events pay for it. However, if a city does get involved with the building of an arena with private-sector partners, understand their commitments, responsibilities, and needs for profit. The completion of the Opera House remains a thorn in the public/private partnership that developed the new Kiel Center. Even a successful partnership can have nagging problems that can extend for years.

2. THE COSTS OF CARTEL POLITICS

Playing ball with the NFL cartel is usually very expensive for cities. St. Louis's efforts raise a number of questions. Should any city agree to provide the level of public support that St. Louis did for wealthy people just to enhance its image and redevelop its downtown area? The justification of the expenditure—to do something dramatic and to finance it in a way that may minimize public expenses—does little to offset the fact that now the NFL can use St. Louis as the model of what it expects from cities. Little comfort can and should be taken from the observation that St. Louis had really provided very little welfare to its sports teams in the past. The subsidies provided to the Rams cannot be justified in terms of the failure to provide assistance in the past. Any way it is packaged, welfare for the rich is welfare. The cost of the dome to the public sector may well be minimized through the financial returns realized as a result of new convention opportunities. Yet, should a successful convention center be operated to provide higher income to NFL owners and players? If the dome in St. Louis could be paid for through fees earned by the convention center, then why not let the NFL develop domed facilities and also utilize them to host conventions? In that way the public sector does not have to be in the position of subsidizing the economically privileged.

Lastly, if you are going to be involved with cartel politics, read the fine print in the lease. After making all of their commitments to the Rams, St. Louis and Missouri will undoubtedly face renewed demands in the future given the need to maintain the facility as a "first-tier" stadium. As such terms are never defined, the Rams can make any number of demands, and if these requests are not met, they could move, again, to another city willing to provide even more welfare to the rich.

9

Sports and Economic Development North of the Border

Baseball Subsidies with a Canadian Flavor and a French Accent

J UST AS IN THE UNITED STATES, sports have been used by Canadian governments in efforts to stimulate economic development and establish civic identities and images. These efforts in Canada have also involved substantial public-sector expenditures to ensure that sports, and major league baseball in particular, would be part of Canadian life, Canada's image, and the economic development policies of cities and provinces. The two most expensive single-site sports projects, both planned to enhance civic images and foster economic development, are found in Canada. Montreal's Olympic Stadium cost more than $1 billion (Canadian), and the Skydome in Toronto had a final price tag in excess of $625 million (Canadian). Even with the very favorable exchange rates that exist between the U.S. and Canadian dollars (favorable for Americans), these two expenditures dwarf the cost of any other facilities built in

North America and maybe even in the entire world. Both projects were initially justified in terms of their potential for economic development and ability to foster a city's image. However, both projects cost far more than anticipated and resulted in huge public subsidies. In reviewing the costs associated with Toronto's edifice, or what one columnist referred to as Ontario's "St. Peter's Basilica" (Stein, 1994), Paul Godfrey, a former chair of Toronto's Metropolitan Government Council, so aptly, and wryly, reviewed the public sector's failure to control expenditures, noting:

> They could have asked for business plans. I don't think they really did their jobs (Van Alphen, 1992).

But they did do their jobs and they built the two most expensive, and subsidized, sports palaces in North America. What they did not do was their homework relative to what sports could do, and they did not provide the oversight and controls needed to build a useful and desirable stadium.

The anticipated or hoped-for return from these investments involved the typical expectations of an enhanced image, expanded downtown development through related private-sector investments, and greater economic growth. Ironically those who benefit from the existence of teams have proclaimed the public's investment as worthwhile. In 1994, Dave Perkins, a columnist with the *Toronto Star,* noted:

> The province [Ontario] has written off the loss and the general public doubtless has better things to get excited about now. Besides, it's here [Skydome] and the roof works and everybody goes to it and many even profess to love it. Plus, it allowed the Blue Jays to make enough money to buy the players to win two World Series and how much was that worth to everyone?

Sarcasm, or are those who benefit from sports simply trying to ensure more subsidies in the future? What did the public sector do north of the border, and what did they accomplish since 1969 when MLB's umpires began yelling "Play ball" in Montreal (*Jouez de balle* might be more appropriate) as the Expos joined the National League. Toronto, frequently in economic and image competition with Quebec's largest city, joined baseball's major leagues eight years later when the Blue Jays became part of the American League. In both provinces, governments tried to outdo each other and build a new wonder for the world's enjoyment. Both succeeded in spending more money than they ever imagined.

It might seem a bit ironic that Canada's largest investments in sports did not focus on hockey facilities. If sports and economic development were to be united in Canada, many would expect hockey to be the centerpiece of any public investments. To be sure, hockey is the "king" of Canadian sports. However, while sports fans in Canada have very deep passions for hockey, both Montreal and Toronto have extensive histories with other sports. The city of Montreal has an illustrious baseball history that begins in the post-Depression days as the city was home to one of the most successful AAA franchises in North America, the Royals. An affiliate of the old Brooklyn Dodgers, the Royals were not only league champions in seven different seasons from 1941 through 1958, but they won three Junior World Series championships during this era and were the team for which Jackie Robinson made his initial inroads into "white" professional sports. Roy Campanella and Don Newcombe were African-American stars who also gained early experience with the MLB system as members of the Royals.

Toronto's history with sports other than hockey is just a bit less storied, but is nevertheless quite extensive. The city was host to one of the charter members of the NBA, the Toronto Huskies, and was actually the site of the first NBA game (played in 1946) after the merger of the preexisting and competing leagues. The Huskies, however, did not survive to play a second season, and the NBA would not return to Toronto until 1995. Toronto was also home to a minor league baseball team prior to the arrival of the Blue Jays. The Toronto Maple Leafs baseball team was a member of the AAA International League from 1912 to 1967. During their existence the Maple Leafs won ten league pennants and one Junior World Series. Six of the pennant-winning seasons took place during the team's last twenty years. The Yankees' first African-American star, Elston

Howard, was a member of the 1954 pennant-winning Maple Leafs team, and Babe Ruth hit his only minor league home run against the Maple Leafs. The baseball Maple Leafs played in a privately owned facility built on the city's harbor front.

As would be expected from this long association with professional baseball, sports fans in Canada have been quite supportive of teams even though their first and most passionate love is hockey. In Montreal, where the Canadiens have won twenty-three Stanley Cup championships, including five in succession in the 1950s, the minor league Royals were able to attract more than 450,000 fans each season during their most successful years. Fans in both Montreal and Toronto have also been quite supportive of winning MLB baseball teams. Indeed, the Toronto Blue Jays were the first MLB team to attract more than four million fans in a single year, and at the height of their success, the Montreal Expos drew more than two million fans (1979, 1980, 1983, and 1984). The Expos might have been able to repeat this success in 1994 when the MLB strike destroyed the team's chance for a divisional title and an appearance in the play-offs.

The public sector in Canada, as will be detailed, has been a lavish and overly indulgent supporter of professional baseball. Large sums of tax dollars have been committed to the building of Skydome in Toronto (built for the Blue Jays) and the Olympic Stadium in Montreal (fitted with a dome for the Expos). Why would Canadian governments be interested in subsidizing baseball? Part of the answer lies in the more willing acceptance of taxes and government involvement in all aspects of life by Canadian voters. However, this was not the overriding factor in either Montreal's or Toronto's decision to subsidize MLB through the building of "signature statement" ballparks. Both governments sought something else. First, each province (Quebec and Ontario) and each city (Montreal and Toronto) wanted to enhance its own prestige and stature within Canada. Simply put, they each wanted to "outdo" the other. A stadium that would become a wonder of the modern world was seen as a vehicle in this effort to be Canada's first city. Second, both cities wanted closer economic and social integration with the United States. What better way to become part of American life than to be part of MLB? What neither community realized is that they would join the society of American cities that have subsidized sports and turn that group into an international fraternity.

As we will see, downtown redevelopment, additional economic growth, closer ties with the United States, and enhanced civic images have all been used by Canadian governments to justify the public sector's expenditures for professional baseball. For example, in explaining Montreal's initial passion and the national government's interest in having an MLB team in Canada in 1969, some leaders pointed to the necessity of integrating Canadian life and Canada into American life and social systems. The United States is such an important economic partner that MLB was defined as a tool for increasing the linkages and associations between the social systems of both nations. Securing a major league franchise—especially for French-speaking Canada—was seen by many as essential for acceptance and participation in U.S. economic, political, and social circles. As Canada's trade and economic future has became more and more linked to the United States, several of the leaders interviewed for this book perceived a critical benefit from being linked to main elements of the culture and social life of the United States. For many Canadians, there is nothing more American than baseball. Consequently, as the two national economies become more and more intertwined, extending these linkages to important cultural institutions seemed not only logical and practical but in the self-interest of both countries. In Quebec, where language and cultural differences exist relative to the United States, having a baseball team served to illustrate the similarity and economic bridges that could be built. As a result, Montreal and Quebec moved first and more quickly to become part of America's national pastime.

Montreal and Toronto have frequently had a level of competition between them; this competition extends through various economic and social circles, including sports. After Montreal secured an MLB team, it was only a matter of time before Toronto would try to become a home to America's pastime. Higgins (1986) notes that "what has distinguished Montréal from the beginning was the city's role on the international scene." This role, however, developed when Canada was a central part of the British Empire and was inexorably linked to the United Kingdom's economic and political status. Economic ties with Great Britain along an east-west Canadian axis were vital for Montreal. After World War II, and with the ascension of the U.S. economy and its political strength, America replaced Britain as Canada's major trading partner. The change from an east-west to a north-south economy favored Toronto within the system of Canadian cities (Gagnon & Montcalm, 1990). As a result, in recent years, Toronto's economic importance has grown, and in the 1970s the city wanted an MLB team to symbolize and illustrate its role in North America and Canada. In addition, for Toronto to underscore its role among Canadian cities, a stadium that "outdid" what Montreal had done for the Expos would be needed. These desires on the part of both Montreal (in the 1960s and 1970s) and Toronto (in the 1970s and 1980s) set the stage for extraordinary levels of public investments and subsidies for MLB.

The experience of Canadian governments in their dealings with professional baseball—and the subsidies they have given to attract and retain baseball—provide excellent examples of how sports teams become part of a community's effort to enhance and change its image. The experiences of both cities also provide important lessons for communities that are considering using sports to improve their economic development. In one example of playing ball in Canada, Toronto may have succeeded in its goals, but only after investing a staggering amount of money. In Montreal, even if baseball fails, the economic success of the community may be virtually unaffected, but the public's extraordinary investment in professional sports will require additional taxes for decades.

THE GROWTH OF CANADA'S GIANTS: SIZE AND COMPETITION NORTH OF THE BORDER

For more than forty years, Canada's two eastern demographic giants, Montreal and Toronto, and Ontario and Quebec provinces, have battled for economic and demographic supremacy. Where once both provinces were about the same size, today Ontario is substantially larger than Quebec. Montreal, Canada's largest metropolitan region through the early 1970s, lost that distinction and is now three-quarters of the size of Toronto (see Table 9–1). While Quebec had an 80 percent increase in the number of its residents from 1951 to 1995, Ontario's population increased 139 percent. Metropolitan Montreal's population increased by 126 percent from 1951 to 1994, but metropolitan Toronto grew by 254 percent. Metropolitan Toronto's population is now 29 percent larger than metropolitan Montreal's, and Ontario's population is 51 percent larger than Quebec's. During the 1980s the population of the Montreal region grew a modest 9.6 percent while the Toronto region's population expanded by 22.1 percent. The number of jobs in Montreal increased by 60 percent between 1971 and 1991, but the total number of jobs in Toronto increased by more than 100 percent.

While metropolitan Toronto and Ontario have now surpassed metropolitan Montreal and Quebec in size, in the 1960s and 1970s both regions were locked in a competitive struggle to be Canada's leading center; sports, expositions, and large public facilities became part of this competition. Montreal established an early lead in this competition by (1) hosting an international exposition in 1967, (2) being selected as a site for MLB with the awarding of the Expos fran-

TABLE 9–1

Population Growth in Metropolitan Montreal and Toronto and
Quebec and Ontario Provinces, 1951–1995

Year	Metropolitan Montreal	Metropolitan Toronto	Quebec Province	Ontario Province
1951	1,471,851	1,210,353	4,055,681	4,597,542
1956	1,745,001	1,502,253	NA	NA
1961	2,109,509	1,824,481	5,259,211	6,236,092
1966	2,570,982	2,289,900	5,780,845	6,960,870
1971	2,743,208	2,628,043	6,027,764	7,703,106
1976	2,802,547	2,803,101	6,234,445	8,264,465
1981	2,828,349	2,998,947	6,438,403	8,625,107
1991	3,127,242	3,893,046	6,895,963	10,084,885
1994	3,322,400	4,281,900	NA	NA
1995	NA	NA	7,300,000	11,004,800

NA=Not Available

chise in 1969, (3) serving as the host city for the 1976 Olympics, and (4) building a stadium for the Olympics that would later become the home of the Expos and the world's first retractable-dome facility (1976 and 1988). It was hoped that this innovative stadium and its retractable roof would make it a wonder of the modern world much as the Astrodome and Superdome had been when they made their debuts. Toronto would then counter these civic achievements by Montreal with the Blue Jays in 1977 and the Skydome—the removable-roof stadium that actually works and that opened for use in 1989.

BASEBALL NORTH OF THE BORDER: THE MONTREAL EXPOS

MLB's long-standing relationship with a successful AAA franchise in Montreal was a clear asset to the city in its quest to be the home for baseball's first franchise outside of the United States. In 1968, the National League was set to expand through the addition of two teams. Montreal was included in a competition with Buffalo, the Dallas/Fort Worth region, Milwaukee, and San Diego. Walter O'Malley, owner of the Dodgers, assumed a large role in the decision to award franchises to both San Diego and Montreal. His long-term association with the city of Montreal through the Royals, the favorable exposure the city had received from its hosting of a World Exposition in 1967, the local political leadership, and the potential market area for the team—more than five million people in the province and in nearby U.S. states—combined to help Montreal edge past Buffalo, Milwaukee, and the Dallas/Fort Worth region as a site for a new team (McKenna & Purcell, 1980; Post, 1993). After all, if a minor league team could attract almost 500,000 fans, a major league team should have no attendance problems. The potential revenues that could be earned by opening Canada as a new market for MLB[1] was not lost on the aggressive business acumen of Walter O'Malley and the other National League owners.

Despite the very favorable demographic characteristics of the Canadian market, Quebec Province, and Montreal, from the very beginning, the finances for a major league baseball team proved to be a challenge for Montreal. While MLB and the city's political leadership was confident that baseball would be a success in French-speaking Quebec, investors were not. To enter the National League the new Montreal franchise had to pay a $10 million franchise fee. Investors were reluctant to commit that much money, and the situation was resolved only when Charles Bronfman agreed to invest $4.5 million in the team in exchange for a tax-investment credit from the Canadian government. The Montreal Expos, then, began with government subsidies, and this reliance on public support did not end with the tax preferences extended to the original investors.

Given certain elements of Montreal's history, the need for subsidies was certainly a bit of a surprise. While the city of Montreal's population declined during the past three decades, the region had grown, and all projections were for even more growth in the future. From 1971 through 1991 the population of Montreal declined from approximately 1.2 million residents to 1 million. The population in the suburbs, however, substantially increased, and the metropolitan area had approximately 3.2 million residents. A population base of this size should be able to support a major league baseball team, especially when there are even more potential fans throughout Quebec and in neighboring American states.

The shift of Montreal's population to the suburbs was related to the changing dimensions of the city's economy. A manufacturing center through the 1970s, the city lost 70,000 jobs, or 36 percent of its industrial base, between the 1970s and 1990s. Jobs first shifted to suburban areas that share the main island with Montreal, and then to suburban areas off the island (Laval and Longueuil). Overall, between 1951 and 1986, the proportion of the metropolitan Montreal workforce employed in manufacturing declined from 37.6 percent to 21.2 percent (Lamonde and Mortineau, 1992). The declining population levels, together with the loss of the traditional base of Montreal's economy, were not the only signs of economic change.

The general decline of industry and commerce affected the financial sector. The Toronto Stock Exchange supplanted the Montreal exchange as the most important in Canada. Toronto was becoming the main site for company headquarters as well. Montreal's diminished role in the Canadian and North American economy was long apparent before the Parti Québecois (PQ) became popular (in the 1970s). Indeed, before turning to separation and the maintenance of the French language and culture, Montreal turned to sports to enhance its image and coupled this emphasis on sports with an entire redevelopment program.

REDEVELOPMENT AND SPORTS: MONTREAL STYLE

While Indianapolis coupled sports and downtown development into one set of policies and programs, Montreal sought to redefine its image through redevelopment and then joined sports to its efforts to maintain the importance of the city. Redevelopment began in Montreal in the 1950s with the widening of major streets to improve east-west traffic flow. Lévesque Boulevard was designed to be a center for corporate headquarters, and Plâce Ville-Marie became "without question, the single most important development in the history of Montréal's downtown" (Nader, 1976). The project's first stage began Montreal's extensive underground pedestrian system and inaugurated the city's era of high-rise building development. Between 1962 and 1967 a number of other large multifunctional office complexes were built in the central business district: Plâce Victoria, Plâce Bonaventure, and Plâce du Canada. Each of these complexes has an extensive underground pedestrian system and set of shopping complexes, but the erosion of Montreal's economic status did not decline.

Just as in several U.S. cities, Montreal joined sports and other festivals to its effort to redevelop its downtown area and change its image. Jean Drapeau, Montreal's mayor from 1960 through 1986, just as Richard Lugar and William Hudnut in Indianapolis were doing at about the same time (1968 through 1991), initiated several other grand projects, including the 1967 World Exposition, the establishment of the Montreal Expos, the 1976 Olympics, a subway,

new highways, and new boulevards. In the latter years of the Drapeau mayoralty and in the progressive administration of Mayor Jean
Doré (1986 through 1994), Montreal tried to revitalize the city with
a number of different policy efforts. To stem the flight of manufacturing to the suburbs, ten industrial parks were created after 1980. A
major effort was made to revitalize neighborhood commercial
arteries with extensive street and sidewalk renovations. The program, Operation 20,000 Houses, was a successful subsidized housing effort for middle-income citizens. Finally, there were attempts to
renew the central business district. Each of these projects was implemented with the hope that Montreal's fiscal stature, image, and economic development would be enhanced. Alas, that did not occur. A
leading downtown department store closed, and Montreal's major
retail area has had a disturbing number of vacancies. For the last fifteen years the Montreal region has had an unemployment rate that
exceeds 10 percent. Recently, Montreal has embarked on a series of
programs to enhance its international image and economic presence. The quest for the Expos was an early precursor of some of
these more recent efforts to make Montreal a leading— if not *the*
leading—city of Canada.

THE MONTREAL EXPOS

The history of the Expos after entering the league in 1969 is relatively lackluster. After twenty-seven years, the team's cumulative
record includes more losses than wins (a .492 winning percentage),
and the Expos are one of only three National League teams to never
have appeared in a World Series during the last four decades.
Indeed, the Expos' only appearance in postseason play came as a
result of the player's strike in 1981 and MLB's use of a split-season
format to determine play-off participants. The history of the Expos
can be divided into three eras: the early or struggling years at Jarry
Park (1969 through 1976), successful years at Olympic Stadium
(1979 through 1983), and the years of decline (1983 through 1995).

When Montreal was awarded its MLB franchise the city had
committed to the building of a new facility for the team. Specific

ideas for a new stadium were slow to evolve; the city was initiating its plans for a proposal to the International Olympic Committee to host the 1976 Summer games. As a new stadium would be needed if Montreal was awarded the games, there was some hope that an Olympic Stadium eventually could become home to the Expos. Until that stadium would be built, however, the team would have to use Jarry Park. Improvements were made to this aging facility, but for the team's first years, its seating capacity was 30,000.

For the Expos' first years playing in a small stadium may have been an advantage as fewer fans had to suffer through the team's poor performance. Indeed, playing in a facility that was similar to those used by some minor league teams might have been appropriate given the team's early records.

In their first year in Montreal the Expos lost 110 games (68 percent), and these losing ways became a tradition and part of the team's legacy. From 1970 through 1978 the Expos never won as many games as they lost, and in 1976 their futility almost matched their pitiful first year (107 losses to 110). Because of the 1976 Olympics the Expos played all of their games on the road for a period of two months. While some believed the extensive road trip contributed to the team's losing ways, others thought the road trip gave the city some relief from the poor play of its baseball team. The team's on-the-field performance, however, did not discourage Montreal's fans. From 1969 through 1974 more than one million fans attended games. Attendance dropped in the Olympic year, 1976, but in 1977 and 1978 more than 1.4 million fans attended games. And this was the precursor to the Expos' glory years (see Table 9–2).

When the Expos moved to Olympic Stadium their fortunes on the field changed. Building on their improved performance in 1977 and 1978, the Expos compiled the best overall record in the National League during the 1979, 1980, 1981, and 1982 seasons. Unfortunately, in no year did the Expos win a pennant. When the Expos became a team that was a potential pennant winner, fan support increased and attendance surpassed two million in four different seasons. The "high-water" marks for the team were 1982 and 1983, when 2.3 million fans were attracted to Montreal's "contending team" (see Table 9–2). The frustration over not winning a title that developed during these years seemed to usher in a period of gradual decline for the Expos, both in their performance on the field and in their presence in the sports life of Montreal and Canada. Ironically, however, their declining popularity may have been as much a result of external forces as it was of their inability to win a pennant.

In 1978, the Molson Companies purchased the Montreal Canadiens and initiated a vastly expanded marketing program. With the Canadiens already having a firmly established fan base, this new emphasis simply made the task of attracting people to other sports more difficult. This new marketing effort was bolstered by renewed levels of success on the ice by the Canadiens, including three new Stanley Cup championships. This success contrasted sharply with the failure the Expos were beginning to endure. Even more disturbing for the Expos was the success of the Toronto Blue Jays and that team's emergence as English-speaking Canada's MLB team. When the Expos were MLB's only Canadian team, they were able to attract substantial fan loyalty from Ontario Province. By the 1980s the Blue Jays were as successful as the Expos, and the Blue Jays, owned by Canada's other large brewery, Labatt, were also extensively marketed throughout populous Ontario Province and the rest of Canada. While Quebec and Montreal are certainly large enough to support a MLB team, the success of the Blue Jays and the marketing of the Canadiens, at a time when the Expos lost more games than they won, initiated a period of sharp decline.

Off the field, the team has had substantial problems with the image created by its players. Two players in the early 1980s admitted to drug use and a third was released when it was suspected that he, too, was using drugs. Gary Carter, in his autobiography, claimed that drugs were frequently used by some Expos players (Carter with Abraham, 1993). The team's manager, Dick Williams, described in his autobiography the use of illegal drugs by players beneath the stands and the sale of illegal drugs in the stadium parking lot. Williams began to check his players for symptoms of drug use before each game and once went so far as to dismantle a hair dryer he thought was a stash for illegal drugs (Williams & Plaschke, 1990). The stories that circulated concerning the use of drugs contributed to the impression that the Expos of the late 1970s and early 1980s were indulgent underachievers. In this atmosphere, fan support suffered, and while some blamed decreasing attendance on the changing economy and the deindustrialization of Montreal, the image created by the stories that circulated about players and the team created substantial fan disenchantment.

When drugs were not undermining the image of the team, the failure of some of the players to embrace the local culture also hurt marketing efforts. Establishing or integrating MLB into the Québe-

TABLE 9–2

Year-by-Year Record and Attendance Levels of the Montreal Expos

Season	Games Won	Games Lost	Winning Percentage	Finish	Games Out	Attendance
1969	52	110	.321	6	48	1,212,608
1970	73	89	.451	6	16	1,424,683
1971	71	90	.441	5	25½	1,290,963
1972	70	86	.449	5	26½	1,142,145
1973	79	83	.488	4	3½	1,246,863
1974	79	82	.491	4	8½	1,019,134
1975	75	87	.463	5	17½	908,292
1976	55	107	.340	6	46	646,704
1977	75	87	.463	5	17½	1,433,757
1978	76	86	.469	4	14	1,427,007
1979	95	65	.594	2	2	2,102,173
1980	90	72	.556	2	1	2,208,175
1981	60	48	.556	-	-	1,534,564
1st half	30	25	545	3	4	
2nd half	30	23	566	1	+0.5	
1982	86	76	.531	3	6	2,318,292
1983	82	80	.506	5	8	2,320,651
1984	78	83	.484	5	18	1,606,531
1985	84	77	.522	3	16½	1,502,494
1986	78	83	.484	4	29½	1,128,981
1987	91	71	.562	3	4	1,850,324
1988	81	81	.500	3	20	1,478,659
1989	81	81	.500	4	12	1,783,533
1990	85	77	.525	3	10	1,421,388
1991	71	90	.441	6	26½	978,076
1992	87	75	.537	2	9	1,731,566
1993	94	68	.580	2	3	1,641,437
1994	74	40	.649	1	6	1,276,250
1995	66	78	.458	5	24	1,292,764

Note: The 1981 season was played in two separate halves as a result of a strike by the players. The Expos were the division champions for the second half of the season.

cois culture is a challenge and an obligation some players were not willing to embrace. While Rusty Staub became proficient enough in French to make public speeches, other players seemed to have a difficult time with Québecois culture and life. Most MLB players are Americans and, similar to the overwhelming majority of residents of the United States, they do not speak languages other than English. With the ever-present possibility of a trade to a team in the continental United States, there is little incentive for players to invest themselves in the French language or the Québecois culture. This, coupled with little commitment to or interest in learning another language or immersing oneself in another culture, created a level of tension between the players and the fans, examples of which abound.

One player's wife was reported to have told many people that she needed to shop in Plattsburgh, New York, because "there are important staples we have to go there for, like Doritos" (Crichler, 1992, p. 6). In 1995, an Expos player complained because the flight attendants spoke French on a team flight. Former Expos manager Dick Williams, an admirer of Montreal as a city, claimed "modern day baseball players don't like Montréal, not because of your city but because they are baseball players. . . . For the modern day player, differences are not to be tolerated. The modern day player doesn't hate Montréal so much as he's afraid of it" (Williams & Plaschke, 1990, p. 205).

Gary Carter, a player who liked Montreal, discussed three problems that players faced. The "hassles" that existed only for members of the Montreal Expos and Toronto Blue Jays included (1) having to pay taxes in both countries, (2) confrontations with customs officials of both countries, and, (3) the language (Carter & Abraham, 1993). Williams and Carter both speak fondly of Montreal. Williams calls it "a wonderful place to spend a summer" (Williams & Plaschke, 1990, p. 206). In Carter's opinion, Montreal is "one of the most beautiful and diverse cities in the Western Hemisphere" (Carter with Abraham, 1993, p. 134).

Not all of the cultural problems between baseball and Québecois culture emanated from the team and its largely American players.

Baseball's fit into Quebec, especially as nationalist pressures developed and a focus upon the preservation of French culture and values began to dominate local politics, was a bit awkward. To reduce this tension the team searched for French Canadian players, but only Claude Raymond, a pitcher who finished his career with the Expos in their early days, and Denis Boucher have been members of the Expos. Neither were stars, but both attracted large crowds to games at Olympic Stadium (Ziniuk & Westreich, 1994).

WHITHER GOES THE EXPOS? MANAGEMENT RESPONDS TO IMAGE PROBLEMS, AND MAKES THE SITUATION WORSE

With cultural and image problems, and declining or low levels of attendance, the Expos seemed to have found themselves in a situation in which reducing payroll costs was the best route to fiscal solvency. While a marketing plan might have helped address some of the team's image and attendance problems, management believed they had to reduce labor costs. As a result, the Expos began to lose free agents to other teams willing to pay higher salaries. Some star players were lost without any compensation, while others were traded to avoid paying higher salaries. From the 1980s through the 1990s, as the Expos' management began to fear high payroll costs, the team lost enough players to form a National League All-Star team (Farber, 1995; see Table 9–3).

The team's fortunes were temporarily reversed in 1994 when it appeared the Expos would likely win their first outright divisional title. Baseball seemed ready to succeed in Montreal, but the season-ending strike ended visions of a World Series in Montreal. Frustrations grew for both team owners and players, and the Expos' management continued its policy of dealing away their most expensive talent. Under instructions from the team's owners, General Manager Kevin Malone tried to reduce the team's payroll from the $18.6 million spent in 1994 to $15 million for 1995. In this environment, Larry Walker, Marquis Grissom, Ken Hill, and John Wetteland all

TABLE 9–3
The Former Expos and Their New Teams

	New Team	Position	Year
Gary Carter	Mets	Catcher	1985
Andres Galarraga	Rockies	First base	1992
Delino DeShields	Dodgers	Second base	1992
Tim Wallach	Dodgers	Third base	1994
Hubie Brooks	Dodgers	Shortstop	1993
Andre Dawson	Cubs	Outfield	1987
Marquis Grissom	Braves	Outfield	1995
Larry Walker	Rockies	Outfield	1995
Ken Hill	Cardinals	Pitcher	1995
Mark Langston	Angles	Pitcher	1990
Randy Johnson	Mariners	Pitcher	1989
John Wetteland	Yankees	Pitcher	1995

left for other teams and the Expos were able to meet their payroll target (see Table 9–3). Not surprisingly, when baseball resumed in 1995, the Expos attracted only 1.3 million fans and the team's fortunes on the field deteriorated. Instead of leading the division, the Expos finished 1995 twelve games below .500 and twenty-four games behind division-leading Atlanta. The Expos' 1996 starting lineup had a salary of $7.0 million, 30 percent lower than in 1995 (Johnson, 1996). The team's total player payroll for 1996 was $15.4 million, the lowest of all twenty-eight MLB teams (Bodley, 1996). However, the Expos again had a team that through September was competing for a play-off berth.

With high-priced players being traded, sold, or signed by other teams, the Expos seemed to exist in a perpetual state of fiscal distress. Throughout 1995 and into 1996 rumors swept through the mania of franchise free agency that the team was destined for northern Virginia or some other large market in the United States. Indeed, in discussing the fate of the Expos, some now consider Montreal a small market for baseball even though the population in the metropolitan area exceeds 3.2 million. Quebec Province has more than seven million residents, and none of these population projections includes potential market areas for the team in northern New York State, New England, and eastern Ontario. Despite this very large market area, the team has sold or traded some of its best talent.

MONTREAL'S VERSION OF
"A MISTAKE BY THE LAKE"

The final cost for Olympic Stadium was in excess of $1 billion, making any further investments impossible. While the Expos were initially required to play in a small facility, Jarry Park, the city had grand plans for its baseball team. Montreal was committed to building a larger and more modern facility, and as the plans for the 1976 Olympic games were already under way, it seemed only logical and practical to have the Expos play their future home games in the new Olympic Stadium. Twenty years later, the city of Atlanta would follow the same course of action when the time came to build a new home for the Braves.

The substantial public investment in Olympic Stadium might have been worth the tangible and intangible benefits if it had not become a symbol of failure. When the project was initiated, there was great hope that the Olympic Stadium would become Montreal's architectural statement, and when the Olympics began in 1976, the stadium received critical acclaim. Jean-Claude Marsan, a leading authority on Montreal's architecture, observed that "if Montréal has any building that merits the title of monument it certainly is the Olympic Stadium. It has all the attributes of Beaux Arts architecture: beauty, clarity of style and function, harmony of the ensemble, which itself is well balanced and rhythmic. Its design is dynamic and vibrant, enclosing spaces by ample movements. The majesty of this structure, particularly from the infield, is impressive" (Marsan, 1981). It seemed that the cost of the stadium might have been worth the benefits; but then the roof literally fell on the project.

The failure that is Olympic Stadium involves its controversial roof. Olympic Stadium was designed to be the first retractable dome stadium. The roof, however, was not completed when the building was opened in 1976. Indeed, the roof was not finished until 1988, and its most telling feature is the mast that was designed to lift a removable section on and off the stadium. It was anticipated that the Expos would play their games in an open-air stadium when weather permitted, and that the roof would descend to cover the field on cold and inclement days. This plan worked for only three seasons, and the giant mast has become a sort of reminder of the trials of the Expos and their stadium.

The mast (or tower) dwarfs the stadium, which is just seven stories high. The mast, fifty-five stories tall, is the world's tallest inclined structure, and is so dominating that it overwhelms the stadium's architecture. During the years that work continued on the roof, 1976 to 1987, Olympic Stadium was an outdoor facility. In 1988, with the roof in place, the team was able to play games in an open-air and protected environment. In 1988 the team played three games with the roof off. In 1989, the roof was removed for thirteen games, and in 1991 the Expos played forty-three games with the roof removed. In 1991, the system for removing the roof was destroyed in a storm. Since that time the Olympic Stadium roof has not been retracted and all of the Expos' games are played indoors. The failure of the retractable roof system has relegated the mast to a tourist attraction (there is an observation deck at its top) and a source of constant humor. The mast is now part of a system that cost millions of dollars and twelve years to design, but is an utter failure and too expensive to fix. The fact that the roof system is too expensive to repair means the stadium's most imposing or defining element is a symbol of failure.

There have been other problems with the stadium. In September 1991, a fifty-five-ton block of concrete fell from the stadium to the street. After two months of repairs, during which time the Expos were forced to play all their games on the road, the Quebec government declared the stadium safe. The Expos returned to play in Olympic Stadium in 1992. But the image of the stadium with the roof that did not work now became the stadium that was collapsing alongside its fifty-five-story symbol of failure.

While many are frustrated with the quality of the stadium, its problems do not result from the lack of interest in spending tax dollars for an architectural wonder. The public's investment in this facility has been quite substantial; indeed, the investment was astronomical even in comparison to those made by St. Louis and Baltimore. The stadium cost the province of Quebec more than $1 billion. This investment created a debt so substantial that it is still being paid off through a special property tax. Even though there is less resentment toward taxes in Canada than there is in the United States, the stadium is a source of resentment, and the stadium's supporters have been forced to ask, "Can architecture be justified regardless of cost" (Marsan, 1981, p. 392). Why did the building cost so much? There was the common litany of overruns: the need to build a special factory for prefabrication, the importing of materials and technicians from France, and the design and shape of the mast. To support the weight of the roof, the inevitable buildup of snow, and the overhang, thousands of extra tons of concrete had to be poured at the base of the mast as a counterweight. The mast alone cost as much to construct as the Kingdome in Seattle.

Cost issues aside, it is difficult to ascertain the reason for complaints about Olympic Stadium. The stadium is located near downtown, and is easily reached on the metro, by bus, or by car. It is certainly easy, cheap, and convenient to reach the stadium. After entering the stadium from the subway, the fan reaches a large food court where relatively inexpensive food is available. Before and after the games, there is always music in the food court, adding to an enjoyable experience for many fans. And while some might object to indoor baseball, sight lines provide an unobstructed view for most fans.

WHAT NOW FOR MLB IN MONTREAL?

The Expos' management would like to relocate to a new downtown stadium. A new stadium might offer additional revenue opportunities with luxury seating and suites. Still, the existing location of Olympic Stadium in the east end of Montreal is very near downtown and other amenities. With the high debt still associated with the existing facility, additional public investments would be very hard to justify. A move to the suburbs might place the team closer to a large concentration of higher-income households, but Olympic Stadium's location and proximity to mass transportation make the facility convenient for all segments of the population. Although there are some minor concerns with the neighborhood adjacent to the stadium, by comparison to other cities, the Maisonneuve area is neither unsafe nor a "slum." The current location of the stadium also meets the important policy objective of anchoring development of the east end of Montreal, an area with a high concentration of French-speaking residents (Francophones). The initial political support for the stadium was tied to the development of this area. In the Maisonneuve neighborhood close to the stadium, three hotels with a total of 516 rooms opened along the major east-west artery (Broadway, 1993).

The need to continue to develop this part of Montreal is but one of the reasons that a new downtown stadium is not likely to be built. In addition, Canada, Quebec, and Montreal are each facing different sets of fiscal problems. Canada's national debt is far greater than that facing the United States (as a percentage of gross domestic production). Provincial debt is even larger, in per capita terms, than Canada's national debt. When the Parti Québecois replaced the Liberal Party in provincial elections in 1993, the province had a deficit of $5.7 billion (Canadian). The PQ pledged to lower the deficit by $2 billion before 1997. Quebec's premier, Lucien Bouchard, has said that deficit reduction will be the priority of his government and that the public must be prepared for sacrifices. The provincial government has been in a retrenchment mode, with hospitals closing throughout the province in 1995. The Montreal area was especially impacted by the hospital closings. As one observer noted, "Is a government that is closing hospitals going to build a stadium?" Moreover, the provincial government refused to provide financial assistance for the Quebec Nordiques (an NHL franchise) and to build a new facility for the team. The Nordiques were then sold and the new owners moved the team to Denver for the 1995–96 season. If the province refused to provide financial assistance for a hockey team within the borders of its capital city, it is unlikely to be willing to provide financial help for a baseball team. The city of Montreal has its own financial challenges. City residents are still paying a tax for the Olympic Stadium, and this does not create a favorable environment for requesting another tax hike. The city's financial situation may even make it impossible to plan for improvements at Olympic Stadium, including the addition of sky boxes.

To put the Expos' fiscal/political situation in harshest perspective, Revenue Québec sued the Expos for payment of a 3.5-percent provincial health-care premium at 100 percent of the Expos' payroll. The government demanded $8 million in taxes. In September 1995, a provincial judge ruled that the team only had to pay for the time the players lived in the province, about 41 percent of the year. This saved the team more than $1 million a year, but still saddles the Expos with an expense not faced by MLB teams in the United States. (The Blue Jays pay their premium to Ontario on a formula similar to that of the Expos.) During the trial the Expos' attorney argued that the players are almost all nonresidents, and that they are treated by team physicians. However, the court still found that the Expos would have to pay the tax.

These fiscal realities are not the only obstacles to the public sector's financial support for baseball. While the value of the baseball team in terms of establishing economic ties to the United States was once a prevailing pressure, independence and the cultural identity of Quebec are, today, far more important issues. Keeping an MLB team is still important to some of the province's leadership, but others are more concerned with other cultural issues besides the economic linkages to the United States. Although baseball in the United States has been a major preoccupation of writers and intellectuals, Quebec is more European in terms of its cultural orientation. The province has a ministry of culture that spends far more per capita than any other province. Quebec has its own national library, and the government spends large sums on theater, museums, and the arts. Québecois buy half the classical records sold in Canada. Quebec is known for its excellent arts festivals, such as the Montreal jazz festival and the folk-dancing festival in Drummondville. Quebec's French-language films are known worldwide as well. In a situation where the survival of French culture and language are of the highest importance, baseball (and its largely American players and English-speaking Canadian fans) is not a priority in an area where culture and a national identity have been fused into a separatist movement. One Expos owner also threatened to move the team out of Montreal if the Parti Québecois succeeded in bringing about Quebec's independence (Richler, 1992), and this has further reduced the public's perception of the team as a permanent part of Montreal's identity and civic culture.

In this environment it is hard to be very optimistic about the future of baseball in Montreal, and the most recent events may provide the best view of the Expos' future as well. In January 1996, Will Cordero, the Expos shortstop, was traded to the Boston Red Sox for Rheal Cormier, a journeyman pitcher. Cordero, twenty-four years old at the time of the trade, has excellent offensive potential. He is an everyday player with speed and power. The Expos couldn't (or wouldn't) pay his salary, which would have been more than $1 million a year. Meanwhile, Cormier, who won seven games in 1995, represents the Expos' eternal quest for the Francophone star. In this case, Cormier is not even Québecois; he is an Acadian from the neighboring province of New Brunswick. Did the desire to reduce salaries or the search for a Canadian star drive the Expos' decision to make this trade? If it is the former, MLB's run in Montreal may be coming to an end. On the other hand, Montreal signed rising star Rondell White to a six-year contract in the spring of 1996. This is the first encouraging sign in a number of years for the future of the Montreal franchise with regard to player development and retention.

THE TORONTO BLUE JAYS AND THE BUILDING OF THE "WORLD'S GREATEST ENTERTAINMENT CENTER"

Toronto had to wait for its entry into MLB until 1977. For eight years, then, the Expos were Canada's baseball team. In 1977, when the American League decided to award Seattle a franchise in response to its lawsuit over the move of the Pilots to Milwaukee, adding a second team to balance the league seemed logical. The benefits of bringing American League baseball into the Canadian market were not lost on team owners. By 1977 metropolitan Toronto had a population of 2.8 million and Ontario had more than 8.3 million residents. In terms of market size, a Toronto-based team would be able to draw fans from a population base larger than what is available to the Cleveland Indians, Baltimore Orioles, Texas Rangers, and Seattle Mariners. By 1977, metropolitan Toronto had a population equal to that of metropolitan Montreal. Baseball seemed to be a natural fit in English-speaking Toronto.

The Blue Jays joined the American League for the rather paltry sum of $7 million. The nation's largest brewery, Labatt, owned 90 percent of the team, and the Canadian Imperial Bank of Commerce (CIBC) purchased the remaining 10 percent. Labatt Limited also owns the Toronto Argonauts football team (Canadian Football League), The Sports Network (a 6.3-million-subscriber, twenty-four-hour cable sports network), and Le Réseau des Sports (a French-language all-sports network). Beer and sports do mix quite well in Canada. The team played its initial seasons in aging Exhibition Stadium, an outdoor facility located on the shores of Lake Erie. From the moment the Blue Jays franchise was awarded, however, the city, as well as the team owners, envisioned a far greater playing facility. Indeed, a stadium was desired that would be a signature statement for the city and one that would surpass Montreal's Olympic Stadium in aesthetics and significance.

FROM AN EXPANSION TEAM
TO BASEBALL'S ELITE

The Blue Jays made consideration of a new stadium relatively easy even if an architectural statement and engineering marvel were not desired or deemed necessary. The Blue Jays, in a relatively brief period, went from an inept expansion team to a championship squad (see Table 9–4). In their inaugural season, similar to most expansion teams, the Blue Jays compiled the worst record in their league. Their 107 losses and winning percentage of .335 were only slightly worse than the Oakland A's performance that year, 98 losses and a winning percentage of .391. The Blue Jays' initial performance was far better than the ineptness of the 1962 Mets, who, in their first season, could manage just forty wins and a winning percentage of

.250. Unfortunately, though, the Blue Jays would get worse before they improved.

The team lost 102 games in 1978, and then, in their third year, lost 109 games as they posted a winning percentage of .327, equal to the performance of the Mets in their third year. A few among Toronto's faithful may have feared that the Blue Jays would be perennial losers; others might have prayed for an amazing turn-around similar to the one that propelled the Mets to the 1969 championship and produced the "Miracle at Flushing Meadow" (Neft & Cohen, 1996, p. 386). Ironically, it was the faithful fans who would be rewarded, as the Blue Jays did indeed turn things around, producing in their ninth season a miracle in the north to rival the Amazin' Mets' eight-year journey from oblivion to stardom. Indeed, the Blue Jays were to accomplish something even the Mets' faithful were denied: a team that competed for championships and pennants for nine consecutive seasons.

The Blue Jays' fortunes began to turn in 1980, their fourth season, as they posted a fourteen-game improvement from 1979 (sixty-seven wins). In the second half of the split 1981 season, the Blue Jays posted a winning percentage of .438, and suddenly major league baseball was a "real" sport in Toronto. Bobby Cox was the manager of the team in 1982, and the Jays began to take on the "look" of a contending team. The Jays won seventy-eight games in Cox's first season and eighty-nine in 1983. In just their seventh season of play, the Jays had become a winning team. In contrast, the Mets never had a winning season prior to their 1969 championship season. In the Blue Jays' ninth season they captured their first divisional title. From the time of their initial winning season, 1983, through 1993, the Blue Jays would win more than a thousand games, post a winning percentage of .563, and capture two World Series crowns. In only one season in the 1984 to 1993 period were the Blue Jays *not* involved in a race for the championship of their division. Three different managers, Bobby Cox, Jimy Williams, and Cito Gaston, led the Blue Jays during this period, and Cito Gaston was their manager during their two championship seasons, 1993 and 1994.

Toronto's baseball fans supported the Blue Jays in both their win-

Table 9–4

Year-by-Year Record and Attendance Levels, Toronto Blue Jays

Season	Games Won	Games Lost	Winning Percentage	Finish	Games Out	Attendance
1977	54	107	.335	7	45.5	1,700,052
1978	59	102	.366	7	40	1,562,585
1979	53	109	.327	7	50.5	1,431,651
1980	67	95	.414	7	30	1,400,327
1981[a]	37	69	.349			755,083
1st half	16	42	276	7	19	
2nd half	21	27	438	7	7.5	
1982	78	84	.481	6	17	1,275,978
1983	89	73	.549	4	9	1,930,415
1984	89	73	.549	2	15	2,110,009
1985	99	62	.615	1	+2	2,468,592
1986	86	76	.531	4	9.5	2,445,447
1987	96	66	.593	2	2	2,778,459
1988	87	75	.537	3	2	2,595,175
1989	89	73	.549	1	+2	3,375,883
1990	86	76	.531	2	2	3,885,284
1991	91	71	.562	1	+7	4,002,527
1992	96	66	.593	1	+4	4,028,318
1993	95	67	.586	1	+7	4,057,947
1994[b]	55	60	.478	3	16	2,907,933
1995	56	88	.389	5	30	2,826,483

Notes: [a]1981 was played as a split season as a result of a strike by the players. The Blue Jays finished in last place, 7th, in both "halves" despite a far better record in the second half of the season. [b]Had the 1994 season been played to its conclusion without a strike, the Blue Jays would have had an additional twenty-two home games. Given their "average" per game attendance, the team could well have attracted 4,154,273 fans, surpassing all of their own MLB attendance records.

Source: The Toronto Blue Jays; Neft and Cohen, 1996; Much and Friedman, 1996.

ning and losing seasons. Indeed, for a region where hockey is king, major league baseball has been quite well supported, and in several years, one could argue that baseball overtook hockey in the hearts of Toronto's sports fans. (It is also possible that their love just increased to adopt another favorite child.) In the Blue Jays' initial year 1.7 million fans were attracted to games, and through each of the team's losing years, 1977 through 1980, no fewer than 1.4 million fans attended games. Attendance declined to 755,083 in the strike-plagued 1981 season, but as soon as baseball got back to normal and the Blue Jays started winning, attendance soared. Nearly two million fans attended games during the Blue Jays' first winning season, and more than two million came in 1984 when the team duplicated its 1983 performance. From 1985 through 1993 the Blue Jays had a winning percentage of .566, and baseball fans in Toronto, Ontario, and other parts of Canada responded to this success and the opening of the Skydome with an unprecedented level of support. The Blue Jays consistently attracted at least 2.4 million fans, and then in 1989, playing more than half of their games at the Skydome, they attracted 3.38 million fans. In 1990, 3,885,284 attended Blue Jays home games.

Then, in 1991, the Blue Jays began a three-year streak of unprecedented attendance, attracting more than four million fans in each year. No major league team had ever drawn four million people to its home games, but during this period the Blue Jays not only achieved this plateau of success, but in each year, 1991 through 1993, they attracted more fans (see Table 9–4). The Skydome has 50,516 seats for baseball. With crowds in excess of four million, the Blue Jays were repeatedly on the verge of selling all tickets to all of their games. In 1991, they played to 97.8 percent of their capacity. This increased to 98.4 percent of capacity in 1992 and 99.2 percent of capacity in 1993. In 1994, the Blue Jays were actually on a pace to play before more than 100 percent of their seating capacity when the strike ended the season with twenty-two home dates remaining for the team. The demand for Blue Jays tickets was so great that all seats and standing room places were being sold even though the team, in 1994, was unlikely to catch the first-place Yankees. If baseball was not first in the hearts of Toronto's and Ontario's sports fans, it was very, very close to hockey. Toronto had proved, beyond a shadow of a doubt, that it was "baseball country." While Montreal launched its involvement with baseball to tie itself to the larger economic and social scene of North America, Toronto had succeeded in making itself a North American center of America's national pastime. Its preeminence over Montreal in terms of relations with America was complete, and it had a stadium whose dome actually worked!!

BUILDING THE WORLD'S GREATEST
ENTERTAINMENT CENTER

Inclement weather in Toronto was always a concern of public officials, the team's owners, players, and MLB. While Toronto's weather is really quite similar to that in Chicago, Cleveland, and Detroit, Toronto's late springs and early falls were part of the justification for considering an indoor stadium. The fact that Montreal had built a stadium with a retractable dome also presented a challenge for Toronto to equal or surpass. When planning the new facility, one of the team's executives retells a story of asking the initial Blue Jay players what they wanted in a new stadium. The overwhelming response from the players was a stadium that could be covered on inclement days but would have a removable roof for the numerous pleasant summer and fall evenings that Toronto enjoys. From that conversation, and the failure of Montreal's retractable roof, was born the ultimate challenge: build a retractable dome that would work. Toronto had its mission and its opportunity to do what Montreal had failed to accomplish. And, if they could be the first to do it in North America, Toronto could establish itself as a truly continental, first-class center.

In June 1983 Ontario's premier, William Davis, proclaimed that a dome was inevitable and needed. A three-person committee was appointed to identify the best site for the new facility, and one year later a public corporation was formed to design and construct it. This corporation was also given the authority to manage and operate the facility. In January 1985 a $150 million plan was proposed. Before construction work was initiated in October 1985, the projected cost of the stadium had increased to $225 million. It took more than three years to build the new facility; the dome did not open until June 3, 1989. The final cost of the stadium was more than $600 million.

To "outdo" Montreal, a design that would solve the architectural and engineering problems associated with a retractable dome was needed. The lure of extensive prestige for Toronto if a retractable dome could be developed was too great a prize to resist. However, Montreal's failure after spending more than $1 billion was a very visible reminder of the prestige losses that would occur if Toronto's dome also failed to open. Ultimately, a design developed by a local firm was chosen that involved a rotating roof pulled by an engine mounted on rails above the stadium and just below the dome itself. And while the enterprising and innovative designers would eventually be forced into bankruptcy, the ability of metropolitan Toronto and Ontario Province to build a design by a local firm added even more prizes to the prestige race with Montreal. The failed Olympic Stadium was designed and partially built in France. Toronto's Skydome would be a Canadian stadium, and it would work even if the designers would be financially ruined.

Toronto, like Montreal, Indianapolis, Cleveland, and St. Louis, also wanted to use the stadium to anchor economic downtown development. Each of these communities was experiencing the slow, but inevitable, decentralization of economic activity to suburban areas, and Toronto too, while sections were booming, had an area south and west of its business and financial centers and near Lake Erie that was not thriving. There was a great deal of land in this area, most of it owned by Canadian-Pacific Railways. If the facility could be built near the new CN Tower, Toronto could have an anchor for this part of its downtown and shoreline. The placement of the stadium in this location would also provide a stunning visual statement, as the facility would loom over the city's major freeway. With Toronto's fixation on mass transportation, the plan for the facility did not include the development of many parking spaces. Fewer than four hundred new spaces were added, as the facility is within easy walking distance of Toronto's subway system and several bus lines. There also is ample parking in several downtown buildings, and through 1996, most fans still relied on mass transportation to reach the Skydome.

Toronto's leadership also developed a very innovative public/private partnership to build the facility. For their investments these firms secured the right to provide services at the new stadium. The public's share of the facility's cost was to be $60 million, with $30 million invested by Ontario Province and $30 million invested by metropolitan Toronto (Reid, 1991). Thirty corporations were initially approached and invited to invest $5 million each in the facility.

These private owners would share in the profits from the stadium (which never materialized) and receive certain business opportunities related to building and operating it. Together with the public's initial investment, the partnership had $215 million of the anticipated or needed $225 million. The shortfall was to have been covered from operating profits, as the public-sector partners agreed to guarantee the total cost of the project. This latter point was extremely crucial. The private-sector partners had limited liability; they would not have to pay more than their $5 million and they would not be responsible for any additional costs. As a public corporation would operate and manage the facility, the $10 million anticipated shortfall became its responsibility.

THE COSTS JUST KEEP ON CLIMBING

In retrospect, the estimated $10 million in extra costs would become the least of the financial problems to beset Skydome. Six months after construction began, the stadium's management company decided to add additional restaurants and recreation venues to the project. This increased the projected cost of the facility by $36 million. In April 1987, then, it was estimated the Skydome complex would cost $261 million. One month later the corporation decided to add a hotel and health club to the complex. The cost of these facilities was estimated to be $57 million, elevating the overall construction project cost to $328 million. (The actual cost of the hotel and health facility would be $112 million.) To accommodate the hotel, seats were removed from the stadium, but several rooms in the hotel do have a view of the playing field. The loss of these additional seats, estimated to be between five thousand and eight thousand, would reduce revenues to the stadium and the Toronto Blue Jays, especially during the team's championship seasons.

As the projected opening day for the stadium began to slip into the 1989 baseball season, the Skydome's management company began to authorize extra overtime to complete the project. At this point, there was no public record of the entire cost of the project, but fears begin to build that the project was substantially over bud-

get. At the end of the saga, and the transfer of the stadium's ownership to the private-sector partners, there would still be very different
estimates of the cost of the stadium. Estimates by different media
analysts placed the cost of the entire facility at $580 million, $600
million, and $628 million. The statement of public accounts issued
by the province of Ontario in 1993 would place the cost of the stadium at $608.9 million. With an original cost estimate of $225 million, a final cost of $580 million would mean the final price tag was
257 percent greater than what had been anticipated. If the final cost
was $628 million, the Skydome would have cost 279 percent more
than expected. The province's own estimate calculated the cost at
271 percent more than anticipated. Regardless of the final cost pro-
jection used, the project cost 2.5 times more than taxpayers were initially told. How did the project's cost get from $225 million in 1987
to its final tally? While a portion of the overrun involved the actual
cost of the hotel and fitness center, $112 million instead of $57 million, and the excessive overtime charges, other costs also began to
accrue as the government decided to sell Skydome and get out of the
stadium business.

ENDING THE PUBLIC/PRIVATE PARTNERSHIP

Approximately one year after Skydome opened, Ontario's provincial
government realized the facility would never generate sufficient revenues to support the interest payments on the money borrowed by
the public sector, much less the principal sum invested by the public
sector. Skydome cost so much that the *daily* interest on the debt was
$60,000. With annual interest charges in excess of $20 million, the
facility's operating profits were simply too small to support the stadium's expenses (Van Alphen, 1991). As a result, each year that the
public sector retained ownership its financial responsibilities and
the cost of Skydome increased. In fact, there was no scenario under
which the revenues from the facility could support the interest
charges much less repay the public for its investment. When the
public's investment was $60 million, the operating revenues from
Skydome would have been sufficient to offset the anticipated inter-

est payments for a $225 million project with an estimated $10 million shortfall. When that shortfall increased by several hundred million dollars, the interest charges alone consumed the facility's operating profit.

With a new political party in office, different from the one that planned, developed, and built the Skydome, the idea that the government should sell the facility to the private owners began to gain considerable momentum. The problem with the suggestion was that no one was interested in paying the full cost of the public sector's investment. There also was no interest in paying the accumulated interest charges that had been accruing on the amount of money spent by the public sector. While the facility was generating an operating profit, that profit was not sufficient to cover the debt payments for the capital construction costs. The operating revenues from Skydome did cover the costs of maintenance. However, when the interest charges associated with the cost of the facility were included in a financial statement, together with the cost of the stadium, Skydome operated at a deficit. The public sector had paid too much for a complex that was far more than a home for sporting events, concerts, and other public gatherings. Skydome included a hotel, a health club, and a series of entertainment venues built into a stadium for baseball and football, and these elements of the greatest entertainment center on earth could not generate sufficient revenues to sustain themselves. While more than six million people attended events at Skydome in some years, the revenue earned was not sufficient to meet the operating and capital costs of the complex. Skydome actually was the site for as many as 256 events in a single year, 1993, but it could not generate sufficient revenue to pay for itself given the large debt associated with the final construction cost.

Within this fiscal environment it might seem prudent to sell the facility for as much as possible to minimize the public sector's costs. But here is where the Skydome story gets even more curious. In 1990, to reduce the public sector's responsibilities for the $60,000 in daily interest charges, Ontario decided to "pay off" the Skydome's debt. In other words, after 1990, the facility had *no public-sector debt*. When Skydome attracted more than six million visitors to 256 event days in 1993, the operating profit from the facility belonged to the province. With the debt "written off," the operating revenues were sufficient to both return a profit and maintain the facility. From an accounting perspective the interest or revenue lost on the debt was still calculated, but that charge was not paid to anyone. In fact, after the bills and bonds were paid in 1990, the interest charges represented what the province would have received had the money for the bonds been placed in a bank and earned interest income for the public sector. Why sell the facility in such an environment?

Any cash that was received would represent income for the province and could be used to offset taxes or the province's own debt, which had escalated throughout the 1980s and 1990s. But, from a strict business standpoint, with the capital cost of Skydome settled, the operating income was returning a profit. The province of Ontario's own records for the Stadium Corporation indicate an operating profit of $29.8 million in 1991 and $34 million in 1992 (see Table 9–5). In each year the government's accountants also placed approximately $18 million in a depreciation fund, leaving an operating profit of approximately $15 million in 1991 and $16 million in 1992. The Stadium Corporation also paid approximately $10 million in taxes to its public-sector owners. However, this represents income for the province and metropolitan Toronto. So, while a "cost" to the Stadium Corporation, it is another source of income for the public-sector partners. As a result, even after depreciation expenses, Skydome was producing more than $15 million in income for its public-sector owners. This "profit" could have remained with the public sector had Skydome not been sold to its private owners.

An agreement to sell Skydome to the private-sector partners was negotiated in 1992. It would take more than two years to finalize the deal as a result of pending lawsuits between several contractors and the Stadium Corporation. One of these lawsuits involved the Toronto partnership that designed the innovative roof system. These two engineers teetered on the verge of bankruptcy as lawsuits, charges, and countercharges were launched. When all of the issues were settled, Skydome was sold for $151 million plus $22 million in interest charges reflecting the delay in the sale. The province also received 60 percent of the free cash flow from the facility after all interest charges (on the new owners' debt), property taxes, maintenance and depreciation costs, and a "base" rate of return for the owners. Both sides publicly conceded this amount of money would be insignificant.

What the owners received for this payment is a facility with the potential to generate an operating profit of more than $24 million. Suppose, for example, the Skydome would be as successful in future years as it was in 1992. In 1992 the facility had a gross profit of $34 million and tax obligations of $10.7 million. That would leave the owners with a net income of $23.7 million before depreciation. The total investment by the private owners that enabled them to receive this income was $173 million. The $23.7 million earned, then, represents a 13.9-percent rate of return ($23.7 million divided by $173 million). The actual rate of return might be less if some money was placed in a reserve account for rebuilding the facility. However, as the private-sector investors could anticipate that replacement of the Skydome would involve another public/private partnership, the placement of from $4 to $5 million in a capital fund each year would probably provide them with sufficient resources to forge another partnership. If $5 million was placed in a capital fund, and discounted from their rate of return, the private-sector partners would still enjoy an 11-percent return on their investment of $173 million. Buying the Skydome was an excellent deal for the private-sector partners.

THE FINAL TALLY: WHAT WAS THE PUBLIC'S INVESTMENT OR SUBSIDY FOR SKYDOME?

What did the Skydome cost taxpayers? The province's records for 1992 indicate the final cost of the Skydome was $608.9 million; these cost estimates were later revised by the province to $628 million (Van Alphen, 1994). The private-sector investors made an initial contribution of $150 million, and the public sector received an additional $173 million when the facility was sold. The total private-sector cost investment in the project was $323 million ($150 million initial investment and $173 million to buy the facility and assume 100-percent ownership), leaving the public-sector share at $305

TABLE 9–5
Income and Expenses for SkyDome, 1992 and 1993

Category	1992	1991
Revenue		
Luxury seating	$22,718,000	$22,909,000
Facility rentals, concessions	13,703,000	12,299,000
Hotel, fitness club, parking	12,452,000	11,257,000
Advertising, other	8,797,000	9,083,000
Subtotal	57,670,000	55,818,000
Expenses		
Hotel, fitness club, parking	9,739,000	10,263,000
Salaries and benefits	7,867,000	7,794,000
Operations	3,890,000	4,893,000
Administration	1,742,000	2,627,000
Marketing	395,000	399,000
Subtotal	23,633,000	25,976,000
Gross Income	34,037,000	29,842,000
Depreciation	18,035,000	17,907,000
Taxes paid	10,682,000	9,740,000
Net Income	5,320,000	2,195,000

Source: Public Accounts, 1992–93, Stadium Corporation of Ontario, Limited, Province of Ontario.

million. From this figure, the taxes paid by the facility prior to its sale should be subtracted. Even though the facility was owned by the public sector, as a separate government corporation it still paid taxes to metropolitan Toronto. The Stadium Corporation paid approximately $27 million in taxes in the three years before the sale, reducing the public sector's cost to approximately $278 million. The *Toronto Star* estimated the public sector's cost at $262.7, but it is unclear if the *Star*'s estimate included the court costs and legal fees associated with several disputes involving the construction of the facility. It also was not possible to verify whether the province's accountants included those legal fees in their final cost estimates. As a result, it is safe to conclude the public sector's cost was no less than $262.7 million, and it may well have been a $275 million excursion into sports wars for economic development and civic pride. This money also becomes a subsidy to the private-sector investors, as that group will earn a handsome return after assuming complete ownership of the facility.

One other factor should be considered in terms of adding up the cost of the dome to the public sector and the total amount of the subsidy provided: the income flow Skydome was generating that now accrues to the private-sector owners. What cannot be dismissed from consideration of the public sector's loss is the point that since the province had "written off" Skydome's debt in 1990, the return the private sector was earning on its cash payments for full owner-ship of the facility could have been earned by the public sector had it chosen not to sell the stadium. In other words, the $173 million received by the province in 1994 from the private-sector owners amounted to anticipated operating profits that would be earned from 1995 through 2002. (Actually, part of 2003 would have to be included to offset the differences in money paid in 1994 for income received in the years 1995 through 2002.) As the private-sector investors will receive income from the stadium for decades after that, the public sector's loss could include the forgone revenue opportunities.

Suppose the public sector had not sold Skydome. What would the public sector have earned? Or, put another way, what is the long-term income value of the Skydome's annual earnings? The private sector paid $173 million when it purchased the Skydome. How much could they have earned on this investment and at what rate of return?

I assumed the facility would continue to earn approximately $24 million per year and calculated the present value of this annual rev-enue stream for the years 1995 through 2020. If the cost of money over those years is assumed to be 7 percent, the income lost by the public sector or gained by the private sector would be $254.3 mil-lion. In other words, had the public sector retained ownership, they would have earned $254.3 million during the years 1995 through 2020. The private sector paid $173 million to earn the $254.3 mil-lion through 2020, for a net return of 47 percent (not too shabby). If the cost of money is set at 8 percent, the present value of Skydome's income through 2020 is $235.6 million. This would generate a return to the private-sector partners of 36.2 percent on their invest-ment. If one used 9 percent as the cost of money, the present value of Skydome's annual income flow is $219.1 million, for a return of 26.6 percent.

It could be argued that the public sector's total loss on Skydome should include this forgone income, or the difference between what the private sector paid, $173 million, and what they will likely earn in the years from 1995 through 2020. The public sector accepted $173 million for an income stream worth between $219.1 million and $254.3 million. The difference between what was received ($173 million) and what could have been earned ($219.1 million to $254.3 million) represents a loss of between $46.1 million ($219.1 million that could have been earned *minus* $173 million or the amount received from the private-sector owners) and $81.3 million ($254.3 million that could have been earned *minus* $173 million or the amount received from the private-sector owners). Now, some might say, what about including, as income, the taxes the facility pays? Well, those taxes would have been earned regardless of which entity owns the stadium. When the Skydome was owned by the government corporation, it still paid taxes. As such, regardless of who owned the facility, the taxes would have been paid. Indeed, even if the stadium had not been built, given the spectacular growth of Toronto it is likely some other set of buildings would have been constructed on the land now used by Skydome.

To measure the total public-sector loss on Skydome, these estimates of forgone income have to be added to the other losses ranging from an estimated $262.7 million to as high as $275 million. Adding in this lost income, Skydome cost the taxpayers not less than $308.8 million and perhaps as much as $356.3 million. Ah, but what did they get for this investment?

THE GROWTH OF METROPOLITAN TORONTO

Numerous chapters have already made the point that sports, by themselves, are not large enough to change economic development patterns. The intangible benefits that sports create can have an impact on an area's reputation, its prestige, and the impression people have of their own community. All of these impressions can subtly influence development. At the micro level, the presence of a facility as large and as popular as the Skydome can also influence the use of buildings and land. This is especially true if more than six million people each year visit a part of a city they did not frequent in the past.

Did the Skydome change the importance of metropolitan Toronto in terms of its economic stature within Canada? Probably not. Metropolitan Toronto has enjoyed a spectacular rate of growth since the 1950s. While Canada's population more than doubled from 1951 to 1994 (an increase of 108 percent), metropolitan Toronto's population increased by 254 percent, or about 2.5 times the rate of growth for the entire country (see Table 9–1). Much of this took place before the Blue Jays ever existed. Toronto has become Canada's economic center, and the presence or absence of the Blue Jays did not influence that outcome. *Financial World* has placed the economic activity of the Blue Jays at approximately $56.4 million. While a business of that size is certainly robust, it cannot propel or even change an economy of a region with more than 4.3 million residents. If the total gross revenues of the Blue Jays are divided across the population of metropolitan Toronto, the team's value amounts to less than the cost of a family of four eating at McDonald's. An impact of this magnitude will not change or influence overall economic development patterns. Within the city of Toronto itself, however, the impact is certainly more substantial. The city of Toronto, in 1991, had 635,395 residents. A business valued at $56.4 million generates a per capita figure of $88.76. For a family of four this is equivalent to an impact of $355 a year, quite a bit more than an evening at McDonald's. Yet, this volume of activity is not sufficient to change economic development outcomes, since the city of Toronto is the destination or focal point for a majority of the region's recreational spending. If the Blue Jays and the Skydome did not exist, some of the revenue collected by the Blue Jays would still be spent within Toronto.

Metropolitan Toronto and Ontario Province are also home, now, to Canada's wealthiest residents. In 1985, average incomes placed Ontario's residents as the second wealthiest in Canada. By 1990, Ontario had the wealthiest residents. In 1985, residents of metropolitan Toronto had incomes below just two other metropolitan areas. By 1990, metropolitan Toronto's residents had the highest average incomes (see Table 9–6). While this growth in income corresponds to the years in which the Blue Jays had their greatest success, the volume of money earned by the Blue Jays was not sufficient to account for the change. Toronto's growth in population and income was related to the spectacular expansion of its economy that included baseball, but it was not driven by baseball.

With these points in mind, does Skydome deserve any credit for changing development patterns within metropolitan Toronto? While there have been no economic or demographic changes that could have been affected by the presence or absence of a baseball team and its playing facility, one factor cannot be easily dismissed. The pressures for suburban development that are so apparent in U.S. cities are also present in Canada and metropolitan Toronto. Indeed, within the Toronto region, one city, North York, has enjoyed spectacular growth at the same time that the city of Toronto has become a smaller and smaller part of the region. In 1951, Toronto had 675,754 residents, and this population comprised 55.8 percent of metropolitan Toronto's population. In contrast, North York had 85,897 residents, comprising 7.1 percent of the region. North York's population was equal to 12.7 percent of the population of the city of Toronto. By the mid-1960s, Toronto's population had increased to 697,422, but this comprised just 30.5 percent of the metropolitan area's population. The city of Toronto had begun to shrink as part of its region. North York, on the other hand, continued to grow. By 1966 it had almost 400,000 residents who comprised 17.4 percent of metropolitan Toronto. By itself, North York's population was now 58.7 percent of Toronto's, and by 1976, North York's population was 88.2 percent of Toronto's. In 1991 the city of Toronto accounted for just 16.3 percent of the region's population, and it had declined in proportion in each population count from 1956 through 1991. In the 1990s, metropolitan Toronto had three cities with populations of at least 500,000: Toronto, North York, and Scarborough. North York, led by an aggressive mayor, was bidding to be the home of each of the region's professional sports. North York's administration had proposed itself as a potential home for the Blue Jays and Maple Leafs. When the Raptors were formed as Toronto's entry into the NBA, North York also proposed a site for a new venue to be built.

TABLE 9–6

Average Income Ranks of Provinces and Metropolitan Areas, 1985 and 1990 (All Figures in Constant Dollars, 1990)

Provinces Ranked by 1985-Income Levels

	1985	1990	Percentage Change
Alberta	$24,474	$24,430	-0.18%
Ontario	24,226	26,216	8.21%
British Columbia	23,117	24,750	7.06%
Canada	*22,640*	*24,001*	*6.01%*
Quebec	21,232	22,391	5.46%
Saskatchewan	20,948	20,638	-1.48%
Manitoba	20,908	21,129	1.06%
Nova Scotia	19,102	19,954	4.46%
New Brunswick	18,511	19,827	7.11%
Newfoundland	17,622	18,769	6.51%
Prince Edward Island	17,103	19,102	11.69%

Metro Areas Ranked by 1985-Income Levels

	1985	1990	Percentage Change
Calgary	$27,138	$27,069	-0.25%
Ottawa-Hull	26,869	28,396	5.68%
Toronto	26,439	28,814	8.98%
Edmonton	24,720	24,554	-0.67%
Vancouver	24,481	26,213	7.07%
Windsor	24,109	24,621	2.12%
Hamilton	23,696	25,635	8.18%
Montreal	22,873	23,935	4.64%
Winnipeg	22,484	22,672	0.84%
Victoria	22,481	24,746	10.08%
Quebec	22,397	23,257	3.84%

Provinces Ranked by 1990-Income Levels

	1985	1990	Percentage Change
Ontario	$24,226	$26,216	8.21%
British Columbia	23,117	24,750	7.06%
Alberta	24,474	24,430	-0.18%
Canada	*22,640*	*24,001*	*6.01%*
Quebec	21,232	22,391	5.46%
Manitoba	20,908	21,129	1.06%
Saskatchewan	20,948	20,638	-1.48%
Nova Scotia	19,102	19,954	4.46%
New Brunswick	18,511	19,827	7.11%
Prince Edward Island	17,103	19,102	11.69%
Newfoundland	17,622	18,769	6.51%

Metro Areas Ranked by 1990-Income Levels

	1985	1990	Percentage Change
Toronto	$26,439	$28,814	8.98%
Ottawa-Hull	26,869	28,396	5.68%
Calgary	27,138	27,069	-0.25%
Vancouver	24,481	26,213	7.07%
Hamilton	23,696	25,635	8.18%
Victoria	22,481	24,746	10.08%
Windsor	24,109	24,621	2.12%
Edmonton	24,720	24,554	-0.67%
Montreal	22,873	23,935	4.64%
Quebec	22,397	23,257	3.84%
Winnipeg	22,484	22,672	0.84%

Source: Statistics Canada.

In this environment, where Toronto has become a smaller part of its metropolitan area and one of a handful of similar sized cities in the region, it is perhaps somewhat easier to understand the fervor and excitement that dominated the Skydome project. Toronto was not only in competition with Montreal and seeking its identification as a leading center in North America; it was also trying to preserve its standing and its centrality in its own region. Focusing people's attention on downtown Toronto for recreation and business and making and maintaining downtown Toronto as the economic heart and cultural center of the region were critical to all the governments that have administered the city of Toronto.

Viewed in this perspective, Skydome has indeed accomplished some very important objectives. First, it is the most popular venue

TABLE 9–7

Population Shares and Changes within Metropolitan Toronto, 1951–1991

| Year/ Change | Metro Toronto's Population | City of Toronto | | | City of North York | | |
		Population	As % of Metro	Population	As % of Metro	As % of the City of Toronto
1951	1,210,335	675,754	55.8%	85,897	7.1%	12.7%
1956	1,502,253	667,706	44.4%	170,110	11.3%	25.5%
% change	24.1%	-1.2%	-11.4%	98.0%	4.2%	12.8%
1961	1,824,481	672,407	36.9%	269,959	14.8%	40.1%
% change	21.4%	0.7%	-7.6%	58.7%	3.5%	14.7%
1966	2,289,900	697,422	30.5%	399,534	17.4%	57.3%
% change	25.5%	3.7%	-6.4%	48.0%	2.7%	17.1%
1971	2,628,043	712,786	27.1%	504,150	19.2%	70.7%
% change	14.8%	2.2%	-3.3%	26.2%	1.7%	13.4%
1976	2,803,101	633,318	22.6%	558,398	19.9%	88.2%
% change	6.7%	-11.1%	-4.5%	10.8%	0.7%	17.4%
1981	2,998,947	599217	20.0%	559,521	18.7%	93.4%
% change	7.0%	-5.4%	-2.6%	0.2%	-1.3%	5.2%
1991	3,893,046	635395	16.3%	562,564	14.5%	88.5%
% change	29.8%	6.0%	-3.7%	0.5%	-4.2%	-4.8%

Source: Statistics Canada.

for sporting events and other forms of entertainment in North America. With 256 event days and more than 6 million visitors, no other single facility on the continent is as utilized. Second, the attraction of 6 million visitors to downtown Toronto has not only redefined portions of downtown Toronto, but entertainment patterns have been irrevocably altered. The Skydome has attracted numerous hotels and restaurants. While metropolitan Toronto's mass transportation system could permit business leaders and their employees to attend events even if facilities were located in North York, the presence of the Skydome may well have influenced some locational decisions. The management of the Toronto Raptors believed their success was dependent on locating their new arena in close proximity to the Skydome. While they politely listened to the options available in North York, in interviews they conceded a suburban location was never seriously considered. To attract the suite and luxury seating crowd, the Raptors wanted to be near existing recreation patterns and corporate centers, and those patterns and locations revolve around Skydome. As important as Skydome was for the locational choice made by the Toronto Raptors, the Toronto Maple Leafs have yet to decide if their future lies in downtown Toronto or in North York. Toronto, in a fashion somewhat similar to Cleveland, invested a huge sum of money to ensure that its downtown area remained a vital hub for the entire region. The costs for Toronto, just as for Cleveland, may have been excessive and could have been minimized. But in Toronto, as in Cleveland, there is an aura of success about the Skydome that cannot be ignored. But was it necessary to subsidize economically privileged individuals and corporations to maintain Toronto's civic stature?

LESSONS LEARNED

The case histories of MLB in Toronto and Montreal offer some important ideas for surviving sports and dealing with the professional sports cartels. Most public officials can probably identify with the reasons both communities undertook their sports projects, and there are clear ways these initiatives could have been managed and planned to avoid the huge subsidies and losses that were incurred.

1. MARKET STUDIES: DETERMINE WHAT IS PROFITABLE AND WHAT IS NOT

The public sector's financial losses in Toronto, and Skydome's clear excesses, were a result of the decision to make the stadium much more than a premier baseball facility. The addition of a hotel and a health club were poorly planned decisions and represent activities that generate no intangible or image benefits for a community. While the value of having a baseball team and the publicity that it generates for a community can be justified despite questions about its role as an economic engine, the presence or absence of a hotel and health club does not define a community's identity.

The private sector can and does build hotels throughout the Toronto region. If additional facilities were needed in downtown Toronto as a result of the success of Skydome, then the private sector would have responded to these market opportunities. No public-sector investments were needed. Furthermore, while one can make an argument that the existence of a stadium will bring people to the downtown area, there are certainly no data available that would support the argument that people will change their recreational patterns if another hotel or health club is developed in a downtown area. It may be true that a stadium in a downtown area shifts recreational patterns, and there may be public purpose or value to such a shift. Hotels and health clubs will not bring those changes. Neither facility was needed, and neither had the potential to improve downtown Toronto's image or standing in the region. However, both facilities detracted from the stadium's assets—seating capacity was reduced—and both cost a small fortune.

If Skydome's management team had performed a market analysis, they would have realized that both the hotel and the health club were not necessary for the project's success. Similarly, the other entertainment venues were also extravagances that could have been avoided. Ironically, had these extras been eliminated, the Skydome would have been a profitable stadium for the public sector and a model for others to replicate. Indeed, Toronto may well be that model if communities can focus on the development of multiuse facilities accommodating a mix of different events. Never, never plan a facility or invest public dollars without a carefully developed market study and business plan that identify what revenues are likely to be produced from a stadium. North America is littered with unsuccessful hotel and entertainment projects. Be sure the market and business plan you develop for your stadium focuses on what services and facilities can be fully developed by the private sector without any public subsidies or "seed capital." Hotels and health clubs existed throughout Toronto. These were clearly something the private sector could build and develop in response to market demands without any participation by the public sector.

2. MUNICIPAL CAPITALISM

Toronto's Skydome also offers a fine example of what I refer to as "municipal capitalism." Municipal capitalism encompasses certain market activities in which the public sector can assume a role and manage a set of financial returns to further publicly declared values. For example, in many communities, cable television firms must negotiate contracts to permit them to deploy their equipment. Some communities have required a share of revenues from the fees collected by cable companies. Some smaller-market cities have also encouraged their cable companies to broadcast basketball and hockey games as part of their basic packages. The companies must pay the teams a fee, and this fee is part of the overall rate set by the city and the company. The public value in this regard is hosting the team. While some might not accept or agree that hosting a team has public benefits, there are those who do believe that using assets such as a cable system can permit smaller communities to host professional sports teams.

Skydome represents probably the best example of a community able to build a facility capable of generating a positive income flow and advancing the image and identity of the community. If Toronto had limited the project to the building of a stadium (without a hotel, health club, and entertainment facility) and refused to authorize the extensive overtime payments to ensure the earlier completion of the facility, Skydome would have been a successful public investment potentially generating sufficient income to retire the public sector's debt. Had that taken place, downtown Toronto would have had its recreational and entertainment anchor, the city and region would have been able to extend its reputation and identity, and the Blue Jays would have been able to maintain their status as one of baseball's most financially successful franchises. A carefully planned facility could have been developed through a public/private partnership. This facility had the potential to generate sufficient income to repay its public-sector partner without generating a set of perverse subsidies.

3. BUILD WHAT IS NEEDED

To a very real extent, ego and the desire for a super project were the "undoing" of both Montreal's and Toronto's entrances into baseball and stadium building. If both communities had built only what was needed, practical dome or outdoor facilities, neither would have encountered the financial problems it did. Both communities sought signature statements or facilities that would become part of their city's logo. Large projects became grand projects, and in each community's rush to outdo the other, "breaking new ground" in design and function created financial nightmares and burdens for taxpayers. All that was needed by both communities to reach their desired goals of economic development and civic identity were baseball facilities that could also accommodate crowds for other events. Montreal needed a stadium for the 1976 Olympics. Toronto wanted a large indoor multipurpose facility. Both built palaces with unneeded and expensive accessories.

If your community is planning to build a new stadium, be sure you build only what is needed. A lesson to be learned from the experiences of both Montreal and Toronto is that wants—we want a signature statement, we want a grand and innovative stadium, we want to be the first to build a retractable dome—quickly became defined as needs. And since the public sector was paying the bill, few questioned whether all wants were really needs. Spend the public's money as if it were your own. Buy what is needed and do not plan what is wanted unless it is really needed.

Montreal's indulgence and romantic attachment to a retractable dome had nothing to do with the Olympics and everything to do with baseball. The retractable dome system could not be completed in time for the 1976 Olympics—remember it took eight additional years to complete the system—and a dome was not needed for the summer Olympics in Montreal. Montreal's summers are quite pleasant. A dome was only needed for early-spring and late-fall baseball games and to impress an American market with a French-Canadian achievement and technology. This was public-sector excess in its most wasteful form.

4. CULTURE AND ECONOMIC FEASIBILITY

The Francophones of Quebec should love baseball enough to make the Expos profitable. The U.S. sports fan should love soccer enough to make it profitable. Are these statements true? One of the lessons to be learned from Montreal's experience with baseball and its extravagant investment for baseball is that culture does matter. Some things and some sports will not fit well into some cultures. Baseball as a sport may be loved by residents of Montreal and Quebec Province, but the sport will be dominated by English-speaking Americans as well as Spanish-speaking athletes from parts of Central America and the Caribbean. Those parts of the world produce the vast majority of players who are likely to be on any MLB team. These individuals will have little incentive to learn another language and adapt to or adopt a new culture. Given that reality, will MLB succeed in Montreal? Will Expos players become mainstays of life in Montreal and Quebec? It hardly seems likely that will occur regardless of the number of residents in the Montreal metropolitan region and their wealth.

If the public sector is to be involved with investments in sports, the community's leadership must be sure the sport fits the community. At the current time several American cities are again joining with investors to launch a professional soccer league. Will this league be any more successful than previous efforts, or is American culture sufficiently dominated by baseball, basketball, football, and hockey to leave little room for another sport? Does the European, Asian, and South American fervor for soccer necessarily mean U.S. sports fans will be as attracted to the sport? And if there is this much uncertainly about its future, should the public sector be making investments in facilities to subsidize soccer teams, or should that investment be left at this time to the private sector? Furthermore, if Europe, Asia, and South America continue to produce the best soccer players because America's youth and best athletes are drawn to other sports, will communities such as Columbus, Ohio, and Kansas City support professional soccer teams enough to justify using the public's tax money to invest in new playing facilities. Or, are communities frustrated at their inability to have certain sports franchises just rushing after the latest fad to enhance their image?

These questions and issues should be raised, as one of the lessons learned from Montreal's experience is that culture matters. Be sure there is support within a community for the sport and that the sport and its athletes fit into the community before spending millions of tax dollars to create an image as an international city or as a city that is a continental center.

10

Can Small Regions Afford Professional Sports?

Cincinnati's and Pittsburgh's Ride to the Rescue or Fade into the Sunset

> I've heard a lot of concerns from the public—things like whether Andy Van Slyke will get a $4 million salary next year. But I think residents realize that having a baseball team keeps us as one of the Number 1 cities in the United States (Barnes, 1994).
>
> —COUNCILMAN JOE CUSICK,
> Pittsburgh, explaining his support for a
> municipal loan to the Pirates

SPORTS TEAMS HAVE ALWAYS been attracted to the largest cities and metropolitan areas. The financial risks for the earliest investors and founders of the professional baseball, basketball, and football leagues were immense. Today, most people believe that all professional sports teams in the four major leagues are financial successes and valuable assets. In each league's formative years, however, teams folded and went bankrupt with a regularity common to any new set of business ventures. As a result, it seemed natural for investors to seek larger communities where more fans might be found. While the spirit, interest, and entrepreneurship that drove the earliest professional sports leagues was first found in small midwestern towns and large eastern cities, few teams in small markets survived.

For the sports entrepreneur the "penetration rate"—the percentage of an area's residents likely to attend a game—applied against the largest possible population base often became the difference between financial success and failure. On balance, with more people in an area, a small penetration rate could still generate a sufficient fan base of ticket buyers to support a team. In smaller communities, team owners needed a much larger and frequently unrealistic penetration rate to achieve financial stability. For example, if it was assumed that 10 percent of all people in a community would be willing to buy a ticket for a baseball or basketball game, then a team could expect a hundred thousand sales in a community with one million residents as opposed to ten thousand sales in a community of a hundred thousand people. Put another way, a team playing in a small market needed either a much larger penetration rate or a much larger repeat sale rate (the number of games attended by fans) to match the revenue potential of teams that played in very large cities. Before the advent of large-scale revenues from broadcasts and luxury seating, the safest way to ensure a team's financial success was to locate in an area with the greatest number of both fans and corporations. From this base, individual game and season-ticket purchases could, hopefully, be secured. Corporations were especially important, as they might be persuaded to buy season tickets, if not large numbers of tickets, to several games. Teams in small-market areas were faced with the challenge of trying to find ways of countering this dynamic and maintaining a profitable operation.

Team movements, overall, have not only *largely* followed a pattern of relocating from smaller- to larger-market areas—there are exceptions to every rule—but there has also been a trend of moving from the eastern half of the United States to the western states, and then from the northern states to the South. For the most part, teams and the professional sports leagues have followed the post–World

War II population expansion and migration patterns in the United States. Just as Americans poured into California and the West Coast and then into Texas and the Southeast, major league sports first moved to California and then spread along the West Coast before moving into Texas and the exploding Sun Belt. These general patterns can be illustrated through a review of the movements of teams in the NBA, NFL, and MLB.

THE NBA AND SPORTS DEMOGRAPHY: BIGGER IS USUALLY BETTER

When the NBA was first organized in 1949 in Fort Wayne, Indiana, its member teams were located in the smaller cities of the industrial Midwest and the large East Coast cities. Several teams in smaller communities such as Anderson (Indiana), Providence, Sheboygan, and Waterloo went bankrupt and faded into history. The survivors slowly, but steadily, moved to bigger cities. In 1951, the Tri-City (Davenport, Rock Island, and Moline) Hawks moved to Milwaukee; four years later they were playing in St. Louis. The move from the Tri-Cities area to Milwaukee represented an increase in market size of 300 percent. The move to St. Louis in 1955 brought another 52 percent increase in market size. Finally, in 1968, the Hawks moved to the expanding South, and for the past twenty-nine seasons Atlanta and its burgeoning population have hosted the Hawks.

After ten years in Fort Wayne, the Zollner Pistons moved to Detroit. This represented a 1,400 percent increase in the size of the market available to the team. While the Pistons have moved twice within the Detroit region, they are still the Detroit Pistons. In 1958, the Rochester Royals moved to Cincinnati, increasing their market size by 834 percent. The Syracuse Nationals were the last small-city team to abandon their initial home. They became the Philadelphia 76ers in 1963, increasing their market area by 910 percent and completing the move of the initial NBA franchises to larger communities. Some larger communities with NBA franchises were also unable to support their teams, and the gradual westward and southern movement continued. The Cincinnati Royals moved to the combined markets of Kansas City and Omaha in 1972 and then Sacramento in 1985. This franchise followed the pattern of first moving to a larger community and then moving west.

These were not the last or only moves by NBA teams. Just before the NBA ended its association with smaller communities in 1963, the Minneapolis Lakers moved to Los Angeles. In 1960, the Minneapolis–St. Paul area had more than 1.6 million residents, making it one of basketball's largest markets. But the burgeoning Los Angeles area already had 7.8 million residents, and it was too profitable to ignore. The Lakers took the leap and moved west at a time when their nearest league member was the St. Louis Hawks. Two years later the Lakers were joined on the West Coast by the Philadelphia Warriors. The Warriors left a market of 5.1 million for the Bay Area's 3.7 million residents. It would take twenty years before the population base of the Bay Area (San Francisco/Oakland/San José) would surpass the population of metropolitan Philadelphia.

There were some countertrend moves as well. Chicago, despite its population base of 6.9 million people, could not support its first NBA team, which moved east to Baltimore in 1963. The Bullets, to take advantage of the entire Washington/Baltimore region, moved to Landover, Maryland, in 1973, but continued to play some games in Baltimore through the 1995 season. San Diego's first NBA franchise also moved eastward to Houston in 1971, but the Houston region was 60 percent larger than the San Diego metropolitan area. Seven years later, the Buffalo Braves would try to capitalize on San Diego's continued growth and followed the general pattern of teams moving to the West. The Braves left a region with 1,243,000 residents for one with 1,862,000 residents, but San Diego was still not a basketball town. In 1984, the Clippers (the San Diego "Braves" did not seem to fit the image of a California basketball team) moved to Los Angeles to share the 11.5-million-person market with the Lakers. There were also other large communities that were just not basketball towns. New Orleans' Jazz found greater success and support in a smaller community, Salt Lake City. The initial teams in several cities that later became home to NBA teams also failed. These include Chicago, Cleveland, Denver, Detroit, Indianapolis, and Toronto.

For the most part, then, teams have always moved to larger communities and have generally followed the migration of people to the West and Southeast. All of the moves of NBA teams are described in Table 10–1, together with the population sizes of the communities teams had left and the population of the communities they selected as their new homes.[1]

The NFL's Demography and the Politics of Stadium Revenue

The movement of NFL teams fits the same general observations made for NBA teams. In recent years, however, there has been a noticeable change as a result of the league's rules for sharing rev-

TABLE 10–1

The Movement of NBA Franchises and the Population of Home Market Areas (Population Figures in Thousands)

Team	First Home	Second Home	Third Home	Fourth Home
Warriors	Philadelphia, 1962 5,131	San Francisco, 1971 3,723	Oakland 4,754	
Rockets	San Diego, 1971 1,358	Houston 2,169		
Clippers	Buffalo, 1978 1,243	San Diego, 1984 1,862	Los Angeles 11,500	
Lakers	Minnpls., 1960 1,661	Los Angeles 7,752		
Kings	Rochester, 1958 176	Cincinnati, 1972 1,468/1,660	K.C., 1985 1,373/1,433	Sacramento 1,481
Spurs	Dallas, 1973 2,352	San Antonio 880		
Jazz	New Orleans, 1979 1,257	Salt Lake City 910		
Hawks	Tri-Cities, 1951 281	Milwaukee, 1955 1,124/1,421	St. Louis, 1968 2,161/2,429	Atlanta 1,684
Pistons	Ft. Wayne, 1957 281	Detroit 4,223		
Nets	Teaneck, 1968 897	Commack, 1969 1,127/1,284	Uniondale, 1977 2,556/2,605	Meadowlands 1,293*
76ers	Syracuse, 1963 564	Philadelphia 5,131		
Bullets	Chicago, 1963 6,935	Baltimore, 1973 1,820/2,089	Landover, 1997 5,440**	Washington, D.C. 5,440**

*From the Meadowlands, the Nets can serve a substantial portion of the fifteen million residents of the New York/New Jersey metropolitan region.
**The Bullets' market within the entire Baltimore/Washington, D.C., region.

enues. In the NFL's formative years several teams played their home games in small communities. Today, just two of these teams still exist and only one continues to play in a small community. The Lions left Portsmith for the Detroit area, but the Green Bay Packers, founded in 1921, still play in this small community, the smallest region in the country to be home to a major league baseball, football, or basketball team. Residents of the other smaller communities that used to host an NFL franchise must now follow teams in nearby larger communities. Akron, Canton, Columbus, Dayton, Duluth, Evansville, Kenosha, Louisville, Marion (Ohio), Muncie, Orange, Pottsville, Racine, Rochester, Rock Island, Toledo, Tonawanda, and Staten Island each had NFL teams for at least one season. In addition, just as in the NBA, some of the NFL's initial teams in larger cities were also unsuccessful. The initial franchises in Baltimore, Boston, Brooklyn, Buffalo, Cincinnati, Dallas, Kansas City, Los Angeles, St. Louis, and Washington, D.C., each collapsed or moved to other locations. Among these cities, however, only Brooklyn and Los Angeles are no longer home to an NFL franchise. Los Angeles will likely receive two franchises in the near future, but Brooklyn's residents have to be content with NFL teams in neighboring New Jersey.

In the NFL's post–World War II years through the mid-1980s the movement of franchises was a rare event. The Cleveland Rams moved to Los Angeles in 1946, leaving the Cleveland market to the upstart Browns, and the Chicago Cardinals left the Windy City for St. Louis in 1959. The American Football League's Dallas Texans left after three seasons to become the Kansas City Chiefs. The popularity of the Cowboys and the NFL was too much for the newer league's team. The Los Angeles Chargers of the AFL also moved to San Diego one year after their creation (1961).

The stability enjoyed by the NFL and its teams was a result of the league's members' sharing equally in the substantial national television revenues it received. This stability endured into the 1980s, marred only by the occasional move of a team within its metropolitan area (e.g., Cowboys, Chiefs, Patriots, Bills, Vikings, Rams, Giants, and Jets). Not until the Colts moved to Indianapolis, the Cardinals to Arizona, and the Raiders to Los Angeles did "franchise free agency" reign in the NFL. The teams that had survived the earliest bouts with bankruptcy nestled themselves in the largest metropolitan regions, and with national media income shared by all teams, the NFL was America's stable sports league for several decades.

The moves by the Raiders, Colts, Cardinals (to Phoenix), Rams (to St. Louis), Oilers (to Nashville), and Ravens (née Browns to Baltimore) were designed to increase each team's access to revenues that were not shared with other league members. Income from luxury seating, seat licenses, and stadium advertising are not shared, and this has produced a spate of moves from larger cities to smaller ones that would build new playing facilities replete with luxury suites. In the NFL, with national media revenues divided equally, the size of any team's individual market is far less important than it is to teams in any other sports. Regions with a population base of one million can fill a stadium with 70,000 fans eight to ten times a year as easily as far larger communities. As a result, the opportunity for any NFL team to earn additional income is a function of the presence, or absence, of luxury seating, restaurants, and advertising within their stadium. With state-of-the-art facilities, some smaller communities have been quite successful in convincing NFL teams to leave larger metropolitan areas. Nashville, with 2.7 million fewer residents than Houston, is the most recent example of this trend.

Baseball's Demography

In the first part of the century, baseball teams quickly moved from smaller to larger communities, with several metropolitan areas having two teams (New York City had three). As the population base of several older metropolitan areas stagnated or as other regions grew, some teams were attracted to new homes. The Boston Braves moved to a smaller region, Milwaukee, in 1952 after more than seventy-five years as Beantown's National League team. While in Boston, the Braves shared a market of 3.1 million residents with the Red Sox. In Milwaukee, they were the only major league team, but they played in a market of only 1.1 million people. Future growth did not materialize, and fourteen years later the Braves headed for the Sun Belt. In Atlanta, they immediately increased their fan base by 6.9 percent; the 1970 population of the Atlanta metropolitan region was that much larger than Milwaukee. However, Atlanta's future growth quickly gave the Braves a very profitable market base. Indeed, given population growth patterns in the nation for the 1970s and 1980s, the Braves' management could be viewed in genius-like terms. By 1980, the Atlanta region's population was 36.7 percent larger than the population of the Milwaukee area. Furthermore, in Milwaukee, the Braves had to contend with competition from the teams in Chicago. From 1966 through the early 1990s the Atlanta Braves were the only major league baseball team in the entire southeast United States.

In a similar manner, the Dodgers played their first games in Los Angeles in 1958, leaving the larger New York City market they shared with the Yankees and Giants. While the Los Angeles market was smaller, the explosive growth of southern California from the 1960s through the 1990s made this move another stroke of genius. The New York Giants moved to San Francisco in the same year, but the population growth there was never quite as spectacular as it was in southern California. The Yankees, of course, were left as the only team in the nation's largest market. While they now share that market with the Mets, the Yankees have been able to exploit their market size with the most lucrative local media contract of any team in professional sports.

There are some examples of reverse migration as well. The St. Louis Browns, for example, moved east to Baltimore in 1954. The Browns had been St. Louis's American League team for fifty years before finding that region too small (2.2 million) to support two teams. Rather than risking a move to the West or South, where no major league teams yet existed, the Browns' ownership sought the relative safety of the populated East, with New York, Boston, Philadelphia, and Washington all within easy commuting distances. The Baltimore metropolitan area had 1.8 million residents, and the team could also hope to attract fans from Washington, D.C., and its 2.2 million people. The move east actually gave the Orioles (née Browns) access to a larger market than their share of metropolitan St. Louis.

The existence of two baseball teams in the metropolitan Baltimore–Washington, D.C., area was a problem, especially given the long losing legacy of the Senators. The stars of "Damn Yankees" decided to abandon the nation's capital in 1961 for Minneapolis–St. Paul (population 1.6 million) and to leave the district's deteriorating downtown area. Unwilling to risk congressional outrage over the loss of the team, another Washington Senators franchise was created. This team lasted for a decade before moving to the Dallas/Fort Worth area. The Texas Rangers, playing in the center of a region with 2.4 million people, was another example of a team leaving a larger area for one that promised more growth. This region did not disappoint the team's owners in terms of future growth. In the Dallas/Fort Worth area, the newly formed Texas Rangers had a market area that extended north through Oklahoma, east through Louisiana, and west to El Paso and New Mexico. To the south, the Rangers shared a market with the National League's Houston Astros, but the combined population base of this market area exceeded what was available to the team in the Washington, D.C., area.

Moving east is clearly the exception to all franchise locations. But, in the 1980s, the Seattle Pilots would move against the flow of America's population growth. After a single unsuccessful season the Pilots replaced the Braves in Milwaukee and became the Brewers. Population demographics would haunt the team as it moved from an area with 1,837,000 residents to one with 1,404,000. In that smaller venue the team would struggle for financial support even though it had reasonable success on the field. The team's financial plight still has not ended, but a new publicly supported retractable dome facility is hoped to have the potential to generate sufficient revenues to make baseball viable in Milwaukee. Seattle, despite its larger size, also struggled with its second baseball team, the Mariners. Poor on-the-field performance did not enhance the team's value, and a threatened move in the 1990s was avoided when a foreign ownership group intervened to save the team. However, even those owners were tempted to move the team in 1995, before a season-ending pennant drive and a spellbinding play-off series victory over the Yankees convinced the state's leaders to support the team. A referendum to build a new stadium was defeated, but state and local government leaders developed a plan that did not require an electoral referendum that convinced the Mariners to remain in Seattle.

BUSINESSES ALWAYS MOVE—SO WHAT'S THE PUBLIC POLICY ISSUE?

The observation that teams, just like other businesses, move to areas with greater profit potential is hardly earth-shattering news. What creates a problem or issue regarding professional sports is that some of America's most storied or famous teams are located in cities that were once "big" but have become second or even third tier in the constellation of America's cities. Cities where the history and memories of baseball and basketball were forged now face an uncertain future with their teams. The social and psychological link between fans and teams, and cities and teams, is being threatened as demographic and economic trends redefine the hierarchy of cities. Those smaller communities—even those that have had teams in their communities for almost a hundred years—are now faced with the very real dilemma of either subsidizing their teams or losing them to larger or wealthier communities. Can these smaller communities keep their teams, or are they destined to lose them? How much will it cost to save the Brewers, Reds, and Pirates—or any team that plays in a small market? Who should pay these costs?

Cincinnati and Pittsburgh are representative of the smaller cities that are struggling to keep their professional sports franchises. The Reds and Bengals in Cincinnati have threatened to leave if new facilities are not built. A similar threat has been posed by the Pittsburgh Pirates. Indeed, that team was unable to find an individual willing to buy the team because the economics of baseball now make it difficult to survive in Pittsburgh without a new and heavily subsidized stadium. Even if a new stadium is built in Pittsburgh, it is not certain that the Pirates will be fiscally viable. The two basic questions posed for this chapter—How much will it cost to save the team? and Who should pay?—are explored against the backdrop of the experiences of the Pirates, Reds, and Bengals.

SAVING BASEBALL IN A SMALL METROPOLITAN REGION

When one thinks of baseball it is hard to imagine the sport without the Cincinnati Reds or the Pittsburgh Pirates. Founded in 1869, the Reds were the first professional baseball team and perhaps the first professional sports team in America. At a time when baseball teams were comprised of unpaid community residents who represented their city, the Cincinnati Red Stockings, as they were then known, took the unprecedented steps of paying their players and not requiring them to live in Cincinnati. In 1880 the Red Stockings were suspended from one of the earliest baseball leagues for both playing games on the Sabbath (Sunday) and selling beer at their ballpark. From 1882 through 1889 the team competed in the American Association, but then joined the National League for the 1890 season. A part of Cincinnati since the post–Civil War days, the Reds have been an institution in the Queen City and an integral part of its culture for more than a century and a quarter. Cincinnati's long-term status in MLB made it the site of the opening game for the National League each season. In more recent times, however, that honor has been shared with other teams. The Reds have won nine National League pennants, and their first World Series victory was the infamous 1919 Series that gave MLB its "Black Sox" scandal. During the 1970s, Cincinnati's "Big Red Machine" was regarded as one of the best teams of all time.

Pittsburgh's relationship with the Pirates is as storied. Founded in 1887, the Pirates have played within the city limits of Pittsburgh for more than a hundred years. The Pirates played in the first World Series (1903), losing to the Boston Red Sox, 5 games to 3. They won their first title in 1909 and have appeared in seven World Series, but none was more memorable than the 1960 series in which Bill Mazeroski's ninth-inning home run defeated the Yankees, 4 games to 3. Never before had a World Series been decided by a home run, and the image of Mazeroski leaping around the base paths remains one of baseball's most endearing and enduring memories. Most middle-age residents of Pittsburgh can still remember where they were when Mazeroski hit his home run. The Pirates were also the team for which two of baseball's most distinguished citizens played. Willie Stargell defined the spirit of the team in the 1970s, and Roberto Clemente's image still shines as an example of what an athlete can represent for a community.

While these memories are both kind and warm, the demographic realities of Cincinnati and Pittsburgh paint a very stark and cold vision in terms of the economics of baseball. Both cities have become small; neither has more than 365,000 residents and both have lost population since 1970. Cincinnati had almost eighty thousand fewer residents in 1990 than it did in 1970, a decline of 17.8 percent. The Cincinnati metropolitan region is not shrinking; in fact, in 1990 it had 131,000 more residents than it did in 1970. Yet, the 1,744,000 residents in the region meant the Cincinnati metropolis was just the twenty-third largest in the United States. Cincinnati's declining size or importance might be best demonstrated by its size within the state of Ohio. In 1970, the population of the Cincinnati metropolitan area accounted for 27.4 percent of the population of Ohio. By 1990, the region, which includes residents of three different states, had a population equal to approximately one-fifth of the state of Ohio. Cincinnati is shrinking in relative size (see Table 10–2).

Pittsburgh has been losing residents at a rate that exceeds the losses that Cincinnati has sustained. Pittsburgh lost 135,539 residents from 1970 to 1990. More important for the economics of baseball and retaining a team, metropolitan Pittsburgh is also shrinking. In 1970, the region had 2,556,000 residents. In 1990, it had 2,244,300 residents, a decline of 311,700 people, or 12.2 percent. In 1970, more than one-fifth of the state of Pennsylvania's population lived in the metropolitan Pittsburgh region. By 1990, the Pittsburgh region accounted for 18.9 percent of the state's population (see Table 10–2). When the Pirates began play in the latter part of the nineteenth century, Pittsburgh was one of America's most important economic centers. By 1990, Pittsburgh was the nineteenth largest metropolitan region and it was very much a shrinking giant. Only two major league teams play in markets that are smaller

TABLE 10–2

The Population Changes in Two Medium-sized Regions

	1990	1980	1970
Cincinnati			
City	364,278	385,409	443,220
Metropolitan area	1,744,000	1,660,000	1,613,000
Ohio	10,847,000	10,798,000	10,657,000
Cincinnati's Population as a Percentage of:			
Metropolitan area	20.9%	23.2%	27.5%
State of Ohio	3.4%	3.6%	4.2%
Metropolitan Cincinnati's Population as a Percentage of:			
State of Ohio	16.2%	15.4%	15.1%
Pittsburgh			
City	366,852	423,959	502,391
Metropolitan area	2,243,000	2,423,000	2,556,000
Pennsylvania	11,882,000	11,864,000	11,801,000
Pittsburgh's Population as a Percentage of:			
Metropolitan area	16.4%	17.5%	19.7%
State of Pennsylvania	3.1%	3.6%	4.3%
Metropolitan Pittsburgh's Population as a Percentage of:			
State of Pennsylvania	18.9%	20.4%	21.7%

than the Cincinnati and Pittsburgh regions: the Milwaukee Brewers and the Kansas City Royals.

Even baseball's newest teams serve larger markets. The Denver metropolitan region has fewer residents than does the Pittsburgh region, but when Colorado Springs (approximately one hour south of the Denver metropolitan area) is included in the population base, the Rockies actually serve a market that is considerably larger than the markets available to either the Pirates or Reds. In addition, the Rockies draw fans from other states making their "home market" substantially larger than the one available to the Pittsburgh Pirates. The combined Phoenix/Tucson region that will become the home market of the Arizona Diamondbacks will also be larger than the population base served by either the Reds or Pirates, and Phoenix's team will draw fans from northern Arizona and from the Yuma area as well. Likewise, the regional population base of the St. Petersburg/Tampa region, home to Florida's second MLB team, will exceed the market bases of both the Reds and Pirates. As a result, both Cincinnati and Pittsburgh represent prime examples from which the question can be answered, Can small regions support and afford professional sports teams?

A FISCAL CRISIS, LIKE BARNACLES, GROWS AND THEN SLOWLY STRANGLES THE PIRATES

The fiscal crisis that has engulfed the Pirates probably began in 1985; signs of the problems to come may have been evident sooner, but they became apparent to everyone and the city's political leadership when John Galbreath attempted to sell the team. Galbreath, a wealthy real estate magnate, had owned the team since 1946. Weak finishes in 1984 and 1985, when the team was in last place in both years, may have convinced Mr. Galbreath the time to sell was fast approaching. More to the point, however, was probably his analysis of baseball's economic situation and where the Pirates stood in relationship to teams in larger markets. Mr. Galbreath's sudden interest in selling might also have been part of his hope that in the absence of local buyers, he could sell the team to investors from other communities.

When no local buyers could be found, a consortium of local institutions joined with the city of Pittsburgh to save the team. The Pittsburgh Associates agreed to buy the team from Mr. Galbreath for $26 million. This group included the organizations listed in Table 10–3.

TABLE 10–3
The Pittsburgh Associates

AlCoA Service Corporation	Carnegie Mellon University
APT Holdings (Mellon Bank)	PNC Financial Corporation
PPG Industries	USX Corporation
Westinghouse Electric	Eugene Litman
John McConnell	Harvey Walken
National Intergroup	Ryan Homes
Frank Schneider	

By 1993, the latter three organizations and individuals were no longer part of the Pittsburgh Associates. The city of Pittsburgh also agreed to loan the team $25 million to increase the team's operating funds. Only $20.8 million of the promised $25 million was ever transferred to the team by Mayor Richard Caliguiri's administration, and the remaining $4.2 million would become part of a lawsuit the team would bring against Pittsburgh. In any event, at the conclusion of 1985, the Pirates were saved, and the city was part of a thirteen-member public/private partnership.

While such a management structure would seem to be a prescription for disaster, the Pirates actually thrived. After failing to draw a million fans in 1985, the team's play improved and attendance soared. In 1991, the Pirates sold 2.3 million tickets, and, through the cessation of play in 1994, had attracted 1,222,520 fans (see Table 10–4). The team was also quite competitive over much of this time period. In the early years of the 1990s, the Pirates had the best record in baseball. The Bucs were Eastern Conference champions in 1990, 1991, and 1992, but in each year they lost the championship series. The 1992 and 1993 losses to Atlanta created some of baseball's best memories of the decade, but nevertheless failed to produce a pennant for the team with the best cumulative record across those three seasons.

While the collection of partners that had purchased the Pirates did not create a management nightmare nor a poorly performing team, the financial record of the team was another matter. Indeed, it began to seem that Mr. Galbreath was correct to sell the team and that the inability to find a single local owner was a function of several people understanding the economics of baseball in Pittsburgh. The team lost money in eight of the nine seasons from 1986 through 1994. Across this period, the team's net loss was $44.6 million (see Table 10–4).

These losses were in addition to the $20.8 million loan from the Urban Redevelopment Authority. Including the loan in an accounting of the team's finances would mean the Pirates' debt could have been as high as $66 million. In the fall of 1994 the *Pittsburgh Business Times* placed the team's debt at $49.1 million (Elliott, 1994), while the *Pittsburgh Post-Gazette* in September 1994 estimated the

TABLE 10–4

Attendance at Pirate Games and Operating Profits and Losses

(Attendance & Tickets in Thousands; Profit/Loss in Millions of Dollars)

Category	Season									
	1986	1987	1988	1989	1990	1991	1992	1993	1994	1995
Attendance	1,001	1,161	1,867	1,374	2,050	2,065	1,829	1,651	1,223	906
Tickets	1,220	1,429	2,160	1,876	2,304	2,376	2,063	1,800	NA	NA
Profit/loss	-$3.4	-$1.8	+$2.8	-$2.0	-$7.1	-$7.6	-$11.8	-$5.0	-$6.1	NA

Sources: Heltzel, 1991; Ruck, 1993; Ozanian, 1995.

debt at more than $60 million (Halvonik, September 1994). Another estimate by the *Pittsburgh Post-Gazette* placed the debt at $62 million (Schmitz, 1994). With figures unavailable for 1995 and 1996, but with the team attracting fewer than one million fans in 1995, it is safe to expect that the team's debt is currently in the $65 to $70 million range if the funds loaned by the city of Pittsburgh are to be repaid.

These financial pressures, while staggering, were not the only problems to beset the prospect of major league baseball in Pittsburgh. As the team's financial situation deteriorated, the Pirates' owners sought additional financial relief from the city. The city of Pittsburgh was encountering its own budgetary shortfalls and was dealing with the very real possibility of raising taxes, eliminating workers, reducing services, or implementing all three of these policy options. In such an environment it is probably not surprising that tempers flared and the city and team were in open conflict with one another. Finding solutions in such an environment is always very difficult.

The financial and political conflict regarding the team's destiny actually began in 1981 when John Galbreath was still the team's owner. Losing money through the operation of Three Rivers Stadium, the team wanted the city to assume responsibility for the playing facility. When the city refused to change the lease, the team sued. The Pirates argued that they should be released from their obligations because the city had failed to develop land adjacent to the stadium and to make needed highway repairs. To "spice up" the lawsuit, team officials met with the management of the Louisiana Superdome. This led to a separate lawsuit against the city of New Orleans by the city of Pittsburgh. The conflicting lawsuits were settled in the summer of 1982 when the city council agreed that the city should assume responsibility for the operation and maintenance of Three Rivers Stadium. The first crisis ended, but the seeds for future conflicts had been sown.

The second stadium crisis began in 1991 and has yet to be resolved. This confrontation began with the "typical" pronouncement that the team was losing money. On February 1, 1991, the Pirates declared they had lost $7.1 million during the 1990 season. While the team's management underscored their desire to remain in Pittsburgh, they were also careful to point out that the team's value to other communities was probably in the range of $100 million. In other words, if the team could leave Pittsburgh, the owners could make a great deal of money, but the team really wanted to stay. However, to be profitable, a new stadium was needed.

As the 1991 baseball season was coming to an end, and the Pirates were in the process of clinching their second straight Eastern Conference championship, Pittsburgh's mayor proposed building a new $100 million baseball-only facility. The mayor conceded that the city already had obligations of more than $100 million for sports as a result of the loans made to the team and money still owed for the building of Three Rivers Stadium, yet she believed a new stadium for the Pirates was a necessity if baseball was to be preserved in Pittsburgh. This stadium proposal lived less than a fortnight. On September 18, 1991, confronted with a $35 million deficit in the city's operating budget, the city council rejected the mayor's proposal, calling it ill-timed and impossible in a year in which workers would be fired and taxes increased.

Both the Pirates and the city were facing financial crises, and the council's complete rejection of the mayor's proposal simply escalated the conflict and the war of words. After the 1991 baseball season ended, the Pirates announced that they wanted their lease revised if no new stadium was to be built. The basis for this request was the city's failure to provide all the funds ($25 million) promised when the current owners bought the team. When there was no progress on these negotiations, the Pirates sued. As the city was in "default" on its payment to the team, the Pirates believed they did not have to make their final lease or rental payment. The Pirates withheld $1.1 million against the $4.2 million the team believed it was owed. The team's action struck a harsh blow to its relations with the city. Mayor Masloff declared that "the team is taking a wrecking ball to the public/private partnership" that preserved the team for Pittsburgh. Her executive secretary, Joseph Sabino Mistick, proclaimed the lawsuit "a slap in the face to taxpayers and baseballs fans in the city. This is the thanks they get for standing by the Pirates all these years."

The Pirates' lawsuit did not end with their demands for the $4.2 million they were promised. The team also claimed the stadium was in need of substantial repairs to maintain the first-class appearance promised in the lease. The Pirates' owners reaffirmed their desire to stay in Pittsburgh, but they argued that their fans needed better facilities. In their oral response the city's leadership pointed to their own budget problems and the $1.8 million annual subsidy they were providing for the facility's operations. The city's administration also noted that the real problem seemed to be the atmosphere the team's president wanted to establish.

Negotiations dragged on through the summer of 1993, and the city responded with a proposal to renovate Three Rivers Stadium and to renegotiate terms of the lease that would increase the team's revenues. In 1994, the city also proposed a second loan of $8 million. However, in exchange for this loan, the city council wanted an additional seat on the team's board of directors and an agreement that the team would stay in Pittsburgh for another twenty years. In addition, the interest rate on the loan was to be 8.69 percent, and the city wanted to receive 53 percent of the net revenues from any sale of the team, ensuring repayment of all loans.

Through July the team reviewed the city's offer, but in August the team's owners rejected the proposal and gave the city six months to find a new owner. If local owners could not be found, the owners reserved the right to sell the team to anyone. A sale of that nature would mean the Pirates would leave Pittsburgh. Several potential owners emerged who promised to keep the team in Pittsburgh, but the six-month period ended without a sale. The city sought and received an extension, and the Pirates' ownership reduced their operating deficit by selling off many of their best players. In 1995 the team attracted fewer than one million fans. In 1994, the Pirates had a winning percentage of .465 as they finished thirteen games out of first place. In 1995, the team's winning percentage was .403 and they finished thirty-two games out of first place. As the 1996 season began, an ownership group for the Pirates had been found; a partnership of twenty-two individuals and corporations, Pirates Acquisition, Inc., was prepared to buy the team. (Members of the partnership include the *Pittsburgh Post-Gazette,* the HJ Heinz Company, one of the city's leading law firms, and several other corporations and individuals.) Led by Kevin McClatchy, who invested $10 million, the partnership would pay $85 million for the team, including the assumption of $60 million in debt. The Pittsburgh Associates then would receive $25 million and be released from responsibility for $60 million of their debts. A local bank also agreed to provide the team and its new owners with a $50 million line of credit. The city agreed to $9 million in stadium lease concessions, and the new management group received the support of the mayor and the governor of Pennsylvania for a new stadium to achieve this level of profitability. This stability did not improve the team's play. Labor Day 1996 found the Pirates in last place with a .417 winning percentage. So, what it will take to make the Pirates profitable and competitive in Pennsylvania? How much does the community and the state have to pay to subsidize a new stadium?

REVENUE SOURCES

As already discussed, baseball teams earn revenues from gate receipts, media revenues, and the sale of items and advertising at their home fields. Luxury seating revenues represent a substantial asset to a team. The national media contracts are shared on an equal basis by all MLB teams, but only the payments for the World Series, play-offs, and All-Star games represent substantial sources of income for each team. Local television, local radio, and local cable television income are not shared. In the National League the home team retains 90 percent of all ticket revenues.

The problems confronted by the Pirates and Reds are probably best illustrated by the cash flow analysis performed by *Financial World* magazine. For the 1994 season it was estimated that the Pirates had gross revenues of $25.6 million, the lowest in MLB (the Cincinnati Reds earned $30.6 million). The average for all teams was $40.4 million, with the Yankees earning $71.5 million, almost $20 million more than the second-highest-grossing team, the Baltimore Orioles. In 1994, the Pirates were able to pay their players $17.0 million, and the Reds' player payroll was $32.7 million ($2.1 million more than they earned). In contrast, the Yankees spent $37.1 million for their players and the Cleveland Indians spent $24.8 million. In 1995, the Pirates had gross revenues of $24.9 million, less than half of the average for all teams. Cincinnati's gross revenues were approximately 80 percent of the league's average.

When the strike-shortened season ended in 1994, twelve teams were in contention for the eight play-off positions that lead to each league's championship series and the World Series. These teams, their records, and their player payrolls are listed in Table 10–5; for a comparison, the records and salary expenditures by the Pirates are also included. The same information for the two best teams in each division are also presented for the 144-game season in 1995. The Reds were leading their division when the strike ended the 1994 season and the Reds again won their division in 1995. Paying large amounts of money for players and earning large revenues do not guarantee a winning team, but they clearly help. Three-quarters of the teams in play-off contention at the conclusion of the 1994 season paid their players more than the MLB average, and two-thirds had gross revenues that exceeded the league average. In 1995, each of the teams that were in serious contention for a play-off position paid their players more than the league average. While paying higher salaries for the best players helps a team's on-the-field performance, as the data in Table 10–5 indicate, the relationship is not linear—you cannot simply pay players more and expect to win more games—as other factors also influence performance. In 1994 the Montreal

TABLE 10–5

Team Performance, Player Salaries, and Gross Revenues

The 1994 Strike-Shortened Season

Division/ Team	Games Won	Games Lost	Winning Percentage	Player Payroll	Gross Revenues
AL East					
NY Yankees	70	43	.619	$37.1 million	$71.5 million
Baltimore	63	49	.563	$30.0 million	$53.1 million
AL Central					
Chicago	67	46	.593	$31.4 million	$45.5 million
Cleveland	66	47	.584	$24.8 million	$41.0 million
AL West					
Texas	52	62	.456	$25.5 million	$50.1 million
Oakland	51	63	.447	$27.3 million	$36.7 million
NL East					
Montreal	74	40	.649	$14.8 million	$25.8 million
Atlanta	68	46	.596	$34.8 million	$55.8 million
NL Central					
Cincinnati	66	48	.579	$32.7 million	$30.6 million
Houston	66	49	.574	$26.3 million	$34.3 million
Pittsburgh	53	61	.465	$17.0 million	$25.6 million
NL West					
Los Angeles	58	56	.509	$28.9 million	$49.5 million
San Francisco	55	60	.402	$33.6 million	$43.1 million
MLB Average				**$25.6 million**	**$40.4 million**

The 1995 Season (144 Games Played)

Division/ Team	Games Won	Games Lost	Winning Percentage	Player Payroll	Gross Revenues
AL East					
Boston	86	58	.597	$32.1 million	$67.9 million
NY Yankees	79	65	.549	$50.5 million	$93.9 million
AL Central					
Cleveland	100	44	.694	$36.3 million	$60.2 million
Kansas City	70	74	.486	$28.3 million	$35.8 million
AL West					
Seattle	79	66	.545	$34.8 million	$36.7 million
California	78	67	.538	$30.7 million	$39.0 million
NL East					
Atlanta	90	54	.625	$44.5 million	$60.7 million
Philadelphia	69	75	.479	$28.4 million	$45.3 million
NL Central					
Cincinnati	85	59	.590	$39.6 million	$40.4 million
Houston	76	68	.528	$31.5 million	$44.4 million
Pittsburgh	58	86	.403	$16.7 million	$24.9 million
NL West					
Los Angeles	78	66	.542	$70.9 million	$32.3 million
Colorado	77	67	.535	$33.4 million	$70.3 million
MLB Average				**$31.2 million**	**$50.4 million**

Source: Financial data from *Financial World*, Web Site.

Expos had the best on-the-field record, but their payroll expenses were the second lowest in MLB. Whatever it was that the Expos learned in 1994 they could not retain, and in 1995, the team's performance substantially deteriorated and the Expos finished the season with a winning percentage of .458, twelve games under .500 and twenty-four games behind the division-leading and eventual world champion Atlanta Braves. In 1996, with a below-average payroll, the Expos, again, had a competitive team.

Those teams that earn the most revenues rely on different revenue sources and mixes to get to their bottom lines. For example, the Yankees play in a facility that is more than fifty years old, and while their total stadium revenues (tickets and other charges) amounted to $93.9 million in 1995, the Bronx Bombers earned more than $57 million from their various media contracts.

In contrast, the Orioles, Rangers, White Sox, Blue Jays, and Rockies were each able to earn more from their playing facilities than the Yankees. Financial stability, then, results from either total stadium revenues or local media contracts. Serving the largest market, the Yankees have media revenue potential that is simply not available to either the Reds or Pirates.

Suppose one accepted the position that a baseball team needed to earn revenues that were similar to those of the more successful teams. For 1995, if 162 games, a full season, had been played instead of 144, teams with a new stadium, such as the Cleveland Indians, Texas Rangers, and Colorado Rockies would have earned at least $64 million to: (1) field a competitive team on a regular basis and (2) produce a reasonable or average rate of return for the owners. Ironically, while not a direct result of their stadium revenues, the Rockies, Rangers, and Indians were each in contention for a play-off spot in 1995 and 1996. Within this assumption of a need for gross revenues of approximately $70 million, we will ignore the observation that professional sports athletes are overpaid or that the profits made by sports are artificially high as a result of the cartel structure of the leagues. Instead, we will focus on the very real political world that mayors, governors, and community leaders face when they try to attract or retain a baseball team for their city. Could the Pirates and Reds earn $70 million? To reach that goal, the Pirates would have needed almost \$42 million in additional revenue (in 1996 based on a 162-game season), the Reds an additional \$25 million.

WHAT WOULD SAVING THE PIRATES COST A SMALL-MARKET CITY?

Returning to the basic sources of revenue for teams, there may be little more the Pirates can expect to earn through media contracts playing in a market of approximately 2.2 million people. Had the 1994 season been played to its conclusion, *Financial World* estimates that the Pirates would have received \$15.5 million from all of their media contracts (local and share of the national contract for the World Series and play-offs). In 1995, the team would have earned \$13.7 million had the entire season been played. Measured against the region's population, this revenue in 1994 was equal to \$6.90 for every resident. Total revenues from the mass media received by teams in several different regions were divided by the population of the home region to produce a per capita figure. (In all instances, the 1990 population count for metropolitan areas was used.) This is a very crude and approximate measure of revenue potential. Advertising agencies would use a far more refined index that included such factors as disposable income and age structure to measure a region's potential. Yet, relying on population levels illustrates the revenue limitations in Pittsburgh.

The Pirates' per capita media earnings (\$15.5 million in 1994 divided by a regional population of 2.243 million) are larger than the revenues received by other teams. For instance, the Philadelphia Phillies' per capita media earnings amounted to \$3.05. For the Houston Astros the comparable figure was \$3.91. The Yankees, even with their very large cable television contract, had a per capita media revenue figure of \$2.90. The Oakland A's, with local games broadcast across the San Francisco Bay region, had a per capita figure of \$3.45, and the Orioles, able to market their games in both the Washington,

D.C., and Baltimore regions, earned $3.19 per person. If the Pirates returned to their winning ways, it is likely they would earn more media revenue. However, it is quite unlikely that they could ever earn enough to produce the additional revenues to equal the gross revenues of the upper tier of MLB teams. Saving the Pirates must therefore involve increasing their revenues from a stadium that includes luxury seating. Yet, if the facility had to generate an additional $42 million for the Pirates, how much could the team afford to pay for the stadium, and how much would the fans and/or public sector have to pay?

SUBSIDIES, OR BUCKS FOR THE BUCS

In terms of planning for a new stadium for the Pirates, let's start with what the Pirates must earn to remain competitive in Pittsburgh. Using data from 1995, and a "low average" estimate of the revenues from smaller market teams with new stadia, revenues of approximately $70 million are needed. This is done even acknowledging that some winning teams earned far less. However, over time, with free agency (players able to move to other teams) and the desire of owners to earn a profit, approximately $70 million in gross revenues is needed. (Of course, if the cartel structure of MLB were ever eliminated, this figure would change. However, in the political world confronted by mayors, governors, and communities that want teams, the reality is that the cartel structure of MLB is not going to go away.)

How much is a stadium going to cost that can produce the level of revenues needed to generate an income of approximately $70 million for the Pirates, given the limits on their income from media? Jacobs Field in Cleveland cost $172 million. The proposed facility for Cincinnati is planned to cost $194.5 million, and Detroit's new proposed facility for the Tigers may cost as much as $240 million (Bradsher, 1996). The proposed new home for the Houston Astros will also cost approximately one-quarter of a billion dollars. The total cost for the Ballpark in Arlington was approximately $195 million. While some of the plans for a new facility in Pittsburgh have included a discussion of building a relatively small stadium with fewer than 40,000 seats, it seems prudent to anticipate a total stadium cost of not less than $172 million. (This is indeed a very low estimate.) Of this figure, if a team is to have gross revenues of approximately $70 million, how much could it afford to pay for the construction of a stadium?

Again, we can look at recent examples for some possible answers to this question. The city of Arlington's obligations for the Ballpark in Arlington were limited to $135 million. All other costs, estimated to be $65 million, were supported by the team. Yet, the team had other assets (land), which it also pledged to the "deal." In terms of "cash" that the team invested in the stadium, the Rangers committed 115 percent of the first year's leases of luxury suites and 5 percent of these revenues in years 2 through 4 of the stadium's operations. Luxury leases generated approximately $11 million in income for the Rangers during their first year, providing $12.7 million for the stadium (Greene, 1995). In the second year of operations, however, the team received about half that amount from its leases (Much & Friedman, 1996). Five percent of that figure for years 2 through 5 would yield $0.67 million (in present value terms). With these approximate figures, the first component of the team's *cash* investment in the stadium was $12.4 million (present value).

There was also a second component to the team's investment in the capital cost of the Ballpark in Arlington. The Rangers pay $1.5 million each year (in addition to their annual rent) to the city of Arlington until the bonds for the stadium are retired. The fixed rental charge for use of the stadium is $2.0 million for the period 1994 through 2024. The present value of the entire *cash* investment by the Rangers in the building of the Ballpark in Arlington, using a discount rate of 8 percent, is approximately $21 million. This figure does not include the base rent the team pays; those funds help defray maintenance and operating costs that the city of Arlington sustains. In addition, the land contributed by the team was not included in this calculation as there were public funds involved in the transfer of that land to the Rangers in the 1970s and 1980s.

The Cleveland Indians also provided a portion of the funds to support Jacobs Field. The initial investment by the team was $20 million, and the club agreed to pay $2.9 million annually for a portion of the facility's debt. The present value of this contribution to the stadium's construction is $31 million. The team's owner also agreed to an annual fee for the naming rights to the stadium. The present value of these annual payments is $5.8 million. In sum, then, the Cleveland Indians will invest a total of $56.8 million in Jacobs Field. While it could be argued the expenditure by the team's owner for naming rights was an optional decision and involves an advertising benefit, the team's investment was $20 million plus an agreed-to annual payment of $2.9 million to retire $31 million of the stadium's debt.

Both the Indians and Rangers generate revenues within the lower reaches of the "target" figure of $70 million. It would seem, then, that the financing of a new stadium in Pittsburgh could be based on a set of financial arrangements similar to those developed by the cities of Arlington and Cleveland. As such, could the city of Pittsburgh expect an investment of between $20 million and $57 million from the team? Well, there are a few other factors to consider.

First, the Rangers earn more revenue from media contracts than do the Pirates ($17.8 million to $15.5 million in 1994 and $19 million to $13.7 million in 1995). Any support from the Pirates for a stadium would have to be adjusted to reflect that revenue differential. Second, and more important, the Pittsburgh franchise has substantial financial debts that must be retired. For the team to remain competitive it must be able to retire this debt, and that may limit what the Pirates can contribute toward building and maintaining a new stadium. If the Pirates were to retire a debt of $60 million over a period of thirty years, and a 9 percent loan could be secured, the team's annual payments would be $5.79 million. If the loan's interest rate was 9.25 percent, the annual payment would be $5.92 million. A shorter-term loan would have higher payments. The team's annual debt payments could be reduced if its creditors agreed to a below-market interest rate or agreed to accept no interest at all. For the purposes of this example, however, it seems useful to include the possibility that the team will have to pay *approximately* $5.8 million per year for thirty years to meet its debt obligations. With these factors in mind it is possible to project the total revenues the Pirates can earn, and then determine how much they could contribute to the operation of a stadium.

Ticket Revenue

To estimate the potential attendance and gate revenues the Pirates could earn with a new stadium, the experiences of the Texas Rangers and the Cleveland Indians were again analyzed. While both teams play in markets that are larger than the one served by the Pirates, both teams needed new playing facilities to improve attendance and create a substantial level of excitement for MLB in their communities. In many ways, the problems faced by the Pirates in terms of attendance levels are similar to the ones encountered by the Rangers and Indians. While the fan base for the Pirates is smaller, the Pirates have had a far more competitive team than either the Indians or Rangers. For example, the Pirates have appeared in postseason play nine times since 1970 (1992, 1991, 1990, 1979, 1975, 1974, 1972, 1971, and 1970). The Pirates have appeared in more postseason series than any National League team. In contrast, prior to 1996, the Rangers had never played a postseason game and, prior to winning the American League pennant in 1995, the Indians' last appearance in postseason play was in 1954. The Rangers and Indians may have larger home markets, but the Pirates have a record of success that would make them the envy of teams in any city. As such, the Pittsburgh franchise, playing in a new facility, might reasonably expect to draw as many fans as either the Rangers or Indians.

Over the past three seasons the high mark in attendance at Rangers games was 2,503,198 fans. During the same years the Cleveland Indians were able to attract 2,842,725 fans (in 1995). With all tickets sold for games in 1996, the Indians will draw 3,472,065 fans. Given the success of past Pirate teams and the building of a new stadium, a lower bound of expected attendance of 2,503,198 fans and an upper limit of 2,842,725 were used. It is reasonable to expect that in years after winning a pennant, the Pirates could also attract three million fans (just as the Indians did). It is also likely that in some years, fewer than 2.5 million fans will attend games. For this example, then, the upper and lower estimates seem reasonable. In 1995, the average price of a ticket to a Rangers game was $12.07, to an Indians game, $12.06. Using these figures, it is likely that the Pirates would collect between $30.2 million and $34.3 million from the sale of tickets.

Other Revenues

Media revenues for the Pirates are expected to continue at their current levels, approximately $15 million (this is based on the average revenue for 1994 and 1995 increased to account for a 162-game season). If a stadium that had amenities similar to those in Jacobs Field or the Ballpark in Arlington were built, and the Pirates were able to have a lease at least as favorable as the ones signed by those teams, the Pirates could expect to generate between $23 million (Rangers) and $14.2 million (Indians) in revenues from stadium operations ($18.6 million is the average of both teams). These stadium revenue figures include the income from the sale of luxury seating and all food and beverages.

A Revenue Comparison

With these figures in mind, the gross revenues available to the Pirates would be between $64 million ($30.4 million in ticket revenue plus $15 million in media revenues plus $18.6 million in stadium operations) and $69 million ($35.4 million in ticket revenue plus $15 million in media revenues plus $18.6 million in stadium operations).

If the Pirates were able to generate those revenues, they would still have to repay their loan. If those payments were approximately $5.8 million a year, the total revenue the team would gross from its operations would be between $58.2 million and $63.2 million (see Table 10–6). How does this compare with the revenues of the Texas Rangers and Cleveland Indians? First, the Rangers, from their 162-game gross of $71.8 million in 1995, must pay rent of $2 million per year. In addition, until the bonds are retired for the Ballpark in Arlington, the team also pays an additional rental charge of $1.5 million. Also, the team paid $21 million in cash (present value terms) for the stadium. To convert this figure to an annual figure, that payment was treated as a loan to the team from its owners.[2] If the Rangers' ownership loaned the team $21 million at 9 percent and expected repayment over twenty years, the team's revenues would be reduced by $2,267,280 each year (annual payments on a $21 million loan). The team's earnings would then be approximately $66 million (see Table 10–6).

A similar set of calculations was made for the Indians. Their down payment of $20 million for Jacobs Field, if loaned to the team at 9 percent for a period of twenty years, would reduce their annual income by $2,159,400. The team also assumed responsibility for a loan with payments of $2.9 million, and the team pays rent of approximately $1.175 million if three million tickets are sold. With each of these costs, the net revenues available to the Indians would be approximately $57.9 million (see Table 10–6).

The net income to both the Rangers and Indians is between $57.9 and $66 million. The net income for the Pirates, after their debt issues are settled, is projected to be between $58.2 and $63.2 million. If it is accepted that $62 million is needed to keep the team competitive and profitable (an average of the income available to the Rangers and Indians after stadium costs), there is no revenue available from which the Pirates could afford to pay for rent and the construction of the stadium, in the absence of any revenue-sharing program between teams, if the Pirates' revenues from attendance matches the Rangers. If the Pirates were as successful as the Indians, slightly more than $2 million would be available each year to help

TABLE 10–6

A Comparison of Potential Revenues for Baseball in Pittsburgh

(All figures in millions of dollars; figures for Indians and Rangers reflect averages for complete 1994 and 1995 seasons adjusted for lease provisions)

Team	Media	Tickets	Revenue From Venue	Capital Investment (Annual Payment)	Rent	Loans	Net Income
Indians	14.6	35.4	14.2	5.1	1.2		57.9
Rangers	18.4	30.4	23.0	2.3	3.5		66.0
Pirates	15.0	30.4 to 35.4	18.6			5.8	58.2/63.2

pay for the stadium. With these costs and income projections in mind, we can now turn to the issue of how much it would cost Pittsburgh, Allegheny County, or the state of Pennsylvania to save the Pirates.

Can a small market like Pittsburgh really afford an MLB team? Using the estimates provided above, if the city were to assume complete responsibility for building the facility, an economically competitive team could exist even in Pittsburgh's small market. However, the team may not be able to even accept maintenance responsibilities for the stadium if a revenue-sharing plan among MLB teams did not exist. It might be possible to assign maintenance responsibilities to a stadium management company who could then raise revenues by "taxing" the sale of food, beverages, and souvenirs. In this manner, the team could retain all earnings from the facility, but they would also be responsible for maintaining it. This is an increasingly common arrangement, and it is the one established for the Cleveland Indians. If a capital asset fund is also a required component of the stadium operations (a fund to pay for remodeling or other needed large-scale improvements in later years), it is possible to have the team handle all aspects of the stadium's operations and retain the integrity of the stadium.

What would it cost the community of Pittsburgh to build a new stadium? If the facility could be built for $172 million, and financed for a period of thirty years, the cost to the taxpayers (assuming an interest rate of 6.25 percent) would be $12,708,840 per year. If the best loan rate available was 6.5 percent, the facility would cost $13,045,970 per year for thirty years. Forty-year financing would reduce the cost of the stadium, but there is substantial risk in financing for that long a period of time, especially if the stadium needs to be rebuilt. How much of a tax increase would this be?

Suppose the Pirates agreed to pay no money each year to the stadium's capital cost but would contribute 50 percent of all revenue earned in excess of the averages achieved by the Texas Rangers and Cleveland Indians (as enumerated here). In that case, the public sector would still have to be prepared to pay approximately $12 million each year, as it is unlikely that the Pirates would ever gross more money than the Indians or Rangers. If we also assume that a 5-percent sales tax were added to all transactions at the stadium, that would generate at least $1.5 million from the sale of tickets and $500,000 from other sales. The public sector could then expect an additional $2 million in each year, reducing the cost of the stadium to aproximately $10 million annually. A revenue-sharing program approved by MLB owners in March 1996 would provide approximately $4 million for the Pirates (Chass, 1996). (Under this plan, teams with large revenues from local media contracts and other sources are required to place some funds in a pool to be redistributed to smaller market teams.) If these dollars were dedicated to the development of the new stadium, the public sector's contribution would have to be approximately $6 million per year if the stadium only cost $172 million.

What does this subsidy represent in terms of the taxes paid in Allegheny County or the city of Pittsburgh? In 1991, Allegheny County collected $289.6 million in taxes from residents. To raise an additional $6 million, taxes would have to increase 2 percent. The city of Pittsburgh collected $238.9 million in taxes. As a percentage of these taxes, $6 million would amount to an increase of 2.5 percent. If the city and county's tax collections were joined together, both units of government would have collected $528.5 million. A $6 million annual subsidy to build the stadium would amount to 1.1 percent of the combined 1991 tax collections of the county and city (excluding school tax collections). Based on a 1990 county population of 1.34 million, the $6 million annual subsidy would amount to a payment of $4.48 for every person in the county to keep the Pirates.

In detailing the subsidy in this manner, other economic benefits and tax revenues are not being ignored. There will be some additional tax revenues collected and other economic benefits produced by building the stadium and having people attend games. However, if the stadium is not built and the subsidy is not provided, consumers likely will spend their $4.48 for other things. Those expenditures will create tax revenues and other economic benefits that will not exist if the stadium is built. Those losses offset the other gains some people want to believe accrue from building the stadium. Leaving aside the potential economic returns or associated economic impacts, residents of the county, it would seem, will have to decide if increasing their taxes approximately 2 percent (excluding school support) and spending $4.48 per person per year is worth the benefit of paying about $13 (ticket prices plus sales taxes) to see the Pirates play baseball.

SAVING PROFESSIONAL SPORTS IN THE QUEEN CITY

No area has been affected by "franchise free agency" more than Cincinnati. For the past several seasons Cincinnati and Hamilton County have listened to the pleas for financial help from the Reds and Bengals, along with their threats to leave the region. After more than two years of squabbles a plan was developed to build a new facility for each team at a cost of just under $545 million (including a new parking facility).[3] The new football stadium would be built on the site of the twenty-five-year-old Riverfront Stadium following its demolition and adjacent to new and renovated parking facilities that would separate the Bengal's home from the new baseball-only facility. In one sweeping action, then, Cincinnati and its county would save major league sports with new local taxes and state aid. In March 1996, the voters were asked if their tax dollars should subsidize professional sports, and more than 60 percent voted in favor of the tax subsidy to save both teams; 58 percent of the voters in the city of Cincinnati also supported the subsidies. This was in sharp contrast to votes in Cleveland and Denver, where a majority of center-city residents generally opposed tax subsidies while suburbanites voted for the welfare program. The Cincinnati vote indicated there was strong support for tax subsidies in the city and in the suburban areas of Hamilton County. How did Cincinnati and Hamilton County get to this juncture? How much will it cost Hamilton County residents to save professional sports for Cincinnati?

Cincinnati overlooks the northern shore of the Ohio River, bordering Kentucky and Indiana. A former industrial center, Cincinnati has seen significant changes in its demographic, political, and economic makeup over the past several decades. A common criticism raised with Cincinnati is that it has few dubious or positive distinctions. This rather "flat" image is what has convinced some community leaders of the need for professional sports teams. Without them, many leaders fear Cincinnati might become indistinguishable from Dayton, Louisville, Lexington, or Columbus, and less prominent than Indianapolis, which has both an NFL and NBA team in its downtown area. Indeed, the campaign for the tax subsidy proposals stressed the need to keep Cincinnati from becoming a Louisville or Lexington. Cincinnati's leaders argued sports were needed to preserve the region's identity (Helyar, 1996).

SHOTS ACROSS THE BOW

Home games for the Bengals and the Reds are played in Riverfront Stadium, which is owned by the county, leased by the city, and subleased to the Reds and the Bengals. Opened in 1970 as a replacement for Crosley Field, both teams now criticize the stadium's saucerlike design and lack of luxury seating and other revenue-generating amenities. These frustrations were first publicly declared by Mike Brown, son of the legendary Paul Brown, after the Bengals' patriarch-owner had died. Mike Brown, as the new owner, wanted a new facility, and the usual set of conflicts between teams and their cities began. First, an announcement was made that the Bengals were losing money and a new facility was required to keep the team. Second, the Bengals needed more revenues immediately and wanted to renegotiate their existing lease. Third, until a new stadium could be built, the Bengals needed a series of renovations to Riverfront Stadium to increase their revenues.

While the team negotiated for its new stadium, complete with club seating, advertising, luxury suites, permanent seat licenses (PSLs), and naming rights, they did receive their new lease. The city also agreed to invest $21 million to improve Riverfront Stadium if the Reds would support the changes. With the Bengals issuing threats and receiving concessions, the Reds decided to play "me too." The Reds refused to agree to any alterations unless the city also agreed to their list of changes. The conflict between the teams and their different demands stalled any of the planned changes and further convinced both teams that they needed their own homes. However, the threat by both teams to move alarmed the Cincinnati Business Committee (CBC), and pressure built for a public-sector response to the possibility that Cincinnati would no longer be home to major league teams. In this atmosphere, the mayor of Cincinnati and the president of the Hamilton County Commission appointed a twenty-seven-member task force to develop plans to "save" the teams for the greater Cincinnati metropolitan area.[4] This task force, composed of regional leaders in Ohio, Kentucky, and Indiana, met intermittently to determine whether two facilities were needed and how the facilities could be financed in a region that includes several counties and parts of three states. One task force member declared, "Our top priority is making sure those teams are happy, that they don't leave and they continue to be the tourism magnets and sources of economic development opportunities for the entire region."

COULD REGIONALISM SAVE SPORTS IN CINCINNATI?

The idea that a regional approach could be used to meet the demands of the teams was unlikely; the region is politically diverse and fragmented. Cincinnati tends to be Democratic while the balance of Hamilton County is Republican. Historically, there has been a poor track record of regional cooperation. The Cincinnati airport is located in northern Kentucky, but few other projects have involved regional cooperation, and the sports task force failed to overcome the regional divisions.

Dealing with the two teams was also a real challenge for the task force. The Reds, as a team, are loved, but their owner is not. The Bengals are not as well loved, but there is great affection for the Brown family. The two owners also failed to cooperate and frequently worked against each other. For instance, while Mr. Brown was negotiating with the city for renovations to the stadium and was working with the task force, Marge Schott, the Reds' owner, refused to attend any of the task force meetings. Eventually, the task force came to her office to receive her input. The situation became even more complex and baffling in May 1994, when Ms. Schott contacted city officials and expressed her interest in buying Riverfront Stadium. She asked for ninety days to evaluate the facility and to develop a financing package. Suddenly, Cincinnati's officials saw a light at the end of the tunnel: The money from the sale of Riverfront Stadium could offset part or all of the cost of a new stadium for the Bengals.

While this unusual twist in events was unfolding, the task force continued to meet and the city hired a local engineering firm to evaluate the costs of rehabilitating a parking garage that would also be sold with Riverfront Stadium. A plan to renovate the stadium to accommodate both teams was also developed. If the city was willing to spend $21 million, club seating and luxury suites could be added. Repairs to the parking garage were estimated to cost $40 million. Thus, the initial cost estimate for meeting the requirements of the Reds and Bengals to stay in Riverfront, or to sell it to Ms. Schott, was $61 million.

Later that same week the consulting firm that Ms. Schott hired to design the renovations she wanted if she bought the stadium released their analysis of the costs to convert Riverfront to a football-only stadium, a baseball-only facility, or to upgrade the facility for joint use. The report projected costs of $48 million for a conversion to a football stadium and $44 million to make Riverfront a baseball facility. The cost of repairing the garages was $40 million. The combined cost of either option was at least $84 million, or 30 percent higher than the public sector's estimates. At this same press conference where the consultants unveiled their findings, Ms. Schott also announced she would not consider buying the stadium unless it was converted to a baseball-only facility.

Regional politics quickly ruptured the public partners in the "save professional sports coalition." First, Hamilton County and the city of Cincinnati fought over who had the rights to secure income from the naming of any stadium. The county thought it had the right, since it owned Riverfront Stadium and wanted ownership of any new facility. The city believed it had the right to any naming fees, since it leased Riverfront from the county and intended to operate any new facility. Cincinnati city councillors claimed the regional task force was an advisory body with no authority to commit the city to any plan. The Reds' owner also upset a regional cooperation agenda by ignoring the task force and openly negotiating her own separate deal with Cincinnati's mayor, Roxanne Qualls.

Mayor Qualls further alienated some suburban officials when she announced that Kentucky residents should assume some financial responsibility for the renovation of Riverfront Stadium, the parking facilities, and any new facility. The mayor wanted a regional sports authority that included three Kentucky counties, one Indiana county, and four Ohio counties. Initially, the task force endorsed this idea, highlighting the additional benefits of regional cooperation, including potential transportation systems, improved museums, an aquarium, and possibly a regional sewer system.

With momentum building for a new, old-style ballpark for the Reds, Mike Brown went to the task force to plead for a new football-only stadium; he did not want to remain in Riverfront Stadium. Mr. Brown presented information indicating the Bengals would earn $5.5 million less than the average NFL team if they remained in Riverfront Stadium. At the same time the Reds began to increase their demands. Ms. Schott continued to refuse to agree to any interim changes to Riverfront and wanted 3.5 times as much as the city was paying Mike Brown not to leave the city (as part of the renegotiated lease arrangement to offset the lack of luxury suites and club seating at Riverfront). In trying to meet Ms. Schott's demands for short-term revenues in excess of what the Bengals were getting, Cincinnati's city manager reported that the stadium fund would be broke by 1996; the city could not afford to keep both teams happy with direct subsidies. This announcement led several city councillors to demand help from the Hamilton County Commissioners. County officials denied the request, adding that Cincinnati needed to manage its money better.

"ME-TOOISM" AND THE POLITICS
OF DEALING WITH TWO TEAMS

A year after Mike Brown renegotiated the Bengals' lease with the city, he announced that the Bengals would not play in Cincinnati after the 1999 season unless a new football stadium was built. He would not accept a renovated Riverfront Stadium; now, both of Cincinnati's teams wanted nothing to do with aging Riverfront. In a classic case of "me-tooism," both teams wanted what had been discussed with the other. The stadium the Bengals wanted would cost an estimated $146 million, not including the rehabilitation or replacement costs of the parking garage. Mr. Brown suggested doubling the county's hotel-motel tax to 6 percent and/or a regional "sin" tax on alcohol and tobacco sales.

The tug-of-war and public relations battle raged with both teams threatening to leave. The city undermined its own negotiating position by promising the Reds $2 million in additional revenue by changing their lease to match some of the changes made for the Bengals. The city was playing into the "me-tooism" game. The Reds escalated their negotiations and threatened to break their lease because they were not satisfied with the progress on the new ballpark plans. MLB raised Cincinnati's anxieties when they announced support for a move of the Reds to other communities in the region that would build the needed stadium. Baseball had now decided to play one government against another by threatening to support a move by the Reds to the suburbs if an acceptable stadium was not built in downtown Cincinnati. In this environment, any hope for a regional plan dissipated. Suburban officials began to oppose new taxes to support the planned facilities for downtown Cincinnati and any form of a regional government. Kentucky residents began to question the need to pay taxes for facilities located in downtown Cincinnati, believing it might be possible to convince the team to move to their suburbs.

In April 1995, the *Cincinnati Enquirer* declared, "Not much left for Bengals but to pack," as the regional task force was to recommend a new facility for the Reds but a renovated Riverfront Stadium for the Bengals. Mike Brown had already declared this plan as unacceptable. Fearing a loss of the Bengals, the Cincinnati city council decided to develop its own plan to save the Bengals. To further encourage the city council, Brown issued his first open ultimatum: If he was not guaranteed a stadium by the end of 1995 he would relocate the Bengals. With the very real possibility that the Bengals would move, the public-sector partners and the CBC had to plan for two new facilities. A 1995 poll of Cincinnati residents found only 37 percent interested in the city's building the new facilities and only 19 percent in favor of a tax increase to do it. Almost half of the supporters wanted another multipurpose facility to replace Riverfront. Yet, in 1996, fearing a loss of both teams, voters eagerly agreed to a tax to build two facilities.

Several plans were developed, including a sports park with a new football stadium adjacent to a new baseball park on the riverfront, and Ms. Schott and her architects presented their ideas for a stadium. None of the plans identified a financing mechanism, but one city councillor discussed using the city's pension funds. When new taxes were discussed, other groups claimed they needed that money. For example, the local teachers union said sales tax money should be used to support schools before stadiums. The local AFL-CIO opposed the use of pension funds on such a speculative investment.

The Kitchen Solution

On June 22, 1995, Republican Hamilton County Commissioner Bob Beddinghaus submitted a plan to the commission to finance two new stadia. In what is evolving into a local urban myth, he was thinking about this issue while sitting at his kitchen table and thought through the revenue that might be generated by a twenty-year 1-percent increase in the county sales tax, raising it to 6.5 percent. His calculations suggested that almost $100 million could be collected annually, of which he would only need $35 million for the bonds to build both of the demanded facilities. The rest of the money became what set the Cincinnati deal apart from that of other cities facing this challenge.

His tax increase would generate $65 million more each year than would be required to build two state-of-the-art sports palaces. Thus, he suggested, a rollback in property taxes that could be offset with some of the additional revenues. Under this plan, sales tax revenues would be used to reduce property-tax levies to support community mental health services, a renewal of the Regional Criminal Information Center, and a new levy for the center. Furthermore, some of the revenues could be directed to cover the costs of building a needed three-hundred-bed jail for the county. The new taxes would be divided:

40%   property tax rollback
35%   stadia costs
15%   three-hundred-bed county jail
6.5%   retire long-term debt
2.0%   reduce real estate transfer tax
1.5%   subsidy for county communications center operations

Another Hamilton County commissioner quickly endorsed the plan and released details to the Cincinnati city council together with a list of "nonnegotiable" items the county wanted in exchange for its lead on the tax increase. This list included a transfer of the city's stadium fund to the county, county ownership of and management responsibility for the Bengals' training facility and Riverfront Stadium, county control over all taxes collected from individuals employed at the stadium, all earnings from the surcharge on tickets, and operational control of the Metropolitan Sewer District (MSD). In Hamilton County, the county government owned the MSD while the city operated it; the county now wanted control over the district. The Beddinghaus plan won immediate support from suburban and business leaders and became the foundation for the plan that was eventually approved by voters.

City councillors were frustrated by the situation and clearly were caught between Mike Brown's threats to enter negotiations with Baltimore and the demands of the county commissioners. For the first few days following the commissioners' demands, all the city councillors groused. Mike Brown set his deadline for June 29. Four days before, the real negotiations began between the city and county. Except on the issues of giving the county the stadium employee earnings taxes, the city capitulated and passed the agreement with a

5–4 vote. All four Republicans voted in favor and Democrat mayor Qualls crossed lines to vote with them. Her fellow Democrats opposed the deal on the grounds that the economic development benefits were speculative and the county's demands were excessive.

The next phase of the story is also rather typical. Prostadium advocates hired a local university to perform an economic impact study that showed the half-billion-dollar investment in downtown was a great deal. An antitax grass-roots group hired another university economist to challenge the prostadium report. The outcome from the dueling consultant reports was to reduce the proposed sales tax increase from 1 percent to 0.5 percent. Ironically, this change had no effect on the amount committed to the sports facilities; the 0.5 percent forgone was to have reduced property taxes. However, in terms of marketing strategy to secure votes for the proposal, the reduction in the tax rate may have been a crucial factor. The tax reduction created the illusion that the public sector was reducing its investment.

WILL THE QUEEN CITY HAVE TO PAY A PRINCELY SUM?

Within this swirling milieu, how much will it take to keep the Reds and Bengals in Cincinnati? Using the target figure of $70 million as the revenue needed by a baseball team, the Reds will need to realize substantial income from their new stadium. Had the 1994 season been played to its conclusion, the Reds would have earned $15.2 million in income from its media sources; $15.3 million in 1995 would have been earned had all games for that seanson been played. This is the equivalent of $8.71 per local resident, a much higher media-to-market ratio than that of Pittsburgh or the larger media markets across the nation. This places Cincinnati in the highest group of media-revenue-earning teams (in per capita terms). It also suggests that additional revenues from media will be very difficult to achieve. The proposed facility for the Reds will cost $194.5 million.[5] Who should or could pay for this stadium?

Again, using the earlier analysis of the Cleveland Indians and

Texas Rangers as a general guide, the city (or county) could expect a present value contribution of between $20 (Texas Rangers) and $50 (Cleveland Indians) million dollars from the Reds for a new ballpark under financial arrangements similar to those involving the new facilities used by the Indians and Rangers. Unlike the Pirates' situation, however, the Reds are not hampered by extensive debts. The money given to the Reds and Bengals were direct subsidies that do not need to be repaid. However, the Reds contribution vis-à-vis the Rangers must be adjusted to account for the difference in media revenues. The Rangers' earnings averaged $18.4 million in 1994 versus the Reds' $15.2 million; in 1995 the differential was $3.2 million. The average difference of $3.2 million will have to be subtracted from the Reds' contribution to the new stadium.

Using the Rangers' and Indians' high-water mark attendance figures from the previous three years, an estimate for the Reds' ticket revenues can be calculated. As with the Pirates, the Reds are a small-market team, so one might argue that they will not have the same draw that the Rangers or Indians can generate. However, the Reds are a consistently strong club like the Pirates, and there is no reason to suspect they could not draw between 2,503,198 and 2,842,725 attendees and earn revenue similar to that of the Rangers or Indians.

Media revenues for the Reds will probably not change as a result of the new facility. Assuming a lease arrangement similar to that of the Rangers, the Reds will probably realize stadium revenues of approximately $13.2 million. Given these ticket, media, and stadium revenues, the Reds could realize total revenues of between $64.2 million ($30.4 million in ticket revenues plus $15.2 million in media revenues plus $18.6 million in stadium operations) and $69.2 million ($35.4 million in ticket revenues plus $18.6 million in media revenues plus $13.2 million in stadium operations). Table 10–7 summarizes these figures and compares them to those of the Indians and the Rangers.

Again, if we assume that it requires $62 million in net revenues to develop a competitive team while owners continue to realize profits (as the experience of the Indians and Rangers suggests), it would appear that the Reds could afford to contribute between $2.2 and $7.2 million toward the annual costs of the stadium. Furthermore, if

TABLE 10–7

A Comparison of Potential Revenues for Baseball in Cincinnati

(All figures in millions of dollars; figures for Indians and Rangers reflect averages for complete 1994 and 1995 seasons adjusted for lease provisions.)

		Revenue From					
Team	Media	Tickets	Venue	Capital Investment (Annual Payment)	Rent	Loans	Net Income
Indians	14.6	35.4	14.2	5.1	1.2		57.9
Rangers	18.4	30.4	23	2.3	3.5		66.0
Reds	15.2	30.4 to 35.4	18.6				$64.2/$69.2

the Reds were to receive some additional income from MLB's new revenue-sharing program, they might be able to afford to pay several million dollars more for their new stadium. Alternatively, if the public sector agreed to finance the entire stadium, then the Reds may become a net contributor to MLB's revenue-sharing program.

One important caveat to note, however, is how much the Reds pay their players compared to what the Indians and the Rangers pay. Though all three teams are competitive, the Reds have the fifth highest payroll in the major leagues, exceeding the Indians' and Rangers' payrolls by approximately 33 percent. Overall, the Reds' payroll exceeded the league average of $36.4 million by $10 million in 1994 and $8.4 million in 1995. If the Reds are unable to bring their player costs more in line with the rest of the league, then the excess revenue from the new facility predicted in this analysis would not be enough to bring the team out of the red, much less provide funds for the team to contribute to the facility.

It is clear that there is substantial room for the Reds to contribute to the new facility if they are willing to be more frugal with their excessive player salaries. Thus, if a governmental unit came forward and led the construction efforts, it is reasonable to expect the Reds to contribute to paying off the debt and to pay for the facility's maintenance and operating costs. According to the task force's report, the new ballpark for the Reds is expected to cost $194.5 million. Assuming, as we did for the Pirates, that the public sector could secure a thirty-year loan at a 6.25-percent interest rate, the annual payments would be $14,370,779. At a 6.50-percent interest rate, the same loan would cost $14,752,529 per year.

If the Reds organization could be convinced to pay between $2.2 and $7.2 million per year of these costs, that would reduce the burden on taxpayers. Furthermore, if a similar 5 percent sales tax on tickets and stadium purchases were imposed by the public sector as a type of user fee, an additional burden of approximately $2 million would be removed. The remaining $4.9 to $10.1 million would have to be paid by the public sector or a portion could come from the team if they reduced their payroll.

How many extra tax dollars does this represent for Hamilton County taxpayers? In 1991, Hamilton County collected $185,616,000 in tax revenue. The city of Cincinnati collected $223,810,000. The $10.1 million in additional revenues to pay for the remainder of the ballpark construction debt would represent an increase in county taxes of 5.4 percent or a 4.5-percent increase in city taxes. Of the combined tax revenues of the city and county, the stadium costs would represent an increase of 2.5 percent. In per capita terms, the $9.7 million would equal an *average* of $11.59 for every man, woman, and child just to have the facility in the region where they might decide to spend additional money for actually attending a game.[6] Is this expenditure worth the value of keeping the Reds?

WAIT, DON'T ANSWER, THERE'S STILL MORE

Before answering, we have to include the cost of a new facility for the Bengals. Pittsburgh's taxpayers have one big advantage: Their football team, the Pittsburgh Steelers, is not yet demanding their own stadium. We can estimate some of these costs relying upon NFL averages from *Financial World,* as it is the only source that has reviewed the financial situations of all teams in a consistent manner over the past several years.

The first important distinction between baseball and football as industries is how revenues are distributed among the owners. The NFL owners have a more aggressive revenue-sharing program in place than does baseball. Thus, the variance between NFL teams in terms of ticket and media revenues is relatively small when compared to that of MLB teams. What distinguishes football teams from one another is the money generated from the unshared revenues derived from the facility in which the teams play. These revenues include concessions, advertising, luxury suites, club seats, and permanent seat licenses. Those teams that get to keep a larger share of those revenues are the teams that have the more valuable franchises and can support more highly paid players, thus circumventing the intent of the salary cap (a current bone of contention among owners). The top four grossing teams in terms of stadium revenues averaged $17.2 million for the 1994 season and $19.2 million for the 1995 season, considerably higher than the overall league average of $5.4 and $6.2 million in 1994 and 1995, respectively.

Financial World estimates that the Bengals earned $1 million from their stadium arrangement (including the city's direct subsidy), which helped produce a $1.1 million profit in 1994. Venue income for the Bengals increased to $1.3 million in 1995, generating $1.3 million in profits. Assuming that a new facility that provided these extra revenue streams could increase the Bengals' stadium revenues tenfold, their total revenues would reach approximately $64 million, $2.2 million above the league average in 1994. The team's profit margin would increase to $11.1 million. Assuming further that the owner redirected $4 million of these profits to bring the team's player costs more in line with the league average (as would be possible under the salary cap), there would still be approximately $7.1 million from which the team owner could contribute to the stadium costs. Given the speculative nature of the increased stadium revenues, I conservatively assume that the Bengals' owner could safely contribute $2 million annually to the facility costs.

The task force in Cincinnati estimated the cost of a new football-only stadium at $205.5 million.[7] A thirty-year loan at 6.25 percent places the annual payments at $15,183,522. If the rate available is 6.50 percent, then the annual payments will be $15,586,862. With a $2 million annual contribution from the Bengals in some form and $2 million from a sales tax on tickets and stadium purchases, the public sector would have to pick up the remaining tab—between $11.2 and $11.6 million. Compared to the 1991 tax revenues of the county, this would represent as much as a 6.2-percent increase in overall taxes or a 5.2-percent increase for the city. Compared to the combined city-and-county-tax revenues, there would need to be a 2.8-percent increase. In per capita terms, every county resident would pay an *average* of $13.38 in additional taxes to build the Bengals a new stadium. Should citizens pay now? Well, there's still more.

All the parties that have been involved in the negotiations have agreed on one thing: the need for new parking at the facilities site. The task force report indicated that to repair the existing parking garage would cost $54 million plus an additional $15 million for new parking at the new ballpark, with architectural and engineering costs bringing the total to $75.9 million. Costs for changes in local infrastructure (including architectural and engineering fees) were estimated to be $11 million.[8] Demolition of the current stadium, land acquisition for the new ballpark, and a payment for the Bengals' playing two seasons on the road would add another $33 million to the remaining construction costs. Finally, taxpayers have an outstanding debt on the current Riverfront Stadium of approximately $25 million. Thus, in addition to the actual facility costs, there are $144.9 million in additional costs for the overall Reds-Bengals project in Cincinnati.

Using the same approach as for the teams, these remaining costs can also be examined in terms of additional taxpayer contributions to the ballpark and stadium. Putting these costs together and securing a 6.25-percent loan over thirty years would require an annual payment of $10,706,045. The payment would be $10,990,445 if the best interest rate is 6.50 percent. Assuming the teams contribute no additional funds to these costs and that the parking facilities can generate $1 million annually toward the construction costs, the remaining amount to be covered by the public sector would be between $9.7 and $10.0 million. At the higher interest rate, this would represent a 5.4-percent increase over 1991 county tax revenues or a 4.5-percent increase over city tax revenues. It represents a 2.4-percent increase over the combined tax revenues of the city and the county. In per capita terms, the higher-interest-rate figure means every county resident would have to pay *on average* $11.53 for these ancillary costs.

Cincinnati and Hamilton County residents will pay a hefty price to retain both teams. Given the assumptions for the teams' contributions to the project and the anticipated revenues from special user fees on tickets, stadium purchases, and parking, a family of four will have to pay almost $150 per year in additional taxes to support the costs of the new facilities and related expenses (see Table 10–8). Of course, if that same family actually wanted to attend a game, that would cost a bit more. And ironically, as the analysis performed here suggests, a very small subsidy was needed to help the Reds stay in Cincinnati. The large subsidy will mean excess profits and higher salaries for players.

LESSONS LEARNED, OR CAN SMALL MARKETS HAVE BIG LEAGUE SPORTS?

Pittsburgh's and Cincinnati's experiences and efforts to save big league sports teams in relatively small metropolitan areas raise critical issues regarding the future of sports in North America as well as important lessons for any city that negotiates with teams for the building of new playing facilities. Much of North America's history with professional sports is associated with small metropolitan areas, or regions that were formerly major urban centers. Can this compo-

TABLE 10–8

Cincinnati's Bottom Line

($ in millions)

	Estimated Cost	Annual Pymt. at 6.5%	Team Contribu-tion	User Fee Contribu-tion	Taxpayer Contribu-tion	% Incr. in Co. Tax Rev.	Per Capita Costs
Ballpark	194.5	14.8	3.1	2.0	9.7	5.2%	$11.14
Stadium	205.5	15.6	2.0	2.0	11.6	6.2%	$13.38
Parking, etc.	144.9	11.0	0	1.0	10.0	5.4%	$11.53
Total	544.9	41.4	5.1	5.0	31.3	16.9%	$36.05

nent of our sports history be maintained? Cincinnati and Pittsburgh are representative of the U.S. cities that are fighting to save their century-old teams. Canada's smaller metropolitan centers have already seen their big league hockey franchises relocate to larger market areas south of the border. Is the future of big league sports and smaller metropolitan areas a history of subsidies?

1. CAN TEAMS SURVIVE IN SMALL MARKETS? NOT WITHOUT REVENUE SHARING

Professional sports teams frequently seek larger markets where it is usually easier to earn profits. This pattern is sometimes changed when new facilities provide teams with luxury-seating revenues and income from the sale of PSLs. Unless the professional sports leagues agree to share revenues to a greater extent than they now do, in many instances competitive teams will be able to exist in smaller market areas only if fans pay higher prices for tickets or the community is willing to assume more and more of the fiscal responsibility for playing and practice facilities. This assumption of fiscal responsibility for building facilities by the public sector permits teams to retain the revenue from luxury seating and PSLs. In the 1950s and 1960s Yankee fans used to joke that the Kansas City A's were their farm team. Financially, the A's were far weaker than the Yanks. Whenever the Yankees needed players, "deals" seemed to be struck with the A's and these trades revolved around star players for journeymen players and the transfer of cash from the Yankees to the A's. The transfer of dollars for players between wealthier and poorer teams is as old as the deal for Babe Ruth that the Yankees engineered with the Boston Red Sox. Red Sox fans still refer to that 1920s sale as the "curse" that prevents Boston from ever winning a World Series.

Recently, MLB's owners have agreed to a modified form of revenue sharing that will increase the dollars available to smaller market teams at the expense of larger market squads. Across two years, $39 million in revenues from ticket sales, concessions, advertising fees, local radio and television revenues, and cable television contracts will be shared. The Kansas City Royals will receive almost $5 million and the Pirates and Brewers will likely receive an additional $4 million. The Yankees will contribute approximately $5.8 million (Chass, 1996). These funds will increase the amount of money the smaller market teams such as Pittsburgh and Cincinnati can pay to build and maintain their playing fields. And as the analysis indicates, this will reduce the subsidy required. Indeed, added to the analysis presented here, these funds could substantially reduce the tax obligations for residents of the Pittsburgh and Cincinnati regions. These dollars will also increase the ability of smaller market teams to attract and retain the best players, but without more substantial revenue sharing, local communities in smaller areas will have to contribute far more dollars to finance playing facilities than will larger communities. In addition, if larger communities decide to subsidize playing facilities, to offset these losses by the larger market teams local communities will have to increase their subsidies. In effect, smaller communities will always have to provide more incentives than larger communities. And then the teams in larger communities will point to these subsidies and demand more in their hometowns. As such, a vicious cycle may continue to exist where smaller cities are always having to increase their subsidies. It must also be remembered that the NFL, NBA, and NHL have also not agreed to share revenue from luxury seating, forcing cities to build new facilities for many teams.

This endless loop will continue until there is either a substantial form of revenue sharing among teams in all sports or all cities agree to limit the subsidies they provide. While MLB has taken the first small steps toward increased revenue sharing, little progress has been made in the NFL, NBA, or NHL for sharing facility revenues. Within this reality there may be little encouraging to pass along; smaller cities can expect to offer larger and larger subsidies to maintain competitive teams or face a future similar to that of the Kansas City A's of the 1950s and 1960s.

2. BUILDING REVENUE SHARING
INTO YOUR MODEL

When the voters went to the polls in Cincinnati to vote for a 0.5-percent increase in their sales taxes to build two new playing facilities, there was little discussion of the impact of a new revenue-sharing program on the fiscal fortunes of the Reds. With MLB implementing a new plan, and other leagues debating the merits of sharing revenues between large- and small-market teams, any new proposal to build a stadium must include these revenues in estimates of the capacity of teams to reduce the public's investments and subsidy. If the Pirates are required to use these funds to build a new stadium, the subsidy required from taxpayers declines by more than $4 million each year. All community leaders must be sure they accurately project the revenues of each team for which they are considering a subsidy to support a new stadium. Only if these revenues are included can an accurate projection be made of the "needed" subsidy. If these revenues are not considered, the public sector's subsidy will be far larger than is necessary. Such is the case in Cincinnati where the team has the potential to assure a considerable portion of the cost for building the stadium. Simply put, Cincinnati's taxpayers are being asked to pay too much for the new stadium even within the cartel-world of MLB.

3. BEWARE OF "ME-TOOISM"

The public sector must develop a unified voice when it negotiates with professional sports teams, especially if more than one team exists in a market. Any deals with any one team will have to be given to the other team. The organized negotiations in Cincinnati left the public sector with no option but to build two facilities. Seattle, reliving Cincinnati's fate, now finds itself with a "me-too" demand from the Seattle Seahawks and the NFL after fixing the revenue problems of the Mariners and Sonics. The public sector must have a "sports policy" and avoid ad hoc responses to each team. An ad hoc framework will lead you to a series of escalating requests from each team as soon as you grant one favor or exception to one team. Know in advance what you want to do, what you are planning to spend, and detail your plan for all concerned. Once your plans and policies are established, do not change them unless you are prepared to offer all teams that exact same set of incentives or rewards.

4. IS REGIONALISM THE ANSWER FOR THE PUBLIC SECTOR'S SPORTS SUBSIDY GAME?

The burden of any subsidy is minimized if it is spread across a larger number of taxpayers and cities. A regional framework for dealing with sports teams also reduces the number of potential governments that can be "played off" each other to secure even larger subsidies. However, be aware that teams and their owners can maximize their positions by threatening to move within a region. When these threats are made, visions of grandeur sweep through the eyes of many suburban community leaders, and many starry-eyed commitments are often made as suburbs seek to build their own identities. Sports team owners are aware of the needs and weaknesses of community leaders and are all too eager to "play this card" if a subtle hint or two might get the desired deal done.

To ensure that communities within a region cannot be played against each other, a commitment to regionalism must exist. Building this spirit of cooperation takes a great deal effort and will not occur when the crisis of negotiating with a team presents itself. If you want a regional approach to the building and financing of facilities for sports teams and a unified sports policy that is agreed to by all governments, develop the needed compacts years before a crisis emerges. Metropolitan areas need to think regionally years before the sports teams issue their siren calls to all communities that seek to build their identities. If you do not build a regional approach to sports, you will pay higher subsidies as the competition between governments to be a home to a professional team will lead to the provision of higher and higher levels of welfare.

11

Fights Within the Family

Suburbs and Center Cities in a Battle for the Intangible Benefits from Sports

During the next week, Arlington will be discovered for all the reasons that it ought to already be known. Having the All-Stars here will establish a national identity we otherwise could never have achieved.

—RICHARD GREENE, mayor of Arlington, Texas, site of the 1995 Major League All-Star game

The [Dallas/Fort Worth] metroplex is so intertwined that there is no one city that really stands independently anymore, whether you're talking about Dallas or Fort Worth or Arlington. The All-Stars are a good thing for all of us.

—TERRY RYAN, executive director, Fort Worth Chamber of Commerce

MOST OF THE ANALYSES in the preceding case studies have focused on economic returns from the existence of teams, the investments made by communities in their efforts to host teams, and the subsidies provided by cities in the hope of securing some level of downtown development. Little attention has been focused on the "intangible" or image benefits that can accrue to cities that host teams for their community. Indeed, a substantial portion of the arguments used by city officials to justify their interest in hosting a team is tied to efforts to establish a major league identity for their community. The argument is frequently made that if a city is home to a major league franchise, the city's identity will be changed, and fame and fortune will most certainly follow. Are the intangible gains from hosting a team worth the subsidies provided? What does a city gain from the intangible or image benefits a team's presence conveys?

There is little doubt that the presence of a team provides a substantial level of publicity for the city that hosts it. Media reports will frequently mention the city even if the team's name does not (for example, Indianapolis and the Indiana Pacers, Irving and the Dallas Cowboys, Arlington and the Texas Rangers). The presence of a team will likely also enhance civic pride and the identity of the city in the minds of its residents. Numerous officials interviewed for this book, even those who were not sports fans, commented on the improved image and feelings of civic pride they believed were the result of the existence of teams. Indeed, these officials frequently noted that they were surprised by the very positive reactions and widespread civic pride in teams and their new arenas and stadia. Professional sports, then, similar to a city's other elements (the arts, parks, schools, universities, and so on) can and do generate positive feelings. But do teams, their playing facilities, and the other intangible benefits lead to any measurable economic returns? The pressing issue for public officials who adopt policies that lead to welfare for teams may well be, "Do the positive feelings from sports produce any tangible rewards?" Earlier, it was noted there was no evidence that businesses decide to locate in an area as a result of the presence of a team. Now it is time for us to look more closely at the intangible benefits—civic pride, and publicity generated by teams—to see if there are any outcomes or changes in a community that can be attributed to a team's presence. While we will not attempt to determine if teams generate more civic pride than other amenities, we will quantify aspects of the benefits from the publicity and civic pride teams generate.

The best setting from which to analyze the actual impact of the intangible benefits of a sports team may be a metropolitan area in which cities have competed against each other to be the "home" for a team. Nowhere is this argument for image benefits more artfully made than when cities within the same region fight among themselves to be the host city for a team that is already part of a region. Frequently, suburban cites in these settings seek teams to achieve a sense of status that would make them feel equal to a larger central city. While the movement of teams between regions attracts the most national attention, numerous franchises have also threatened to move or have moved from one city to another within the same metropolitan region. The willingness of public officials from suburban and central cities to provide a subsidy to a team is always tied to the supposed image benefits that will result from the team's presence. Does a team's choice of one city over another within a metropolitan area change economic development patterns or the locational choices of individuals? Does the prestige, publicity, or pride that comes from hosting a team translate into any real benefits that can be measured? We focus on these questions through a review of the competition for teams within the Dallas/Fort Worth region. Here, where the spirit of Texas, capitalism, and individualism often work against regional cooperation, several suburban cities have battled Dallas to be home to the region's professional teams. Just what did Arlington, home to the Rangers, and Irving, home to the Cowboys, get when they became "major league cities"?

In focusing on the Dallas/Fort Worth area it should be remembered that the fighting within this regional family of communities is similar to the battles that have taken place in other areas. Community leaders in Cleveland, St. Louis, Toronto, Cincinnati, and Indianapolis, as detailed in previous chapters, have either worried about the movement of teams to suburban areas or have seen teams move from center cities to the suburbs. St. Louis feared the Blues might leave for the suburbs, and the Cavaliers did leave Cleveland for suburban Richfield only to return, years later, for a king's ransom. Both of Kansas City's major league franchises play in the suburbs, and the Washington Redskins have announced their plans to play in suburban Maryland. Detroit has lost two of its franchises to the suburbs, and their fear of a potential move by the Tigers has made them very willing to provide subsidies. In a response to Detroit's latest incentives, not only will the Tigers remain in the city, but the Lions are coming home. The concern that a team could move within a region is not limited to these "smaller" center cities. New York, Chicago, and Los Angeles, the nation's largest center cities, have each listened to threats by their teams that they might leave their borders for the friendly confines of the suburbs. The Giants and Jets did move to suburban New Jersey, and the Rams moved to Anaheim before heading to St. Louis. In an effort to reassert itself, Los Angeles has now developed a proposal to bring the Lakers and Kings from Inglewood to downtown. New York City now faces the potential loss of the Yankees if the city is not willing to "invest" in a new home for the team. This fear has led to New York City entertaining a $1 billion proposal for a new Yankee Stadium. The Bears also have toyed with the idea of moving to northwest Indiana or Chicago's western suburbs. The control over the supply of teams by the sports leagues means that the competition among cities within a region can be manipulated because the suburban and center cities' leaders well understand that it is unlikely that a second team will exist within their region. As a result, when major league teams cast a roving eye within their region, there are always one or two suburban cities that are all too willing to provide the desired subsidies and a king's ransom in the hope of achieving a mythical level of status.

Staying in an existing metropolitan area, but orchestrating a competition between cities within that area, has a number of attractions for owners and players. First, without going through all of the public ridicule and political battles that accompany moves to other regions, team owners still can receive the subsidies they want by simply suggesting they have an interest in moving to another city within their market area. Invariably, suburban cities will offer very favorable incentive packages to attract teams in the hope of achieving major city status, and these inducements frequently rival anything that could be provided by a city in another region. In this manner the team's owner can reap substantial awards and not risk the ire of other owners or fans that moves to other regions generate. Intraregional competition (and manipulations) can produce the same level of returns with far less grief and anxiety for the owners.

Second, while frequently able to secure the desired inducements from the competition between center and suburban cities, owners face virtually no risk of losing existing and lucrative local cable, television, or radio contracts. Yankee fans throughout metropolitan New York would still want to receive telecasts and broadcasts even if the Bronx Bombers were the Manhattan Maulers or the Jersey Jolters. If a team has developed an extensive television or cable network of subscribers, staying in an area means this source of revenue does not have to be redeveloped in a new region. Third, movement within a region does not require league approval and frequently reduces the likelihood of any legal challenges. Fourth, with few or no moving costs, team owners can utilize virtually all of the inducements provided to increase profit levels. Players, too, can remain in their existing homes and continue to pursue any local business and advertising interests without any disruptions in their lives. With an increase in profits as a result of the inducements provided by the city in the region that ultimately wins the battle to provide welfare and subsidies to the team, the players also benefit from the increased revenues available from which higher salaries can be paid. Intraregional competition between cities for teams is very, very good business for team owners and players. But is it good business for cities, or a risky venture unlikely to produce any gains for the city that ultimately bears the costs of the subsidies it provides?

It is certainly clear why owners and players are interested in having cities within their market area fight for them. Why do suburban cities do it? Simply put, smaller cities have always sought to achieve status or a level of acceptance equal to that accorded center cities. Many suburban leaders believe "major league" city status can be obtained *only* by hosting an NFL, MLB, NBA, or NHL team. This status, many believe, will lead to the attraction of businesses and residents who want to be associated with a major or "big league" community. Can any city within a region that hosts a team capture the "image benefits" that teams supposedly generate? Without questioning whether or not these benefits exist (Bale, 1989; Zimbalist, 1992), an analysis of growth and development in the Dallas/Fort Worth area will demonstrate that the intangible benefits, if they do exist, cannot be captured by any one city that offers inducements or subsidies. Fights within the family of cities in a region do nothing more than increase taxes and the subsidies provided to teams.

THE DALLAS/FORT WORTH "METROPLEX"

Unlike some of the other regions that have tried to keep and attract teams, the Dallas/Fort Worth area has neither been shrinking in population nor stagnating. Indeed, the Dallas/Fort Worth metroplex has been one of the nation's fastest-growing areas. In 1970 the region had 2.4 million residents. By 1980 the population had increased by 24.6 percent to 2.9 million people. Another decade of growth in the 1980s, a 32.6-percent increase, brought the region to 3.9 million inhabitants in 1990. Today, the U.S. Bureau of the Census estimates the region's population to be 4.5 million people. Few areas of the country have grown as quickly as the Dallas/Fort Worth region, now the eighth largest media market in America.

In terms of its image, the region has adopted the name "the Dallas/Fort Worth metroplex." The term *metroplex* is used to describe the sort of triplex combination of cities that also defines the competition for sports teams. The end points of the metroplex are the region's two center cities, Dallas and Fort Worth. Unlike the Minneapolis–St. Paul area, however, these cities would hardly be described as "twins." They are more like feuding cousins who have spawned even more feuding family members.

At the region's eastern pole is the central city of Dallas, in Dallas County. There are two large suburbs to Dallas's east, but in terms of the concept of a "metroplex," it is useful to think of Dallas as one end of the region. Approximately forty miles to the west is the region's other center city, Fort Worth, which is the region's western anchor. Fort Worth, far smaller than Dallas, with fewer than five hundred thousand residents, is the central city of Tarrant County. There are but a few small communities to Fort Worth's west, and none of these suburban areas are as large as Dallas's eastern suburbs. In the middle, between the two large central cities, are a series of suburban

cities sometimes called the "Mid-Cities." There are also some important and growing suburban cities to the north of both central cities.
The two central cities and the suburban cities represent the three-
tier structure of cities in the region, or a sort of triplex of cities in a
single metropolitan area (hence "metro" for *metropolitan* and "plex"
for *triplex*).

The metroplex cities have a history of competing against one
another to attract economic development, and this spirit of individualism and a lack of regional cooperation have created a very fertile
environment for sports teams seeking the best possible deals. The
feuding between cities in this region, while sometimes bitter and
sometimes comical, is always present. Although the initial fighting
for economic dominance of the region occurred between Dallas and
Fort Worth, two or three of the larger suburban cities have now
joined this family feud. The competition is based, in part, in the very
different images the two center cities have of each other and of
themselves.

For Dallasites, Fort Worth is a sleepy, provincial, and backward-
looking west Texas "cow town." Dallas's old-time residents take great
satisfaction from a story that had one of their leaders venturing into
the "frontier" of downtown Fort Worth only to find it so quiet that a
panther was sleeping on Main Street. Some still refer to Fort Worth
as the Panther City. In later years Fort Worth was able to capitalize
on this reputation with a restored stockyards section of old Fort
Worth that has become a popular tourist attraction. An old "drovers'
house" has been refurbished into a restaurant, and a hotel was
restored to its nineteenth-century grandeur. Several restaurants,
bars, nightclubs, and western clothing and saddle shops are also part
of this section of Fort Worth. However, when Dallasites speak of a
cow town, they are referring not to the tourist center but to a Main
Street where a panther could well enjoy an afternoon nap.

Fort Worth's citizenry see Dallas as eastern, not unlike New York
City and the East Coast of the United States. These attributes, of
course, are frequently discussed or described in quite disparaging
terms and contrasted with Fort Worth's western and more commu-
nity-oriented values. For many Fort Worth residents, Dallas is the
New York City of Texas and the prime example of all that is wrong

with life in Texas or America. Amon Carter, Fort Worth's civic and economic icon, countered the sleeping panther tale by carrying his own lunch to Dallas whenever he had to attend meetings. He argued there was no restaurant in the city able to satisfy his dining needs.

As the Dallas/Fort Worth area has grown to a region of more than four million people, the competition between cities has expanded to include suburban cities. At first, this competition was at a more distant or secondary level. The growing suburban cities fought with one another to be "the" bedroom community and to attract some of the area's largest employers to their business parks. However, as the region and its suburbs began to grow, new "giants" were created in the area between Dallas and Fort Worth and to Dallas's north, and these suburban cities sought to enhance their images and become "big league" cities in their own right.

The city that would most decidedly change the urban competition between Dallas and Fort Worth into a three-way battle, especially for sports teams, was Arlington. A nineteenth-century stage coach stop, and a sleepy home to a small military academy in the early part of the twentieth century, Arlington, even in 1970, was little more than a footnote to the Dallas/Fort Worth area. Located virtually midway between Dallas and Fort Worth, its population in 1970 was less than one-quarter of Fort Worth's. In the early 1970s, Arlington was not even the biggest suburban city in the region; but the seeds for Arlington's growth had been planted and cultivated years earlier with the election of Thomas Vandergriff as mayor. To foster development, the young mayor, who was to lead the city across three decades, helped secure the political support for building a large lake within the city and on its western border with Fort Worth. Having secured access to water, a necessity for any city in Texas that wishes to thrive, Arlington was able to attract a large General Motors assembly plant, and its growth became nothing short of spectacular.

Arlington has been the beneficiary of several other factors or assets that have sustained its more than three-decade-long growth spurt. First, Arlington's location has been a great asset. At the virtual midpoint of the region, two interstate highways crossed Arlington from east to west. Two north-south state highways linked the city to the Dallas/Fort Worth Regional International Airport, and one of these roads eventually became a limited-access freeway. Second, Arlington's political and community leadership was well organized and concentrated in its dynamic leaders. Although two of its mayors held sway over tightly knit growth machines and a regime, Tom Vandergriff and Richard Greene (the latter of who was mayor of Arlington when the Ballpark in Arlington was built) provided strong leadership and developed a vision of Arlington as a major league city across a substantial portion of the period of Arlington's extraordinary growth. Third, Tom Vandergriff did not stop his efforts to build Arlington with the establishment of Lake Arlington or the attraction of the GM plant. With these successes under his belt, he next focused on enhancing Arlington's educational resources. When it became apparent that the state would create a University of Texas system with a campus in the Dallas/Fort Worth area, Mayor Vandergriff was able to use the competition between Dallas and Fort Worth and his own substantial political acumen to "suggest" Arlington as a possible compromise site. In 1967 Arlington State College became the University of Texas at Arlington (UTA); today, more than 25,000 students attend UTA. Other companies also sought locations in the expanding Arlington area, including Bell Helicopter. With new corporate and educational resources, Arlington was on an economic development roll.

Fourth, Mayor Vandergriff shifted his economic development focus to recreational enterprises as a way to further elevate Arlington's image. The Six Flags (over Texas) amusement park opened in Arlington, as did an unsuccessful marine life park. Mayor Vandergriff was also able to convince the Washington Senators to move to the city (this will be discussed in greater detail later in this chapter), and when the Dallas/Fort Worth Regional Airport opened just to Arlington's north, Arlington became far more than an edge or suburban city. With an expanding, affluent population attracted to the city's largely homogeneous neighborhoods, Arlington became a retail and urban center for the Dallas/Fort Worth metroplex. Fifth, Arlington is the largest city in the United States without any form of public transportation. This policy, robustly supported by the residents and their elected officials, minimized the number of lower-income people who could live in the city. Even today, the city has refused to join any of the region's transportation districts. While this would appear to be a limitation rather than an asset for attracting sports teams, the less than friendly environment the lack of transportation creates for lower-income households protects Arlington's fiscal stability and status. Sixth, with its central location, Arlington became a prime location for retail development. Retail trade in Arlington produces more than $48 million in annual tax revenues for the city (1995 and 1996 revenue levels). Seventh, surrounded by unincorporated land, Arlington has also been able to annex all the area it has wanted for residential and retail development. Finally, Arlington's mayors (and the city councils) also hired leading professionals as city managers to propel Arlington's image as a sophisticated and efficiently managed community. A series of excellent city administrators ensured the stability of the political leadership through the efficient delivery of services. A small example of this technical expertise is projected by Arlington's home page on the World Wide Web. Arlington's presentation on the information highway is substantially more sophisticated than the home pages designed by most other cities in the metroplex or elsewhere in North America.

Arlington's success and popularity is best illustrated by the meteoric rise of its population. From 1970 to 1995 Arlington attracted more new residents to its boundaries than did any city in the Dallas/Fort Worth region. During this twenty-five-year period, 189,371 people moved to Arlington. In contrast, 185,749 people moved to Dallas despite its larger geographic size, and Fort Worth's population increased by just 77,125 people. In 1995, Arlington's total population of 279,600 made it the largest suburban city in the region, the seventy-first largest city in America, and the seventh largest in Texas. From "just another 'burb," Arlington, at the cusp of the twentieth and twenty-first centuries had become major league in every way. It was and is a major competitor for economic development with Dallas, Fort Worth, and every other city in Texas and the southwest United States.

Arlington was not the only suburban city to emerge as a major competitor of Dallas and Fort Worth. While perhaps not as large as

Arlington, four communities in Dallas County also became important "players" in the economic destiny of the region. The population
of Irving, located immediately west of Dallas and adjacent to the
Dallas/Fort Worth International Airport, grew from 97,260 to
165,950 in 1995. Of greater significance for the development of Irving, however, was the building of the Las Colinas office and residential complex. A virtual "edge city," or city within a city, Las Colinas
became the home office for several of the Dallas/Fort Worth region's
largest employers. Complete with a canal, hotels, a golf course, and
luxury housing, and with close proximity to the Dallas/Fort Worth
Regional International Airport, Las Colinas is a prime location for
financial and computer technology firms. Approximately 30,000
people now work in the Las Colinas "edge city" complex. Richardson, north and east of Dallas, saw its population increase by 62 percent from 1970 to 1995. The home of the University of Texas at Dallas, Richardson now has 78,200 people. Plano, a prime residential
suburb north of Dallas, increased its population by a whopping 845
percent from 17,872 in 1970 to 168,900 in 1995. Plano was easily the
region's and state's fastest growing city, and Garland, an older suburb to Dallas's east, remains quite large. In 1970 Garland had 81,437
residents; in 1995, 192,200 people called this suburb home.

It is also critical to point out that virtually all of these suburbs
have been able to attract some of the region's wealthier residents,
concentrating lower-income people in both center cities. In Dallas,
in 1989, 14.7 percent of all households had incomes at or below the
poverty level; in Fort Worth, 13.6 percent of all households had
incomes this low. In contrast, in both Richardson and Plano, just 3.1
and 2.2 percent of the population had incomes this low. In Arlington, 5.7 percent of the households had incomes at or below the
poverty level. This unequal distribution of lower-income households meant that the center cities, as is typical in many metropolitan
areas, had a greater challenge in terms of attracting and retaining
businesses and residences while also generating any revenues
needed to provide inducements to attract or retain professional
sports teams. There would also be a natural attraction for professional sports teams to locate in faster-growing suburban areas. Not
only were the more affluent fans to be found in these cities, but with

the explosive growth of the Las Colinas and Arlington areas, as well as the areas in close proximity to the Dallas/Fort Worth Regional Airport, many of the region's most important businesses were to be found in the suburbs.

The competitive environment of the metroplex is now defined by battles for the attraction of businesses and sports teams between Dallas, Fort Worth, Arlington, Irving, Richardson, Grand Prairie, Addison, and Plano. There are even smaller suburbs that also frequently throw their hat into the ring when an opportunity arises. To be sure, there are some important examples of regional cooperation. The North Central Texas Council of Governments produces a series of reports and analyses helpful in managing the region and fostering its economic development. And while both Dallas and Fort Worth fought to be the site of the regional airport that became the Dallas/Fort Worth Regional International Airport, when the federal government intervened to specify the site, both cities and their elected representatives worked together to develop a facility that has become second only to Chicago's O'Hare airport in terms of the number of daily flights. These examples of cooperation, however, do not minimize the competition that characterizes the relationships among and between the cities in the Dallas/Fort Worth region. Perhaps the spirit of Texas and the emphasis on rugged individualism contribute to the difficulty in developing regional perspectives and more intensive and extensive examples of cooperation.

SPORTS AND THE METROPLEX

The Dallas/Fort Worth region's history with major league professional teams began in 1960. The upstart AFL, eager to challenge the more established NFL, targeted rapidly growing areas that did not have teams and placed one of its charter franchises, the Texans, in Dallas. The NFL, in an effort to protect potential markets, quickly responded with its own expansion and awarded the Dallas Cowboys franchise in the same year. The older league, with greater prestige and the ability to attract more fans as a result of its established and popular teams with many star athletes (such as the Chicago Bears, Green Bay Packers, and New York Giants) was far more successful in this new market, resulting in the Texans' move to Missouri in 1963, where they became the Kansas City Chiefs.

Dallas, with the region's only NFL-caliber stadium, became the home of the first major league franchises. Arlington, however, was the home of the region's minor league baseball team, and it would use its existing baseball facility to attract the Washington Senators in 1971. Arlington first tried to secure a baseball team when the National League expanded in the late 1960s. The Dallas/Fort Worth area was in the running for a team when the Montreal Expos and San Diego Padres were created. With Houston already home to a National League team, the Dallas/Fort Worth area seemed more likely to be an attractive site for an American League team. However, with no expansion planned by that league, the Dallas/Fort Worth area needed to attract an existing team. Tom Vandergriff, with the support of all cities in the region, began the arduous process of convincing an existing team to move. In 1971, Mayor Vandergriff was able to convince Bob Short to relocate his floundering Washington Senators to the center of the Dallas/Fort Worth region. In 1972 the Texas Rangers began play in Arlington Stadium, a facility initially developed for a minor league team, but adjacent to Interstate 30 and at the geographic and transportation center of the region. As part of the agreement with the Washington Senators and Bob Short, Arlington agreed to expand its minor league stadium to accommodate 50,000 fans. Arlington would never be able to fulfill that part of its original contract with the team, and that failure would be part of all future negotiations between the team and the city.

The NBA made its appearance in the Dallas/Fort Worth area with the awarding of the Dallas Mavericks team franchise in 1980. The team has played in Reunion Arena in downtown Dallas since its inception. Reunion Arena, built for an NBA team, was opened in 1980 and provided the city with its initial "first-class" enclosed facility capable of competing with Fort Worth's Tarrant County Convention Center (located at the opposite end of Interstate 30 in downtown Fort Worth). Dallas built Reunion Arena for the Mavs, and while the facility does not have any suites or luxury seating, the team pays rent equal to $10,000 per game plus 5 percent of gross ticket revenues in excess of $324,000. If receipts are less than this amount, the team pays, per game, seven percent of the gross or $10,000, whichever is less. The team also receives a small portion of all advertising and concession income.

The NHL did not come to the Dallas/Fort Worth region until the 1990s. In 1994 the Minnesota North Stars moved to Reunion Arena and began play as the Dallas Stars. The Stars received a lease that was virtually identical to the one given the Mavs. Minor league hockey had long been a staple in the region with teams in both Fort Worth and Dallas. While those teams changed owners and names, the two minor league hockey teams are still part of the sports world of the metroplex. The Fort Worth Fire play at Will Rogers Auditorium, a small venue on Fort Worth's west side. The Dallas Freeze play their home games approximately five miles east of Reunion Arena.[1] Dallas has also been home to several other sports, including indoor and outdoor soccer teams. The Dallas Sidekicks, the region's indoor soccer team, while encountering some severe financial problems, continue to play their home games at Reunion Arena. Dallas was also selected to be home to one of the franchises in the new outdoor soccer league that began play in 1996.

The attraction of the Dallas Cowboys, Texas Rangers, Dallas Mavericks, and Dallas Stars was seen as major image and economic development coups for the Dallas/Fort Worth region. Both soccer teams were also viewed as providing even more attractions for the region. Sports provided a conduit through which a new image could be shaped, and the success of the Cowboys certainly helped to create other perspectives of Dallas. While Dallas's attachment to the Cowboys and the extensive fan following are a result of the two sustained periods of success the team has enjoyed, there may well be other reasons Dallas cherishes its relationship with "America's team." The popularity of the Cowboys during their first period of substantial success coincided with the aftermath of the assassination of President Kennedy and the death of Lee Harvey Oswald while he was in Dallas police custody. The success of the Cowboys seemed to have the potential for changing the image of Dallas. In the 1960s, the name Dallas, for many people, rekindled their memories of the chaos and murder that followed the assassination of President Kennedy. The image of Jackie Kennedy's bloodstained suit seemed to be a prominent part of Dallas's image; and it was a perspective or view the region wanted to discard. The Cowboys and their success were a first step in that effort.

The relocation of the Washington Senators, at about the same time that the region opened the Dallas/Fort Worth Regional International Airport, continued the process of redefining the images of the region. Dallas, indeed the entire Dallas/Fort Worth region, seemed to be an area on the move and destined for substantial economic growth. As the Cowboys became America's team, the metroplex came to typify the growth and expansion that embodied so much of America's view of itself. In the Dallas/Fort Worth metroplex, with the Cowboys winning, a new airport, new sports teams, and expanding economic growth, one could hardly wait for tomorrow, for it was destined to be better than today. The Cowboys' winning ways underscored the region's success and provided the whole metroplex with an image and swagger that the teams, and the Cowboys in particular, epitomized. When the Cowboys added their cheerleaders to the equation, the entire region was seen as beautiful, brash, and successful, hardly the dreary, backward section of America where a president was murdered.

WANDERING EYES AND IMAGE BENEFITS

When any of the cities in the region first attempted to bring a new sports franchise to the metroplex, there was a high level of cooperation to ensure that the team would come to the area. However, as soon as any of the teams began to cast a wandering eye about the region for a better stadium or arena, cooperation gave way to a battle to achieve a "major league image." In the same order they appeared in the region, the teams began to seek improved stadia and arenas and to encourage a competition between the cities. The spirit of cooperation quickly gave way to a spirit of individualism and the hope of achieving the mythical status of a major league city.

The Cowboys played their home games at Dallas's historic, but aging, Cotton Bowl, which lacked many of the modern amenities teams and fans sought in the late 1960s. In addition, the Cotton Bowl was and is located in a predominantly minority, declining neighborhood, which continues to suffer from high crime levels and economic disinvestment. In the late 1960s the Cowboys and the city of Dallas exchanged ideas and plans for a new downtown facility or a facility north of downtown. Four separate plans were developed, but none could be supported by all parties. Frustrated with the pace of negotiations and the city's seeming lack of concern or appreciation for the needs of the team, the Cowboys began to look for alternatives. When no agreement could be reached with the city of Dallas, the team initiated negotiations with the city of Irving. While some of Dallas's leadership could hardly imagine a football team in Irving, the Cowboys and the city of Irving reached an agreement to build Texas Stadium, where the Cowboys have played since 1971. As had so many other teams of that era, the Cowboys left the center city for the suburbs. The actual site of the stadium was less than half a mile from the city of Dallas's border, but the new location was in the midst of suburban sections of the region and far removed from the inner-city world of the Fair Park area, the Cotton Bowl's neighborhood.

In contrast to today's stadium deals, the city of Irving stole the Cowboys for a song. Although they did subsidize the move and the team, in comparison to today's standards the price was a bargain. Construction costs for Texas Stadium were $35 million. Municipal bonds were sold to season-ticket holders; each seat required the purchase of a $250 bond. This raised $15 million; the city paid $10 million for the land, and the balance of the money, $10 million, was raised by selling a municipal bond to the Cowboys' owner (Rosentraub, 1988). The city of Irving retired all these bonds from its general revenues. All revenues from Texas Stadium were assigned to the team, but the Cowboys do pay a small rental charge each year to the city of Irving. Irving, then, got itself into the professional sports business for a paltry $35 million, minuscule by comparison to the investments now required. Of course, the Cowboys' current owner is thinking about a new stadium; Irving's investment may increase in the future if the Cowboys are to be kept from roaming through the range of the Dallas/Fort Worth region for another home. Despite the bargain price Irving paid, the building of Texas Stadium and the subsequent lease given the Cowboys still represented a substantial subsidy to the team.

Unfortunately, the Texas Rangers and the city of Arlington had a long history of problems with Arlington Stadium. Designed to serve a minor league franchise, the stadium was not only small, with inadequate food-and-beverage facilities, but a large proportion of its seats were outfield bleachers. The city made two major sets of renovations, including the construction of a new upper deck that provided more seating around home plate, but the facility could never seat the promised 50,000 fans. With only 42,500 seats, more than one-third of them outfield bleachers, the revenue potential for the team was extremely limited.

As a small-market team, the Rangers began to encounter the range of problems common to other teams: too little revenue from the facility and too little revenue from local media. If the team was to survive, the owners were convinced that an entirely new stadium was needed. Such a decision had substantial implications, as the city of Arlington had yet to retire all the bonds sold for the expansion of Arlington Stadium and the attraction of a team from Washington, D.C. These fiscal challenges aside, the failure of the city to provide a stadium of the size the team and the city had agreed to in 1972 weakened Arlington's bargaining position. As the team had never received what they were promised, Arlington, if it was to keep the team, had little choice but to build a signature-statement stadium that both the team and the city would enjoy. The Rangers, of course, engaged in a series of tactics to ensure the city's cooperation in this effort. But, realistically, Arlington had few options. It had made a series of commitments when it entered into the world of professional sports and it failed to fulfill one of the most critical—provide the team with a 50,000-seat stadium. Furthermore, the city's robust fiscal status and wealth also meant that building the facility would not be a major fiscal problem. The situation was clearly ripe for the provision of a substantial set of incentives and welfare payments that would increase the wealth of the owners and players.

In the early 1990s the Rangers began to explore their options, which included a new facility in Arlington, a stadium in Dallas, a stadium in one of Dallas's northern suburbs, or a possible move to St. Petersburg (Florida) and its Sun Coast Dome.* However, the Rangers were unlikely to want to leave the nation's eighth largest media market, and so the team's attention was focused on Arlington, Dallas, and Dallas's northern suburbs. A competition of sorts was initiated. Dallas wanted to discuss three sites with the team. One was located about five miles east of downtown and south of Texas Stadium, within the city of Dallas. This site was at the nexus of an east-west freeway (Interstate 30) and a state highway, Loop 12. A second site was in an area in close proximity to Reunion Arena, just east of the downtown core area. The third site was east of downtown. All of these sites had locational disadvantages and would require substantial infrastructure improvements. It was also possible that environmental problems would make some of these sites unacceptable or impractical. A location in one of Dallas's northern suburbs would have moved the team far from its fans in Arlington and Fort Worth. More important, the transportation linkages to these northern suburbs were not as convenient as those that existed at the Arlington Stadium site. The best outcome for the team was to remain in Arlington, but the best deal to that end could be negotiated only if Arlington thought the team might leave.

Negotiations between the Rangers and the city of Arlington eventually developed into the plans that led to "the Ballpark in Arlington," a facility widely proclaimed as one of the finest in America. The deal that was negotiated, and summarized in earlier chapters, involved the investment of $21 million by the team (present value). In addition, the Rangers pay the city of Arlington $2 million per year as their rental fee for use of the stadium. The city of Arling-

---

*The Florida city had built the dome stadium without a commitment from any team. The Rangers and the Chicago White Sox both used the threat of a move to the Sun Coast Dome to secure new facilities (Mier, 1993).

ton agreed to spend $135 million to finance the new stadium. These funds were raised from a 0.5-percent increase in the local sales tax, and when voters were asked to ratify this proposal, more than two-thirds of them did. In fact, the voter turnout when the new stadium financing proposal was on the ballot was the largest in Arlington's history for a local election. A report issued by the state of Texas's comptroller assured voters that as much as 60 percent of the sales taxes paid in Arlington was paid by nonresidents. This helped to convince the voters to support the proposed financing program. As a retail center, Arlington is able to export a great deal of its sales taxes to nonresidents, as these nonresidents pay the sales taxes for the stadium each time they buy anything in the city of Arlington. As such, while the public sector did pay for a large portion of the Ballpark in Arlington, that public included residents from all cities and communities in the Dallas/Fort Worth region. Arlington has been so successful in financing its commitment through this sales tax that the bonds sold will likely be paid five years sooner than anticipated. This success means the city has the tax capacity to consider other investments if it were to decide to ask voters for permission to maintain the 0.5-percent sales tax increment.

While Arlington has been quite successful in retiring its debt earlier than anticipated, it is still doing that with taxes and not revenues earned from the stadium itself. As is typical in most deals involving cities and teams, after the initial year, the Texas Rangers retain virtually all revenues generated at the stadium, including 100 percent of all advertising and parking revenues, 100 percent of all luxury seating revenues, and all concession profits. The city of Arlington owns the stadium and is responsible for all maintenance. The Rangers' rental fees will likely support most if not all of these maintenance costs. The team's ability to retain virtually all revenues from the stadium substantially increased its value. By 1996 the Texas Rangers were estimated by *Financial World* to be the ninth most valuable MLB franchise despite being the only team in MLB (through 1995) to never play a postseason game. The team's lack of success on the field, reversed only in 1996, did not detract from its financial value.

The competition between cities in the region for the Rangers set the stage for another round of sports wars involving the Mavericks and Stars. Reunion Arena, while relatively new, does not have the luxury suites and club seating that have increased the profitability of several NBA and NHL teams. In addition, the arena's capacity is less than that of the newer facilities that several cities have developed. Indeed, indoor arenas now frequently have more than 20,000 seats or are at least 15 percent larger than Reunion Arena. In 1993 the Mavericks' ownership began to explore the possibility of a new arena with the city of Dallas. At the same time the team was negotiating with Dallas, the team's owner purchased land in a northeast suburb in an effort to consider a move from Dallas to the city of Lewisville. Lewisville's voters narrowly defeated a proposition to implement a local sales tax to support their investment in the arena, but then Arlington signaled its interest in building a new arena for the Mavericks and Stars by hiring a consulting firm to perform a feasibility study regarding the financial viability of an indoor arena located in Arlington that *could* serve as home for the Mavericks and Stars. The favorable results of this assessment were released to the media and discussed at a city council meeting that was extensively covered by the region's television and radio stations and newspapers.

While the city of Arlington's official position was that it would not make a proposal to the Mavericks and Stars until such time as a deal was not feasible in Dallas, Arlington's officials did nothing to conceal their excitement in attracting both teams. In the first half of 1995, then, a sports war broke out in the Dallas/Fort Worth region for the Dallas Mavericks and Stars. In late 1995 it seemed as if the Mavericks would indeed land in Arlington. However, when the team was sold to an ownership group that included Ross Perot, Jr., Dallas's fortunes improved. Although the final site for a new arena had not been chosen by mid-1996, the new owners clearly prefer a location in Dallas. Arlington, however, waits in the wings, ready and quite fiscally able to build a premier facility. With its sales tax for the Ballpark in Arlington set to expire, the city could easily raise $100 million for a new arena by simply extending the tax for a few years.

SPORTS FRANCHISES AND THE BENEFITS FROM BEING A "MAJOR LEAGUE CITY"

Each of the cities that provided incentives to attract or retain teams did so with the hope and expectation that their enhanced image and the status conferred by hosting the teams would result in economic development. Indeed, if there was a value to hosting a team, then one would expect to find higher levels of population growth, economic development, and a higher concentration of high-income and high-skill occupations in cities that became "major league." By looking at these changes, then, we can determine what image benefits are generated from a community's investment in sports and the provision of subsidies to teams.

Population Growth

The population growth in Dallas, Arlington, and Irving was compared to that of all other communities in the region. There was no statistically different rate of growth in these cities as compared to the other communities in the region. Indeed, several other cities in the Dallas/Fort Worth region grew at considerably higher rates than the cities that invested in sports. In terms of both nominal percentage changes and net local growth (that is, nominal growth less the national growth of cities of the same size class), the region's noninvestor cities did better on average than the investor cities. From 1970 to 1980, Arlington grew considerably, but four other suburbs grew at a higher rate; from 1980 to 1990, six noninvestor suburbs grew at a higher rate than Arlington. From 1970 to 1980, Irving ranked thirteenth among all seventeen cities examined here, but did manage to exceed the rate of growth in six of the noninvestor cities in the 1980s. Overall, however, these population data do not support the proposition that sports franchises attract people to the "host" investor city faster than to other noninvestor cities within the same region (see Table 11–1).

TABLE 11–1

Population Change, by City and Sports Investor Class, Dallas/Fort Worth Metropolitan Area, 1970–80 and 1980–90

	Pop 1970 (1)	Pop 1980 (2)	Change 1970–82 (3)	Nat'l Percentage Change (4)	Nat'l Growth by City Size (5)	Nat'l Net Local Growth (4–5)	Pop 1990 (6)	Change (7)	Nominal Percentage Change (8)	Nat'l Growth by City Size (9)	Nat'l Net Local Growth (8–9)
Investor cities											
Arlington	90,229	160,113	69,884	77.5%	8.6%	68.9%	261,717	101,604	63.5%	15.1%	48.4%
Dallas	844,401	904,078	59,677	7.1%	-16.1%	23.2%	1,007,618	103,540	11.5%	-7.3%	18.8%
Irving	97,260	109,943	12,683	13.0%	8.6%	4.4%	155,037	45,094	41.0%	15.1%	25.9%
Average growth				32.5%		32.2%			38.6%		31.0%
Non-Investor cities											
Bedford	10,049	20,821	10,772	107.2%	12.5%	94.7%	43,762	22,941	110.2%	2.6%	107.6%
Euless	19,316	24,002	4,686	24.3%	12.5%	11.8%	38,149	14,147	58.9%	8.9%	50.0%
Farmers Branch	27,492	24,863	(2,629)	-9.6%	17.2%	-26.8%	24,250	(613)	-2.5%	2.6%	-5.1%
Fort Worth	393,455	385,164	(8,291)	-2.1%	12.4%	-14.5%	447,619	62,455	16.2%	20.3%	-4.1%
Garland	81,437	138,857	57,420	70.5%	8.6%	61.9%	180,635	41,778	30.1%	15.1%	15.0%
Grand Prairie	50,904	71,462	20,558	40.4%	8.6%	31.8%	99,606	28,144	39.4%	20.5%	18.9%
Grapevine	7,049	11,801	4,752	67.4%	9.0%	58.4%	29,198	17,397	147.4%	2.6%	144.8%
Hurst	27,215	31,420	4,205	15.5%	17.2%	-1.7%	33,574	2,154	6.9%	8.9%	-2.0%
Lewisville	9,264	24,273	15,009	162.0%	9.0%	153.0%	46,521	22,248	91.7%	8.9%	82.8%
Mesquite	55,131	67,053	11,922	21.6%	8.6%	13.0%	101,484	34,431	51.3%	20.5%	30.8%
N. Richland Hills	16,514	30,592	14,078	85.2%	12.5%	72.7%	45,895	15,303	50.0%	8.9%	41.1%
Plano	17,872	72,331	54,459	304.7%	12.5%	292.2%	127,885	55,554	76.8%	20.5%	56.3%
Richardson	48,405	72,496	24,091	49.8%	17.2%	32.6%	74,840	2,344	3.2%	20.5%	-17.3%
Southlake	2,031	2,808	777	38.3%	9.0%	29.3%	7,082	4,274	152.2%	0.7%	151.5%
Average growth				69.7%		57.7%			59.4%		47.9%

Note: 1. National growth by city size (cols. 5 and 9) is total population growth in all U.S. cities of this size class during the period.

Source: North Central Texas Council of Governments, annual population estimates, 1970–1991; U.S. Statistical Abstract, various years.

Comparative Fiscal Benefits

Many cities that attain major league status by attracting a team expect to enjoy improved local finances. Because sports-related facilities are often fixed-capital investments, city officials anticipate higher property values around such sites, which in turn are expected to generate more property taxes for the municipality. However, city officials pay less attention to the debt impacts of sports facilities. Fixed sports investments require the use of public debt to finance these facilities, so we would also speculate that investor cities may exhibit higher levels of debt. On the other hand, because these fixed investments bring in fans, and presumably create entertainment complexes around stadiums, more sales tax revenue in investor cities might also be expected. Finally, investment in sports facilities is expected to affect the operating expenditures of investor cities; that is, if higher property taxes and sales tax revenues are being generated, there may be more revenues to support higher levels of public municipal spending. Conversely, if revenues are not increased, the expenditure requirements of sports franchises and their fixed investments may detract from expenditures available for general government services. Either way, we expect to see different spending patterns by investor versus noninvestor cities.

In a previous study of the 1970 to 1978 period in Dallas/Fort Worth, it was found that Arlington and Irving were not able to capture a larger share of fiscal benefits than other Dallas/Fort Worth cities after the Rangers and Cowboys moved in the early 1970s (Rosentraub & Nunn, 1978). As the new suburban franchise locations matured during the 1980s, however, new entertainment and business complexes may have resulted in comparatively better fiscal performance in the two suburban cities. The same may be hypothesized for the city of Dallas because of the Mavericks franchise.

As Table 11–2 shows, differences in fiscal performance from 1980 to 1991 do indeed exist, but not always in the direction expected for the investor cities. Investor cities do have statistically higher levels of per capita debt than noninvestor cities: Per capita debt is nearly 20 percent higher on average in Dallas, Arlington, and Irving than in the noninvestor cities. Arlington's per capita debt is exceeded only

TABLE 11-2

Mean Per Capita City Finances, by City and Sports Investment Class, Dallas–Fort Worth Metropolitan Area, 1980–1991

	Assessed Property Value	Property Taxes	Sales Taxes	Total Debt	Total Expend.
All Cities	51,162	196	152	1,083	818
Investor Cities	43,445	207	160	1,246	806
Arlington	32,341	162	127	1,479	726
Dallas	50,804	266	200	1,449	1,009
Irving	47,190	194	155	811	683
Noninvestor Cities	53,119	193	150	1,042	821
Euless	24,806	120	79	484	389
Farmers Branch	106,790	432	400	1,201	1,362
Fort Worth	28,705	226	133	1,325	1,001
Garland	31,649	149	74	1,323	1,278
Grand Prairie	35,778	164	101	875	671
Grapevine	57,853	219	214	1,435	1,317
Hurst	31,695	155	184	463	542
Lewisville	36,723	168	110	1,195	501
Mesquite	29,491	142	116	643	638
N. Rich. Hills	28,873	122	108	846	574
Plano	77,256	219	111	1,171	785
Richardson	144,917	201	173	1,545	794
F-score	1.69	0.75	0.41	3.97	0.04
Probability	ns	ns	ns	0.05	ns

Notes: (1) All figures expressed in constant 1992 dollars; (2) All figures represent twelve-year averages for each city, except for Grand Prairie, which reflects a ten-year average; (3) F-score and probability refer to differences between investor and noninvestor city groups (ns=not significant).

Source: U.S. Census, City Government Finances, various years; Moody's Municipal and Government Manual, various years.

by that of the city of Richardson. Since Dallas, Arlington, and Irving were not the fastest-growing cities in the region (see Table 11–1), these higher debt levels are not driven completely by population growth; other factors, which are likely to include the fixed-asset financing and service requirements of professional sports facilities, must also underlie these debt figures.

Although no other statistically significant differences exist, the nominal per capita differences are still intriguing. First, noninvestor cities had higher per capita assessed property valuations than investor cities. Second, in terms of property and sales tax revenue per capita, the investor cities did somewhat better than noninvestors, although the differences are not statistically significant. Furthermore, seven noninvestor cities exhibited a average annual property tax per capita higher than that of Arlington, while five noninvestors collected more sales tax per capita on average. Irving did somewhat better in these two revenue categories, but a number of cities without franchises still exceeded its twelve-year averages.

Overall, this fiscal comparison lends additional empirical support to the proposition that investor cities cannot prevent the leakage of public tax and revenue benefits of sports investment to other cities in the metropolitan region. In terms of these fiscal indicators, there is not a great deal of difference between investor and noninvestor cities, or at least very little that is statistically significant. This suggests that if the presumed fiscal largesse of the sports franchises is real, the region as a whole appears to share in it, even though the costs of the sports investments are localized within the three investor cities.

It was also possible to secure updated reports on the sales tax revenues received by the investor and noninvestor cities in the Dallas/Fort Worth region for the years 1992 through 1995 from the Texas Comptroller's Office. Focusing on sales taxes alone in this time period permits inclusion of the potential benefits of Arlington's new ballpark for the Texas Rangers. Again, however, there was no significant difference in the sales tax revenues earned by investor cities when compared to noninvestor cities. Separate analyses were also performed comparing Arlington to all other suburban cities, as it was the city that made the most recent investment. For no pairing of cities could any statistically significant difference be found. Table 11–3 illustrates the per capita sales tax revenues cities in the Dallas/Fort Worth region collected in the years 1992 through 1995.

Comparative Attraction of High-Skill Employment

Many advocates of the value and importance of professional sports teams point to the image and prestige effects of sports franchises; the familiar refrain is that these benefits are important to a city because of the people that will want to live in the community. Thus, one is not just hoping for an improvement in the "quality of

TABLE 11–3
Per Capita Sales Tax Revenues by City, 1992–1995

	1995	1994	1993	1992
Irving	179	176	151	136
Arlington	180	178	160	145
Dallas	149	143	134	124
Fort Worth	112	106	96	89
Euless	121	114	81	59
Garland	73	69	64	60
Farmers Branch	410	395	332	323
Grand Prairie	139	131	106	85
Grapevine	155	146	130	123
Hurst	236	229	173	159
Lewisville	208	172	142	125
Mesquite	188	179	162	103
N. Richland Hills	26	25	23	22
Plano	184	164	149	121
Richardson	220	185	171	173

life" per se when competing for professional sports teams. On the contrary, the quality-of-life arguments used to evoke public incentives to attract or keep sports teams are frequently underpinned by the hope that professional sports teams will lure highly skilled, highly paid employees to the host (investor) cities. This proposition can be tested by examining the proportion of each Dallas/Fort Worth city's occupational workforce that is classified as executive-administrative-managerial, professional, or technical. Of all the standard labor force occupational classifications, these reflect the "high-skill" occupations that presumably seek the high quality of life to which professional sports are believed to contribute.[1]

Changes in high-skill occupations in the Dallas/Fort Worth region, classified by city and sports investment class, are shown in Table 11–4. Once again, several noninvestor cities in the Dallas/Fort Worth area fared as well as and often better than Dallas, Arlington, and Irving. Looking only at the average proportion of high-skill employment, the investor cities exceeded noninvestors in 1970 only, and by 1990 noninvestor cities averaged 35-percent high-skill workforce, compared to 33 percent in the investor cities. On an individual basis, noninvestor cities like Plano, Richardson (home to the University of Texas at Dallas and several computer firms), Garland,

and Farmers Branch have consistently had proportions of high-skill occupations similar to those of the investor cities. Of the investor cities, however, Arlington has maintained its proportion of high-skill occupations at approximately one-third of its labor force, exceeding both Dallas and Irving in 1970, 1980, and 1990. In 1990, Arlington ranked third behind Plano and Richardson. (Arlington is also home to the University of Texas at Arlington.) Similar findings are exhibited in terms of the decade-by-decade growth of high-skill employment. Several noninvestors (such as Plano, Lewisville, Grapevine, and Euless) indicate more growth than the investor cities. This was certainly true in 1970 to 1980 and 1980 to 1990 when comparing the *average* growth in high-skill occupations between the investor and noninvestor cities as two separate groups. Moreover, individual noninvestor cities had ten-year growth rates far exceeding those of investor cities. With respect to attracting and keeping high-skill occupational classes, then, the investor cities in the Dallas/Fort Worth region do not show clear evidence of doing a better job than many of the noninvestor cities.

SPORTS TEAMS AND THEIR INTANGIBLE WORTH

The experiences of Arlington, Irving, and Dallas clearly indicate that if there are intangible benefits from hosting a team, they do not accrue to any single city. If Arlington, Dallas, and Irving became "major league" because they invested in facilities that helped support professional sports teams, they did not receive any more returns or benefits than other cities that did not invest. It is possible that the intangible benefits accrued to the entire region, and that Arlington, Dallas, and Irving shared in the economic and social gains that all communities enjoyed. However, the outcomes in the metroplex clearly indicate that no one city can capture any image or quality-of-life benefits when hosting a team. These benefits, if they exist at all, are available to all communities in a region. The decentralized and integrated nature of America's urban economies makes

TABLE 11–4

Changes in High-Skill Occupations, by City and Sports Investment Class, Dallas–Fort Worth Metropolitan Area, 1970–1990

	1970		1980		1990		Percent Change in high-skill occupations	
	Number in high-skill occupations	As percent of city's employment	Number in high-skill occupations	As percent of city's employment	Number in high-skill occupations	As percent of city's employment	1980	1990
Investor Cities (mean)		29.8		26.9		32.9	45.2	75.2
Arlington	15,689	39.1	27,149	31.2	51,805	35.4	73.0	90.8
Dallas	91,431	24.4	122,570	26.4	162,567	31.8	34.1	32.6
Irving	11,047	25.8	14,190	23.3	28,668	31.4	28.5	102.0
Noninvestor Cities (mean)		26.6		27.8		35.3	131.4	113.4
Euless	1,908	24.4	3,156	23.4	7,631	33.0	65.4	141.8
Farmers Branch	2,767	23.9	3,981	27.7	4,274	32.2	43.9	7.4
Fort Worth	29,524	18.4	41,616	23.2	60,644	29.3	41.0	45.7
Garland	8,865	25.8	20,418	27.9	31,451	32.0	130.3	54.0
Grand Prairie	4,599	21.5	6,730	19.3	14,107	27.8	46.3	109.6
Grapevine	645	22.8	1,753	26.8	6,942	41.6	171.8	296.0
Lewisville	879	21.6	3,081	24.6	9,451	34.2	250.5	206.8
Mesquite	4,301	19.5	6,294	18.2	16,163	29.7	46.3	156.8
N. Richland Hills	2,036	29.7	4,594	28.5	8,493	33.3	125.6	84.9
Plano	2,777	37.4	15,026	42.3	34,688	48.2	441.1	130.9
Richardson	9,280	47.8	17,019	44.2	19,269	46.7	83.4	13.2

Notes: (1) "High-skill occupations" include executive/administrative/managerial, professional, and technicians; (2) "City's employment" refers to employment of the individual city only.

Source: U.S. Bureau of the Census, "General Social and Economic Characteristics, Texas," various years.

it impossible for any single city to capture a disproportionate share of these benefits. At a minimum, then, if any investments are to be made in sports facilities, they should be shared by an entire region and they should not be the responsibility of any single community.

LESSONS LEARNED FROM THE DALLAS/FORT WORTH REGION

1. Do Intangible Benefits Exist? There seems to be little doubt that the presence of a team produces intangible benefits. Civic pride probably increases for many people, and a substantial amount of publicity is undoubtedly generated by the team for a city. Do any of these intangible benefits attract business, economic development, or people? If the experiences of the investor cities in the Dallas/Fort Worth area offer any advice, the intangible benefits do not offer any special economic returns to investor cities. Do sports teams make cities "major league"? If "major league" means "attract more people or investment," the answer is no. It is possible, however, that the intangible benefits from teams still accrue to a region, but no one city in that region seems able to capture a disproportionate share of those benefits. It may well be appropriate for taxpayers to question whether or not the status conveyed by teams is more myth than reality and worth the substantial subsidies provided.

2. If You Are Going to Do Sports, Use a Regional Tax. With no city able to contain the economic or image benefits from a team's presence, and if you are in a situation in which you believe you must subsidize a team, use a regional tax. Arlington's sales tax approximates such a tax because it is a regional shopping center. However, most of its shoppers are from the western half of the region. In that sense, then, those who live in the eastern half of the region pay less for the benefits than do those people who shop in Arlington. Of course, residents of the region can avoid any payment for the stadium by simply refusing to shop or dine in Arlington. The point here is to suggest that the best possible approach to financing a regional effort is through a tax paid by all or most residents of the region, not a tax paid by residents of a single city. In that sense, then, the tax used by Arlington comes far closer to creating a balance between the liability for the costs and the sharing of benefits. In contrast, Irving, paying for its investment from its property tax, may well concentrate a larger proportion of the tax on the residents and businesses of Irving.

Given the small cost today of that investment, the issue is hardly worth discussing. Yet, if another investment must be made, public officials should focus their attention on a regional tax, not local property taxes.

3. *If It Quacks, It Is Still a Duck.* The success Arlington has had in financing its shiny new ballpark and the regional nature of the tax do not obscure the conclusion that the city and taxpayers across the region are subsidizing wealthy owners and players. Sales taxes paid by lower-income people produce excess profits that are divided between players and owners, all of whom enjoy salaries about which the taxpayers can only dream. A subsidy spread across hundreds of thousands of people amounts to a small charge each year. It is still, however, a transfer of wealth from the lower and middle classes to the upper class. It is still welfare in a state that abhors life on the dole; it is still a subsidy in a state that defends capitalism and the spirit of the free market. Arlington may well have found the least offensive tax, but it is still a tax and it is still welfare for the rich. And, as Arlington (and Irving) secures no tangible or intangible benefits from the presence of a team, each city is providing welfare. Perhaps it's time to see if other investments (schools, public safety, family recreation, and so on) could make a city "major league" and produce the same level of tangible benefits that the intangible benefit of teams seems to produce.

12

Surviving Sports

Sports are an integral part of U.S. and Canadian societies, and they will continue to be an important component in the lives of most men, many women, and hundreds of communities. Teams and the games they play provide entertainment, opportunities for countless numbers of discussions and debates (especially around water coolers and over lunch and coffee), and an escape from the demands of daily life. Teams also engender community spirit and help establish an identity for many regions and people (for example, the Dawg Pound, Pacer People). Recognizing these as benefits in addition to the economic gains possible from a team, how can or should states, provinces, cities, and the taxpayers respond to the demands placed on them by teams? While it is possible for governments and their taxpayers to support and benefit from professional sports, the practices and policies of cities and states must change. Taxpayers and community leaders have to do their homework and understand the very small economic returns that result from professional sports as well as the elusive and regional nature of the intangible or quality-of-life benefits they create. The subsidies currently provided are not needed, cannot be justified, and the system that produces them can be changed. This does not mean that sports are unimportant in the life of people or should not be part of the public sector's agenda. But it does mean that negotiations between the public sector and sports teams have to start from an understanding of what sports leagues and their teams can and cannot do for a community.

The material presented in the previous eleven chapters has established that the issue of sports and cities has really six components or dimensions.

1. SPORTS ARE AN IMPORTANT PART OF LIFE

The extraordinary interest in hosting teams is a direct result of the *exaggerated* importance our society places on sports. From politics to social relations, numerous aspects of our lives revolve around sports. Holiday celebrations include sporting events; political statements are made through sporting events; even dating is tied to the high school sports scene. Fathers and their children develop relationships through sports, and increasingly women are also involved in team sports, building for them a cherished set of memories. Even our language is replete with metaphors drawn from sports. With the extreme social significance of sports it is not hard to imagine that their importance is magnified and exaggerated by public officials and leaders who begin to believe that if one does not have or host a team, his or her city is somehow not "major league." This emotionalism drives many sports subsidies. Although many of us may think this attention to sports is not deserved, is overly exaggerated by men, and does not sufficiently account for the negative aspects of sports (violence, gambling, the role of women, and so forth), one must recognize that the sociological importance of sports to millions influences the behavior, attitudes, and beliefs of community leaders. If you want to know why so many leaders do not do their homework on the real economics of sports, it is because they "believe" sports are a good thing for families, for young people, and for a community.

2. SPORTS ARE IMPORTANT TO THE MASS MEDIA

Sporting events and games provide an endless supply of mini-dramas for television and radio to broadcast to viewers and listeners. As such, the broadcast media underscore the importance of sports in our lives through their seemingly endless broadcasts and the inordinate coverage provided to "big games." There are now pregame and postgame shows as well as entire news shows devoted to sports scores and stories. The United States, Canada, and Europe already have complete sports networks (which, through satellite systems, are available worldwide), and ESPN's success has led to the formation of ESPN2 so that more than twenty-four hours of sports programs can be broadcast each day. CNN regularly offers its sports addicts a full news program every night, and ESPN will shortly launch its new sports news network. This extraordinary level of coverage becomes a subtle reminder that if your city does not have a team, it cannot host "big games" and thus is suddenly not a "big city."

The print media also report, in great detail, sporting news and events. Sports are a profit center for most newspapers, and an inordinate amount of newspaper space is devoted to sports. This is possible because each game is different and the news from each game can be gathered at relatively low cost and retold to fans. Previews of upcoming games also can fill space, and advertisers are particularly attracted to the demographic characteristics of the audience that follows sports. With the newspapers striving to cover sports, community and elected leaders are further reminded of the importance of teams and the value brought to the mayor or governor who either "saved the team" or brought them a new team. With the large amount of press sports teams can generate for elected officials, there is little wonder that elected officials believe they are important (and worthy of public support). Even the most fiscally conservative mayor or governor does not want to be in office when a team leaves. On the other side of the coin, mayors and governors would love to be in office when they have saved the team or brought a team to an area. The photo opportunities are quite numerous for these events.

3. SPORTS ARE THE ECONOMY'S SMALL POTATOES

While sports are important to the mass media and a critical component of life for many people, their economic importance is small. In no county in the United States do sports account for more than one-half of 1 percent of all jobs or all payroll dollars, and the most financially successful sports teams have budgets that would be less than one-third of the expenditures made by a typical urban university. Sports may attract a great deal of attention, but they are not an economic engine, they will not generate a great number of jobs, and they will not revitalize a city's economy. Even in cities that advertise themselves as "entertainment centers," sports and the related spending at hotels and restaurants are never the largest component of a community's economy. In addition, while sports are an important part of a community's quality of life, many things contribute to the quality of life in a city. As such, businesses do not decide to relocate to an area because of the existence of a team.

4. "BASEBALL BEEN BERY, BERY GOOD TO ME"

A character created by *Saturday Night Live*'s troupe in the 1980s used to repeatedly declare, "Baseball Been Bery, Bery Good to Me." We can now modify that line for players and owners alike: "Sports been bery, bery good to us." Players, once abused and held hostage by teams, are now earning the salaries they deserve relative to the income their teams earn. Players in each of the four major sports have to be considered among the most economically privileged people in the world. Some have amassed fortunes that are almost incomprehensible, and contracts exceeding $20 million (for more than one year of service) now exist. Rising costs of ownership have not discouraged people from trying to buy teams or from trying to join the professional sports leagues when expansion is considered. Although some teams may be losing money, the vast majority are not.

5. WELFARE IS ALIVE AND WELL
WHEN IT COMES TO SPORTS

Candidates for public office may pledge themselves to reform welfare, but this spirit of fiscal restraint has not been extended to professional sports. Taxes are routinely raised to provide money to build facilities so owners and players can share more income. And this interest in providing welfare for sports teams, their owners, and their players extends across party lines and occurs in virtually every corner of North America. Canadian governments have increased taxes for sports, and taxes have been increased for sports in many U.S. states, including Maryland, Ohio, Florida, Texas, Missouri, Wisconsin, Illinois, Indiana, California, Arizona, and Washington. When it comes to welfare for sports it almost seems as if we should change Winston Churchill's legendary remark after the air battle for Britain, "Never have so many owed so much to so few," to "Never have so few received so much from so many."

6. PLAYING FACILITIES ALWAYS COST MORE

The public sector's experience with sports facilities has not been limited to the provision of huge subsidies to owners and players. The cost overruns and mismanagement of facility development have created some legendary stories. Projects are planned and taxpayers are asked to vote on proposals at one price, only to learn years later that the price paid was substantially more. Cynically, one can almost suggest that whatever price is discussed the final tally will be no less than 40 percent more once all of the infrastructure investments, related costs, and other subsidies are included.

Recognition of these concluding observations is not meant to devalue the excitement that successful teams can create for some communities, the civic pride and spirit that does develop and is strikingly evident when teams win, and the positive media exposure that can result for cities, regions, and downtown areas from the presence of a successful team. I am not oblivious to the fact that the residents of Cleveland and Detroit, as well as sports fans around the nation, now consider those cities winning places to be because of the success of the Indians and Red Wings. I also recognize that my colleagues at Hebrew University in Israel knew far more about the Indiana Pacers, and Reggie Miller, not to mention Indianapolis, because of basketball than they would have had the Pacers moved to some other city. Indeed, as I poignantly described, Indianapolis has been a lavish recipient of some very favorable media coverage and image enhancement as a result of sports. However, that exposure and the transformation of Indianapolis's image did not herald a period of substantial economic growth for the city. Cleveland, too, has millions of people coming to its downtown area since the opening of "the Jake" and Gund Arena. The movement of people to downtown Cleveland for their recreational hours has neither transformed that city nor addressed the employment, crime, and education issues that still plague many inner-city communities. Indeed, almost half of Cleveland's population would still be classified as low income even though Albert Belle wants to be the highest-paid player in baseball. Sports are fun, good theater, and provide excellent opportunities for favorable exposure for a community from the mass media. Sports, however, are not an economic engine or a social elixir for either the tangible or intangible necessities of life. Sports do not need to be subsidized to create whatever benefits you believe they generate.

The starting point for every negotiation with a professional sports team must be that the presence or absence of a team will have very little economic or social impact. The presence of a team will generate a certain type of media exposure, but that exposure itself, no matter how satisfying, does not attract firms, make the city safer, or make the workers in the city better paid or educated. The publicity from sports teams and the "winning image" a team creates does not change any of the cost factors that influence economic development and growth. With these facts and observations completely understood and accepted, communities and their leaders can then begin to think about what they want and can really anticipate from any subsidy of a professional sports team. If a community seeks economic development from any subsidy given to a team, very little should be provided by the public sector to a team unless the public sector can share in the revenues produced by the team. If a community *believes* that the presence of a team will convey prestige and name recognition, then the issue that should be debated is how much would you be willing to pay for those intangible benefits? If a community wants to change recreational patterns so people come to the downtown area to see games and other events, then the issue should be how much is it worth to you to change recreational patterns?

To help taxpayers and their community leaders develop a strategy for surviving and even benefiting from their investments in facilities for professional sports teams, this last chapter contains a series of recommendations organized into three sections. First, if governments are to put an end to the madness of the welfare payments to rich owners and highly paid athletes, a "Brave New World" is needed. In this Brave New World for professional sports teams, owners would need to operate their teams in a free market without any welfare payments from governments and their taxpayers. In this Brave New World professional sports teams would be treated as any other form of entertainment and would not receive any preferential treatment or subsidies.

Second, if a Brave New World cannot be created, but if certain limitations could be placed on the powers of the professional sports leagues, it may still be possible for cities and taxpayers to realize a return on their investments in professional sports. Options for increasing the protection of cities from the power of the sports leagues are described in the second part of this chapter, "Come As Close As You Can: A Bill of Rights for Taxpayers Who Subsidize Professional Sports." What is proposed here is a "Bill of Rights" for cities and taxpayers if teams accept money from taxpayers.

Third, if all else fails, and the world of professional sports is not changed and the welfare payments continue to flow, there are still some dos and don'ts taxpayers should keep in mind when the fear of losing their team, or the euphoria of attracting a franchise, grips their politicians and community leaders. These suggestions are detailed in the section "Same Old, Same Old, No More."

A BRAVE NEW WORLD FOR CITIES AND TOWNS: USING THE MARKET TO END WELFARE

Think the unthinkable; imagine a world where professional sports teams had to operate without any subsidies or welfare payments. Investors who wanted to own teams did so, and they paid players and built the playing and practice facilities they needed. Can such a world exist? Of course it can, and did. There is no need for governments to be involved in the economics of professional sports.

When students enroll in public finance and budgeting classes, one of the first principles discussed is the concept of public goods. Here we try to explain what the government should do, why it needs to ensure that certain services be delivered, and what services or products it should not produce or provide. When markets fail, or when more efficient solutions can be achieved through government activity, we tell our attentive students that public-sector intervention is needed. When markets do not fail, and when greater efficiencies are not possible, there is no need for government action. Are there any markets failing in the world of professional sports? Team owners are earning impressive returns on their investments, networks are paying hundreds of millions of dollars to broadcast games, players are earning several million dollars for a single season of play, and fans are flocking to games in record numbers despite escalating ticket prices. Is there any rational human being who could describe these outcomes as examples of market failure? Indeed, this appears to be the perfect example of a well-organized market. Investors and players are well compensated and fans (consumers) seem overjoyed; they want more sports, not less, and they are more than happy to pay relatively high prices for the performances they attend.

Could the sports business be operated more efficiently if the government were to intervene? The answer to this question is also no!! When the Chicago Bulls win seventy or so games in a single season and the Dallas Cowboys appear in three or four Super Bowls in a

five-year period, does any one really believe that the government needs to help teams operate more efficiently? Does this situation sound like a market in failure? No!! Sports represent a set of very healthy private-market relationships that do not require government subsidies or interventions.

With no need for government participation or intervention, why are so many states, provinces, and local governments tripping over themselves to help finance professional sports? Governments are involved because the number of cities that want teams exceeds the supply. The sports cartels prohibit markets from operating properly. Consumers want more goods (teams and the games they play), but the market cannot provide them because of the artificial constraint imposed by the existing leagues. Faced with this situation, fans organize themselves through their governments to offer inducements to convince teams to come to their communities. The owners of the teams have the ability to control the number of teams that exist, and no one seems inclined to take this power away from them. But the market can be made to work for fans and cities. How? Follow me in this argument and recommendations for creating a Brave New World for cities and professional sports teams.

I've already illustrated how many teams should exist if the cartels or leagues could not artificially control the supply. If there were no cartel control there would be more teams in the United States and in our largest markets, Los Angeles and New York. If there were more teams in each of these two metropolitan regions, the revenues from media contracts enjoyed by the existing teams in the largest markets would decrease. With more teams for fans to follow, each of the existing teams in the New York or Los Angeles areas would receive lower revenues from local media contracts, as fans in their areas would have more teams from which to choose. With more teams, some of the existing Yankee and Dodger fans would now want to watch these newer franchises' games. This would produce lower individual incomes, resulting in no need to subsidize teams in smaller metropolitan areas.

The argument that is frequently made is that teams in smaller markets need large revenue flows from luxury suites and club seats to offset the gains made by the Yankees, Knicks, Lakers, and Dodgers

from local media contracts. If the city or region in a smaller market pays for a large portion of the construction cost of a new stadium with luxury seating, and the team is permitted to retain the revenue from this luxury seating, the team's revenues obviously increase. These increases can be substantial enough to offset the local media revenue earned by teams in larger markets. If the larger local media contracts of a few teams in larger markets no longer existed, smaller market teams would not "need" the subsidies they currently demand, as there would be less differential in income between teams. In a similar fashion, if the Dallas Cowboys began to earn a great deal of money from the luxury seating in their facility, other teams might develop in the Dallas/Fort Worth area to challenge them for part of that market. If some fans attended the home games of teams in Arlington or Fort Worth, there would be less interest in paying the suite fees now collected by the Cowboys. In the case of the NFL and the Dallas Cowboys, television revenues are shared, but the current popularity of the Cowboys and football in the Dallas/Fort Worth region, combined with a favorable lease arrangement for that team, generates substantial extra profits for the team. However, if other investors could penetrate the Cowboys' market, those extra profits would decline, reducing the pressure on cities elsewhere to subsidize their teams to make them competitive with the Cowboys. Markets work if the markets are free and not controlled by a cartel. When markets do not work or are controlled by a cartel, excessive profits and higher costs for consumers will always result. These higher costs will always take the form of subsidies and welfare payments unless the current system is changed.

IMAGINE MORE TEAMS: HOW MANY CAN NORTH AMERICA'S POPULATION SUPPORT?

In chapter 3, I used *four* different illustrations to demonstrate how many more teams would likely exist if sports operated in a free market. Zimbalist (1992) used the increasing population of the United States to describe the supply of players for more teams. In 1990, with a population of 250 million people, America would be able to produce one-thousand major league baseball players using the proportion of athletes to the general population that existed in 1903. With approximately twenty-five players on each team, the population of the United States is sufficiently large to produce enough players for forty teams. I then used the changes in the population in the United States to illustrate how many markets that could financially support MLB and NFL teams existed. That analysis indicated there should be at least thirty-five major league baseball teams, or five more than currently exist (two expansion teams have been approved for play later this decade). There probably should be as many as forty-two NFL teams, or twelve more than currently exist. With the expansions planned for Cleveland (a new Browns team to replace the Ravens, who were the Browns) and Los Angeles (two teams, assuming that no existing team moves there), the NFL should probably have at least nine more teams.

The analysis performed by the *New York Times* found nine areas without MLB that could definitely support a team, five areas that could possibly support a team, and as many as five areas that could support at least one *additional* team. With twenty-eight teams based in the United States (including the Phoenix and St. Petersburg teams), the *New York Times* analysis would suggest that MLB should have at least thirty-seven teams, and possibly as many as forty-seven in the United States alone (Ahmad-Taylor, 1995). Lastly, the population growth in Los Angeles and New York has been sufficient to support *seven additional* MLB franchises (four more teams in the New York City metropolitan area and three more in the Los Angeles region), since both areas have only two teams.

With too few teams relative to the number of cities able to support teams, and with an adequate supply of talent, an *undersupply* of teams exists, increasing the competition for franchises and raising the level of subsidies cities are willing to provide. These four approaches to measuring the demand for teams illustrate how the market is failing—the demand for teams exceeds the supply—because the cartel structure of professional sports has developed leagues not unlike those that the oil-producing nations created. MLB, the NFL, the NBA, and the NHL are the OPEC of the 1990s, at least as far as taxpayers and professional sports teams are concerned.

Just as the oil-producing nations held the oil-consuming nations hostage to high prices in the 1970s, the sports leagues and their players are holding cities and their taxpayers hostage today. We need an excess profits tax on this cartel too, or a commitment to let the free market work to the advantage of consumers.

What Would Happen If More Teams Existed?

First, there would be more jobs for players. For each baseball team added, at least twenty-five additional major league players would be needed. Football teams, with more than fifty players each, would also create more jobs for members of the NFL Players Association. NBA teams require far fewer players, twelve, but there would also be more jobs in that industry. Second, with more teams, revenue from national media contracts would have to be shared among more league members. Furthermore, if the number of teams in the New York region were increased to six, the local media revenues received by the Yankees would also likely decrease. The existence of more teams would likely lead to price competition, resulting in reduced ticket prices and creating additional benefits for sports fans. With lower ticket prices, more fans might be able to attend games and take their families to games. A common lament in past years is that professional sports has become a "rich person's form of entertainment." When it costs more than $100 for a family to attend a baseball game, there is indeed a great deal of truth to the observation that major league sports are no longer games for the average person or an affordable form of family entertainment. More teams would create more competition for fans' sports dollars. Just as the existence of more airlines, automobile manufacturers, fast-food restaurants, and mutual fund firms creates lower prices and higher service for consumers, fans can expect more teams to mean lower prices and more affordable opportunities to take their families to games.

The declining revenues per team would also result in less profit. The value of teams would decline, and with that, the salaries paid to individual players would decrease. There would be more jobs, but competition would drive prices and salaries to lower *market* levels. This might mean a .300 hitter would not earn $3 million per season, and some basketball players who average twenty points per game would not earn in excess of $6 million in a season. But should players earn that much? They can earn that much if the supply of teams is limited and cities offer subsidies to attract teams. Those subsidies lower the cost of operation (teams do not have to build their own stadia or arenas), and the money that owners would have used to pay for the playing facilities is now left to be divided between the players and owners.

Taxpayers and community leaders must now understand that the players and their unions are as much a part of the cartel ownership group of sports as are the team owners themselves. More teams will mean less revenues per team and therefore less revenue that any one player can receive even though there will be more jobs, more teams, and the need for more players. If price competition is introduced into the world of sports cartels, then all those who benefit from the existing cartel structure could receive lower salaries and profits. Fans, on the other hand, would have access to more teams and more games at lower prices. More teams having less money will mean even Michael Jordon and Shaquille O'Neal will earn less than $25 and $12 million per year for playing basketball.

The existence of the subsidies has also permitted the owners of professional sports teams to earn handsome profits. At the same time that cities are being asked to make these investments, it is important to underscore that the profitability of sports for team owners is substantial. To be sure, some teams are losing money, but far more make a profit. The value of teams has escalated substantially.

Franchise revenues grew by nearly 12 percent per year from 1970 to 1991, a 6.3-percent annual growth rate over and above the rate of inflation. Increases were not, however, equally distributed among all franchises. . . . The Baltimore Orioles, a profitable team, were sold for $12 million in 1979, $70 million in 1989, and again for $173 million in 1993 (with the benefit of a new stadium complex financed by Maryland taxpayers). The Seattle Mariners, long a financially weak team, were sold in 1981 for $13 million and again in 1988 for $89.5 million ($77.5 million changed hands, with the buyer taking over $12 million in liabilities). In 1992, they were sold again for $106 million to a group of local businesses that offered to invest an additional $19 million in the team. The Texas Rangers, also a weak team, were sold for $10.5 million in 1974 and for $79 million in 1989 (Cox & Zimmerman, 1995, p. 4).

Since 1991, the value of the average NBA team has increased 81.4 percent. NFL team owners have enjoyed a 31.8 percent increase in value, and NHL owners have also seen an average increase in value of 68.2 percent. The value of MLB teams has fallen 5 percent as a result of their labor problems, but that state of affairs may be only temporary. With both players and owners enjoying substantial salaries or returns, there are clearly excess profits to enjoy, and no need to subsidize professional sports. Creating more teams would reduce the value of teams and the salaries earned by players to their appropriate market levels from the inflated levels that were created as a direct result of the cartel structure of sports and the subsidies extracted from governments and their taxpayers.

The Rights of the Owners of a Private Business

At this point in our journey toward a Brave New World you might think a slight contradiction exists. If professional sports teams are privately owned corporations, why should they not have the right to form leagues and limit the number of members of the leagues? Indeed, earlier in this book I made the point that sports are different from any other business in that they require competitors organized into leagues. To be successful, sports teams require other competitors who agree to follow a common set of rules and regulations. This need is what establishes the requirement for leagues. The professional sports leagues have then tried to use this need to limit the number of teams that exist. While sports leagues can more easily establish accepted rules, schedules, and a process for crowning a champion, they do not need to control the number of teams. Granted that authority, the leagues have limited the number of the teams that can exist, establishing an atmosphere within which cities offer ludicrous welfare payments to attract and retain teams. But wait, should not any owner or individual have the right to form a league and exclude people? In other words, if team owners wish to operate private businesses, form leagues, and limit the number of teams, is that not their right?

It may not be their right, however, if that power creates a monopoly and that monopoly generates excessive profits and limits competition. We could debate the monopoly issue for several chapters, but the purpose of this book is not to create a debate or forum for lawyers to discuss the extent to which MLB, the NFL, NBA, and NHL are or are not unfair monopolies violating the spirit or intent or antitrust laws or the tenets of capitalism and the free market. Rather, I am striving to raise several basic points regarding the cartel structure of sports.

First, if the demand for teams drove supply and investors could respond to the demand for teams and join the existing leagues as they wished, the number of teams that would exist would be far greater.

Second, the supply of players is more than adequate for the number of teams that would exist under a free-market scenario, leading to the development of many more teams.

Third, the increasing population size of the United States would lead to the creation of far more teams if the cartel-like power of the leagues did not control and restrict the number of the franchises that are granted.

Fourth, the creation of more teams would create price competition, especially in areas with more than one team. This price competition would lead to lower ticket prices.

Fifth, with lower ticket prices, profits would be less, and there would be less money available to pay players the salaries they now enjoy because of the absence of a free market. Unlike the early years of professional sports, the players are now equal partners with the owners in the operation of a cartel and welfare system that holds cities and their taxpayers hostage and transfers wealth from the lower classes to the economically privileged.

Sixth, by refusing to consider a market response—allow the number of teams that exist in any sport to rise to meet the demand that exists—salaries and profits will remain artificially high and an environment in which subsidies exist and welfare is provided will continue. Whenever the supply is far less than the demand, prices will rise, as those who own or control the coveted resource will charge and receive more than the [real free-market] value of their product and service.

Do you want to end the welfare system that inflates the salaries paid to athletes and the profits earned by owners? Here are two possible suggestions or recommended policies that would use a market-based approach to end the sports welfare game.

Recommendation #1: *The National Governors' Association and the U.S. Conference on Mayors should establish a binding compact among all its members that prohibits the use of tax dollars and all other revenues collected by governments or publicly created authorities (such as user fees, grants from other governments, lottery proceeds, and so forth) for the building or maintenance of venues used by professional sports teams. In addition, the National Governors' Association and the U.S. Conference of Mayors should also agree that no public resources can be used to assemble or provide the land upon which venues used by professional sports teams are built. The public's investments in professional sports should be limited to the building and maintenance of public transportation infrastructure (including streets and roads) that is needed to facilitate the development of sports venues.*

What's the justification for such a resolution? The professional sports leagues have used their power to form leagues to develop cartels that (1) restrict the supply of teams and (2) lead to a system in which the existing teams can extract welfare payments, subsidies, and other incentives from the cities that do not have teams. Cities and states must form a similar cartel and refuse to deal with the professional sports leagues. If such a cartel is not formed by the cities and states, the welfare system will continue and the subsidies will flow.

The implementation and support for this resolution will not only end the sports welfare machine, but it will also protect taxpayers from efforts to circumvent the intent of the resolutions. By excluding all taxes, user charges, lottery revenues, grants, or fees collected by any government or publicly created authority, there would seem to be a fairly firm rule that no funds from the public sector can be used to subsidize professional sports. Furthermore, without such a resolution all mayors and governors fear one of their colleagues will offer an incentive package forcing them to provide welfare to teams.

If this resolution were accepted by all cities and states, the sports welfare system would come to a screeching halt. With owners having to pay for their playing facilities, there would be less cash available for players' salaries and owners' profits. The value of each team would also decrease. Players' salaries would decline to actual free-market levels, as would team values and the profits realized by owners. But would ticket prices decline? Possibly not, if the cartel still limited the supply of teams to ensure its profit levels. While Recommendation #1 ends the sports welfare game, it does not require the formation of new teams if populations increase or other communities want teams. Recommendation #1 does not address the frustrations of cities such as Indianapolis, Columbus, San Antonio, Orlando, Louisville, Nashville, and the suburban areas of New York and Los Angeles that want teams but would be unable to attract them if the subsidies were prohibited and nothing was done to end the power of the sports cartels.

Recommendation #2: *In any community where investors have sufficient resources to pay an admission or franchise fee equal to the average value of all teams in a professional sports league, each of the professional sports would be required to admit this team to the league. Credentials for team ownership would be limited to the fiscal requirement stated above and the conditions attached to ownership in the league that are binding on all existing owners.*

What's the justification for such a law, which would have to be passed by the U.S. Congress? Professional sports are an integral part of American society. They are seen as a mechanism through which civic identity is established.[1] Restricting the availability of teams limits the ability of any city to enhance its reputation and attractiveness by hosting a professional sports franchise. While the benefits of a team may be small or could be achieved by other means and assets, permitting a small group of owners to control the number of franchises works against the public's interests and the clear preferences of a large number of citizens and communities to have teams.[2]

What would happen if such a law existed? The number of teams in each of the professional sports leagues would increase to meet the demand. More teams would eliminate the market clout of the New York Yankees or Los Angeles Dodgers. With numerous teams in those markets, the local media revenues of existing teams would likely decline. There would be fewer small-market teams with financial problems. With more teams in larger markets, the ability of those teams to accrue large cash surpluses to attract the best players would decline. All teams would, in a sense, be playing in similar-size markets. (With more teams in larger markets, each existing team in a league would have a similar-size fan base although multiple teams in larger markets would still have an advantage in that fans could support two or more teams. While that is possible, the situation would be far more balanced than what currently exists.) This is not to suggest that the population of New York would shrink. Rather, with six teams in the metropolitan area, the Yankees would have far less advantage and opportunity to earn money than they do now relative to the Pirates, Indians, or Brewers. The team that was the best managed or coached and got the best performance (most return) from their players would likely earn the most revenues.

Would this lead to a proliferation of teams? There would be more teams, but not necessarily a proliferation. New teams would only be created if the investors were able to pay a franchise fee equal to the average value of all teams in the league; as a result, while franchise values would decline over the years, substantial investments would be required to gain admission to a league. For example, if the values established by *Financial World* were used to secure an MLB franchise, investors would need $115 million (average 1996 value of all MLB teams). An NBA franchise would require a $127 million investment; an NFL team would cost $174 million; and an NHL franchise would cost $74 million. Again, these prices would decline over time, but large investments would still be needed. After paying this fee, investors would still need money to pay players and a staff, establish offices, and develop playing facilities. Investing in a professional sports team is a $100 to $200 million investment; it is definitely not for those who dislike risk, and a large amount of capital is required. As such, there would be more teams, but not necessarily a plethora of teams flooding the market.

This proposal also protects existing team owners. Each team that is admitted to the league would provide league owners with a substantial amount of income (franchise fees would be divided equally among existing team owners). That money would remain with the owners even if the new teams failed. Furthermore, while the new teams would be permitted to draft one player from the existing teams, each team could protect a number of players by following the same procedures that are currently used when the leagues expand. Team owners would be required to share league resources with the new teams, but the franchise fees are payments for those income flows. The system proposed here in a Brave New World would create income for existing owners (the franchise fees paid by individuals who joined the leagues), increase the supply of teams (provide more games and opportunities to see those games for fans while creating more jobs for players), and create the potential for market forces to determine the number of teams that exist. The power of the leagues to declare which cities or regions could have teams and how many teams can exist in any region would be eliminated. With more teams, a form of price competition would emerge as the newer franchises sought to attract fans. With more teams and price competition, profit levels of the existing teams would decline. However, the franchise fees received by those teams would compensate them for losing the profits they have received only because of the existence of the cartels.

As the profitability of each individual team declined and price competition emerged, teams would have fewer dollars to pay individual players. The inflated salaries of some players would decline. There would then be some lost income opportunities for some players. To offset these losses, existing players should be permitted to share in the income from the franchise fees paid by new teams. In much the same way that players share in the revenues earned by the leagues today, these franchise fees should be added to the revenue pool. For example, if a league currently pledges that players receive 52 percent of all income earned by the teams, that formula should also include income from franchise fees. In that manner, both the existing players and owners would receive windfall income from the increase in the number of teams. As this income offsets the loss in future income, players and owners are compensated for the change to a market-based system.

In the Brave New World proposed here, the current players and owners are protected from excessive losses as they receive income from the franchise fees paid by new team owners. Cities and states are freed from paying unneeded welfare-reducing taxes. Fans will see lower ticket prices, more realistic salaries for athletes, and more teams. There will be greater access to all major league sports. Fans, players, owners, and taxpayers all gain in the Brave New World, and we create more jobs or playing opportunities for young people (maybe even women's teams would develop) who want to be ballplayers. Sounds too good to be true? It's not; it is just a reasonable set of outcomes from the use of market forces to permit the number of sports team to rise to meet the demand. In some games everyone is a winner!!!

COME AS CLOSE AS YOU CAN: A BILL OF RIGHTS FOR TAXPAYERS WHO SUBSIDIZE PROFESSIONAL SPORTS

How radical are the ideas encompassed in Recommendation #1 and Recommendation #2? They are not extremist views, but merely amplifications, modifications, and extensions of some of the ideas voiced by others. Across three decades, Howard Cosell called for the regulation or oversight of sports to prevent franchise movement and the ability of teams to hold cities and their taxpaying residents as fiscal hostages (Cosell, 1985). Cosell's "telling it like it is" attitude mirrors repeated calls from the National Governors' Association and the U.S. Conference of Mayors for cities not to bid against each other for teams and other corporations or economic development opportunities. I am not recommending a regulatory framework or suggesting there is a need to create a new bureaucracy. I am suggesting that the market establish the number of teams that can and should exist in every region and in each sport and that governments agree not to provide welfare for successful businesses. This would eliminate the ability of teams to hold cities hostage through their threats to leave. The investment of each of the existing owners would also be preserved through the requirement that franchise fees be paid for access to the league's resources.

More recently, the Federal Reserve of Minneapolis's annual report for 1994 called for congressional action to halt the economic war between the cities for businesses such as professional sports teams (Burstein & Rolnick, 1995). Yet, teams continue to move or threaten to move, and cities continue to bid against each other and offer extensive subsidies to professional sports teams, without any national or state-level oversight of sports. Indeed, rather than provide oversight, some states (including Florida, Ohio, and New York) have had legislation introduced to provide statewide support (subsidies) for any city that uses its own tax revenues to support professional sports franchises. In other words, in Florida, Ohio, and New York legislation was introduced that called for the use of state tax dollars to supplement local dollars used to attract and retain professional sports franchises. Both Florida and Ohio passed their laws and now subsidize wealthy owners and players with taxpayers' dollars from the state if local tax dollars are also invested. In both states a situation where local governments have an incentive for spending their tax dollars to attract and retain teams has been created. If they commit their dollars as part of a sports welfare program, the state will also provide funds. The rich get richer and the poor and middle class pay more in taxes to provide this welfare for the wealthy. Despite calls for recommendations similar to those I have proposed, nothing has yet been done to end the welfare mess that is professional sports.

Okay, let's assume a Brave New World for professional sports cannot be created. How close can we come to that Utopia? We can take several steps. Let's assume neither Recommendation #1 nor Recommendation #2 is accepted, and that the power of the leagues to admit or to refuse to admit teams continues to exist as it does in its present form. What can communities do to at least minimize their welfare payments or secure real value for their investments? There are several items that could be implemented as part of a taxpayers' Bill of Rights.

Recommendation #3: *If a team agrees to play in a facility in which there is any form of public investment in the facility itself or in the infrastructure that provides access to the arena or stadium (this would include any and all improvements to streets, roads, and freeways), then the league in which the team plays has to guarantee the city an expansion franchise if the team leaves the boundaries of the city. The expansion franchise will be permitted to begin play within twenty-four months of the movement of a franchise. The new team must be owned by local investors; and the franchise fee charged the new owners will not exceed 75 percent of the average value of teams in that league. This guarantee of a new franchise is waived only if attendance at games has fallen below 75 percent of the average attendance of other teams in the league (attendance measured as a percent of capacity).*

What's the justification for a recommendation of this nature? This protects any public investment in a playing facility or the infrastructure to support a facility by guaranteeing the community that it will have a team to play in that facility as long as the community continues to support that team by purchasing tickets.

Recommendation #3 establishes a set of rights for a community if it invests in the playing facilities that teams demand and the fans in the community continue to support the team through ticket purchases. The recommendation also protects team owners and their investments in the team by requiring a minimum level of attendance. If attendance declines, a team owner should have the right to move to a more profitable location. A community's support of the team should be measured by the percentage of seats it purchases in a season. My suggestion is that a community's support should be measured as a percent of capacity. If the league's average attendance is equal to 90 percent of the capacity of any facility, then a community would be judged as supporting its team as long as its attendance level was 75 percent of the league average (90 percent of capacity multiplied by 75 percent would equal 67.5 percent of capacity). If a basketball team played in a facility that had 20,000 seats, for its forty-one home games the total capacity figure would be 820,000 tickets. If the league's average attendance was equal to 90 percent of capacity, a team with 820,000 seats would be expected to sell 738,000 tickets. If a team sold less than 75 percent of this figure, 553,500 tickets, then they could move without the league being forced to award another franchise to the community that lost the team.

Requiring a league to award a community a new franchise at 75 percent of the average value of all teams creates a strong incentive for all owners to resolve issues before any team is given permission to move to another location. Each time a new franchise is awarded existing owners receive less revenue from all sources of revenues that are shared by league members (national media contracts). In addition, if that entrance fee is reduced to 75 percent of the value of all teams, each league owner has a vested interest in finding a solution that would involve payment of a full franchise fee and in avoiding the move. In this manner, then, there is a cost to all members of the league if any one team moves. This establishes a strong incentive for the league to attempt to develop a solution to a team's fiscal needs without encouraging a move to another region.

Recommendation #4: *If a community agrees to pay for a portion of the cost of a new arena or stadium, it should be entitled to that proportion of the increment in a team's value. When new facilities are constructed, complete with luxury seating, the value of most teams increases. Since a substantial portion of that increased value is a function of the revenue sources built into the facility, the public sector should share in the wealth it creates. If state and local governments paid 50 percent of* *the cost of a new facility, then they should be entitled to receive 50 percent of the increase in the team's value if the team is ever moved.*

One substantial inequity results when public funds are used to increase the wealth of a small group of rich individuals by investing in new playing facilities and giving teams control of most revenues generated by these facilities. If a team is valued at $90 million before a stadium or arena is constructed, and after construction its value increases to $120 million, the $30 million increase in value should be shared in proportion to the funds spent on the facility. If the public sector paid 50 or 60 percent of the cost of project, then the public sector should be entitled to 50 or 60 percent of the increase in value (50 percent of $30 million is $15 million). This addition to the Bill of Rights for taxpayers and local governments ensures a fiscal return to the taxpayers for the specific form of wealth their taxes have created. When taxes are used to create wealth, the public sector should be entitled to a return on that investment similar to the return enjoyed by any other property owners.

There are many ways to establish or assess the value of a team. A community and a team owner could agree to accept the estimates made by *Financial World*. The community (represented by a mayor or governor) and the team could also agree to each select one expert appraiser and to have these experts on team valuation appoint a third expert. All three could then assess the team's value prior to the building of the facility, and the average of all three figures could be the asset base agreed to by all parties. Increments to this base, again determined by a reassessment in the future (following the same procedures used for the initial assessment), would establish the growth that took place from the time the new facility was built.

This return to the public sector could be described as asset valuation financing. For participating in the financing of the stadium or arena the public sector receives a *proportionate* share of the value it generates in relationship to its share of the cost of a new playing facility. *The public sector, however, does not receive its share of the wealth unless the team moves from the community.* If the team never moves, the public sector never receives its increment. This provision would permit the sale of the team to other investors, but the team would have to remain in the city or the government would have to receive its share of the wealth generated. At the time of the move the cash must be paid to the public sector. This would create a substantial disincentive for any team to move after the public sector has made an investment.

Some would argue that the public sector does receive a return on its investments in new playing facilities through the taxes paid by the team owners and the other taxes paid by individuals who attend games and events. In most circumstances those returns do exist. (They may not exist if the local government collects mostly property taxes; then changes in the income of owners as a result of the existence of a new stadium or arena might not generate any new tax revenues for the local government.) However, when a government becomes an investor in a facility that is essentially a private enterprise (sports facilities and entertainment, for example), the public sector's return should be related to market forces and not just taxes used to provide public services. If the public sector assumes the risks of investing in a stadium or arena that makes a team more profitable or valuable, the public sector becomes a part owner. As a part owner it should receive direct returns on its investment.

Recommendation #5: *If a team threatens to leave a community, and the public sector has paid at least 50 percent of the cost for constructing or rebuilding the playing facility used by the team within the past fifteen years, the public sector entity that made the investment in the facility will have the right to purchase the team for its market value, less any proportion of that value that is already assigned to the public sector.*

What's the rationale for this proposal? With communities frequently spending in excess of $100 million to build playing facilities for professional sports teams, public entities have substantial financial interests in a team's continued presence in a community. In addition, taxpayers have both a financial and emotional investment in a team. After making these investments, if a team still elects to leave, the city should have the right to purchase the team to ensure its continued presence in the community and at the facility. The team could still be managed by professionals in much the same manner as are many other public assets, including port authorities, airports, water companies, and the Green Bay Packers.

This proposal also has substantial symmetry in terms of the benefits it provides for communities and team owners. First, it protects a community against a possible move and the payment of any forgone rent by another city. Remember that when the Browns franchise moved to Baltimore and the Rams moved to St. Louis, both teams fulfilled the financial obligations of their leases, but both Cleveland and Anaheim lost their teams. The dollars for these rent payments came from the new home cities, which were only too happy to subsidize the move to immediately have a team in their community. Second, the proposal also protects the owners from a city that refuses to invest in a needed stadium or a needed set of improvements. The fifteen-year clause would mean the right to purchase a team by the community *does not exist* unless the public sector has recently made a substantial investment in a playing facility. The economics of sports change quickly; as a result, it is reasonable to expect that teams need facilities with both the most current amenities and the most recent sources of revenues. If a community is to have a right to buy a team, then it must also have the responsibility for ensuring that the existing facility offers owners the amenities and revenue streams available to other teams.

Additional protection for the owners could be developed if my proposed fifteen-year investment rule included a provision that the in-stadium revenues from a facility must equal at least 95 percent of the average revenues received by all teams from their playing facilities. In other words, if the economics of sports changes to the point where any facility does not produce for its team revenues equal to 95 percent of the average income received by all teams in the league from their facilities, then renovations or a new facility is needed. Under these circumstances, if revenue from a playing facility did not equal 95 percent of the league's average, and if a city and team could not form a partnership to enhance a playing facility, the team would be able to move to another city and the city that lost the team would not be guaranteed a new franchise. Why choose 95 percent of the league's average revenues from playing facilities? In this manner, a team must be assured of a base of income, independent of performance, that permits it to attract the best players.

This provision in a Bill of Rights for taxpayers and fans would provide substantial protection from the loss of perceived intangible benefits. For example, when teams leave one area for another, while they may have sufficient resources (or subsidies from the other city) to prepay their lease obligations for the old playing facility they used, what compensation does the community that loses the team receive for its perceived psychic loss? There are legendary stories regarding the sense of loss felt by residents of Brooklyn when the Dodgers left and by the citizens of Baltimore when the Colts headed to Indianapolis. How do these communities receive protection from these losses? What is their compensation or rights after providing years of support by purchasing tickets and cheering from the stands?

My proposal, that communities be permitted to purchase the teams, would mean that if a team owner could find a more profitable location, he or she would be required to sell the team to the public sector in its existing home for the value of the team in that other location. But the sale would have to be to the public sector in the original community. In this manner, the owner does not suffer any economic loss—the value paid by Baltimore for the Colts would be the agreed value of the team in their new home (reflecting the income they could have earned in Indianapolis), and the value paid for the Browns would be their value once located in their new, 100 percent subsidized stadium in Baltimore.

How could these values be measured? The appraisal process to be used is the same one described earlier. This is not the difficult part of implementing this recommendation. What is difficult is the alteration that must be made in league procedures. What need to be changed are the provisions in each sports league that effectively prohibit public-sector ownership of teams. This is done by requiring that an individual own at least 50 percent of the team. Since teams mean more to communities than their meager economic benefits, that provision needs to be changed and cities need to have the right to buy the teams. Ironically, the investments made by many communities in playing facilities far exceed the cost of the team. In this regard, the public sector could increase its total investment in sports by a relatively small proportion and pay for both the stadium or arena and the team itself. If it did that, team movement would be a distant memory and not a relatively fresh news item for each day's papers.

Finally, if any public-sector entity had to be given the right to buy the team, think about the incentives for the other owners to disapprove any move. Wanting to keep teams in the hands of the private sector and individuals, the leagues would have an incentive to develop solutions that restricted team moves. In such an environment the era of franchise free agency might end.

SAME OLD, SAME OLD, NO MORE

What options exist for communities to survive sports if none of the changes recommended can or do take place? While my fervent hope is that the financing of facilities for professional sports teams will change and the provision of welfare and incentives to teams will end, if there are neither changes in nor ends to the subsidies provided, cities and states can still take steps to reduce their fiscal commitments for sports. Let's assume none of the ideas already presented can be implemented. What other principle should be followed? The guiding idea or notion should be that users of the facilities—sports fans—should pay for their costs and any subsidies provided to teams. General revenues (lottery funds for example) or broad-based taxes (food and beverage, hotel, car rental, and sales taxes) should not be used to support a team or its playing facility.

CHARGE THE USERS

If people want to spend money for sports facilities and want money spent on sports teams, let them. Communities have a wide range of possibilities that could be used to pass the costs of the new facilities along to fans. First, consider an admissions or entertainment tax on all tickets sold. Team owners and players have passed the higher costs of player salaries and their profit needs to fans. The public sector should do the same thing for the new playing facilities. The users of the facility should pay for the facility. The public sector's responsibility for the financing of a stadium or arena and any subsidies provided to team owners should be met by sports fans and not the general public. An admissions tax could be a step in that direction.

Second, establish a special sales tax for all goods and services sold or provided within the stadium and within the immediate area surrounding the stadium or arena. This special tax, something in the order of 5 or 10 percent, would be paid by facility users and attendees. These revenues should also be part of any public-sector responsibility for a team. The exact area affected by the tax would differ from city to city. In some communities, restaurants within two or three blocks might be the appropriate special tax zone. In other areas a wider or smaller zone might be developed. Remember, the goal of this zone is to increase the share of the cost of the stadium or arena that is paid by the fans who attend games and visit the playing area where playing facilities are built.

Third, extend the admissions or entertainment tax to all those who witness games through the mass media. Remember, an arena or a stadium is a stage upon which a performance occurs. Some of the fans enjoy this play in person. Others enjoy it on television or on the radio. The fees charged by the teams and the income they receive from cable television operators, the major television networks, radio networks, and individual television and radio stations should be subject to the same admissions tax charged to fans that attend a game. Let's suppose a community agrees that the admissions tax should be 5 percent of the ticket value. That tax ought to be applied against the agreed fee accepted by the team or league for the broadcast of all games, and these fees should be used to finance the public sector's obligations for a stadium, arena, or any other subsidy provided.

LIMIT INCENTIVES TO INCREMENTAL TAX GROWTH

If user charges cannot support the entire amount of the investment in a stadium or arena required by the public sector or of the other incentives that the public sector must provide, then public officials should limit the additional investment to the *incremental* tax growth related to the team's presence. As discussed, under the worst of conditions, approximately 12 percent of the spending associated with a team's presence represents real economic development. That growth will produce some new tax revenues for a community. Those revenues should be calculated, and once established, that level can become the limit placed on the subsidy a government could provide to a team. In this manner, the public subsidy would be limited to the tax revenues collected that are directly related to the presence of a team.

Notice, however, that this proposal would target the *real economic development* and *not the total aggregate spending that occurs as a result of a team*. At several points in this book I have gone to great lengths to demonstrate that most of the spending associated with teams would occur even if the team was not in the city. This occurs because people still spend money for recreation regardless of the presence of a team. As such, a careful analysis must be performed to estimate the real incremental development or growth that occurs to establish the actual limits for any subsidies.

Sports can be survived. None of the recommendations made here will be easy to implement. But they are necessary steps. An excessive welfare system has been created and it transfers large sums of money to the most economically privileged groups in our society. It can be stopped. It should be stopped. We live in an era in which people want more individual responsibility and lower taxes; sports should not be excluded from the "reinvention" process that is so much a part of today's politics and business world. Sports subsidies must be "downsized." After all, the examples we set through sports seem to attract a great deal of attention.

We cannot continue to let the interest in and "hype" generated by sports take money from taxpayers. Sports teams can financially support themselves and do not deserve welfare. Cities should not be held hostage to demands issued by team owners and players for subsidies that do not make sporting events more available to citizens but simply increase profits and salaries. It is time for cities, their taxpayers, and their civic leaders to recognize the leagues and sports for what they are. Leagues are cartels that ensure profits and salaries. Sports are a diversion, not a public good or service that requires tax support.

NOTES

Chapter 3: Maintaining Scarcity

1. To be sure, important critics of major league sports and their control over the supply of teams have also suggested that other factors could limit the number of teams. At least one leading student of baseball's economics has suggested that there is *in*sufficient talent available to sustain quality and add baseball teams. Scully (1989) notes that in 1952 there were 364 minor league teams; that number had dwindled to 145 by 1987. However, while there were clearly fewer teams, that does not necessarily mean there is insufficient quality to sustain playing levels. First, each year MLB needs between 90 and 120 new players. With 145 minor league teams now existing, there are as many as 3,500 players from which these new major leaguers can be drawn. Fewer than one-half of 1 percent of all minor league players are thus needed to cover retirements from major league squads. Second, the decline in minor league teams may be a result of media penetration and the availability of fans to see televised games, both of which reduce the need for many minor league teams.

2. In some instances when teams have been admitted to one of the professional leagues, they were expressly told they would not share in certain league revenues for a specific number of years. When this occurs, the new owners actually pay a franchise fee for future revenue flows they must wait to enjoy. The operating losses sustained by the Jacksonville and Carolina franchises in the NFL in 1995 were a result of their reduced share of the league's media contacts.

Chapter 4: What Do Teams Really Mean for a City's Economy?

1. The U.S. Department of Commerce does produce other multipliers. For example, in addition to the earnings multiplier, a total output to total

output multiplier is created. Total output includes labor and all materials. That multiplier is usually greater, but for the category that includes sports it was only 2.3 for the entire state of Texas. As a result, the multiplier of 3 discussed in the consultant's report would seem to be an overestimation of the impact of the recreation sector on a city the size of Arlington, Texas.

Chapter 5: How Do Governments Make Money from Sports

1. The bond rating of Allegheny County and the state of Pennsylvania is considerably higher than the rate the city of Pittsburgh could secure. As such, if those units of government guaranteed the bonds, the interest rate would be less than if the city of Pittsburgh were the sole guarantor. It should be noted, however, that interest rates for bonds sold to build a stadium would be higher than the rate that could be secured by any public entity that is negotiating bonds whose interest is exempt from federal income taxes.

Chapter 7: Sports and Downtown Development II

1. The cost for Jacobs Field, Gund Arena, and the Commons Area that surrounds both facilities was approximately $420 million. The parking garages that surround the area cost $42 million and serve both facilities as well as the downtown area near the facilities.

2. The financial package to support the proposed $175 million renovation of Cleveland Stadium consisted of a tax on parking in downtown Cleveland, an excise tax on cars rented in the county, and an extension of the tax on tobacco and alcohol products. The taxes on parking and rental cars comprised the majority of the financing, and that part of the "package" was approved in the late spring of 1995. As there was no remonstrance to the County Commission's action, no election was required to approve these measures. The "sin tax" extension did require the voters' approval, and that vote occurred on election day in November 1995. From testimony presented at a U.S. Senate committee in November 1995 it became clear that Mr. Modell actually initiated his negotiations with the state of Maryland after the Cuyahoga County Commission had approved their portion of the financing plan for the renovation of Cleveland Stadium.

3. A majority of the events at Gund Arena, home of the Cleveland Cavaliers, involve other forms of entertainment. Sports are an important component of the total number of events, but it must be noted that there are more nonsports events at Gund Arena than there are games. However, the main purpose in building the arena was to attract the Cavaliers back to

Cleveland. Indeed, Mayor White's support of the entire Gateway concept rested on the attraction of the Cavaliers to downtown Cleveland.

4. The owner of the Cavaliers in the 1970s, Nick Maletti, has claimed that he wanted to keep the team in downtown Cleveland. He reports that he was willing to build a new facility with his own funds, as he did in Richfield, Ohio, but he needed help from the city of Cleveland to assemble a large enough tract of land for the new project. He asserts the city would not or could not help in this effort, whereas there was a substantial amount of vacant land in suburban Richfield.

5. The proposed use of a property tax also became an important local political issue as a local official who supported the stadium proposal and the use of the property tax as the financial instrument was opposed by another local politician with strong links to Ohio's governor. This political backdrop contributed to the defeat of the stadium proposal and the unseating of the local official who was a very visible advocate of the stadium.

6. The Cavaliers did make an "up-front" payment of $4 million against their future obligations. In addition, at the time of this writing, negotiations were ongoing to convince the Gund Brothers to assume some of the fiscal responsibility for the construction overruns. It is possible the Gunds might decide to pay an additional $9 million for the cost of the facility. That would lower the overall investment by the public sector.

Chapter 8: Reviving the Glory of Days Past

1. Any increase in prices may lead to a reduction in consumption. While there is universal attraction to taxes paid by tourists, it needs to be remembered that although these taxes are paid by nonresidents, when anyone pays higher taxes they have fewer dollars to spend on other items. This reduced availability of funds for other purchases can lead to lower levels of employment as fewer workers are needed to produce services. When that occurs, the "tax" is paid by service-sector workers in the form of fewer jobs or reduced working hours.

Chapter 9: Development North of the Border

1. It is also important to note that each of the U.S. cities had problems that Montreal did not. Milwaukee was engaged in legal battles with MLB involving the move of the Braves to Atlanta. The Houston Astros did not want another Texas team that might erode their television revenues. The Buffalo area could not provide an MLB team with a suitable playing facility.

Chapter 10: Can Small Regions Afford Professional Sports?

1. The dates following each city indicate the year of a move (e.g., the Rockets moved, in 1971, from San Diego to Houston). Population figures are reported for communities in each move using the count from the more recent U.S. Census. When teams have moved twice, and the moves took place in different census periods, both population figures are reported: the population at the time of the first move and the population at the time of the second move. For example, when the Kings arrived in Cincinnati from Rochester (as the Royals), the population of Cincinnati was 1,468,000. When the team moved to Kansas City, the population of Cincinnati was 1,660,000.

2. Owners frequently loan their teams money for various activities, including the payment of franchise fees and the construction of playing facilities. These loans are then repaid and represent substantial sources of income to team owners.

3. The data on stadium costs are from the Regional Stadium Task Force, Stadium Financing Presentation made by Public Financial Management, Inc., June 22, 1995, p. 5.

4. The work of the Regional Stadium Task Force was being underwritten by a grant from the state of Ohio's capital improvements budget in excess of $1 million.

5. The report estimated the stadium construction cost at $160 million for the retro-style ballpark plus 10 percent for "soft costs," which include architectural and engineering costs. The report counted the luxury suites, build-out, and scoreboards separately at $37 million for both new facilities. Half of this amount is included in the total stadium cost for the Reds. The other half will be included in the stadium costs for the Bengals.

6. Note also that this simplified analysis does not account for issues regarding the distribution of tax burdens or benefits.

7. The report estimated the stadium construction cost at $170 million for a new football stadium on the current site of Riverfront, plus 10 percent for "soft costs," which include architectural and engineering costs. As mentioned earlier, the report counted the luxury suites, build-out, and scoreboards separately at $37 million for both new facilities. Half of this amount was included in the total stadium cost for the Reds while the other half is included in the stadium costs for the Bengals.

8. In a footnote in the task force report, there is mention of the possibility of having to move two other public right-of-ways. If this becomes necessary, the construction costs associated with these moves would increase the overall costs between $60 and $120 million.

Chapter 11: Fights Within the Family

1. As in several markets, minor league hockey, with its lower ticket prices, remains economically viable and even a complement to NHL teams, which typically charge far more for tickets.

Chapter 12: Surviving Sports

1. As already discussed, this benefit or advantage is not only difficult to quantify, it may not even exist. Yet many mayors, governments, taxpayers, and corporate leaders believe it exists. Whether or not the benefit actually exists is, at this point, secondary to the power to restrict the presence of teams to a group despite the needs, wants, and beliefs of others.

2. Some have argued that such a law is not needed because investors could form competitor leagues. Indeed, this has happened in the past, and such an effort to create a new baseball league only recently failed. However, relying upon the hope that new leagues would form to increase the supply of teams may be a relatively naive perspective. The existing leagues have substantial informal powers that can be used to discourage the formation of competitors. For example, cities that agree to host a team in a new league might fear their permanent exclusion from existing leagues if the upstart league failed. There are always factors that can be used to justify a cartel's decision not to grant a new franchise. Would a city risk its chances for a team by agreeing to host an upstart franchise? Furthermore, if the existing leagues were not required to admit new teams, they possess a number of other tools to inhibit the formation of competing leagues. For example, league owners could agree, informally, not to hire players who agreed to play in a competing league. In addition, the leagues could favor networks that elected not to bid on broadcast packages of competing leagues. While these actions are probably illegal, they are difficult and expensive to prove in court and establish a powerful set of incentives to stop efforts to develop new leagues. In such an environment where it is very difficult to prove unfair practices, it seems best to simply require the existing leagues to accept new team members.

REFERENCES

Ahmad-Taylor, Ty. "Who Is Major Enough for the Major Leagues?" *New York Times,* April 2, 1995, Section E, p. 5.

Ahmadi, Mossoud. "Economic and Fiscal Impacts of Baltimore Orioles' 1992 Season in Maryland." Office of Research, Maryland Department of Economic and Employment Development, State of Maryland, Baltimore, Maryland, unpublished, 1992.

Ahmed, Safir. "Escape from St. Louis." *The Riverfront Times,* January 24–30, 1996, pp. 18–21.

Ahmed, Safir. "Phantoms of the Opera House." *The Riverfront Times,* February 7–13, 1996, pp. 20–23.

"Angry Fans See a Game and Maybe a Team Lost." *New York Times,* November 6, 1995, p. B5.

Applebaum, Rhonda, David Casey, Michael Grant, Kristin Hahn, Phil McGivney, Barton Phillips, Damon Shanle, Dominic Wiker, Lamar Willis, and Patrick Larkey. *Ballpark Systems Synthesis Project, Final Report.* Pittsburgh: H. John Heinz III School of Public Policy and Management, Carnegie Mellon University, 1995.

Arthur Anderson and Company. "Economic Impact: Report on Target Center." Report for the City of Minneapolis, unpublished, 1994.

Associated Press. "Browns' Modell Indicates Team Will Move to Baltimore." *Indianapolis Star,* November 4, 1995, p. B7.

Baade, Robert A. and Richard F. Dye. "Sports Stadiums and Area Development: A Critical Review." *Economic Development Quarterly* 2, no. 4 (1988), pp. 265–75.

Baade, Robert A. "Stadiums, Professional Sports, and City Economics: An Analysis of the United States Experience." In John Bale and Olaf Moen, eds. *The Stadium and the City.* Keele, England: Keele University Press, 1995.

Baade, Robert A. "Stadiums, Professional Sports, and Economic Development: Assessing the Reality." Heartland Policy Study, Number 68, Chicago, IL: The Heartland Institute, April 4, 1994.

Bale, John. *Sports Geography.* London and New York: E. & F. M. Spon, 1989.

Barnekov, Timothy, and Daniel Rich. "Privatism and the Limits of Local Economic Development." *Urban Affairs Quarterly* 25 (1989), pp. 212–38.

Barnes, Tom. "Council, Bucs Reach Loan Accord." *Pittsburgh Post-Gazette,* June 28, 1994, p. 1.

Bartik, Timothy J. *Who Benefits from State and Local Economic Development Policies?* Kalamazoo, Michigan: W. E. Upjohn Institute, 1991.

Bartimole, Roldo. "Gateway Cost: $750,000,000." *Point of View* 26, no. 15 (1994).

Bartimole, Roldo. "$600,000 Gund Gateway Apartment." *Point of View* 28, no. 2 (1995), pp. 1–4.

Bartimole, Roldo. "Gunds Sandbag Politicians." *Cleveland Free Times,* August 16, 1995, p. 3.

Beauregard, Robert A., Paul Lawless, and Sabrina Deitrick. "Collaborative Strategies for Reindustrialization." *Economic Development Quarterly* 6, no. 4 (November 1992), pp. 418–30.

Becker, Bob, and Lou Mio. "Baseball Chief Opposes City Losing Indians, But Says Move Is Possible." *Cleveland Plain Dealer,* May 3, 1990, pp. 1, 10.

Bennett, C. "Moving Can Be Hell." *Times-Picayune,* May 12, 1994, Section C, p. 12.

Birch, David et al. *Entrepreneurial Hot Spots: The Best Places in America to Start and Grow a Company.* Cambridge, Mass: Cognetics, 1993.

Blum, Debra E. "Sports Programs Continue to Lose Money, Survey Finds." *Chronicle of Higher Education* 41, no. 2 (September 7, 1994), p. 58.

Bodley, Hal. "Baseball Payrolls Increase by Only 1.8%." *USA Today,* April 5, 1996, pp. C1, 14.

Bowen, Ezra. "Blowing the Whistle on Georgia." *Time,* February 24, 1986, p. 65.

Brace, Pete. "Blockbuster Wins 'Special District.'" *PA Times* 17, no. 11 (November 1, 1994), p. 1.

Bradsher, Keith, "Football Team Plans to Return to Detroit," *New York Times,* August 2, 1996, p. A8.

Broadway, Michael J. "Montréal's Changing Tourist Landscape." *Canadian Journal of Urban Research* 2, no. 1 (June 1993), pp. 30–48.

Buchanan, James. "Principles of Urban Fiscal Strategy." *Public Choice* 4 (1971), pp. 1–16.

Burstein, Melvin L., and Arthur J. Rolnick. "Congress Should End the Economic War Among the States." *The Region* 9, no. 1 (March 1995). Publication of the Federal Reserve Bank of Minneapolis.

Carter, Gary, with Ken Abraham. *The Gamer.* Dallas: Word Publishing, 1993.

CCRC. *First Annual Report.* St. Louis, MO: Civic Center Redevelopment Corporation," March 29, 1993.

Chass, Murray. "Baseball Owners Approve Revenue-Sharing Plan." *New York Times,* March 22, 1996, p. B17.

Chass, Murray. "Budig See New Parks in 6 Cities." *New York Times,* June 7, 1995, p. B10.

Chass, Murray. "Pirates Left at Gate in Many Ways." *New York Times,* May 16, 1995, p. B11.

City of Arlington, Texas, Office of the City Manager. "Questions and Answers About the Sales Tax Referendum and Proposed Texas Rangers," unpublished memorandum.

Cobb, Steven, and David Weinberg. "The Importance of Import Substitution in Regional Economic Impact Analysis: Empirical Estimates from Two Cincinnati Area Events." *Economic Development Quarterly* 7, no. 3 (August 1993), pp. 282–86.

Colcord, Frank C., Jr. "Saving the Center City." In Elliot Feldman and Michael A. Goldberg, eds. *Land Rites and Wrongs: The Management, Regulation and Use of Land in Canada and the United States.* Cambridge, MA: Lincoln Institute of Land Policy, 1987, pp. 75–124.

Coopers & Lybrand. "City of St. Louis: An Analysis of Net New Fiscal Benefit Generated from the Construction and Operation of the Expanded Cervantes Convention Center." Done for the St. Louis NFL Corporation. Dallas, TX: Coopers & Lybrand, February 27, 1991a.

Coopers & Lybrand. "State of Missouri: An Analysis of Net New Fiscal Benefit Generated from the Construction and Operation of the Expanded Cervantes Convention Center." Done for the state of Missouri. Dallas, TX: Coopers & Lybrand, February 27, 1991b.

Coopers & Lybrand. "Analysis for a Proposed Multi-Purpose Arena in Arlington." Report Prepared for the Arlington City Council, 1994.

Coopers & Lybrand. "Review of the Sources and Uses of Funds for the Development and Operation of The Gateway Sports Complex." Cleveland, OH: Cuyahoga County Auditors Office, 1992.

Cosell, Howard. *I Never Played the Game.* New York: William Morrow, 1985.

Cox, William A., and Dennis Zimmerman. "Baseball, Economics, and Public Policy." Washington, D.C.: Congressional Research Service, The Library of Congress, 1995.

Crothers, Tim. "The Shakedown: Greedy Owners Are Threatening to Move Their Teams If Demands for New Stadiums, Betters Lease Deals, etc., Aren't Met." *Sports Illustrated,* June 19, 1995, pp. 77–82.

Cummings, Scott, C., Theodore Koebel, and J. Allen Whitt. "Redevelopment in Downtown Louisville: Public Investments, Private Profits, and Shared Risks." In Gregory D. Squires, ed. *Unequal Partnerships: The*

Political Economy of Urban Redevelopment in Postwar America. New Brunswick: Rutgers University Press, 1989.

Cuyahoga County. "Cuyahoga County Commissioners Approve Financial Package for the Economic Development of the Central Market Gateway Project." Press Release, March 21, 1990.

Cuyahoga County Auditor's Office, Gateway Revenue Memo, 1995.

DeLater, Laurie. "Big Profits Prove Hard to Come by for New Stadiums." *Cleveland Plain Dealer,* April 29, 1990, pp. 1–2.

DeLater, Laurie. "It's Official—Cavs Would Play at Gateway." *Cleveland Plain Dealer,* May 3, 1990, pp. 1, 10.

Dion, Stephanie. "The Dynamic of Secession: Scenarios After a Pro-Separatist Vote in a Québec Referendum." *Canadian Journal of Political Science* 28, no. 3 (September 1995), pp. 533–51.

Doeringer, Peter B., and David G. Terkla. "Japanese Direct Investment and Development Policy." *Economic Development Quarterly* 6, no. 3 (August 1992), pp. 255–72.

Drier, Peter. "Economic Growth and Economic Justice in Boston: Populist Housing and Jobs Policies." In G. Squires, ed. *Unequal Partnerships.* New Brunswick: Rutgers University Press, 1989, pp. 35–58.

Dvorchak, Robert. "It's State Against State in a Battle for New Jobs." *Indianapolis Star,* October 4, 1992, Section B, pp. 1–2.

East-West Gateway Coordinating Council (EWCGG). *How We See It.* St. Louis, MO: East-West Gateway Coordinating Council, May 1992.

East-West Gateway Coordinating Council (EWCGG). *Where We Stand.* St. Louis, MO: East-West Gateway Coordinating Council, December 1992.

Edwards, Harry. *Sociology of Sport.* Homewood, IL: Dorsey Press, 1973.

Eisinger, Peter K. *The Rise of the Entrepreneurial State.* Madison: University of Wisconsin Press, 1988.

Eisinger, Peter. "State Economic Development in the 1990s: Politics and Policy Learning." *Economic Development Quarterly* 9, no. 2 (1995), pp. 146–58.

Elliott, Suzanne. "City Willing to Share $6 Million to Keep Pirates at Three Rivers." *Pittsburgh Business Times,* October 10–16, 1994, p. 1.

Euchner, Charles C. *Playing the Field: Why Sports Teams Move and Cities Fight to Keep Them.* Baltimore: Johns Hopkins University Press, 1993.

Farber, Michael. "Stars Are Out." *Sports Illustrated,* April 17, 1995, pp. 32, 35.

Financial World. "Team Values." Financial World Web Site.

Fort, Rodney. "Direct Democracy and the Stadium Mess." In Roger Noll and Andrew Zimbalist, eds., *Cities and Stadiums.* Washington, D.C.: Brookings Institution, forthcoming, 1997.

Gagnon, Alain, and Mary Beth Montcalm. *Quebec: Beyond the Quiet Revolution.* Ontario: Nelson, Canada, 1990.

Gateway Economic Development Corporation. "Lease Agreement by and Between Gateway Economic Development Corporation and Cleveland Indians Baseball Company Limited Partnership." July 3, 1991.

Gateway Economic Development Corporation. "Lease and Management Agreement by and Between Gateway Economic Development Corporation and Cavaliers Division of Nationwide Advertising Service, Inc. December 20, 1991.

George, Thomas. "Rams Get Green Light to Proceed to St. Louis." *New York Times,* April 13, 1995, p. B7.

Ginsburg, David. "Modell Bids Cleveland Goodbye." *Indianapolis Star,* November 7, 1995, pp. C1, 10.

Gittell, Ross. "Dynamic Development Cycles and Local Economic Management." *Economic Development Quarterly* 6, no. 2 (May 1992), pp. 199–210.

Gorman, Jerry, and Kirk Calhoun. *The Name of the Game: The Business of Sports,* New York: John Wiley and Sons, 1994.

Goyens, Chrys, and Allan Turowetz. *Lions in Winter.* Toronto: McGraw-Hill Ryerson, 1994.

Grabowski, John J. *Sports in Cleveland.* Bloomington, Indiana: Indiana University Press, 1992.

Greco, Anthony L. "Sports Value More Myth Than Reality." *Standard and Poor's Creditweek,* July 26, 1993.

Greene, Richard, personal correspondence between Richard Greene, Mayor of the city of Arlington and the author, 1995.

Halvonik, Steve. "Rooneys Looking to Buy Pirates." *Pittsburgh Post-Gazette,* September 16, 1994, p. A–2.

Halvonik, Steve. "Pirates' Lease Their Own Fault." *Pittsburgh Post-Gazette,* August 30, 1994, p. 1.

Hamilton, Arnold. "Bricktown Boomtown." *Dallas Morning News,* March 5, 1995, p. 41.

Hamilton, Bruce, and Peter Kahn. "Maryland Big League Stadiums." In Roger Noll and Andrew Zimbalist, eds. *Cities and Stadiums,* Washington, D.C.: Brookings Institution, forthcoming 1997.

Harding, Charles P. *Industrial Development* 33, no. 3 (May/June 1988), pp. 24(682)–27(685).

Hellinger, Daniel. "Finally Flim-Flam Football." *The St. Louis Journalism Review* 25, no. 176 (May 1995), pp. 1ff.

Hellinger, Daniel. "Most Reporters Were Uncritical Promoters of Stadium Financing." *The St. Louis Journalism Review* 25, no. 177 (June 1995), pp. 1ff.

Helyar, John. "A City's Self-Image Confronts Tax Revolt in Battle on Stadiums." *Wall Street Journal,* March 19, 1996, p. 1.

Helyar, John. "Canadian Clubs Appear to Skate on Thin Ice Amid Hockey Lockout." *Wall Street Journal,* November 15, 1994, p. 1.

Helyar, John. "Newly Cool NHL Skates on Some Thin Ice." *Wall Street Journal,* January 19, 1995, p. B6.

Helyar, John. "Pro Basketball Loses Its 'Feel Good' Image in Nasty Labor Dispute." *Wall Street Journal,* August 7, 1995, p. 1.

Helyar, John. *Lords of the Realm: The Real History of Baseball.* New York: Ballantine Books, 1994.

Higgins, Benjamin. *The Rise and Fall? of Montréal.* Moncton: Canadian Institute for Research on Regional Development, 1986.

Hirsch, Werner. *Urban Economic Analysis.* New York: McGraw-Hill, 1973.

Hudnut, William H. III. *The Hudnut Years in Indianapolis, 1976–1991.* Bloomingtion, IN: Indiana University Press, 1995.

Humber, William. *Diamonds of the North: A Concise History of Baseball in Canada.* Toronto: Oxford University Press, 1995.

IDA, Industrial Development Authority of the City of St. Louis. "Preliminary Official Statement" for bond issue dated October 27, 1992, Prudential Securities Incorporated.

"In Nashville, A Beer Ban Ends." *New York Times,* June 8, 1995, p. B8.

Johnson, Arthur T. "Local Government, Minor League Baseball, and Economic Development Strategies." *Economic Development Quarterly* 5, no. 4 (1991), pp. 313–23.

Johnson, Arthur T. "Rethinking the Sport-City Relationship: In Search of Partnership." *Journal of Sport Management,* forthcoming.

Johnson, Arthur T. *Minor League Baseball and Local Economic Development.* Chicago: University of Illinois Press, 1993.

Johnson, Chuck. "Montréal, Alou Rebuild-Again." *USA Today,* March 11, 1996, p. 4c.

Kearns, Gerry, and Chris Philo, eds. *Selling Places: The City as Cultural Capital, Past and Present.* New York: Pergamon Press, 1993.

Keating, Dennis W. "Cleveland and the 'Comeback' City: The Politics of Redevelopment Amidst Decline." Levin College of Urban Affairs, Cleveland State University, 1995.

Keating, Dennis W., Norm Krumholz, and John Metzger. "Cleveland: Post-Populist Public-Private Partnerships." In Gregory Squires, ed. *Unequal Partnerships: The Political Economy of Urban Redevelopment in Postwar America.* New Jersey: Rutgers University Press, 1989.

Kieschnick, M. *Taxes and Growth: Business Incentives and Economic Development.* Washington, D.C.: Council of State Planning Agencies, 1981.

Kissling, Catherine L. "Details About Gateway Plans Still Sketchy." *Cleveland Plain Dealer,* April 15, 1990, p. 16a.

Kissling, Catherine L. "Gateway Arena Costs Soaring." *Cleveland Plain Dealer*, May 26, 1994, pp. 1, 11.

Klacik, Drew, and Mark S. Rosentraub. *The Economic Importance and Impact of IUPUI as a Major Urban University for Indianapolis and Central Indiana.* Indianapolis: Center for Urban Policy and the Environment, School of Public and Environmental Affairs, Indiana University–Purdue University Indianapolis, 1993.

Koff, Stephen, and Evelyn Theiss. "Mayor Offers 4th Stadium Plan." *Cleveland Plain Dealer*, June 2, 1995, p. 1.

Koff, Stephen. "Gateway Financial Disclosure Sought." *Cleveland Plain Dealer*, December 15, 1994, p. 1b.

Korr, Charles. "Sports and Recreation." *St. Louis Currents.* St. Louis, MO: The Leadership Center of Greater St. Louis, 1992, pp. 139–46.

Kotler, Philip, Donald H. Haider, and Irving Rein. *Marketing Places.* New York: The Free Press, 1993.

Kruckemeyer, Thomas J. *For Whom the Ball Tolls.* Jefferson City, MO: Kruckemeyer Publishing, 1995.

Lamonde, Pierre, and Yvon Mortineau. *Desindustrialization et Restructuration Economique: Montréal et les autres grandes metropoles nord-américanes, 1971–1991.* Montréal: INRS-Urbanisation, 1992.

LaPointe, Joe. "Red Wings' Rebirth Helps Enliven Detroit." *New York Times*, June 18, 1995, p. 18.

Larkin, Brent. "No Threat, Just Facts from Jacobs." *Cleveland Plain Dealer*, April 17, 1990, p. 1d.

Land Clearance for Redevelopment Aurthority (LCRA). "Downtown Sports Stadium Project Redevelopment Plan." St. Louis, MO: Land Clearance for Redevelopment Authority, revised 7/20/65.

Land Clearance for Redevelopment Aurthority (LCRA). Bond issue prospectus, Prudential Securities Incorporated, 1992.

Lederman, Douglas. "Do Winning Teams Spur Contributions? Scholars and Fund Raisers Are Skeptical." *Chronicle of Higher Education* 34, no. 18 (January 13, 1988), pp. 1–2.

Levine, Marc V. "The Politics of Partnership: Urban Redevelopment Since 1945." In G. Squires, ed. *Unequal Partnerships.* New Brunswick: Rutgers University Press, 1989, pp. 12–34.

Lipsyte, Robert. "Why Sports Don't Matter Anymore." *New York Times Magazine*, April 2, 1995, pp. 51–57.

Lipsyte, Robert. *SportsWorld: An American Dreamland.* New York: New York Times Books, 1975.

Logan, John R., and Harvey L. Molotch. *Urban Fortunes: The Political Economy of Place.* Berkeley: University of California Press, 1987.

Lund, Leonard. *Locating Corporate R&D Facilities.* Washington, D.C.: The Conference Board, Inc., 1986.

MacAloon, John J. "Missing Stories: American Politics and Olympic Discourse." *Garnett Center Journal* 1, no. 2 (Fall 1987), pp. 111–42.

"Marge Disgusted By Stadium Report." *Dayton Daily News,* February 12, 1995, p. D12.

Marsan, Jean-Claude. *Montréal in Evolution: Historical Analysis of the Development of Montréal's Architecture and Urban Environment.* Montréal and Kingston: McGill-Queen's University Press, 1981.

McKenna, Brian, and Susan Purcell. *Drapeau.* Toronto: Clarke, Irwin and Company, 1980.

McNabb, David. "TCU Football Program Faces Loss of 25 Scholarships over Two Years." *Dallas Morning News,* April 24, 1986, p. B1.

Meserole, Mike, ed. *The 1996 Information Please Sports Almanac.* New York: Houghton Mifflin, 1995.

Meserole, Mike, ed. *1995 Information Please Sports Almanac,* Boston: Houghton Mifflin, 1994.

Michener, James A. *Sports in America.* New York: Random House, 1976.

Mier, Robert. *Social Justice and Local Development Policy.* Newbury Park: Sage Publishers, 1993.

Miklasz, Bernie. "Commentary." *St. Louis Post Dispatch,* January 22, 1995, p. 1f.

Miller, James Edward. *The Baseball Business: Pursuing Pennants and Profits in Baltimore.* Chapel Hill: North Carolina University Press, 1990.

Miller, Laura. "Why Dallas Shouldn't Replace Reunion Arena." *Dallas Observer,* October 20–26, 1994, pp. 17–29.

Mills, Edwin S. "Should Governments Own Convention Centers?" Chicago, IL: The Heartland Institute, January 21, 1991.

Milward, H. Brinton, and Heide Newman. "State Incentive Packages and the Industrial Location Decision." *Economic Development Quarterly* 3, no. 3 (1989), pp. 203–18.

Miranda, Rowan, Donald Rosdil, and Sandy Yeh. "Growth Machines, Progressive Cities, and Regime Restructuring: Explaining Economic Development Strategies." Paper presented at the 88th Annual Meetings of the American Political Science Association, Chicago, 1992.

Molotch, Harvey. "The City as a Growth Machine." *American Journal of Sociology* 82, no. 2 (1976), pp. 309–30.

Molotch, Harvey. "The Political Economy of Growth Machines." *Journal of Urban Affairs* 15 (1993), pp. 29–53.

Montréal Expos. *Guide 1995.* Montréal, 1995.

Much, Paul J., and Alan Friedman. *Inside the Ownership of Professional Sports Teams.* Chicago: Houlihan, Lokey, Howard, and Zukin, 1995.

Much, Paul J., and Alan Friedman. *Inside the Ownership of Professional Sports Teams.* Chicago: Team Marketing Report, Inc. 1996.

Mullin, Bernard J., Stephen Hardy, and William A. Sutton. *Sports Marketing.* Champaign, IL: Human Kinetics Publishers, 1993.

Nader, George. *Cities of Canada,* Vol. 2. Toronto: Macmillan of Canada, 1976.

Neft, David S., and Richard M. Cohen. *The Sports Encyclopedia: Baseball, 1996.* New York: St. Martin's Griffin Press, 1996.

Noll, Roger G. "Professional Basketball: Economic and Business Perspectives." In Paul D. Staudohar and James A. Morgan, ed. *The Business of Professional Sports.* Chicago: University of Illinois Press, 1991, pp. 18–47.

Noll, Roger, and Andrew Zimbalist, "The Economic Impact of Sports Teams and Facilities," Roger Noll and Andrew Zimbalist, editors, *The Ecomonic Impact of Sports,* Washington, D.C.: Brookings Institution, 1997.

Norton, Erle. "Football at Any Cost: One City's Mad Chase for an NFL Franchise." *Wall Street Journal,* October 13, 1993, p. A1.

O'Connor, Michael. "Officials' Ratings Local Improvements Underscore Importance of Quality of Life." *Site Selection* 32, no. 4 (August 1987), pp. 778–84.

Oates, Wallace. *Fiscal Federalism.* New York: Harcourt, Brace, Javanovich, 1977.

Ozanian, Michael K. "Suite Deals: Why New Stadiums Are Shaking Up the Pecking Orders of Sports Franchises." *Financial World,* May 9, 1995, pp. 42–56.

Peck, John E. "An Economic Impact Analysis of South Bend's Proposed Class A Baseball Stadium." South Bend: Bureau of Business and Economic Research, Indiana University at South Bend, 1985.

Penne, Leo R. *Art Spaces and Economic Development: Experiences in Six Cities.* Washington, D.C.: Partners for Liveable Places, 1986.

Perkins, Dave. "It's Time to Cut SkyDome Losses and Walk Away." *Toronto Star,* January 5, 1994, p. C1.

Peterson, Iver. "The Mistake Wakes Up, Roaring." *New York Times,* September 10, 1995, p. 9.

Peterson, Paul. *City Limits.* Chicago: University of Chicago Press, 1981.

Picard, Andre. "Expos Win Big in the Courtroom." *The Globe and Mail,* September 2, 1995, p. A19.

Picard, Andre, "Bouchard Vows Not to Raise Taxes When He's Premier." *The Globe and Mail,* December 7, 1995, p. A5.

Porter, Michael E. *The Competitive Advantage of Nations.* New York: The Free Press, 1990.

Post, Paul W. "Origins of the Montréal Expos." *The Baseball Research Journal* 22 (1993), pp. 107–10.

Price Waterhouse. "1994 Arena and Stadium Managers' Annual Report." Price Waterhouse Sports Facilities Advisory Group, Volume II, Tampa, Florida, 1994.

Quirk, James, and Rodney D. Fort. *Pay Dirt: The Business of Professional Team Sports.* Princeton, NJ: Princeton University Press, 1992.

Radich, Anthony J. *Twenty Years of Economic Impact Studies of the Arts: A Review.* Washington, D.C.: National Endowment for the Arts, Research Office, 1993.

RCGA, Regional Commerce and Growth Association. "Annual Economic Impact of the NFL Rams on the St. Louis Region." St. Louis, MO: RCGA, March 28, 1996.

Reese, Laura A. "Local Economic Development in Michigan." *Economic Development Quarterly* 6, no. 4 (November, 1992), pp. 383–93.

Reid, Susan. "Toronto Seeks Public Inquiry into Financing of SkyDome." *Toronto Star,* September 18, 1991, p. 2.

Richler, Mordecai. *Oh Canada! Oh Canada!: Requiem for a Divided Country.* New York: Alfred A. Knopf, 1992.

Rosentraub, Mark S., and David Swindell. "Just Say No? The Economic and Political Realities of a Small City's Investment in Minor League Baseball." *Economic Development Quarterly* 5, no. 2 (May 1991), pp. 152–67.

Rosentraub, Mark S., and David Swindell. "Fort Wayne, Indiana." In Arthur T. Johnson, ed. *Minor League Baseball and Local Economic Development.* Chicago: University of Illinois Press, 1993, pp. 35–54.

Rosentraub, Mark S., and Samuel Nunn. "Suburban City Investment In Professional Sports." *American Behavioral Scientist* 21 (1978), pp. 393–414.

Rosentraub, Mark S. "Public Investment in Private Businesses: The Professional Sports Mania." In Scott Cummings, ed., *Business Elites and Urban Development.* New York: State University of New York Press, 1988, pp. 71–96.

Rosentraub, Mark S., David Swindell, Michael Przybylski, and Daniel R. Mullins. "Sport and Downtown Development Strategy: If You Build It, Will Jobs Come?" *Journal of Urban Affairs* 16, no. 3 (1994), pp. 221–39.

Rubin, Herbert J. "Shoot Anything That Flies; Claim Anything That Falls: Conversations with Economic Development Practitioners." *Economic Development Quarterly* 2, no. 2 (May 1988), pp. 236–51.

Rushin, Steve. "The Heart of a City." *Sports Illustrated,* December 4, 1995, pp. 59–70.

Sandomir, Richard. "New Jersey Working to Keep the Devils." *New York Times,* May 17, 1995, p. B10.

Sandomir, Richard. "Yankees Cool to Stadium Renovation." *New York Times,* March 9, 1995, p. B8.

Sandomir, Richard. "Devils Plan to Stay in New Jersey for a Year." *New York Times,* July 14, 1995, p. B11.

Schaffer, William A., Bruce L. Jaffee, and Lawrence S. Davidson. *Beyond the*

Games: The Economic Impact of Amateur Sports. Indianapolis: Chamber of Commerce, 1993.

Schmenner, Roger. *Making Business Location Decisions.* Englewood Cliffs, NJ: Prentice Hall, 1982.

Schmitz, Jon. "Ballpark May Be the Key to a Deal." *Pittsburgh Post-Gazette,* August 4, 1994, p. A–1.

Scully, Gerald W. *The Market Structure of Professional Team Sports.* Chicago: The University of Chicago Press, 1995.

Scully, Gerald W. *The Business of Major League Baseball.* Chicago: The University of Chicago Press, 1989.

Shanahan, James L. "The Arts and Urban Development." Center for Urban Studies, University of Akron, 1980.

Sperber, Murray. *College Sports, Inc.* New York: Henry Holt and Company, 1990.

Squires, Gregory D., ed. *Unequal Partnerships: The Political Economy of Urban Development in Postwar America.* New Brunswick: Rutgers University Press, 1989.

St. Louis Regional Convention and Sports Complex Authority. *1994 Annual Report.* St. Louis, MO: Sports Complex Authority, 1995

Stainer, Harry. "Gateway, Indians Produce Agreement." *Cleveland Plain Dealer,* December 9, 1990, pp. 1–2.

Stein, David Lewis, "Selling Off Our St. Peter's Basilica Is Profane." *Toronto Star,* April 6, 1994, p. 23

Stephenson, M. O., Jr. "Whither the Public-Private Partnership." *Urban Affairs Quarterly* 27 (1991), pp. 109–127.

Stevens, John. "The Rise of the Sports Page." *Garnett Center Journal* 1, no. 2 (fall 1987), pp. 1–11.

Stuteville, George. "Lugar Labels Himself Ripken of GOP field." *Indianapolis Star,* September 10, 1995, p. 1.

Suskind, Ron. "How the Inner Circles of Medicine and Sports Failed a Stricken Star." *Wall Street Journal,* March 9, 1995, pp. A1, A14.

Swanstrom, Todd. "Semi-Sovereign Cities." *Polity* 21 (fall 1988), pp. 83–100.

Swanstrom, Todd. *The Crisis of Growth Politics: Cleveland, Kucinich, and the Challenge of Urban Populism.* Philadelphia: Temple University Press, 1985.

Swindell, David W., and Mark S. Rosentraub. "Issues Involved in the Selection of Tools for Public Policy Analysis." *Economic Development Quarterly* 6, no. 1 (1992), pp. 96–101.

Swindell, David. "Public Financing of Sports Stadium: How Cincinnati Compares." Dayton, Ohio: The Buckeye Center, 1996.

Taylor, Humphrey. "Evaluating Our Quality of Life. "*Industrial Development* 32, no. 4 (March/April 1987), p. 2(299).

Thompson, Lyke, and Mark S. Rosentraub. "Growth Poles and Lending Patterns in a Conventional Mortgage Market." *Social Science Journal*, 17, no. 1 (1980), pp. 73–86.

Tiebout, Charles. "A Pure Theory of Local Expenditures." *Journal of Political Economy* 65 (1956), pp. 416–24.

Turner, Dan. *The Expos Inside Out*. Toronto: McClelland and Stewart, 1983.

Van Alphen, Tony. "Final Dome Tally: $263 Million Lost." *Toronto Star*, September 29, 1994, p. 1.

Van Alphen, Tony. "How SkyDome's Debt Soared Through the Roof." *Toronto Star*, August 2, 1992, pp. 1, 10.

Van Alphen, Tony. "Public Will Never Know Final Score on SkyDome." *Toronto Star*, November 25, 1991, p. B1.

Warren, Robert. "National Urban Policy and the Local State." *Urban Affairs Quarterly* 25 (1990), pp. 541–61.

Weber, Michael J. *Industrial Location*. Beverly Hills, CA: Sage Publications, 1984.

Whitford, David. *Playing Hardball: The High Stakes Battle for Baseball's New Franchises*. New York: Doubleday, 1993.

Whitt, J. Allen. "The Role of Performing Arts in Urban Competition and Growth." In Scott Cummings, ed. *Business Elites and Urban Development: Case Studies Critical Perspectives*. Albany, NY: State University of New York Press, 1988.

Will, George. "Baseball Owners Abuse Their Power." *Dallas Morning News*, December 30, 1994, p. 25a.

Williams, Dick, and Bill Plaschke. *No More Mr. Nice Guy: A Life of Hardball*. San Diego: Harcourt Brace Jovanovich, 1990.

Williams, Huntington. "The News in Network TV Sports." *Garnett Center Journal* 1, no. 2 (fall 1987), pp. 25–38.

Wilson, John. *Playing by the Rules: Sport, Society, and the State*. Detroit: Wayne State University Press, 1994.

Wolff, Alexander. "Broken Beyond Repair." *Sports Illustrated*, June 12, 1995, pp. 20–26.

Wolman, Harold. "Local Economic Development Policy: What Explains the Divergence Between Policy Analysis and Behavior." *Journal of Urban Affairs* 10 (1988), pp. 19–28.

Zimbalist, Andrew. *Baseball and Billions*. New York: Basic Books, 1992.

Ziniuk, Dan, and Daniel Westreich. "L'Equipe de Denis Boucher: The Montréal Expos and Nationalism in Québec." Paper presented at the Cooperation Symposium on Baseball and American Culture, Cooperstown, New York, June 8–10, 1994.

CONTRIBUTORS

SAM NUNN is an associate professor of public and environmental affairs and associate director of the Center for Urban Policy and the Environment in the School of Public and Environmental Affairs at Indiana University (Indianapolis). Dr. Nunn's research has appeared in the *Journal of the American Planning Association*, the *Journal of Urban Affairs*, *State and Local Government Review*, *Public Works Management and Policy*, the *American Review of Public Administration*, *Policy Studies Journal*, the *Journal of Policy Analysis and Management*, *Economic Development Quarterly*, and several other journals and collections. Before returning to the academy, Dr. Nunn worked for several years in the public sector in Texas. His research interests include the economic development impacts of local government initiatives, infrastructure issues, and telecommunications policy.

DON PHARES is a professor of economics and public policy at the University of Missouri–St. Louis. He has published four books, more than sixty professional articles, and more than one hundred reports for various government agencies and businesses. He served for eight years as co-editor of the *Urban Affairs Quarterly* and two terms on the Governing Board of the Urban Affairs Association. His research and professional activity focuses on public policy issues related to urban development, urban government structure, and urban finance. His research has focused on the economic development impacts of gaming, recreation, and sports.

MICHAEL PRZYBYLSKI is a senior research scientist at the Center for Urban Policy and the Environment, School of Public and Environmental Affairs, Indiana University, Indianapolis. His research has focused on the economic development impacts of various public/private partnerships and recreational facilities. His published work has appeared in *Economic Development Quarterly*, the *Journal of Urban Affairs*, and the *Nonprofit and Voluntary Sector Quarterly*.

DAVID SWINDELL is an assistant professor in the Department of Urban Affairs and Geography and a research scientist at the Center for Urban and Public Affairs at Wright State University. In addition to his work on sports in public policy, he also is involved with research on micro-level community economic development and the development of alternative delivery options for public services. He has provided testimony to state and local governments that are considering constructing new sports facilities. His work has appeared in such journals as *Economic Development Quarterly* and the *Journal of Urban Affairs,* as well as numerous newspapers and periodicals across the nation.

ROBERT WHELAN is a professor of urban studies and associate dean at the College of Urban and Public Affairs, the University of New Orleans. An urban scholar with publications in numerous journals, Dr. Whelan has been involved in studies of Canadian urban politics and economic development for more than two decades. He has also worked with Quebec and Ontario Provinces as well as local governments throughout the United States.

INDEX